Failure in High Command

The Canadian Army and the
Normandy Campaign

Failure in High Command

The Canadian Army and the Normandy Campaign

John A. English

Foreword by Gunther E. Rothenberg

The Golden Dog Press
Ottawa – Canada – 1995

Original Copyright Acknowledgements

The author and publisher gratefully acknowledge permission to reprint the following materials:

An extract from the poem "Ice," by Sir Charles G. D. Roberts. Reprinted by permission of McGraw-Hill Ryerson Ltd.

Extracts from the Alanbrooke Papers. Reprinted by permission of the Trustees of the Liddell Hart Centre for Military Archives, King's College, London.

Extracts from Field Marshal Sir Bernard Montgomery's papers in the collection of the Imperial War Museum, London. Reprinted by permission of the Montgomery Collections Committee of the Trustees of the Imperial War Museum.

Extracts from personal letters of Field Marshal Sir Bernard Montgomery. Reprinted by permission of Viscount Montgomery of Alamein, CBE.

An extract from W. B. Yeats, "Under Ben Bulben," *W. B. Yeats Collected Poems* (London: Picador, 1990), p. 401. Reprinted by permission of Pan Books Ltd.

Canadian Cataloguing in Publication Data
English, John A. (John Alan)
          Failure in High Command: the Canadian Army and the Normandy Campaign
Previous edition published by Praeger, New York, 1991
          under title: The Canadian Army and the Normandy Campaign.
Includes bibliographical references and index.
ISBN 0-919614-60-4

1. World War, 1939-1945 – Campaigns – France – Normandy.
2. Canada. Canadian Army – History – World War, 1939-1945.
3. Normandy (France) – History. I. Title.

D756.5.N6E54 1995   940.54'2142   C95-900661-3

Distributed by: Oxford University Press Canada, 70 Wynford Drive, Don Mills, ON, Canada, M3C 1J9

Cover design: The Gordon Creative Group
Cover photo: National Archives of Canada, #PA 132194
Printed in Canada by AGVM Inc.

The Golden Dog Press is an Imprint of Haymax Inc.

To the Memory of My Father,

JOHN PERCIVAL ENGLISH,

Proud Albertan, Patriotic Canadian,

Who Every 24th of May and 1st of July

Flew the Red, White, and Blue,

and, Finally,

Went to His God like a Soldier

Contents

Figures and Maps

FIGURES

MAPS

Foreword

Forty-seven years ago this summer allied armies stormed the Normandy beaches, only to find that after the initial landing phase, progress toward the D-Day objectives became slow indeed. This, too, was the experience of the First Canadian Army on the road to Falaise in the summer of 1944. If the ultimate test of the combat effectiveness of an army is the battlefield, then the performance of the Canadians, including the many non-Canadian formations in this army, while brave beyond dispute, was disappointing.

The author, a long-serving infantry and staff officer in the Canadian land forces, does not question the historical record; he does seek to discover the "reason why." He challenges the widely accepted explanation that inexperienced troops and, on occasion, inadequate regimental officers were no match for the fanatic, combat-experienced Germans. Instead, he places ultimate responsibility for the operational shortcomings revealed in Normandy on the Canadian high command. During the lean interwar years, Canadian senior commanders, overly concerned with keeping a skeleton army alive in a hostile political environment, neglected the essence of their profession and forgot the lessons of 1914–1918. But the British high command and army were in much the same predicament, as were the armies of Canada's sister dominions. None was adequately prepared, either mentally or in materiel, for war in 1939.

Most Canadian formations, however, were not engaged until the summer of 1944. This provided adequate time for realistic training, and some effort was made to profit from combat experience gained in Sicily. However, as the author shows, Canadian senior officers in England, caught up in routine, all too often failed to make good use of this opportunity. Peacetime habits and ways of thinking are always hard to shed, and for three years the

Canadian high command failed to understand and adjust to the new dynamics of war and the new operational requirements.

This is a serious charge which undoubtedly will raise some hackles in Canada and which requires substantial proof. I think that the author, relying on immediate primary evidence, often as close to "real time" as possible, has made his case. Many brave men needlessly lost their lives in Normandy. Though the author does not say so outright, some blame must accrue to the politicians who starved the armed forces far too long, but high-ranking officers share the blame. For the sake of soldiers who in all probability will have to face combat somewhere, sometime in the future, I hope that the wider lesson of this book will be studied and absorbed in command and staff colleges and in other institutions of higher military learning. Ultimately the high command is responsible for the preparation of its troops for battle, and if it fails to do so adequately, it "hath a heavy reckoning to make."

Gunther E. Rothenberg
Purdue University

Preface

The First Canadian Army was the only field army ever to fight under Canadian command and staff direction. It was also the last great British imperial army. Within a force structure that encompassed "units"—that is, battalions and regiments, and the progressively higher "formations" of brigade, division, corps, army, and army group—the First Canadian Army lay just below group, of which there were but three on the Western Front in the Second World War. This was the Canadian army's most recent experience at the *operativ* or operational level, that gray zone lying somewhere above tactics and below military strategy once called "Grand Tactics," the tactics of large formations. For a military organization that has not fought since Korea, when but one Canadian brigade was deployed, it is didactically important that the operations of Canada's first army continue to be the subject of serious professional study. As Carl von Clausewitz so astutely pointed out, despite the essential unity of all military activities, command at the higher formation level usually calls for a greater measure of imaginative intellect. Gaining a better understanding of how large field forces function is thus an important step toward avoiding a repetition of past mistakes.

This work, presented in two parts, endeavors to explain Canadian Army operations in Normandy during the Second World War against a backdrop of organization, training, and fighting style developed before actual battle. It explores the Great War experience, the British connection, the interwar period, force development, equipment, staff structure, and doctrine. More specifically, it traces the development of the Canadian overseas army, describes the workings of this roughcast yet complex fighting force, and critically appraises the subsequent performance of Canadian formations in

Normandy. Major attention with respect to the last focuses on land operations after the consolidation of the bridgehead, since Canada's second great expeditionary force trained principally for action expected to follow the amphibious landings on the Continent. While these operations naturally relate to the controversial closure of the Falaise Gap, it must be stressed that this aspect in itself is of but collateral concern to the present study. The scenario nonetheless remains highly significant, for had the First Canadian Army achieved its objectives along the road to Falaise, it would undoubtedly have attained a military renown equal to Lieutenant-General George Patton's more famous Third U.S. Army. It might even have spearheaded the subsequent advance of Field Marshal Sir Bernard Montgomery's 21st Army Group instead of being left to plug along the difficult and essential, but plainly unglamorous, northern seaboard through Holland.

What happened to Canadian arms in the Norman summer of 1944 cannot, of course, be explained in terms of that season alone. Yet, the accepted rationalizations, which have attributed battlefield reverses to German fanaticism, inferior tanks, or the greenness of Canadian troops and the inadequacies of their regimental officers, do border on this simplistic approach. By delving deeper into the past and looking further afield, especially to the experience of the British Army with which the Canadian was so closely integrated, one is driven to conclusions of a different order. Indeed, as Peter Paret has so convincingly stated:

> The . . . operations of any war can be understood only in the light of conditions of the ten or twenty years before its beginning. Technology, organization, doctrine, training, command and staff appointments—all the essentials of action in war—are put in place and developed in peacetime. The testing experience of combat will bring about change, but prewar elements continue to affect many events throughout even the longest of conflicts.[1]

In the course of establishing the connection between the summer of 1944 and the preceding winters of Canadian Army development and growth, it will be demonstrated that high command shortcomings seriously impaired Canadian fighting performance. The Canadian field force was from its inception compromised by a military leadership that had for too long concentrated on bureaucratic, political, stratego-diplomatic, and technical pursuits to the neglect of its operational and tactical quintessence. Having forsaken its Great War professional legacy and military *raison d'être* during the interwar years, the Canadian high command proved incapable of conducting worthwhile training in Britain. The overseas army thus largely wasted its time and had to be retaught by others the business of war, which truly professional armies had long recognized was more profitably studied in peace. The frenzied rhythm that characterized Canadian training activity from the start unfortunately continued to de-emphasize the need for all arms cooperation, with the result that some higher commanders in Normandy unknowingly and unnecessarily cast the lives of their soldiers away.

Obviously, given the exceedingly complex and multifaceted nature of the foregoing subject area, there existed a practical need to limit the scope of this study. For this reason, only the combat arms—armor, artillery, and infantry—and the command and staff function have been considered in any depth. The intent was not to discount the importance of engineers, signals, tactical air, maintenance, logistics, or other support services, but merely to suggest that they require separate specialist analyses. In short, this work does not pretend to be definitive either from the standpoint of scope or primary evidence, the full depths of which have by no means been plumbed by scholars. The study does, however, break new ground on staff and tactical training through a reading of archival records, particularly Montgomery's personal correspondence with Lieutenant-General H.D.G. Crerar on the state of Canadian training three years into the war. In one sense *The Canadian Army and the Normandy Campaign* illustrates the cumulative nature of history, for its argument could not have been raised up without the firm foundations provided by Colonel C. P. Stacey's official and unofficial histories and Professor R. H. Roy's indispensable *1944: The Canadians in Normandy*. The more one reads Stacey, the more one is struck by the sheer magnitude of his scholarly achievement. Undoubtedly, his dominance of the field will grow stronger with the years as other formerly more fashionable Canadian historians continue to fade. Having toiled through war diaries and operations logs, I can also appreciate better than most the value of Professor Roy's painstaking research.

As always in the production of a book, there are many whose help and assistance must be publicly acknowledged. First, to Professor James Pritchard of Queen's University I owe a special thanks for his great patience in reading my manuscript and offering wise and friendly advice. I shall remain ever grateful to him for introducing me to the Braudelian perspective of the *longue durée*, the broad sweep of history, which influenced my investigative approach. I am similarly indebted to Professor Barry Hunt of the Royal Military College for reviewing chapters and providing many constructive criticisms. I might add that ever since studying under Dr. Hunt on the RMC War Studies course, I have heavily relied upon him as a mentor. A man of unparalleled naval and military knowledge, he has been the best possible friend a serving officer could ever hope to have.

It has also been my good fortune to have had the opportunity to conduct the 1989 and 1990 battlefield tours of Normandy for the Canadian Land Forces Command and Staff College. For this I sincerely thank my former commandant, Major-General Clive Milner, who had a fine vision of what a staff college should be, and my current commandant, Brigadier-General T. F. de Faye, who enthusiastically promoted the study of military history. I am furthermore beholden to the hero-veterans who contributed so much to the success of our Normandy field studies, namely Brigadier-General "Rad" Radley-Walters, Oberst Helmut Ritgen, Colonel Tom Bond, Lieutenant-Colonels Lockie Fulton and Bob Lucas, Wing Commander "Papa" Ambrose, Major William Whiteside, and former SS-*Sturmbannfuehrer* Hans Siegel. Lieutenant-Colonel Roman Jarymowycz deserves special mention for unselfishly sharing the results of his veteran interviews and archival research, which related most particularly to the agony of Verrières Ridge.

For secretarial and graphics support I am much obliged to Captain John McComber and his staff, especially Sergeant Norm Ramsay, Corporal Sherry Goundry, Eileen Wood, Mary Ferguson, Linda Gauthier, Louise Owen, and Chris Heffernan. I owe additional thanks to Lieutenant-Colonels John A. Macdonald and John A. Selkirk, Major Mitch Kryzanowski, and Captains Alan Balfour and Hugh Egener for reading chapters and suggesting fresh ideas and material. To my other colleagues on the Directing Staff who lent continuous moral support throughout this long ordeal, I also say thanks and *Tam marte quam Minerva*. I furthermore wish to express my gratitude to Mr. Serge Campion, David Willis, Theresa O'Neill, and Glenyss Turner of the Fort Frontenac Library for their excellent service. Keith Crouch and Benoit Cameron of the RMC Massey Library, as always, assisted above and beyond the call of duty. Between them, these two libraries present the greatest concentration of military books in the Dominion.

Among others who offered valuable assistance were Dr. Bill McAndrew, who suggested the topic, Ben Greenhous, Owen Cooke, and Carl Christie of the Directorate of History. Major Bob Caldwell, Major Al Fowler, and Sharon Babaian gave especially good military and historiographical advice. Professor Dominick Graham, who has been commissioned to write the biography of Lieutenant-General Simonds, likewise shared his considerable experience and knowledge with me. I am additionally most appreciative of information proffered by Dr. Robert Fraser, Dr. Jane Errington, Dr. Brian McKercher, and Captain Al English. The late Colonel Stacey, who would probably not have agreed with many of my conclusions, and Professor Martin Blumenson, who does, also read parts of my work and offered encouragement. Colonel Hans von Luck, formerly of the 21st Panzer Division, and Colonel Hubert Meyer, formerly of the 12th SS Panzer Division, both provided early information for which I remain thankful.

Across the Channel, the staff of the Public Record Office, Kew, and Miss Patricia Methven, archivist of the Liddell Hart Centre for Military Archives at King's College, were most helpful with my researches in London. Mr. Roderick Suddaby, the Keeper of the Department of Documents, and his able assistants at the Imperial War Museum all went out of their way to make my visits there especially pleasant and productive. I, of course, remain grateful to the Montgomery Collections Committee of the Trustees of The Imperial War Museum and the Trustees of King's College, University of London, for allowing me access to their respective collections. Viscount

Montgomery of Alamein, CBE, kindly gave permission to reproduce extracts from his father's personal letters. Nearer to home, I received absolutely outstanding service from the staff of the Queen's University Archives and the National Archives of Canada, both institutions of which Canadians can be proud.

On a less nationalistic note, however, I would be most remiss if I did not mention my especial indebtedness to Messrs. Ron Chambers and Dan Eades of Praeger Publishers, who ever since taking a chance on my first work have stuck by me like the truly good friends they are to bring this book to fruition. Finally, despite all the disruption they have undergone and the many outings they have forfeited, my family to the last lent unstinted support. My wife, Valerie, helped on the computer, my mother cut the lawn, and my daughters, Shannon and Laura, provided light entertainment. My Irish setter, Cromwell, remained pensive throughout. Princess, the rabbit, stayed out of my way.

NOTE

1. Foreword by Peter Paret in Harold R. Winton, *To Change an Army: General Sir John Burnett-Stuart and British Armoured Doctrine, 1927–1938* (Lawrence, Kans.: University Press of Kansas, 1988), p. vii.

The Canadian Army
and the
Normandy Campaign

Prologue

Of Ignorant Armies

"Write the history of a battle? As well write the history of a ball." So growled the Duke of Wellington[1] in what surely has come to be recognized, historiographically, as a perceptive assessment. Similarly, Count Leo Tolstoy brilliantly argued in the second part of his epilogue to *War and Peace* that "there was no possibility of describing the movement of humanity" without taking into account "the history of *all*, without one exception, *all* the people taking part in an event."[2] Clearly, in the writing of history, particularly military history that deals with the movement of masses of men within limited space and time frames, one can only aim at the most rudimentary reconstruction of past events. The historian is thus challenged like some benighted staff officer at a distant headquarters to piece together as reasonably accurate a picture as possible from the "confused alarms of struggle and flight."[3]

It has been further asserted that the writer who lacks personal experience of combat cannot know what happens on the battlefield. In his latter-day account of infantry life in the Great War, veteran front line soldier W.H.A. Groom takes issue with the work of "front rank historian" John Terraine on the grounds that he "was not in the war and has no knowledge of the mental strain of the front line."[4] Yet, as Sandhurst historian Paddy Griffith sensibly counters, "no one man in battle can see very much of what is going on, nor will he have the leisure to weigh the significance of what he does see." He concludes that, in fact, the "vast majority of battles leave . . . but few useful eyewitness accounts, and it is rare for any two observers to describe exactly the same event."[5] No less revealing is Arthur Swinson's discovery in the course of researching the battle of Kohima of "more than once . . . instances where both parties were convinced that they were on the left (or right) of each other."[6] Obviously, while there appears to be general agreement that the most accurate impression of what really happened can only be gained through the circumspect use of first-hand accounts rendered by participants, lack of personal combat experience, as John Keegan has so brilliantly shown, need not disqualify the historian.[7]

Colonel C.P. Stacey, the Canadian official historian, rightly suggested that in the matter of weighing evidence, "the vital element is that of time," the validity of a written account or interview being directly related to the elapsed passage of time between the event and its recording. "The best historical evidence," Stacey declared, "is evidence recorded *at the time*." Allowing that in order to fill gaps it may be necessary to interview participants long after an event, he nonetheless counseled, "it is something that should be done only when the contemporary written evidence fails"; even then, it "should be checked with care against such contemporary written records as are available." Concerning "reminiscences... thirty or forty years on,"[8] Stacey was much kinder than British historian A. J. P. Taylor who savagely warned such could "degenerate into 'old men drooling over their youth'...forget[ting] truth and manufactur[ing] myth."[9] Stacey pointedly referred, however, to a study by historians of the European Theatre of the U.S. Army on "how long it took a soldier's memory of a battle ...to fail." Their conclusion was that this occurred in six days. More recently, military historian Dominick Graham sounded the alarm that memory "is particularly unreliable after a subject has talked to other people, compared notes and repeated his story many times. By then, he may no longer tell truth from fiction."[10]

Naturally, it makes great sense to exercise the same care in determining the worth of written evidence, and again the most important factor is elapsed time. Official correspondence, private letters, and especially personal diaries written shortly after an action are thus most valuable. War diaries fall into the same category, except that entries were often made days after events occurred. According to Stacey, the "one document superior to all others as a source of information" is the operations log maintained at various headquarters not for "historical purposes, as a unit or formation war diary is, but as an instrument for fighting the battle." The log is also a preferable source because it is impersonal[11] and, though checked, is rarely rewritten; war diaries, on the other hand, are subject to approval and possible alteration by those in command. As for regimental histories, quality tends to vary with authorship, but even when written by trained historians little is generally said to the detriment of regimental performance. Indeed, the purpose of a regimental history is not so much to present the unvarnished truth, which is generally attempted, as to promote pride in achievements, traditions, and *esprit de corps*.[12]

The student of Second World War history can take some consolation, of course, from the knowledge that all shots have been fired, all efforts spent, and all decisions taken. The cumulative nature of history written since the report of the last round has also provided him with a reasonably firm foundation upon which to build. In short, many of the facts having already been established, he can now in Stacey's words, "go on to the perhaps more important tasks of establishing *why* . . . [they] happened."[13] That events took the course they did, however, does not mean that they had necessarily to follow this course; there is, after all, nothing inevitable about history, even though no replay is ever allowed. To examine with a critical eye those events that did occur is nevertheless instructive for the academic and military professional alike.

For a Canadian Army whose reputation relected the illustrious fighting record of the Canadian Corps in the Great War, the Norman summer of 1944 appears in retrospect disappointingly lackluster. In recent years, moreover, whereas historical accolades have continued to accrue to the Canadian Corps, historical aspersions have increasingly been cast upon the combat performance of the First Canadian Army on the road to Falaise. That the charges are not insignificant is evident from the conclusion of Eversley Belfield and Brigadier H. Essame that "the Canadians' advance was frustratingly sluggish and, in retrospect, it was unfortunate that the better trained British 2nd Army could not have been employed to close the Falaise Gap."[14] American Lieutenant-Colonel Carlo D'Este also noted "the inability of the Canadians to develop their actions more quickly,"[15] and repeated Stacey's admonition in the official history that

> It is not difficult to put one's finger upon occasions in the Normandy campaign when Canadian formations failed to make the most of their opportunities. In particular, the capture of Falaise was long delayed, and it was necessary to mount not one but two set-piece operations for the purpose at a time when an early closing of the Falaise Gap would have inflicted most grievous harm upon the enemy and might even, conceivably, have enabled us to end the war some months sooner than actually was the case. A German force far smaller than our own, taking advantage of strong ground and prepared positions, was able to slow our advance to the point where considerable German forces made their escape. That this was also due in part to errors of judgment south of the Gap should not blind us to our own shortcomings.[16]

British journalist Max Hastings is more critical, claiming that "even within the Canadians' own ranks, [few] disputed that the principal cause of the Allied failure [to close the Gap] was the feeble performance of First Canadian Army"; the British official history, in his view less frank than the Canadian, pointedly "evades the central fact that the ragged remains of two German divisions and a handful of tanks held all Crerar's [First Canadian] army for 13 days, from the opening of [Operation] TOTALIZE to the crossing of the gap at Chambois, a distance of barely thirty miles."[17] To quote General Charles Foulkes, former commander of the 2nd Division,

"When we went into battle at Falaise and Caen we found that when we bumped into battle-experienced German troops we were no match for them. We would not have been successful had it not been for our air and artillery support."[18] Even Major-General Harry Foster, who rarely saw eye to eye with Foulkes, agreed that Canadians

> were no match for Germans once they were dug in. It could be argued that everything being equal, defenders always hold an advantage over attackers. But in Normandy everything wasn't equal. We held the advantage; in the air, at sea and on the ground. Yet every time our troops got beyond the range of supporting artillery or sour weather grounded our fighter-bomber cover, the Germans stopped us cold.[19]

It has been claimed, moreover, that never once during operations in northwest Europe did Anglo-American forces ever succeed in decisively breaking through organized German defences. The enemy seemed always able to fall back, regroup, and reestablish a cohesive defensive posture. By way of comparison, the Red Army from the summer solstice of 1944 attained its greatest triumph on the Eastern Front: the destruction of Army Group Center. While Canadian land forces ground their way toward Falaise, Russian troops swept to the banks of the Vistula, covering some 450 miles in four weeks. The Soviets purposefully delayed this mighty offensive, aptly called Operation "Bagration," until 22 June, the anniversary of the Hitlerian and Napoleonic invasions of Russia. Masters of the art of encirclement by this time, the Russians refused to dissipate their armor in the marshy, forested terrain of the "Byelorussian Balcony"; the subsequent objectives of the First Baltic and Second Byelorussian Fronts (equivalent to Anglo-American army groups) were also defined in terms of lines of advance rather than specific limited objectives. The Soviet high command "deliberately took the risk of not immediately giving the troops set objectives for the whole depth of the strategic operation because . . . [it] would have inevitably meant the relatively rigid use of men and material on the selected line of advance, whereas the situation demanded just the reverse—the preservation of all opportunities for flexible and rapid manoeuvre."[20] In the words of Major-General F.W. von Mellenthin, former Chief of Staff of 48 Panzer Corps, "Army Group Center . . . broke to pieces before the onslaught . . . Twenty-five German divisions simply disappeared."[21]

Despite obvious limitations, the foregoing comparison does lend a certain perspective to Canadian operational participation in northwest Europe. It has often been voiced by the more nationalistic, for example, that Canada by the end of the war possessed the fourth-ranking army in the world. While this may be true, one should again try to keep this claim in perspective. In terms of divisions deployed against the Third Reich, which mustered more than 300, the Soviet Union fielded around 450 on the Eastern

Front. Of the roughly 90 Allied divisions that fought their way across Western Europe, the Americans provided 61, the British 14, the French eight, the Canadians five, and the Poles one.[22] If, as Basil Liddell Hart estimated, the British contributed "barely 6 percent of the forces arrayed against Hitler in the final campaign,"[23] the Canadian contribution must appear even smaller. Given the nature of the Anglo-American direction of the war, moreover, Canadians served in northwest Europe under a theater headquarters composed mainly of Americans and Britons in turn subordinate to an exclusive Anglo-American Combined Chiefs of Staff. Had Canada fielded "ten divisions instead of five," ventured Stacey, "she would probably not have been welcomed [to membership] at that board, but she might have fought her way in."[24] As it was, Canada was effectively excluded from participation in any higher strategic direction of the war.

In real terms, her influence came largely to depend, as it had in the Great War and might well again, upon the operational and tactical prowess of her expeditionary forces.[25] Indeed, the decision to dispatch the 1st Canadian Infantry Division and the 1st Canadian Army Tank Brigade to the Mediterranean in June 1943 was made partly out of concern that Canadian influence in the postwar world might suffer "if no demonstrable contribution to victory" were made. The questionable decision to have the 5th Canadian Armoured Division and 1 Canadian Corps join them in Italy, of course, ensured the greater polygot composition of the First Canadian Army when it undertook operations in northwest Europe. With 1 British Corps and the 1st Polish Armoured Division under command, as well as 14 percent of its headquarters officer establishment British, it remained less than half Canadian until 1 Corps rejoined it from Italy but a month before the German surrender.

Being the most international of all such formations that fought in northwest Europe, the First Canadian Army has often been compared to the more famous British Eighth.[26] That there were Canadian corps in both, however, is probably less significant in this respect than the fact that within the empire that spawned them they were the last of an imperial line. Indeed, until the last two months of the war, there were more British troops in the First Canadian Army than in the Eighth at Alamein. During the early stages of the Battle of the Rhineland in February 1945, nine British divisions fought under the command of the First Canadian Army. With an aggregate strength of nearly 400,000 men, this was the largest field force ever led by a Canadian.[27] Yet, size alone has not historically proven to be a major determinant of Canadian battlefield success; at Vimy and Amiens it was the relatively superior tactical skill of Canadian arms that won the admiration of the world.

The intention in Book Two of this work is neither to attack nor defend the Canadian record, but to subject it to critical analysis, which, to employ the wisdom of Carl von Clausewitz, involves the application of theoretical truths to actual events. The former being determined by "inquiry . . . the most essential part of any *theory* . . . the task of . . . [which is] to study the nature of ends and means," the resultant "arch of truth" may even produce certain principles and rules. Yet, cautions Clausewitz, "these are less likely to yield an algebraic formula for the battlefield" than to "provide a thinking man with a frame of reference for the movements he has been trained to carry out; it is highly improbable that they could serve as a guide which at the moment of action lays down precisely the path he must take."[28] In this Clausewitzian view, theory is neither "a positive doctrine, [nor] a sort of *manual* for action"; instead, it "exists so that one need not start afresh each time." Intended to "educate the mind of the future commander . . . to guide him in his self-education," it is not meant "to accompany him to the battlefield; just as the wise teacher guides and stimulates.a young man's intellectual development, but is careful not to lead him by the hand for the rest of his life."

Theory, according to Clausewitz, "becomes a guide to anyone who wants to learn about war from books." In the critical, as opposed to plain narrative, approach toward historical events, "which merely arranges facts one after another," he recommends three intellectual steps. The first, historical research proper, involves discovering and interpreting the "equivocal facts" and has little to do with theory. The second, "*critical analysis proper*," is to attempt to trace effects back to their causes, of which there are usually more than one. The third and final step, which for the military professional is most important, remains "the investigation and evaluation of the means employed" using theoretical measurements as appropriate, which is described as "criticism proper, involving praise and censure . . . [and] the lessons to be drawn from history." In war, as Clausewitz warns, however, "the facts are seldom fully known and the underlying motives even less so," which is "why critical narrative must usually go hand in hand with historical research."

As previously indicated, it is not proposed in this work to examine Canadian Army operations in their totality, but to study the second phase of the Battle of Normandy in light of Canadian preparations for land warfare on the Continent. Not surprisingly, these preparations cover more winters of peace than a summer's fighting. Indeed, what happened in Normandy, though it remains our focus, can only be explained in terms of what went on before. It is of course realized, as Keegan reasoned, that

> Action is essentially destructive of all institutional studies; just as it compromises the purity of doctrines . . . War, the good quartermaster's opportunity, the bad quartermaster's bane, is the institutional military historian's irritant. It forces him . . . to combine analysis with narrative—the most difficult of all the historian's arts. Hence his preference . . . for the study of armed forces in *peacetime*.[29]

In examining high command, force structure, equipment, doctrine, and battle and staff training in Book One, however, it is expected that appropriate connections to operations can be drawn.

No apologies are offered for this essentially "drum and trumpet" approach, for military history "must in the last resort be about battle."[30] Indeed, as the distinguished American military historian, Russell Weigley, reminds, "it is to prepare for and to wage war that armies primarily exist, and for the military historian to fail to carry his studies . . . to the test of war is to leave his work grotesquely incomplete." This is neither to deride the acknowledged impact that political, social, and economic forces work upon the exercise of arms, nor to decry the moral and psychological aspects of military history. In fact, where apposite, efforts will be made to consider these dimensions. In the main, however, the intent will not be to "avoid venturing into the heat of battle," for as Weigley contends: "A day's trial by battle often reveals more of the essential nature of an army than a generation of peace."[31] It is to be hoped that dispassionate analysis of Canadian operational performance in the Caen-Falaise battles will bear this out.

NOTES

1. Richard Holmes, *Firing Line* (London: Jonathan Cape, 1986), p. 9; and also John Keegan in Introduction to Paddy Griffith, *Forward into Battle* (Chichester: Antony Bird, 1981).

2. Count Leo Tolstoy, *War and Peace*, trans. Constance Garnett (New York: Modern Library, undated), pp. 1118–1131.

3. Matthew Arnold, "Dover Beach," line 36. *The Golden Treasury of the Best Songs & Lyrical Poems in the English Language*, selected by Francis Turner Palgrave, 5th ed. (Oxford, U.K.: Oxford University Press, 1990), p. 365.

4. Holmes, *Firing Line*, p. 9; and W.H.A. Groom, *Poor Bloody Infantry: A Memoir of the First World War* (London: William Kimber, 1976), p. 22.

5. Griffith, *Forward into Battle*, p. 8.

6. Arthur Swinson, *Kohima* (London: Cassell, 1966), pp. xiv-xv.

7. Holmes, *Firing Line*, pp. 8, 15.

8. Col. C.P. Stacey, *A Date With History* (Ottawa: Deneau, 1983), pp. 229–230.

9. Holmes, *Firing Line*, p. 10.

10. Stacey, *Date*, p. 229; and Dominick Graham, "The First World War on Land," *British Military History. A Supplement to Robin Higham's Guide to Sources*, ed. Gerald Jordan (New York: Garland, 1988), p. 279.

11. Stacey, *Date*, p. 230. The log is a minute-by-minute record of all information and orders sent out and received by a headquarters. The purpose of the war diary "is to furnish a historical record of operations and to provide data upon which to base future improvements in army training, equipment, organization and administration." Stacey noted that war diaries often contained irrelevant "chitchat" and "errors of fact," commonly the result of their being written up after the event; he found roughly one-third of all war diary map references to be inaccurate. C.P.

Stacey, "War Diaries: Good, Bad and Indifferent," *Canadian Army Journal* (hereafter *CAJ*), 3 (Summer 1950): 17–24.

12. Swinson found that: "Regimental histories and Divisional histories are often so inaccurate and disagree completely as to dates, times and disposition of units; war diaries are notoriously inaccurate also" (Swinson, *Kohima*, pp. xiv–xv).

13. Stacey, *Date*, p. 230. Reference to all shots being fired is taken from Isaac Deutscher, *Stalin* (Harmondsworth.: Penguin, 1984), p. 13.

14. Eversley Belfield and H. Essame, *The Battle for Normandy* (London: Pan, 1983), p. 233.

15. Carlo D'Este, *Decision in Normandy: The Unwritten Story of Montgomery and the Allied Campaign* (London: Pan, 1984), p. 457.

16. Col. C. P. Stacey, *Official History of the Canadian Army in the Second World War* , Vol. III: *The Victory Campaign: The Operations in North-West Europe, 1944–1945* (Ottawa: Queen's Printer, 1966), pp. 275–276.

17. Max Hastings, *Overlord: D-Day and the Battle for Normandy, 1944* (London: Pan, 1984), p. 358.

18. Stacey, *Victory Campaign*, p. 276.

19. Tony Foster, *Meeting of Generals* (Toronto: Methuen, 1986), p. 366.

20. Terry Copp and Robert Vogel, *Falaise* (Alma, Ont.: Maple Leaf Route, 1983), p. 116; Gen. Sergei Shtemenko, "Bagration Operation Byelorussia, 1944," *Main Front* (London: Brassey's, 1987), pp. 189–193; and Bryan Perrett, *Lightning War: A History of Blitzkrieg* (London: Panther, 1985), pp. 265–266.

21. Maj.-Gen. F.W. von Mellenthin, *Panzer Battles: A Study of the Employment of Armor in the Second World War*, trans. H. Betzler, ed. L.C.F. Turner (Norman: University of Oklahoma Press, 1983), pp. 282–283. Forty-nine German commanding generals were also lost.

22. Col. C. P. Stacey, *Arms, Men and Governments: The War Policies of Canada, 1939–1945* (Ottawa: Information Canada, 1974), p. 200. Eight French divisions, armed and equipped by the Americans, participated in the later stages of the campaign in northwest Europe. Australia raised by the spring of 1943 a relatively enormous army of 12 divisions, most on home defense duty in Australia and three on garrison duty in Papua-New Guinea (Ibid). The Canadian Army in northwest Europe advanced a total of some 450 miles (Stacey, *Victory Campaign*, p. 641).

23. B. H. Liddell Hart, *Defence of the West: Some Riddles of War and Peace* (London: Cassell, 1950), p. 215.

24. Stacey, *Arms, Men and Governments*, pp. 180, 196. The Americans were apparently responsible for the decision not to allow Dominion representation, even as observers, in Anglo-American military conversations. The matter of Canadian membership on the Combined Chiefs of Staff would doubtless have entailed giving similar representation to Australia, France, and perhaps even Brazil, which provided one division to the Italian theatre in autumn 1944 (Ibid., pp. 159–163, 200–201). According to J. L. Granatstein, the "Canadian generals were probably not high-powered enough to merit a seat on a supreme strategy board, even if Canada's military contribution might have justified such representation" [J. L. Granatstein, *The Ottawa Men: The Civil Service Mandarins, 1935–1957* (Toronto: Oxford University Press, 1982), p. 129].

25. On the diplomatic front, Canada developed the "theory of functional representation," whereby size of contribution to the war effort in certain specific areas

rather than overall power status determined the corresponding degree of representation. Canada was the sole country outside of Britain and the United States to gain direct representation on the Combined Food Board and the Combined Production and Resources Board. She was not granted membership on the Munitions Assignment Board. (Stacey, *Arms, Men and Governments*, pp. 171–172, 179–180; and Granatstein, *Ottawa Men*, pp. 93, 125–126, 131–132).

26. Stacey, *Arms, Men and Governments*, pp. 41–42, 229, and *Victory Campaign*, pp. 30–34, 545; and Lt.-Col. G. W. L. Nicholson, *Official History of the Canadian Army in the Second World War*, Vol. II: *The Canadians in Italy, 1943–1945* (Ottawa: Queen's Printer, 1956), pp. 20–27, 340–343. It was originally intended that on completion of Operation "Husky," the invasion of Sicily, Canadian formations would return to the United Kingdom, bringing to the First Canadian Army the benefit of their battle experience. Canadian insistence instead on increasing the commitment to a small two-division corps, which included an armored division that the Allied theatre commander did not want, took on sillier proportions when the Canadian government asked for its return before it had even fought a corps battle. Ibid.

27. Stacey, *Victory Campaign*, p. 642; Jeffrey Williams, *The Long Left Flank: The Hard Fought Way to the Reich, 1944–1945* (Toronto: Stoddart, 1988), p. 18; and Ralph Allen, *Ordeal by Fire* (Toronto: Popular Library, 1961), p. 452. Canadian field force strength in northwest Europe by the war's end was about 170,000.

28. Carl von Clausewitz, *On War*, ed./trans. Michael Howard and Peter Paret (Princeton, N.J.: Princeton University Press, 1976), pp. 140–142, 156–157.

29. John Keegan, *The Face of Battle* (New York: Viking, 1976), p. 29.

30. Ibid.

31. Russell F. Weigley, *Eisenhower's Lieutenants: The Campaign of France and Germany, 1944–1945* (Bloomington, Ind.: Indiana University Press, 1981), p. xv.

Book One

Long Forgotten Winters

When Winter scourged the meadow and the hill
And in the withered leafage worked his will,
The water shrank, and shuddered, and stood still,—
Then built himself a magic house of glass,
Irised with memories of flowers and grass
Wherein to sit and watch the fury pass.
                                    Sir Charles G. D. Roberts, *Ice*

Chapter 1

The Canadian Corps and the British Mold

The Great War terminated with the military forces of the Empire a unified fighting organization. This army dispersed to its homes and the different portions of the Empire set about the task of readjustment to meet the conditions of peace. . . . When war again threatens, however, . . . our responsibility as soldiers stands clear—against that day to prepare the military machinery of the Empire for its highest effectiveness.

Lieutenant-Colonel H. D. G. Crerar,
"The Development of Closer Relations Between
the Military Forces of the Empire"[1]

As the British Empire blasted its way to victory during the "Hundred Days" in 1918, it seemed the greatest power on earth. At the signing of the Armistice it possessed the grandest fleet, the largest air force, and one of the strongest armies in the world. Yet, though unrecognized at the time, the Great War marked the last, greatest heave of the world's farthest flung imperium. In the Hall of Mirrors at Versailles the stage was set for Greek tragedy, for as is now recognized, it was the Romanic American rather than the Hellenic British presence that proved decisive. As James Morris so dolorously put it, "the sacrifices of the Great War . . . were given to a cause that was already receding into history, like those discredited grey battleships [off Gallipoli], their smoke-pall filling the sky, hull-down on the Aegean horizon."[2]

The illusion of Britain's omnipotence hastened her imperial eclipse during the Second World War as even American bankers and businessmen, believing the Empire still affluent and rival, aggressively sought to undermine the economic and political foundations of their closest ally.[3] Canada, whose nascent efforts to preserve the sway of the British Empire actually made good national sense, was concomitantly caught up in the pull of the quickly shifting foundations of imperial power within the Anglo-American world. So would be, in time, more distant Australia and New Zealand. Had Britain but managed to retain even a portion of the relative power it once enjoyed, it is doubtful that Canada would have gravitated quite so quickly into the American orbit. Indeed, the path eventually taken by Canada was less a conscious national choice than the inevitable consequence of the irresistible attraction that greater powers have always exerted upon lesser ones. As it was, Canada fought the Second World War as part of an empire in decline, and it is against this background that her participation must be viewed.

The shape of Canadian land forces between the wars, while bearing the double stamp of neglect and Depression, also manifested both the legacy of the first Canadian Expeditionary Force (CEF) and the impress of continued imperial association. If four years of fighting had not produced a distinctive Canadian way in warfare, they had at least fostered a truly professional military approach, albeit one characterized by a pronounced reliance on artillery and a lesser emphasis on maneuver. The heightened sense of professionalism that became the hallmark of the CEF was nonetheless substantially eroded by postbellum reorganization that saw the reemergence of the traditional Canadian Militia in its various regimental guises and ugly hues of political patronage. Widespread war weariness and Britain's growing imperial dilemma further complicated Canadian defense posture at this time. Canadian land forces during the interwar period, in fact, somewhat reflected the plight of the British Army, especially in respect to expeditionary force roles, armored warfare theory, regimental structure, interservice rivalry, and even defense priorities.

Canada emerged from the Great War well on the road toward becoming a fully autonomous and industrialized state. The feats of the Canadian Corps in Flanders had gained her Prime Minister a voice in the Imperial War Cabinet, earned her diplomats enhanced status on the British Empire Delegation at Versailles, and firmly laid the cornerstone of nationhood itself. It is unlikely that any Canadian leader has since enjoyed greater relative prestige and access to the inner sanctums of world power politics than Prime Minister Sir Robert Borden who, in the absence of David Lloyd George, "regularly acted as chairman of the meetings of the British Empire Delegation."[4] For a Dominion of not yet eight million souls, the cost had been enormous: more than 60,000 dead, one-third again as many as perished in all her armed forces in the Second World War.

At the beginning of the Great War, the Canadian Non-Permanent Active Militia (NPAM) or reserve force fielded 59,000 all ranks, while the Permanent Active Militia (PAM) or regular force numbered around 3,000. In 1939, by way of comparison, the reserves numbered about 51,000 and the regulars somewhat more than 4,000.[5] On balance, it is difficult to refute

Stacey's claim that the "creation of the Canadian Corps was the greatest thing Canada had ever done."[6] Like most great commitments, however, fielding an armed force of over 600,000 men called forth substantial national effort that lamentably resulted in the infamous conscription crisis of 1917, which served to foster similar cleavages in the Second World War.[7] On a more positive note, Canada had managed to embrace, by accident if not design, the enviable strategic luxury of waging her wars on the shores of the enemy.

Ironically, for place of birth has never been a prime determinant of Canadian nationality, some historians have implied that the mainly British immigrant composition of the original Canadian Corps demonstrates that the "war to end all wars" was not Canada's war. The coincident but disturbing thought that superior battlefield performance could also be a function of this factor has fortunately not been so avidly suggested. It is nonetheless fact that most of the soldiers in the first overseas draft of the CEF were British-born immigrants; of 36,000 troops, less than 30 percent were born in Canada. By war's end, after heroic recruiting measures and the imposition of conscription, the percentage of Canadian-born in the entire CEF had risen to but 51 percent. Magnificently, the province of Manitoba with a sizable non-British foreign-born population provided the highest proportional contribution, some 40 to 61 percent of its eligible manpower.[8]

Although the officer corps was never less than 70 percent Canadian-born, for much of the war most of the key general staff appointments within Canadian field formations were filled by British officers. At one time a third of all staff officers were British. In its most celebrated victory, the Canadian Corps was also commanded by a British general, Sir Julian Byng, whose leadership was of such sterling quality that Canadian troops long after the war insisted on calling themselves the "Byng Boys." While less popular Canadian Lieutenant-General Arthur Currie replaced Byng in June 1917, the former insisted upon retaining British officers in the three senior staff appointments at his corps headquarters; indeed, he singled out the most senior, his Brigadier-General, General Staff (BGGS) N. W. Webber, for particular personal praise. At the divisional level, the first Canadian senior operations staff officer or General Staff Officer Grade 1 (GSO 1) was not appointed until November 1917, and, by the Armistice, one of Canada's four fighting divisions still had a British GSO 1.[9]

It is true, of course, that Canadian military tradition, rooted in loyalist mythology dating from the War of 1812, called for part-time soldiering in a volunteer militia that harbored a resentment, even scorn, of regulars. Recognition of the latter's incompetence in the Boer War allegedly prompted the Minister of Militia and Defence, Sam Hughes, to reject general staff mobilization plans in 1914 and to resort to patronage in appointing officers to senior command in the CEF. This precipitous action by a fanatical militiaman[10] had the particularly important, if unintended, effect of ensuring that the Canadian Corps was formed not from traditional units existing within the Canadian regimental system, but, instead, on the basis of entirely new composite numbered units. Ironically, whatever informal connection the CEF did have with the peacetime volunteer militia practically ceased to exist on the adoption of compulsory service in 1917. Despite the chaos engendered on initial mobilization, however, the exclusion of the old militia, indicted by the Governor-General in 1913 as "the worst force in the empire," may indeed have been a blessing in disguise.[11]

Some British military historians have attributed superior Canadian operational performance in the Great War to their being "unhindered by such prejudices" as are often fostered by peacetime military structures that tend to lay, in the name of regimental spirit, proprietary claim to weapons and combat functions. The aversion of traditional arms or corps like cavalry and artillery to the creation of new ones was thus not so strong as to discourage Canadian pioneering efforts in machine-gun employment. Likewise, because he was "not so obsessed with arms institutionalism," the Canadian soldier more readily embraced new weapons like the mortar than, say, the British gunner who preferred not to exchange his horse for something that resembled a drain pipe. Still, as William Stewart has so convincingly demonstrated in his excellent study, the Canadian Corps essentially adopted and refined British methods. Detailed planning, thorough preparation, and exhaustive training more than any innate superiority underpinned Canadian fighting efficiency.[12]

Much of the operational effectiveness of the Canadian Corps also sprang from the skill of its high-quality British staff officers, three of whom rose to become Chief of the Imperial General Staff (CIGS). In a highly positional war that left little room for strategic maneuver, tactical innovation effected through meticulous staff work was critical. By 1918, moreover, Canadian divisions had ten more staff officers than their smaller British equivalents. Of greater import than its oft touted national spirit, the Canadian Corps additionally possessed the inestimable advantage of having permanently allocated divisions. This enabled it to develop a military cohesion and operational capacity that can only ever result from soldiers constantly working together. British corps were not afforded this luxury as the division remained the basic fighting formation, which meant that corps composition had regularly to be altered as the operational situation demanded.[13]

That there were many outstanding British divisions commanded by exceptionally able general officers is of course worth recalling. Among these must be counted Liddell Hart's patron, the "hard-swearing" Major-General Ivor Maxse, whose 18th (Eastern) Division on the bloody first day of the Somme seized its objectives in less than an hour with comparatively light casualties. Unfortunately, divisions such as the 18th and 30th that escaped the firestorm that day were ultimately done in anyway, as the reputation they had gained ensured their use as "stormers" for the remainder of the war.[14] The inescapable logic that the longer a soldier stays in combat the more likely he will be killed was accordingly demonstrated, and thus did Britannia begin to exhaust her manpower. The great advantage of the Canadian Corps was that it was always kept up to strength. Its spirit throughout the war was never that of "an army that felt betrayed or let down by its government."[15] Currie insisted on maintaining Canadian divisions of three brigades each of four battalions, moreover, when the British, partly due to manpower shortages, were obliged to reduce theirs to three brigades each of three battalions.[16]

If Morris is to be believed, "most people agreed . . . that the Canadians were the best troops on the western front."[17] An Australian might protest, however, that this merely reflected a British judgment based less on actual fighting performance than acute senior officer aversion to an Australian desertion rate four times the norm. The Canadians, it seems, were much better disciplined. Yet the Australians comprised only nine percent of British Empire forces, but accounted for over 20 percent of all prisoners, guns, and ground captured by all Allied forces, and more than the Americans, in the offensives launched from April to October 1918.[18] Despite the obvious subjectivity of such assessments, it is nonetheless possible to note certain characteristics of the Australian and Canadian approaches. The latter were quite correctly regarded as the leaders in machine-gun tactics, proving particularly innovative in massing their heavy variants in batteries and fighting them as tactical entities to support attacks as well as defenses.[19]

The Canadian officer most responsible for the foregoing development appears to have been a French emigrant and engineer, Raymond Brutinel, who on declaration of war obtained ministerial approval to raise the 1st Canadian Automobile Brigade, a small armored car unit later named the 1st Canadian Motor Machine Gun Brigade. Eventually, a Canadian Machine Gun corps was established with Brigadier-General Brutinel in command. The machine-gun art was subsequently refined to a highly sophisticated degree that included the use of indirect or "barrage" fire. Given the positional nature of the Great War, however, it was not until the great German offensive of March 1918 that Brutinel's motor machine-gun concept based on armored car mobility proved its worth. Following this experience General Currie approved the formation of an additional motor machine gun brigade (actually battalion size) that with the 1st Canadian Motors, one field artillery battery, an engineer company, a cyclist battalion, and a mortar unit constituted the Canadian Independent Force commanded by Brutinel. This mobile force, it has been claimed, "was the first mechanized formation in the Commonwealth armies and the forerunner of the armoured division."[20]

At the other end of the maneuver scale, Canadian artillery officers were incorporating the advantages of air reconnaissance, flash-spotting, and sound-ranging into counterbattery work. Brigadier-General A. G. L. "Andy" McNaughton, strongly influenced by Lieutenant-Colonel A. G.

Haig of 5 (British) Corps and a cousin to Field-Marshal Sir Douglas Haig, exploited these developments to create a matchless counterbattery organization within the Canadian Corps. McNaughton, it should be stressed, also held that the solution to difficulties associated with the attack in the Great War lay "in a preponderance of artillery sufficient to crush out of existence a wide section of the enemy's defensive system, entrenchments and defenders alike, thus creating a gap through which troops could be thrown to work around the exposed flanks." Significantly, because he later became Canadian Chief of the General Staff (CGS), he had serious reservations about Brutinel, especially the latter's advocacy of machine-gun indirect fire and quite possibly his penchant for maneuver. The failure of Brutinel's innovative, but unfortunately careless, motor machine-gun attack down the Arras-Cambrai road to seize a bridgehead over the Canal du Nord in September 1918, served to confirm the principle "to pay the price of victory in shells and not the lives of men." The Canadian Corps fired about one-quarter of the shells used by the BEF in the "Hundred Days."[21]

A Canadian proclivity for intense preparatory fire and heavy barrage cover for assaulting infantry stood somewhat in contrast to the "peaceful penetration" tactics that saw Australian troops "glide about in the night like cats." Essentially a process of aggressive defense characterized by opportunistic large and small group patrolling that gained ground gradually, "peaceful penetration" negated the need to undertake the hateful, formal raids so reminiscent of the nightmare of trench warfare. Instead of relying on lengthy artillery bombardments that often compromised surprise, the Australians infiltrated forward in speedy, stealthy fashion, winkling Germans out of position and nibbling away at their lines. When considered necessary, artillery support usually took the form of short, sharp engagements designed either to suppress or distract the enemy and drown out the noise of patrols. These tactics were so successful, in fact, that when it came time to prepare a full-scale attack on the Villers-Bretonneux plateau in July, over one-quarter of the objective had already been taken by "peaceful penetration." The Australians were later to claim that "it was by the Peaceful Penetration of the four months, April to July, . . . that the Battle of Amiens was decided."[22]

If a more pronounced artillerist bent did distinguish Canadian Corps operations, it was also indicative of an increased professionalism. Having suffered Hughes's impulsive and often ill-considered interventions, the great majority of CEF senior officers, regular and reserve, had become convinced of the value of a nonpartisan approach toward the conduct of war. Four years of trial by fire had seen fighting ability and knowledge displace political patronage as the basis for selecting leaders and commanders. The Canadian Corps had of necessity become the most militarily professional ever of Canadian forces, which previously had tended to be highly political. On repatriation, a strong case was advanced to have the CEF serve as the foundation of a restructured land force based on an equitable, if politically unrealistic, system of universal military training. It was "better that a dozen Peace [militia] Regiments should go to the wall," declared one veteran commander, "than the C.E.F. units be lost."[23] A committee headed by septuagenarian Major-General Sir William Otter was accordingly constituted in 1919 to make recommendations as to the incorporation of CEF units into the militia "so as to perpetuate them and make sure that none of the traditions which were gained at so much cost overseas were not lost to the future."[24]

This proved to be a rather complicated, tedious, and controversial undertaking, since it involved the award of coveted battle honours won by CEF numbered battalions to those militia units that had furnished them with wartime drafts of soldiers. The original idea of fusing the CEF and militia that would have led to the reform as well as reorganization of the latter was quickly effaced during interviews and meetings that revealed the "parochial nature of Canadian militia officers and their obsessive interest in their own regiments and units." The lessons of the Great War with respect to large armies, the role of cavalry, machine guns, tanks, and the need for mechanization were in the throes of demobilization hardly discussed. Little concern was expressed about the purpose and object of military forces or their future role in the defense of Canada. Despite various public calls for a force "designed for war purposes, not as a social edifice to be kicked over as soon as real soldiering [wa]s demanded," the Otter Committee accomplished little more through its deliberations than a return to the prewar situation, wherein the militia was less a war machine than a social organization. In this respect, it reflected the opposition to reform among older veterans of the militia, many of whom had not served overseas and feared that traditional volunteer service would be supplanted by something akin to a continental standing army.[25]

No final written report was tendered by the Otter Committee, but it generated through a series of decisions and memoranda a reversionary, largely notional, land force establishment. Essentially, it was a patchwork effort in which the discordant relationship of widely dispersed militia centers, constituent political support, and government spending figured prominently. Within the infantry, the battle honors and traditions of 50 fighting and some 260 reinforcement battalions of the CEF were scattered among 112 authorized units. Those of the four Canadian Mounted Rifle (CMR) battalions that had actually taken the field were perpetuated by seven CMR units added to a cavalry establishment that included 26 prewar regiments. Only in the artillery did CEF units supersede traditional organizations, with the bulk of prewar batteries being redesignated with CEF numbers. Conspicuously, two of the four most influential officers appointed to the Otter Committee were CEF gunners, one of them the ubiquitous McNaughton. All told, the Otter Committee in 1920 called for a paper force of eleven infantry and four cavalry divisions with an appropriate number of ancillary or supporting troops. This was considered the minimum strength required to hold hostile American forces at bay, in event of war with the United States, while awaiting the arrival of imperial reinforcements. As for the politically unpopular question of dispatching an expeditionary force to deliver other imperilled areas of the Empire, the committee advocated a structure strikingly similar to that of the legendary British Expeditionary Force: one cavalry and six infantry divisions.[26]

Yet the imperial sands were shifting for Canada, the ebb of Britannic power being nowhere better illustrated than in the case of the Anglo-Japanese Alliance of 1902, which year also marked the withdrawal of Royal Navy squadrons from North America. In its time this pact saw Japanese troops considered for employment on India's Northwest Frontier, and, during the Great War, units of the Imperial Japanese Navy supporting Royal Navy minesweeping operations in the Mediterranean and Canadian coastal defenses on the Pacific. Its renewal in 1911 was hailed by then Prime Minister Sir Wilfrid Laurier as a "happy event." By 1921, however, despite Admiralty and vehement Australian objection, Prime Minister Arthur Meighen was urging abrogation of the alliance to assuage growing American hostility toward it. According to Correlli Barnett, Meighen's "resolute opposition" finally sunk the agreement, which amounted to Canada exercising "a decisive influence" in "one of the most crucial national-strategic decisions England had ever to reach in her history." At the Washington Naval Disarmament Conference of 1921–1922, the Anglo-Japanese Alliance was finally terminated, superseded by a nebulous four-power treaty.[27]

At the same conference Britain accepted naval parity with the United States, giving up with respect to the Republic all pretensions of maintaining her traditional two-power standard. The Washington Treaties, inasmuch as they forbade the fortification of Hong Kong and the Philippines, also had the effect of leaving Japan the dominant Pacific power. Britain and her Antipodean dominions were thus left facing a spurned, resentful, and now unconstrained Nippon; in effect, for U.S. goodwill, an ally had been converted into an enemy. Bereft of alternate allies in the Far East and with American strength confined to Hawaii, the British Empire turned its attention to Singapore on which hung the imperial lifeline to Australia and New Zealand. This focus on a "Singapore strategy" to safeguard the British Far Eastern Empire, it has been argued, spawned a policy of strategic appeasement essentially based on bluff, since British power alone could not deal simultaneously with Japan in the Far East, a resurgent Germany in Europe, and Italy in the Mediterranean. Not since the American Revolution had Britain faced such a potentially overwhelming array of enemies.[28]

Canadian defense policy, though far less grim and complicated, exhibited certain characteristics of the wider imperial predicament. Just as public revulsion at the perceived loss of a generation of finest manhood led, in

Britain, to bitter condemnation of the expeditionary force commitment to the Continent, so it did in Canada. While British generals were pilloried as incompetent, sanguinary fools, the Canadian government meted out a disgracefully shabby welcome to returning General Currie; he was later accused on the floor of the House of Commons of cowardice and wasting the lives of Canadian soldiers. Likewise, pressures to repatriate troops from Allied intervention in the Russian Civil War and reduce military forces to prewar levels proved similarly irresistible in Canada and Britain. As if to reinforce this point, demobilization mutinies occurred in both armies. An isolationist trend also developed in Britain, though it was not considered by most to be a realistic option in light of British national involvement in the League of Nations, and, by 1925, the umbrella Treaty of Locarno that principally guaranteed the Franco-Belgian-German frontier established by the Treaty of Versailles. Indeed, Britain maintained an army in the Rhineland until 1930.[29]

With German power eliminated, however, only Bolshevik Russia and Japan were regarded as major threats for most of the 1920s. The potential danger of air attack by France was for a brief period between 1921–1923, not entirely for service reasons, taken seriously by the Royal Air Force (RAF). It had been assumed from August 1919, nonetheless, that for purposes of framing service financial estimates, "the British Empire . . . [would] not be engaged in any great war during the next ten years, and . . . no Expeditionary Force . . . [would be] required." In July 1928 this so-called Ten Year Rule, essentially a Treasury control measure that sparked intense inter-service rivalry for funds, was put on a "moving day-by-day basis."[30] The military thus once again assumed the traditional role of garrisoning India and protecting the Empire. In essence this represented a reversion to the 1872 Cardwell system that placed the regiment, a "linked" battalion at home feeding drafts to another one abroad, in the central position. It also meant gelding the Home Army mainly to sustain the autonomous Army in India, which with its focus on the Northwest Frontier and internal security was less receptive to mechanization. To Barnett, this relegated the British Army to little more than "a colonial gendarmerie with no major role to play or plan for."[31]

While the complexities of British defense policy between the wars will not be examined in any depth, as many of the scholars consulted have done in admirable detail, certain aspects for their influence upon Canadian military thinking should be considered. Foremost among these must be the recognition that the British people, with the slogan "never again" upon their lips, actively searched through successive governments for alternate means of waging or, preferably, avoiding war to enhance their security. To much of the war-weary British electorate, mechanization merely equated to another continental commitment of land forces. According to the Commandant of the British Staff College, Major-General Edmund Ironside, writing to the head of the Canadian forces in 1923, changing military conditions also militated against the dispatch of another BEF:

> As far as an [sic] European war is concerned, there will be absolutely no chance of an Expeditionary Force leaving Great Britain while intensive air action is going on. It would hardly be a practical military project to begin with, and secondly, no politician would allow it to start. There was difficulty enough in getting the politicians to let the force go in 1914, when there was no danger. This intensive air action will, therefore, go on until one side has quietened or softened the others' air action. Then, and then only, will the Army be able to embark for Europe if that is what is required, and so the Army will definitely have a good time in which to complete itself.[32]

"The first principle of defense," Ironside concluded, was "anti-aircraft," to which role he saw the Territorial Army entirely committed. He further advocated increasing the air force, a stance more enthusiastically embraced by the Canadian Deputy CGS, McNaughton, who saw this service as "the *first line of defense.*"[33] Indeed, in both Canada and Britain the air force seemed the one form of rearmament acceptable to the ordinary taxpayer. The bombing of London in 1917 had left a deep impression on the public, which, frightened by Prime Minister Stanley Baldwin's 1932 declaration that "the bomber will always get through" and an anticipated casualty rate of 150,000 souls per week, eagerly embraced the apostles of air power and the highly delusory strategic bombing doctrine they preached. Based more on political requirements than experience, and intimately linked to justifying the RAF as an independent force, this doctrine threatened any potential attacker with economic dislocation through retaliatory bomber strikes that also sought to crush morale. That the RAF was technologically incapable of fulfilling this role against Germany in 1934 and had no capacity to deliver even in 1938, seems not to have lessened the attractiveness of this "Trenchard (after Marshal of the RAF Viscount Trenchard) Doctrine." Indeed, uncritical acceptance of the military value of the *Luftwaffe*'s terror bombings of Guernica and Barcelona in the Spanish Civil War appears to have heightened its appeal.[34]

The 1932 publication of Liddell Hart's seminal work, *The British Way in Warfare*, provided an intellectual basis for protagonists of the deterrent approach and those who yearned for a return to Britain's traditional "blue water" strategy with its emphasis on blockade and the use of the army as a "projectile fired by the navy." Mobility and surprise were seen as the essence of a distinctive British way in warfare that sought to avoid major military effort on the Continent. To this Liddell Hart applied his strategy of the indirect approach and, coincidentally, the doctrine of limited liability that proposed committing only minimal British land forces to the direct assistance of European allies. This doctrine had powerful appeal for a variety of reasons, among them still vivid memories of Great War slaughter, mistrust of the French, crude interservice rivalry, arrant army unpreparedness for Continental operations, an accepted military need to buy time, and perhaps most importantly, Treasury concern for financial and economic stability. Ironically, for Liddell Hart was a tank advocate, limited liability favored mechanization more than armored force development—that is to say, simply harnessing the internal combustion engine as opposed to utilizing armored fighting vehicles in battle. Imperial policing, to be sure, was more amenable to the former.[35]

Lacking the traditional esteem of the Royal Navy, the novel appeal of the RAF, and the perceived deterrent capacity of either, the 200,000-man British Army soon came to consider itself the "Cinderella" service. As Michael Howard has suggested, however, government parsimony and electoral pacificism were not the only factors contributing to the general malaise of what has been described as "a comatose army."[36] In his view, the army was "still as firmly geared to the pace and perspective of regimental soldiering as it had been before 1914."[37] Major-General J. F. C. Fuller's caustic crack that the War Office after the Great War "plunged into a battle for the red coat, khaki not being considered military enough for peacetime soldiering"[38] was thus not far off the mark. That the military profession demanded as much intellectual dedication as the practice of law or engineering does not seem to have been fully appreciated:

> Too many . . . senior officers regarded it as a comfortable sanctuary from industrial society to welcome even the limited measures of streamlining and mechanisation which were forced on them after 1937 by Leslie Hore-Belisha, with Liddell Hart . . . his unofficial but powerful adviser; and a whole military generation went to its graves cursing the two men who tried to drag it, kicking and screaming, into the twentieth century.[39]

Here the central issue remains the British Army's failure to progress beyond pioneering stages in the field of armored warfare. While other explanations besides social interpretations have been offered, none alone seems entirely convincing. It has been argued by Brian Bond, for example, that the hitherto touted conservatism of the officer corps was less a detrimental factor than the army's lack of a definite European role toward which to train. In this regard he is supported by Howard and D.C. Watt. At the same time, others like Shelford Bidwell and Dominick Graham have insisted that lack of military professionalism more than public antipathy and government economy accounted for British Army shortcomings. Robert H. Larson, following in the footsteps of Fuller and Liddell Hart, has further submitted that the army remained wedded to an attrition doctrine that denied their concept of inducing strategic paralysis through powerful armored thrusts deep into an enemy's rear. Not surprisingly, Harold R. Winton in a masterly synthesis more recently concluded that military conservatism, political and social indifference, and the imperial mission were the primary factors that impeded continued British armored development.[40]

Canadians, as British subjects, found neither the British military scene nor that of the Empire at large entirely foreign. From the Imperial Defence Conference of 1909 up to 1937, a direct channel for exchanging military information existed between the CIGS in London and the CGS in Ottawa. By the 1920s the Canadian General Staff received on a regular basis a veritable flood of documents from the War Office, Army Headquarters in India, British South China and Malaya commands, Australia, New Zealand, and South Africa. As much of this correspondence related to technical matters and training, Canadian officers of the interwar period did not have to look far to determine what thoughts preoccupied their colleagues overseas. In addition, the practice of attaching Canadian officers to the War Office recommenced in 1925. Further dissemination of information related to British military developments occurred in the editorial pages of the *Canadian Defence Quarterly(CDQ)*. Specific British exercises received comprehensive coverage in the "Service Notes" section, while "Notes on Service Journals" impressively highlighted selected excerpts from the *Army Quarterly*, the *Journal of the Royal United Service Institute*, the *Cavalry Journal*, and the *R.A.F. Quarterly*.[41]

The Canadian military establishment thus learned firsthand from Gen. Sir George Milne, CIGS 1926–1933, that although he had supported the mechanized experiment in 1927, it had unfortunately diverted attention from "actualities." For this reason he urged officers not to think too much about mobility or the pace of maneuver. Milne also expressed concern in 1932 that "tactical conceptions still tended unduly in the direction of those which were acquired in the later stages of the Great War." He therefore made it abundantly clear that the British Army at home had "no single predominant objective towards which its training c[ould] be categorically directed." Instead, its assigned roles embraced in order of probability the four broad categories of imperial policing, minor expeditions and guerilla warfare, major expeditions, and a national war. Milne accordingly concluded that troop training would normally be most profitably focused on "wars of different degrees against a second class enemy." To ensure against the "remote" contingency of a national war, he advocated "special studies" and the development of a "military mentality" based on "minds open to scientific possibilities, and as wide a knowledge of all sorts and conditions of men as is possible."[42]

Remarkably, the British Army did not initiate any study of the lessons of the Great War until the 1931–32 Kirke (after Lieutenant-General Sir Walter Kirke) Committee. Though hastily assembled, partly in response to Liddell Hart's prodding, it produced a farsighted report highly critical of the British conduct of the Great War. Unfortunately, the committee findings were judged too progressive and potentially embarrassing by General Sir

Archibald Montgomery-Massingberd, CIGS 1933–1936, who insisted that the army role was not to fight in a major war but to defend and police the Empire. Like many other top army officers, he was unwilling in light of the politico-economic climate to face the issue of a possible Continental commitment. As a proponent of the notion that the next conflict would be an updated version of the Great War, he also took steps to suppress the Kirke Report, which advocated armored expansion in preparation for mobile warfare. Limiting distribution to only the most senior officers, he subsequently had produced an expurgated, and distorted, version for wider circulation within the army for discussion purposes. The result was that the lessons of the combined arms operations conducted so impressively during the "Hundred Days" were largely forgotten.[43]

Although Montgomery-Massingberd was not the criminally incompetent reactionary depicted by his bitterest critics, his imposition of a rigid centralization stifled progressive development. He adamantly refused to accept armored warfare theory and clung to the belief that cavalry still had a limited role in war, perhaps for reasons related to preserving the social fabric of the army. Like Montgomery-Massingberd, Field-Marshal Sir Cyril Deverell, CIGS 1936–1937, appears to have placed excessive emphasis upon loyalty as a determinant of an officer's worth, when in fact it was actually but a useful tool for the suppression of unwelcome criticism. "The army must stand together" was the cry, even as Deverell, who strongly supported a Continental commitment, disastrously hindered the development of armored forces. According to Brian Bond, "When everything possible has been said in mitigation of the Army's inefficiency in the inter-war period, it is still difficult to deny the essential truth . . . [that its] . . . higher direction . . . between the two wars was on the whole deplorable."[44]

Bond additionally considered the regimental system the very "root of the malaise" afflicting the army during the interwar years. Despite its evident worth in promoting unit *esprit de corps* and cohesion, the system intrinsically fostered an extreme parochialism and narrowness of view that stultified professional thought and ultimately obstructed reform. The British Army remained what it was in Sir John Fortescue's day, "not an army at all, but only a collection of regiments." According to Howard, the real benefit of the regimental system was more political than military in any case; though an "obstacle to full professional efficiency," it served to tame the soldier, "fixing . . . [his] eyes on minutiae, limiting . . . [his] ambitions, teaching . . . a . . . gentle, parochial loyalty difficult to pervert to more dangerous ends."[45] To Fuller, the regimental system throttled good officers, making them "no more than members of social clubs," rather than part of a greater army. Likening it unto the "Hindu caste system," he saw its "totemic ritual of life" that had "nothing to do with war or peace," usurping intelligence and professional knowledge as the universal military catalyst. "Once a black-button man," he charged, "you cannot become a brass-button man, you are black-buttoned for life; and just as a mandarin's yellow button used to get him a job, so will the five black buttons on your . . . tunic get you one."[46]

The only military institution capable of reining in a regimental system with the bit literally in its teeth would have been a properly constituted general staff. As will be shown, however, the British General Staff was but one component of an Army Council whose military membership to a degree reflected corps and regimental affiliations. While these were in the main infantry and artillery rather than cavalry as often supposed,[47] General Staff direction seems to have been inversely proportional to the heat generated by intercorps rivalry. Milne's vacillation in the area of armored development, where Britain for a brief period led the world, was especially unfortunate as it produced repercussions that echoed for far too long. Simply put, the perceived intransigence of the traditional arms drove the impatient armored apostles, whose truly reformist message espoused radically different approaches toward war, to adopt extreme positions. As so often with men of high intellect, these "rude mechanicals" unfortunately came to regard all those who did not think like them as obstructionist and unprogressive.[48]

A major consequence of this schism was the growth of an "all tank" approach that considered artillery support redundant, and, in the absence of any self-propelled capability, even a brake upon armored mobility. Since tank supporters also identified artillery with the attrition warfare of 1916 and 1917, which saw *l'artillerie conquiert, l'infanterie occupe*, they increasingly come to view it as a rival instead of an ally. At the same time, widespread gunner indifference to military thought that emphasized armored maneuver led to the abandonment of pace-setting, self-propelled (SP) gun trials in 1928. The armored school meanwhile promoted the development of a two-pounder tank main armament, the underlying idea being that small rounds could be carried in such a quantity that constant resupply would be unnecessary and hence mobility enhanced. Although a high explosive (HE) shell was produced, the firing of solid armor-piercing shot received extreme emphasis in anticipation of tank versus tank battles. One result of this fixation was that antitank gun development received less than the attention it deserved; another, that no British tank had any effective (i.e., HE) means of dealing with enemy antitank guns when hidden or entrenched. Ironically, when the two-pounder on a wheeled carriage was offered to the infantry for antitank defense, it was initially rejected. The artillery thus found itself in 1938 responsible for first-line antitank defense with an inadequate weapon. In sum, the British Army went to war without an SP artillery piece or a tank with an adequate gun. Worse yet, it had failed to develop a common doctrine for the cooperation of tanks and field guns, and, just as important, tanks and antitank guns.[49]

British Army hesitancy to embrace new fighting techniques was matched by, and mirrored in, its neglect of higher formation exercises. The first large-scale maneuvers since before the Great War occurred in September 1925 and involved over 40,000 troops. Significantly, these were observed by more than a dozen Canadian officers, including their defense chief, who subsequently published a report of his impressions in the *CDQ*.[50] Though world attention during 1927–1928 fixed upon the Experimental Mechanized Force, not as many personnel were involved. Incredibly, conservative concerns for "safeguarding" the morale and training of the traditional arms led to Milne's abrupt disbandment of this force in 1928. Given the expense of tanks, armored machine-gun carriers henceforth came to be increasingly viewed as the best means of restoring infantry and cavalry offensive capability. The idea of an armored force using its firepower and shock action in independent operations gave way to a "cavalry concept" that envisioned tanks merely replacing horsemen in their traditional mobile role.

The 1929 maneuvers, restricted to small-scale exercises, presaged the nadir of the army in 1931, which year saw Britain's export trade decline by 30 percent and financial estimates fall to their lowest level. An entirely tracked and wireless-equipped tank brigade was nonetheless temporarily assembled under Brigadier Charles Broad, whose 1929 seminal work, *Mechanized and Armoured Formations*, had been carefully studied by the Germans. As his well-drilled brigade's success in tactical maneuver appeared more staged than radio-directed, however, it caused many onlookers to feel they were victims of an elaborate hoax. Fortunately, the process he had instigated of infiltrating tank units to Egypt so as to circumvent political objections continued unabated.[51] At the same time, the complexities of armored development, the Cardwell system, and other related facets of modern military thought in Great Britain received amazingly thorough coverage in the editorial section of the *CDQ*. The expressed hope was that while Canada lacked the means to conduct such experimentation, it could with fewer actual problems than the British benefit equally as much.

The year 1932 witnessed the reconstitution of the tank brigade and the rescision of the Ten Year Rule. During the 1933 exercises, tanks performed solely in the infantry support role within imperial small-war or guerilla scenarios, assessed by military observers as the dullest maneuvers ever. The following year saw the 1st Tank Brigade established on a permanent basis under Brigadier Percy Hobart, who now rejected operations in cooperation with infantry in favor of semi-independent offensive missions against the enemy rear. The apparent defeat of Brigadier George Lindsay's armored force that same year by an infantry-cavalry formation unfortunately dealt a severe blow to the advocates of an armored theory of war. Montgomery-Massingberd now made the fateful decision to mechanize the cavalry and motorize the infantry rather than create an armored striking force around the Royal Tank Corps at the expense of the traditional arms.[52]

This action underscored the tank as an infantry support weapon rather than the core of an offensive force capable of all arms operations. In its lighter version it was seen as a means of assisting a rejuvenated cavalry in traditional reconnaissance, raiding, and security screening roles. The 1935 maneuvers, the largest since 1925, focused on the employment of infantry divisions in preparation for a possible European conflict. Tank battalions mainly provided close support as "Infantry" or "I" tanks, a "new idea in tactics" that was not, significantly, applauded by the editor of the *CDQ*, who much preferred the machine-gun carrier for such purposes.[53] The tank brigade again assumed infantry support tasks in the 1936 maneuvers, and military training generally became less rather than more realistic with the approach of war. In November 1937 the commander of Southern Command remarked that none of his formations was fit to take the field against a first-rate military power. The 1937 creation of the Mobile Division (later re-designated the 1st Armoured Division) reinforced the "cavalry concept" of armored operations insofar as its role, like the Cavalry Division in 1914, was to cover the advance of a field force. The decisive blow was still to be struck by the infantry supported by heavy tanks.[54]

The War Office, faced with the reorganization of the army, decided in December 1937 to adopt a two-year training cycle intended to address, in turn, techniques for controlling units and higher direction in war. The first cycle, completed in 1938, concentrated on brigade and unit training, leaving the more senior officers to participate in a series of limited map exercises. The year 1939, which was to have seen maneuvers on the scale of 1925 and 1935 in which none of the senior officers of 1939 had participated in key appointments, was instead taken up with adjustment problems associated with conscription and equipment acquisition. Thus, though the Second BEF that arrived in France may well have been, as often stated, the most mech-anized of all belligerent field armies, it critically lacked the all-arms punch of the largely horse-drawn German army. Mustering but 196 light tanks, 50 infantry tanks, and some 38 armored cars in operational units on the outbreak of war, the British Army was, as might be expected, better suited for imperial policing than warfare on a continental scale.[55]

That this situation should have developed is hardly surprising, for on 22 December 1937 the government of Prime Minister Neville Chamberlain formally adopted a limited liability defense policy that established four strategic priorities: first, defense of Britain; second, protection of sea routes; third, defense of overseas territories; and fourth, cooperation with allies in defense of their territories. Largely because of its perceived deterrent value, the RAF received first priority in rearmament, with the navy and army following second and last in order. Within two years the RAF would receive 41 percent of the defense budget and more than 20 percent of total gov-ernment expenditures. Fear of a devastating "knockout blow" from the air, however, prompted Sir Warren Fisher of the Treasury wisely to insist, despite Air Staff opposition, upon the creation of Fighter Command and the award of production priority to fighters over heavy bombers. The army's responsibilities were now decreed to be in descending order of priority: the Air Defence of Great Britain (ADGB); imperial garrison duty; provision of a field force for general purposes; and, last of all, commitment to the Continent. As the Territorial Army inherited the air defense role, no reserve army was available to undertake field force duty. The ADGB role, in fact, absorbed most of the Army's funds and negated the need for heavier tanks.

At this point, British military strategy essentially consisted of a combination of defensive isolationism and imperial commitments in which service Chiefs of Staff actually acted as strategic appeasers trying to buy time. As late as October 1938 Chamberlain repeated that his government would not introduce conscription in peacetime. The persistent aggressions of Adolf Hitler put an end to this brief euphoria, however, and by February 1939 the British government officially abandoned the policy of limited liability and once again accepted a Continental commitment. Conscription, hurriedly enacted in May 1939, was less militarily significant than a symbol of this renewed, albeit belated, undertaking. If anything, the sudden extensive changes forced by calling up masses of "militiamen" for 32 divisions "created conditions of near chaos" in the British Army. By the summer of 1939 it was in a "profound state of disarray."[56]

Canadian defense posture about this time reflected, somewhat in the manner of men's fashion, the stance assumed by Great Britain. Although the Ten Year Rule was never formally adopted by Canada, it served in fact as the basis for preparation of financial estimates by the Department of National Defence (DND) to 1935. While the British commenced limited rearmament in that year, Canada followed suit only in 1937. As late as April 1939, but two months after the British had reluctantly accepted a Continental commitment, the government of Prime Minister W. L. Mackenzie King established an order of defense service priorities that closely resembled that associated with Chamberlain's limited liability policy of December 1937. The development of the Royal Canadian Air Force (RCAF) was accorded primacy over the Royal Canadian Navy (RCN), which service was given priority "so far as possible" over the Militia, as the army was yet called.

The suspicion that Mackenzie King may have himself decided upon these priorities[57] is not without foundation for he manifested an abiding aversion to conscription as counterproductive to the Canadian war effort and an apparently unshakable conviction in the efficacy of appeasement. With some good reason he regarded European war with Great Britain a belligerent as the ultimate catastrophe. Coercive collective security action was thus simply too high a price to pay for curbing Italian violation of the Covenant of the League of Nations or German abrogation of the terms of Versailles or Locarno. In Mackenzie King's view, it was "sometimes well to leave sleep-

ing dogs to lie . . . especially . . . where they happen to be the dogs of war."
At the 1937 Imperial Conference, where a common system of military
organization and training was agreed, he had eagerly embraced the appeasement stance of Chamberlain. After Munich, he basked in the same
limelight as illuminated the British Prime Minister for avoiding war over
"a far away country," and surrendering without a shot 40 Czech divisions.
When Chamberlain finally abandoned appeasement on the German occupation of what remained of the Czechoslovak Republic in March 1939,
Mackenzie King did not.[58]

NOTES

1. Lt.-Col. H. D. G. Crerar, "The Development of Closer Relations Between
the Military Forces of the Empire," *Canadian Defence Quarterly* (hereafter referred
to as *CDQ*), 4 (July 1926): 426, 432.

2. James Morris, *Farewell the Trumpets: An Imperial Retreat* (Harmondsworth,
U.K.: Penguin, 1980), pp. 201, 210–211. See also Correlli Barnett, *The Collapse of
British Power* (New York: William Morrow, 1972), pp. 71–73, 249. By the end of
the war, the British Empire had fielded 80 infantry and eight cavalry divisions on
active service outside the United Kingdom and India, of which 61 infantry and three
cavalry were on the Western Front. The Royal Air Force possessed 22,000 aircraft.
The Royal Navy had more battleships (61) than the American and French fleets
combined and twice as many as the Japanese and Italian navies together. It had
nearly twice as many cruisers (120) and destroyers (466) as the American and French
total and nearly three times as many destroyers as the Japanese and Italians combined.

3. Christopher Thorne, *Allies of a Kind: The United States, Britain and the War
Against Japan, 1941–1945* (Oxford, U.K.: Oxford University Press, 1978), pp. 136–
141, 280–281, 365, 388, 503–507, 536–541, 675–676, 699–701, 725; and his *The Issue
of War: States, Societies, and the Far Eastern Conflict of 1941–1945* (New York: Oxford
University Press, 1985), pp. 121–220. For further insight into the American hum-
bling of British world power, see Barnett, *Collapse of British Power*, James R. Leutze,
Bargaining for Supremacy: Anglo-American Naval Collaboration 1937–1941 (Chapel Hill,
N.C.: University of North Carolina Press, 1977), and D.C. Watt, *Succeeding John
Bull: America in Britain's Place, 1900–1975* (Cambridge, U.K.: Cambridge University
Press, 1984).

4. Col. C. P. Stacey, *Canada and the Age of Conflict: A History of Canadian External
Policies*, Vol. I: *1867–1921* (Toronto: Macmillan, 1977), pp. 170–171, 202–217, 238–
256, 265. See also Col. C. P. Stacey (ed.), *Historical Documents of Canada*, Vol. V:
The Arts of War and Peace 1914–1945 (Toronto: Macmillan, 1972), p. 381. The
Americans were the most "determined opponents" of Canadian international representation at the armistice, viewing it as but another "limb of the spreading British
imperial tree." When at Versailles U.S. Secretary of State Robert Lansing inquired
as to "why Canada should be concerned in the settlement of European affairs,"
Prime Minister Lloyd George replied "because some hundreds and thousands from
the Dominions had died for the vindication of the public right in Europe and that
Canada as well as Australia had lost more men than the United States in . . . [the]
war" (Stacey, *Age of Conflict*, I, 246, 273). It is worth comparing Borden's position

with that of Mackenzie King as tea server at the "Quadrant" Conference, Quebec City, in August 1943; Roosevelt, in fact, vetoed Churchill's suggestion that King and the Canadian Chiefs of Staff attend the plenary sessions of the gathering [C. P. Stacey, *Canada and the Age of Conflict: A History of Canadian External Policies, Vol. II: 1921–1948, The Mackenzie King Era* (Toronto: University of Toronto Press, 1981), pp. 14–15, 334].

5. Col. C.P. Stacey (ed.), *Introduction to the Study of Military History for Canadian Students* (Ottawa: Directorate of Training, Canadian Forces Headquarters, undated), pp. 23–29, 35. The total army casualties in all theaters was 232,494, of which 59,544 were fatal. In the Second World War fatal casualties amounted to 41,992 [Col. G. W. L. Nicholson, *Official History of the Canadian Army in the First World War: Canadian Expeditionary Force 1914–1919* (Ottawa: Queen's Printer, 1962), p. 535].

6. Stacey, *Age of Conflict*, I, 238.

7. The conscription issue was really more symptom than cause. In Australia voluntary enlistment alone sufficed to split "the male population of the country into those who joined up and those who did not," producing a socio-political cleavage that "tore out Australia's heart, shattered the community and caused untold mental agony" [L. L. Robson, *The First AIF: A Study of its Recruitment 1914–1918* (Melbourne: University of Melbourne Press, 1970), pp. 2–3].

8. J. L. Granatstein and J. M. Hitsman, *Broken Promises: A History of Conscription in Canada* (Toronto: Oxford University Press, 1977), pp. 23–24. According to one estimate, Canada had by 1917 enlisted only 9.6 percent of its male population. Of 800,000 British-born Canadians, however, 37.5 percent had already enlisted, the highest proportion for any group within the British Empire. Only 1.4 percent of French-Canadians enlisted and but 2.4 percent of Quebec's population, compared to 9.5 percent for British Columbia (Ibid., p. 62; and Stacey, *Age of Conflict*, I, 235–236). See also C. A. Sharpe, "Enlistment in the Canadian Expeditionary Force 1914–1918: A Regional Analysis," *Journal of Canadian Studies*, 3 (Fall 1983): 15–27.

9. Col. C. P. Stacey, "The Staff Officer; A Footnote to Canadian Military History," *CDQ*, 3 (Winter 1973/74): 47–48; and Kenneth Charles Eyre, "Staff and Command in the Canadian Corps: The Canadian Militia as a Source of Senior Officers" (unpublished M.A. thesis, Duke University, 1967), pp. 120–121.

10. Queen's University Archives (hereafter QUA), Brig. James Sutherland Brown Papers (hereafter SBP), Box 8, File 178, "The Expansion of the Canadian Militia for War 1914–1918," pp. 6–13, 19; Col. C. P. Stacey, "Canada's Last War—and the Next," *University of Toronto Quarterly*, 3 (April 1939): 250–252; William Beahen, "A Citizens' Army: The Growth and Development of the Canadian Militia, 1904 to 1914" (unpublished Ph.D. thesis, University of Ottawa, 1979), pp. 2, 108–110, 146–147, 156, 193–194; and Ronald G. Haycock, *Sam Hughes: The Public Career of a Controversial Canadian* (Ottawa: Wilfred Laurier University Press/Canadian War Museum, 1986), pp. 180, 189–191, 266–272, 275–284, 299–301, 317–321.

11. Beahen, "Citizens' Army," p. 117. In 1910 Field Marshal Sir John French officially reported that the Militia was not in a fit "condition to undertake active operations" [General Sir Ian Hamilton, *Report on the Military Institutions of Canada* (Ottawa: Government Printing Bureau, 1913), p. 34]. On mobilization and field force structure, see Nicholson, *Canadian Expeditionary Force*, pp. 18–26, 545–550; Haycock, *Hughes*, pp. 178–184; "The Canadian Militia Before the Great War," *Canadian Historical Review* (hereafter *CHR*), 2 (June 1923): 98–104; and Stephen John

Harris, "Canadian Brass: The Growth of the Canadian Military Profession" (unpublished Ph.D. thesis, Duke University, 1979), pp. 141, 146–148, 157–168. The last, an impressive work, was subsequently published as *Canadian Brass: The Making of a Professional Army 1860–1939* (Toronto: University Press, 1988), but because of significant differences in text and references, the original is separately cited.

12. Shelford Bidwell and Dominick Graham, *Fire-Power: British Army Weapons and Theories of War 1904–1945* (London: Allen and Unwin, 1982), p. 123; William F. Stewart, "Attack Doctrine in the Canadian Corps, 1916–1918" (unpublished M.A. thesis, University of New Brunswick, 1982), pp. 247–248, 228–229; Dominick Graham, "Sans Doctrine: British Army Tactics in the First World War," *Men at War: Politics, Technology and Innovation in the Twentieth Century*, ed. Timothy Travers and Criston Archer (Chicago: Precedent, 1982), p. .75; and D. S. Graham, "The Ascendancy of Firepower," *The Mechanized Battlefield: A Tactical Analysis*, ed. Lt.-Col. J. A. English, Maj. J. Addicott, and Maj. P. J. Kramers (Washington: Pergamon-Brassey's, 1985), pp. 57, 60, 65–66.

13. Stacey, "Staff," p. .48; Stewart, "Attack Doctrine," pp. 230–231, 255–256; and Jeffery Williams, *Byng of Vimy: General and Governor General* (London: Leo Cooper, 1983), p. 115. Field Marshals Lord Ironside, Sir John Dill, and Sir Alan Brooke all served with the Canadian Corps as staff officers.

14. Martin Middlebrook, *The First Day of the Somme, 1 July 1916* (Harmondsworth, U.K.: Penguin, 1984), pp. 146, 179, 268, 279; and Maj.-Gen. E. K. G. Sixsmith, *British Generalship in the Twentieth Century* (London: Arms and Armour, 1970), pp. 92–98.

15. Harris, "Canadian Brass," p. 196.

16. A. M. J. Hyatt, *General Sir Arthur Currie: A Military Biography* (Toronto: University of Toronto Press, 1987), pp. 98–102; Stewart, "Attack Doctrine," pp. 235–238, 241; James Arthur Mowbray, "Militiaman: A Comparative Study of the Evolution of Organization in the Canadian and British Voluntary Citizen Military Forces 1896–1939" (unpublished Ph.D. thesis, Duke University, 1975), pp. 253–268; and SBP, Box 8, File 178, "Expansion of the Canadian Militia," pp. 24–25.

17. Morris, *Farewell*, p. 213.

18. Roger A. Beaumont, *Military Elites* (Indianapolis, Ind.: Bobbs-Merrill, 1974), p. 28; and Peter Firkins, *The Australians in Nine Wars: Waikato to Long Tan* (New York: McGraw-Hill, 1972), p. 158. The Canadians did not countenance desertion, for which crime 22 soldiers were executed by firing squad [Desmond Morton, "The Supreme Penalty: Canadian Deaths by Firing Squad in the First World War," *Queen's Quarterly*, 3 (Autumn 1972): 348].

19. Bidwell and Graham, *Fire-Power*, p. 123; and Lt.-Col. G. S. Hutchinson, *Machine Guns: Their History and Tactical Employment* (London: Macmillan, 1938), pp. 175–176.

20. Larry Worthington, *Worthy: A Biography of Major-General F. F. Worthington* (Toronto: Macmillan, 1961), pp. 89–91, 116; Hutchinson, *Machine Guns*, pp. 177–189, 193–200, 223–316; Lt.-Col. W. K. Walker, "The Great German Offensive, March 1918, with Some Account of the Work of the Canadian Motor Machine Gun Brigade," *CDQ*, 4 (July 1926): 399–412; and Brereton Greenhous, *Dragoon: The Centennial History of the Royal Canadian Dragoons, 1883–1983* (Ottawa: Guild of the Royal Canadian Dragoons, 1983), pp. 176–177, 227–228, 273.

21. Maj.-Gen. A. G. L. McNaughton, "The Development of Artillery in the Great War," *CDQ*, 2 (January 1929): 160–171; John Swettenham, *McNaughton* (Toronto: Ryerson, 1968), Vol. I, pp. 68–83, 129–130, 150–153, 157–161, 165–166; Stewart, "Attack Doctrine," p. 225; and Nicholson, *Canadian Expeditionary Force*, pp. 404, 429, 432, 435–438. The Canadian Corps often fired more than double the amount of ammunition expended by British formations. McNaughton's views of the limited effectiveness of indirect machine-gun barrage fire in the Great War appear at variance with those expressed by Hutchinson, Bidwell, and Graham. See also Capt. Bruce I. Gudmundsson, "The Lost Art of Indirect Machine Gun Fire," *Marine Corps Gazette*, 9 (September 1988): 43–44. Brutinel deserves more attention. See also Hyatt, *Currie*, pp. 121–122.

22. C. E. W. Bean, *The Official History of Australia in the War of 1914–1918*, Vol. VI: *The Australian Imperial Force in France During the Allied Offensive, 1918* (Sydney: Angus and Robertson, 1942), pp. 40–46, 57–59, 344–346, 363, 439–440; and Firkens, *Australians*, pp. 124–127, 136–143. The term "peaceful penetration" was taken from commonplace pre-war British press phraseology that claimed German trade policy aimed at gaining the British Empire by "peaceful penetration."

23. Harris, "Canadian Brass," pp. 169, 173–174, 189–193, 198–208, 227–260; Haycock, *Hughes*, pp. 180,308; Hyatt, *Currie*, pp. 71–73; and National Defence Headquarters, Directorate of History (hereafter DHist) 82/468, Stephen Harris, "A Matter of Influence: The Canadian General Staff and the Higher Organization of Defence 1919–1939," pp. 1–3.

24. National Archives of Canada (hereafter NAC), McNaughton Papers (hereafter MP), MG 30, E133, Vol. 347, Remarks by Maj.-Gen. McNaughton to the Canadian Infantry Association Annual Meeting, 18 January 1930; and SBP, Box 8, File 178, "Expansion of the Canadian Militia," pp. 25–26.

25. Capt. Robert Stewart Reid, "The Otter Committee: The Reorganization of the Canadian Militia, 1919–1920" (unpublished M.A. thesis, Royal Military College, 1970), pp. 6–12, 24, 33–39, 93–96; Beahen, "Citizens' Army," pp. 2–3, 212, 221, 253; Hyatt, *Currie*, p. 133–135; and Harris, "Canadian Brass," pp. 234–235.

26. MP, Vol. 109, Otter Committee Papers; Reid, "Otter Committee," pp. 27–35, 42, 49–53, 82–83, 88–91, 94–96; Swettenham, *McNaughton*, I, 179–182, 188–189; Col. C. P. Stacey, *Official History of the Canadian Army in the Second World War*, Vol. I: *Six Years of War: The Army in Canada, Britain and the Pacific* (Ottawa: Queen's Printer, 1966), pp. 4–5, 31; Mowbray, "Militiaman," pp. 312–323; George F.G. Stanley, *Canada's Soldiers: The Military History of an Unmilitary People* (Toronto: Macmillan, 1974), pp. 339–340; Desmond Morton, *The Canadian General: Sir William Otter* (Toronto: Hakkert, 1974), pp. 355–362; and Col. G. W. L. Nicholson, *The Gunners of Canada: A History of the Royal Regiment of Canadian Artillery*, Vol. II: *1919–1967* (Toronto: McClelland and Stewart, 1972), pp. 3–7. Original Otter Committee members Major-General A. C. Macdonnell and Brigadier-General E. A. Cruikshank had little influence compared to their replacements, Major-General Sir Edward W. B. Morrison, former commander corps artillery, and Major-General W. G. Gwatkin, the CGS. The BEF, originally conceived as a strike force of six infantry divisions and one cavalry division, fielded four infantry divisions and one cavalry division when dispatched to France in 1914 [Correlli Barnett, *Britain and Her Army 1509–1970* London: Allen Lane, 1970), pp. 364, 371].

27. John Gooch, *The Plans of War: The General Staff and British Military Strategy*

c. 1900–1916 (London: Routledge and Kegan Paul, 1974), pp. 192–193; Barnett, *Collapse of British Power*, pp. 254, 264–266, 585; and Stacey, *Age of Conflict*, I, 139, 160, 334–354 and *Historical Documents*, pp. 392–405.

28. Barnett, *Collapse of British Power*, pp. 251–258, 263–279, 345–353, 441–446; and Thorne, *Allies*, pp. 19–20, 33–36. For a further look at the British strategic dilemma and the vagaries of "concession through strength," see also L. R. Pratt, *East of Malta, West of Suez: Britain's Mediterranean Crisis, 1936–1939* (Cambridge, U.K.: Cambridge University Press, 1975) and Martin Gilbert, *The Roots of Appeasement* (London: Weidenfeld and Nicholson, 1966). An excellent treatment of the "Singapore strategy" may be found in Arthur J. Marder, *Old Friends, New Enemies* (Oxford, U.K.: Clarendon, 1981).

29. Hyatt, *Currie*, pp. 125–127, 129–132; Desmond Morton, *A Peculiar Kind of Politics: Canada's Overseas Ministry in the First World War* (Toronto: University of Toronto Press, 1982), pp. 179–198; Eric J. Leed, *No Man's Land: Combat and Identity in World War I* (Cambridge, U.K.: Cambridge University Press, 1979), pp. 201–202; and James Eayrs, *In Defence of Canada: From the Great War to the Great Depression* (Toronto: University Press, 1967), pp. 7, 23–24, 41–42. The British Dominions, largely at Canada's insistence, were exempted from the provisions of Locarno, which through the Rhineland Pact provided a collective guarantee of the Franco-Belgian-German border by France, Germany, Britain, Belgium, and Italy.

30. Brian Bond, *British Military Policy Between the Two World Wars* (Oxford, U.K.: Clarendon Press, 1980), pp. 15, 20–25, 31–38, 74–77, 82–83; and Peter Dennis, "The Reconstitution of the Territorial Force 1918–1920," *Swords and Covenants*, ed. Adrian Preston and Peter Dennis (London: Croom Helm, 1976), p. 192. While the Ten Year Rule has its defenders, Bond considers its confirmation in 1928 indefensible (Bond, *British Military Policy*, pp. 96–97).

31. Correlli Barnett, *Britain and Her Army 1509–1970* (London: Allen Lane, 1970), pp. 306–310, 410–411; John Keegan, "Regimental Ideology," *War, Economy and the Military Mind*, ed. Geoffrey Best and Andrew Wheatcroft (London: Croom Helm, 1976), pp. 7–15; Maj.-Gen. J. F. C. Fuller, *The Army in My Time* (London: Rich and Cowan, 1935), pp. 46–48, 201–203; Lt.-Gen. Sir A. A. Montgomery-Massingberd, "The Role of the Army in Imperial Defence," *The Army Quarterly*, 2 (January 1928): 240–241, 246; and Bond, *British Military Policy*, pp. 38, 98–126.

32. MP, Vol. 109, Maj.-Gen. W. E. Ironside to Maj.-Gen. J. H. MacBrien, 27 January 1923. Ironside, a gunner, held the prize appointment of Commandant Staff College for four years from 1922.

33. MP, Vol. 109, McNaughton memo to MacBrien, 13 March 1923.

34. Bond, *British Military Policy*, pp. 251, 261–262; Barnett, *Collapse of British Power*, pp. 474–475, 494–497; Charles Messenger, *"Bomber Harris" and the Strategic Bombing Offensive, 1939–1945* (London: Arms and Armour, 1984), pp. 15–28; and Allan D. English, "The RAF Staff College and the Evolution of RAF Strategic Bombing Policy 1922–1929" (unpublished M.A. thesis, Royal Military College, 1987), pp. 2–3, 29, 66–70, 75. The estimate of 150,000 casualties per week (there were 147,000 in the entire war) produced fear of the "knockout blow." For an examination of the perceived air threat, see Uri Bailer, *The Shadow of the Bomber: The Fear of Air Attack and British Politics, 1932–1939* (London: The Royal Historical Society, 1980).

35. Barnett, *Collapse of British Power*, pp. 497–505; Montgomery-Massingberd,

"Role of the Army," pp. 249–250; Bond, *British Military Policy*, pp. 1, 41, 177, 189, 215–243, 256; and Harold R. Winton, *To Change an Army: General Sir John Burnett-Stuart and British Armoured Doctrine, 1927–1938* (Lawrence, Kans.: University Press of Kansas), pp. 2, 24. See also B. H. Liddell Hart, *The British Way in Warfare* (London: Faber and Faber, 1932); and Michael Howard, *The British Way in Warfare: A Reappraisal* (London: Jonathan Cape, 1975). In fairness to Liddell Hart, he did not expect limited liability to starve the army of equipment; on the contrary, he envisioned the establishment of a small, but highly mobile tank army capable of intervening on the Continent at a critical juncture [Robert H. Larson, *The British Army and the Theory of Armored Warfare, 1918–1940* (Newark, Del.: University of Delaware Press, 1984), pp. 205–211.

36. Barnett, *Britain and Her Army*, p. 411. See also Bond, *British Military Policy*, pp. 9, 30, 33, 35, 41.

37. Quoted in Brian Bond and Williamson Murray, "The British Armed Forces, 1918–39," *Military Effectiveness*, Vol. II: *The Interwar Period*, ed. Allan R. Millet and Williamson Murray (Boston: Allen and Unwin, 1988), p. 100.

38. Fuller, *The Army in My Time*, p. 175. "For once," observed Fuller, "Finance did the Army a good turn and stopped this tomfoolery" (Ibid.).

39. Michael Howard, "Liddell Hart," *Encounter*, 6 (June 1970): 40. That Hore-Belisha also made powerful competent enemies is clear from Gen. Sir Alan Brooke's observation on encountering the former in 1943 that he was "looking more greasy and objectionable than ever" [Liddell Hart Centre for Military Archives, King's College London (hereafter LHC), Alanbrooke Diary (hereafter AP), 24 February 1943]. For another view of Hore-Belisha, see J. P. Harris, "Two War Ministers: A Reassessment of Duff Cooper and Hore-Belisha," *War and Society* 1 (May 1988), pp. 64–78.

40. Winton, *To Change an Army*, pp. 1–2, 225–227; Bond, *British Military Policy*, pp. 6, 188–189; D.C. Watt, *Too Serious a Business: European Armed Forces and the Approach to the Second World War* (London: Temple Smith, 1975), pp. 63–64, 71, 81, 132; Bidwell and Graham, *Fire-Power*, pp. 152, 166, 227, 247; and Larson, *Armored Warfare*, pp. 15–33, 38, 104, 211–212, 240–241.

41. Eayrs, *Great War*, pp. 89–92; "Service Notes" and "Notes on Service Journals," *CDQ*, 3 (April 1933): 365, 516; "Military Notes," *CDQ*, 1 (October 1931), 128; "Service Notes," *CDQ*, 1 (October 1932): 111; and "Editorials," *CDQ*, 1 (October 1931), 1 (October 1933), 3 (April 1933), and 1 (October 1934).

42. SBP, Box 9, File 196, Army Training Memorandum No. 4A Guide for Commanders of Regular Troops at Home 1932, and Box 8, File 173, Address to the Officers of the Mechanized Force by the C.I.G.S. at Tidworth, 8 September 1927. According to Bidwell and Graham, Milne "has been treated horribly by historians and deservedly so" because of his vacillation on army reform (Bidwell and Graham, *Fire-Power*, p. 155). Winton disagrees (Winton, *To Change an Army*, pp. 225). On Milne, see Brian Bradshaw-Ellis, "Seven Lean Years: The Organization and Administration of the Imperial General Staff, 1926–1933" (unpublished M.A. thesis, University of New Brunswick, 1976).

43. Bidwell and Graham, *Fire-Power*, pp. 130–133, 140, 145–146, 187–189; Larson, *Armored Warfare*, pp. 159–161; Winton, *To Change an Army*, pp. 127–131, 225, 231; Sixsmith, *British Generalship*, p. 176; and Bond, *British Military Policy*, pp. 35–38; Bond and Murray, "British Armed Forces," p. 106.

44. Bond, *British Military Policy*, pp. 55–56, 138–143, 162–163, 195–196; Larson, *Armored Warfare*, pp. 172–179, 185–187; Winton, *To Change an Army*, pp. 225,229; and Anthony John Trythall, *'Boney' Fuller: Soldier, Strategist, and Writer 1878–1966* (New Brunswick, N.J.: Rutgers University Press, 1977), pp. 144, 178.

45. Bond, *British Military Policy*, pp. 58–71; and Keegan, "Regimental Ideology," p. 15.

46. Fuller, *The Army in My Time*, pp. 37–38. According to Bidwell, "one of the greatest dangers of any army like the British Army, fragmented as it is by the regimental system from which it derives much of its fighting spirit, is lack of sympathy between arms and the growth of inter-unit jealousy" [Shelford Bidwell, *Gunners at War: A Tactical Study of the Royal Artillery in the Twentieth Century* (London: Arms and Armour, 1970), p. 30].

47. Larson, *Armored Warfare*, pp. 18–19.

48. Barnett, *Britain and Her Army*, p. 415; A. J. Smithers, *A New Excalibur: The Development of the Tank 1909–1939* (London: Grafton, 1986), pp. 235–274; Bond, *British Military Policy*, pp. 130–132; and Winton, *To Change an Army*, pp. 27–30.

49. Bidwell, *Gunners*, pp. 64–65, 68–71, 79–80, 94–96; Larson, *Armored Warfare*, pp. 80–81; Sixsmith, *British Generalship*, pp. 177–179; Kenneth Macksey, *A History of the Royal Armoured Corps and its Predecessors 1914 to 1975* (Beaminster, U.K.: Newtown, 1983), pp. 49–54 and his *Armoured Crusader: A Biography of Major-General Sir Percy Hobart* (London: Hutchinson, 1967), pp. 82–85, 98–108, 125–126; Ian V. Hogg, *Amour in Conflict: The Design and Tactics of Armoured Fighting Vehicles* (London: Jane's, 1980), pp. 103–104; and Brig. A. L. Pemberton, *The Second World War, 1939–1945, Army, The Development of Artillery Tactics and Equipment* (London: War Office, 1951), p. 9. In 1938 the deficiencies of the two-pounder were recognized and design of a six-pounder commenced. After Dunkirk, the decision was made not to start production of the latter, which would have involved a delay, so as to enable the quicker, mass production of the former. Here the Germans had the jump as all of their 37-mm equivalents had been produced before the war. See also Lt.-Gen. Sir Gifford le Q. Martel, *Our Armoured Forces* (London: Faber and Faber, 1945), p. 26; and Sixsmith, *British Generalship*, p. 179.

50. Maj.-Gen. J. H. MacBrien, "The British Army Manoeuvres September, 1925," *CDQ*, 2 (January 1926): 132–150.

51. Bond, *British Military Policy*, pp. 37, 138–151, 154–172; Larson, *Armored Warfare*, pp. 122–123, 133, 137–167, 172; Winton, *To Change an Army*, pp. 111–118, 142–167; Macksey, *Royal Armoured Corps*, pp. 49, 54–55; and SBP, Box 9, File 196, Extracts from Report on Collective Training 1927 Aldershot Command.

52. Ibid; "Editorial," *CDQ*, 1 (October 1931): 6; "Service Notes," *CDQ*, 1 (October 1932): 111–112; "Service Notes," *CDQ*, 3 (April 1933): 364–365; Bradshaw-Ellis, "Seven Lean Years," pp. 17–18; and Winton, *To Change an Army*, pp. 177–179, 180–183, 226–231.

53. Lt.-Col. A. G. Armstrong, "Army Manoeuvres, 1935," *The Journal of the Royal United Service Institution* (hereafter *JRUSI*), 520 (November 1935), p. 807; and "Editorial," *CDQ*, 3 (April 1936): 260.

54. Bond, *British Military Policy*, pp. 172–181, 187–190; Larson, *Armored Warfare*, pp. 171–178, 186–191, 199, 203–208, 212–222; and Martel, *Our Armoured Forces*, pp. 48–50.

55. Ibid.

56. Bond, *British Military Policy*, pp. 72–75, 251, 257–263, 269–271, 312, 338; Barnett, *Britain and Her Army*, pp. 417–419, 423. On the Territorial Army and rise and fall of "limited liability," see Mowbray, "Militiaman," pp. 293–318 and Peter Dennis, *Decision by Default: Peacetime Conscription and British Defence 1919–39* (London: Routledge and Kegan Paul, 1972), pp. 53–55. On the role of Warren Fisher, air defense, and the disparity in British service strategies, see Watt, *Too Serious a Business*, pp. 47, 55–56, 72–77, 97–102.

57. Col. C. P. Stacey, *Official History of the Canadian Army in the Second World War*, Vol. I: *Six Years of War: The Army in Canada, Britain and the Pacific* (Ottawa: Queen's Printer, 1966), pp. 7–13, and *Historical Documents*, p. 533.

58. Eayrs, *In Defence of Canada: Appeasement and Rearmament* (Toronto: University of Toronto Press, 1965), pp. 29, 44–47, 54, 60–61, 69–71, 73–74, 77–78, 226–231; J. L. Granatstein, *Canada's War: The Politics of the Mackenzie King Government 1939–1945* (Toronto: Oxford University Press, 1975), pp. 4–5; and "Editorial," *CDQ*, 1 (October 1937): 7.

Chapter 2

The Bellows of Peace

The need to fight quickly led man to invent appropriate devices to gain advantage in combat, and these brought about great changes in the forms of fighting. . . . They have to be produced and tested before war begins; they suit the nature of the fighting, which in turn determines their design. Obviously, however, this activity must be distinguished from fighting proper; it is only the preparation for it, not its conduct.

Carl von Clausewitz, *On War*[1]

The trials and tribulations of the British Army between wars obviously influenced those Canadian militia officers who, through official and unofficial channels, professional journals, and personal contacts, monitored developments overseas. Like the British, the Canadian military establishment endured a want of clear direction about its roles and, except with respect to personal pay and allowances, a dearth of government funds. Indeed, Canadian military unpreparedness in 1939 has usually been explained largely in terms of equipment shortages and political neglect. Yet, as the German army demonstrated by training with mock tanks and antitank guns, military prowess is not necessarily a function of matériel alone. Neither was lack of resources during the 1930s the sole cause of later British Army operational and tactical weaknesses.[2]

The interwar Canadian militia was diverted from its professional essence by its own leadership's preoccupation with the bureaucratic battle for the budget slice and the politics of mere survival. Keeping alive the art of war fighting, especially against a first-rate enemy, does not appear to have been as high a priority. Judging from the hefty $10,000 per annum paid the

CGS in 1932, when a doctor, dentist, or lawyer earned but $1,500, the Canadian public had every right, despite itself, to expect more of its professional military establishment. As one student of the period put it, "in the absence of any governmental direction . . . the Canadian Militia really had no idea what to do with itself, other than to keep itself going."[3] Clearly, however, electoral blindness can hardly excuse professional military myopia; neither is it entirely fair to hold peacetime societies more responsible than their retained soldiers for failing to remember that the chief purpose of any army, in the final analysis, is to fight its country's wars and fight them well.

Understandably after so bloody a conflict as the "war to end all wars," neither the people, including the rank and file soldiers, nor the government of Canada were prepared to take seriously the matter of fielding a force calling for up to 300,000 men in arms. While the established ceiling of the regular force was raised to 7,000 all ranks in 1919, it was reduced to 5,000 in 1920. At no time over the next few years did it ever exceed a peak strength of 4,125 attained in 1920. With the election of Mackenzie King's Liberal government in 1921, militia expenditure dropped substantially, though under the powerful direction of J.L. Ralston as Minister of Defence from 1926, it resurged to 1920 levels. Still, by 1929, the reserve forces mustered but 4,443 officers and 29,905 other ranks within respectively authorized ceilings of 10,509 and 117,273. Compared to her sister dominions and other nations, Canada had not given much priority to defense. Whereas Canadian defense expenditure for the fiscal year 1923–24 amounted to $1.46 per capita, New Zealanders spent an equivalent $2.33, Australians $3.30, South Africans $4.27, Americans $6.51, Britons $23.04, and Frenchmen $24.66.[4] But then, none of the foregoing peoples was so happily shielded by deterrents like the Royal Navy and Monroe Doctrine.

Here it must be stated that disillusionment, frustration, and uncertainty largely characterized the Canadian domestic scene in the aftermath of the Great War. The year 1919 witnessed increasing agrarian unrest and the worst labor strife ever. An economic slump left over 15 percent of the work force unemployed by 1921, which year also saw for the first time a Canadian population divided almost equally between urban and rural dwellers. By the middle of the decade, however, markets for Canadian goods and staples reappeared, and the industrial and agricultural sectors of the economy began to experience rapid growth. Much of this new-found prosperity was undoubtedly due to an overflow of wealth from the United States, which now replaced Britain as Canada's most important trading partner. Unhappily, the Great Depression that struck in October 1929 shattered the export economy, which garnered a third of national revenue from abroad, throwing thousands out of work with no hope of relief, social welfare, or unemployment benefits. By 1933 one-third of the labor force was unemployed. Mass emigration to the United States and a declining birth rate that reached a low in 1937 further sapped Canadian confidence; not until 1938 would national revenue exceed that of 1929. In the eyes of many, it was because Canada had paid so dearly in the Great War that she had been laid so low by the Depression.[5]

In keeping with its policy of retrenchment, the Mackenzie King government from 1922 placed all Canadian services under a single Department of National Defence (DND). This move, strongly supported by the militia, now precipitated an interservice struggle of shameful dimensions. In what was clearly a power play, the CGS, Major-General J. H. MacBrien, managed to get himself appointed Chief of Staff (COS) with broad powers of coordination over air and naval plans and programs. Subsequent resistance by the RCN so consumed the COS, however, that matters pertaining to militia preparedness and defense planning were neglected. Indeed, effective leadership of any kind was lacking from 1924 to 1927 within the land forces. On MacBrien's resignation in 1927, the position of COS was allowed to lapse and that of Chief of the Naval Staff created. When Major-General A. G. L. McNaughton became CGS in January 1929, he strove unsuccessfully for reinstitution of the COS position and worked incessantly for a reduction in naval funding. In McNaughton's view, air power had rendered traditional concepts of sea power obsolete, especially in the realm of coastal defense.[6]

What McNaughton thought and advocated was most important, since he was to remain CGS until 1935 and eventually be called back to command the expeditionary force in the Second World War. He was unquestionably the most influential soldier in militia service during the period leading up to that conflict, for which reason alone he merits special attention. Although representative of the new professional corporateness spawned by the CEF, he also epitomized the citizen-soldier. As a member of the Otter Committee, he concurred in the initial assessment that the "principal peril" to national security was "the danger of the overthrow of Law and Order" by foreign or Bolshevik agitators. McNaughton likewise held that the key to dealing with this threat was "to have immediately available an efficient military body with which to overawe this unruly element, and secondly, by education, to convert them from their perverted ideals to a true conception of citizenship."

In fact, the regular force, "maintained constantly ready"[7] for such action, was deployed in aid of the civil power duties once in Quebec City in June 1921 and three times in Sydney, Nova Scotia during 1922–1923, "most spectacularly" on the last occasion when over 1,000 permanent force troops were involved. During 1932 and 1933 soldiers were also used to quell disturbances in Oshawa, St. Catherines, and Stratford, Ontario.[8] Regardless of whether the Canadian regular force was even principally structured for internal security duty, however, it is virtually a truism that such employment remains ultimately inimical to military professionalism and in no way prepares an army for war. Ironically, the very specter of Bolshevism related indirectly to the incipient disintegration and degradation of professionalism that occurred in the Czarist army while it was engaged in internal security duties during the critical years 1905–07.[9]

Preoccupation with aid to the civil power was not the only unprofessional focus of the militia in the few years between wars moreover. During a nationwide tour in the summer and fall of 1932, McNaughton became convinced of the pressing need to address the plight of some 70,000 single, transient, unemployed men who were last in priority for relief. On his return to Ottawa, he approached the Minister of Labour with an outline plan of action that, in reasonably short order, the Cabinet charged DND to administer on behalf of the Department of Labour. Within days, the energetic McNaughton had a crash program of relief camps in operation. Under its terms, fit and eligible unemployed men were housed, fed, clothed, and paid 20 cents a day in return for their labor on projects such as road and airfield construction, forestry work, historical building maintenance, new barracks erection, and rifle range and military training area development. Between 1932 and 1936 more than 170,000 men, and up to 20,000 at one time, were gainfully employed on 144 various projects.[10] Though debate is unlikely to subside over the success or failure of this scheme and the actual reasons for its institution, DND seems to have paid a price for involvement. As a public relations venture it was a disastrous failure, for in the words of McNaughton's biographer, "Rarely . . . has any scheme been so criticized and from so many sides."[11]

The "Royal Twenty Centres," as they were disparagingly called in reference to the daily allowance, quickly drew the fire of opposition parties, labor unions, capitalists, and inmates alike. The camps themselves acted as magnets for agitators, with the result that major disturbances rocked many of them between 1933 and 1935. They became, in short, a liability to the government. Although DND was in the end officially praised for the "non-political and non-military fashion," in which it administered the camps, the Canadian public remained largely of the opinion that they were but a form of militarism that aimed at dragooning slave labour. A comparable U.S. program administered by the Civilian Conservation Corps with limited input from the War Department proved during the same period more readily acceptable to the American public. Certainly it ranked among President Franklin D. Roosevelt's most popular initiatives.

While the Canadian military undoubtedly acquired some useful infrastructure from this venture, and possibly certain training benefits for its administrative and engineer branches, it gained more public enmity than practice in the art of war. The combat arms benefited little, and for the militia at large it consumed an excessive amount of time.[12] The personal involvement of the CGS in this affair was such, moreover, that he barely had time to see his Director of Military Training, who headed one of the few DND directorates not involved in unemployment relief. A more savage indictment by Brigadier James Sutherland Brown, who personally considered the complaints of relief camp workers justified, held that McNaughton deliberately manipulated the situation as a ploy to ingratiate himself with political leaders and draw attention away from the poor state of the militia for which he was responsible.[13]

It has been suggested that because McNaughton's personal interests were so extensive, he may not have been "able to give all of his time to the main function of his office."[14] To be sure, the unemployment relief scheme had been his idea, his concept alone, which he defended to the last. Described as "a forceful dynamic thruster" with "a tornado-like intellect,"[15] he reputedly "dominated his colleagues in the military establishment as a great oak dominates a scrub forest." Such a leader, James Eayrs has argued, could obviously not have been expected "to remain within the compound of conventional military wisdom."[16] On the other hand, McNaughton has also been called "a master military bureaucratic politician" and one "preoccupied by military problems of a scientific nature such as air burst ranging."[17] During meetings he seems regularly to have had "attacks of the gadgets."[18]

Credited with the invention of the cathode ray direction finder in the interwar years, McNaughton had also promoted the extension of the Northwest Territories and Yukon Radio System, which had the beneficial side effect of garnering additional civil appropriations for Royal Canadian Corps of Signals training. The attraction of northern development further enabled McNaughton to obtain similar funding for RCAF operations in the North, especially in the field of aerial survey and mapping. Evidently fascinated by the potentialities of aviation, he as well played a key role in the formulation of an agreement on a Commonwealth transatlantic air route. In 1933 he chaired the deliberations of the Inter-Departmental Committee on Trans-Canada Airways that led to the air bridging of the Dominion. It is also a matter of record that McNaughton, a close personal friend of Prime Minister R.B. Bennett, revised drafts of the latter's 1930 campaign speeches and reviewed his 1935 radio addresses.[19]

According to Eayrs, the "military field then [existing in Canada] offer[ed] little scope for...[McNaughton's] talents...[so he] employed them in non-military affairs" to become the most powerful civil servant in the nation.[20] While this does not say much for McNaughton's recognition of the art of war as a field for serious study, it does say something about the Canadian military scene. A prevailing attitude expressed by McNaughton was that the "foundations of military efficiency" rested on the education of citizens in their respective privileges and responsibilities related to defense and the "creation of a national spirit." Given such circumstances, "technical efficiency in the various arms and services...[would] readily follow, [it being]...merely a matter of drill and training combined with careful selection of suitable material."[21] In short, McNaughton's faith in a citizen militia still remained strong.

Indeed, he personally considered it a mistake to use regular forces as a basis for expanding national armies, since

> They may have the highest technically trained officers in the world, but they are *trained to handle trained men*, and I doubt very much if they would make as much success in a war of the "Nation in Arms" type as [reserve] officers . . . who, while less qualified technically, nevertheless have in general a wider experience of men and affairs, and are used to getting results from semi-trained personnel. The competition of private life is a school for training in initiative through which the regular officer does not pass.[22]

In 1931 McNaughton reiterated the view that "a Citizen Militia . . . [was] the proper type of Land Defence Force for Canada," with a small regular force acting as an "instructional corps." In line with his 1923 statement that there would be "no large expansion of fighting forces on mobilization," he expected armies of the future to be smaller, more mobile, harder hitting, and better trained than those of the past.[23]

At the root of all such issues, of course, lay the matter of under what conditions Canadian troops were liable to fight. Sensibly, for it is ultimately the planner rather than the plan that counts, the General Staff began to develop certain contingency measures. Fear of the United States, as a traditional enemy and potential violator of Canadian neutrality in event of an American-Japanese conflict, prompted the first: Defence Scheme No. 1, a plan for war with America. Circulated for comment in April 1921, it called for denying the initiative to the Americans and gaining time for imperial forces to intervene in strength. As British Empire defense had always been based on a capacity to generate a strategic offensive after a tactical defensive, this much debated plan was never really quite so ludicrous as it has since been painted.[24]

Even after the termination of the Japanese alliance, McNaughton continued to regard the United States "a [potential] danger . . . [as] their foreign policy . . . consistently Imperialistic, . . . aimed at the hegemony of the Americas." He nonetheless assumed that "timely aid from other portions of the Empire" would render "the [Canadian] case far from hopeless."[25] When British Prime Minister Ramsay MacDonald announced in 1929 the dismantling of Royal Navy facilities in Halifax and the Caribbean, however, McNaughton charged that the British action compromised Canada's defense against the United States and cast the Dominion into the latter's sphere of influence. At the same time, though he remained concerned that America might abrogate Canadian neutrality in any war with Japan, McNaughton recognized it was folly to continue planning for a full-scale war in North America. MacDonald's initiative had, in a Canadian context, laid Defence

Scheme No. 1 to rest and with it the rationale for maintaining an excessively large military establishment of 15 divisions.[26]

Defence Scheme No. 2, which considered war with Japan and, later, defense of Canadian neutrality in an American war against Japan, figured less prominently in militia planning than Defence Scheme No. 3, which, approved in January 1932, addressed the dispatch of an expeditionary force overseas. On scrapping Defence Scheme No. 1 in May 1931, McNaughton hinted that one cavalry and six infantry divisions, properly manned and equipped, should now suffice to meet all contingencies. Cleverly, he managed to link this recommendation to Canadian force reduction proposals for the 1932 League of Nations Disarmament Conference in Geneva. It had been recognized for some time, of course, that reserve force structure was inflated and unnecessarily costly. It was eventually reduced from 35 to 20 cavalry units, which included four armored car and two mechanized regiments, and from 135 infantry and machine gun units to 91, of which six were reorganized as armored units sans tanks. Artillery and engineer units were at the same time increased, the number of field batteries rising from 67 to 110.

Militarily valid as this decision may have been, because it meant the demise of many regiments, it took some time to sell to the various corps associations, the political power of whose part-time soldier representatives remained formidable. Since the Depression-beset Bennett government lost its nerve and failed to proceed with restructuring, McNaughton retired leaving a militia still organized for home defense, deficient in modern weapons, and, sadly, in worse condition than when he was appointed CGS. On his departure, he produced an oft-quoted memorandum entitled "The Defence of Canada" that warned of severe equipment and weapon shortages; Canada, it stated, possessed but 25 obsolescent aircraft, not a single anti-aircraft gun or air bomb, and artillery ammunition sufficient only for "90 minutes' fire at normal rates for . . . field guns inherited from the Great War."[27]

In the same document, McNaughton acknowledged that the Ten Year Rule, which "relieved [the British Chiefs of Staff] of responsibility for lack of preparation in the event of war," had since 1919 been used unofficially as the basis for preparing estimates for the funding of the militia.[28] Like most regular officers, McNaughton kept himself abreast of British developments through the many intelligence, operational, and personal contacts Militia Headquarters maintained with the War Office;[29] in fact, most of McNaughton's addresses were little more than informative discourses on aspects such as the latest divisional organization and experiments with mechanization. Broadly convinced of the merits of the latter, he also believed that the lead Britain had established in this field would "be difficult even for other civilized powers to make up." McNaughton remained additionally confident that Canadians were naturals at "handling machinery of all kinds" and hence could be expected to outperform others on the technological battlefields he anticipated would mark the next war. Yet, he was not in 1929 an "advocate of extensive re-equipment," since the "rate of development would make . . . [such] equipment obsolescent before . . . [it got] into the hands of troops."[30]

McNaughton's philosophy, exactly like Milne's, was instead to devote scarce funds to officer, NCO, and specialist training, while urging all ranks to "think . . . about the effect of . . . new weapons of war and prepar[e] . . . [their] minds for the conception of tactics which they involve." In his view, if you had a good plan with which everyone was familiar, "you would usually be able to extemporize the material resources to carry it out." He was, above all, "an earnest advocate of moral preparation which . . . [was] largely thought and . . . cost . . . little." McNaughton further held that training was mainly a matter of education, which for a "highly scientific army requir[ing] highly trained personnel . . . [could] be best obtained quite outside the army itself."[31] There were in Canada, he claimed in 1931, adequate numbers of personnel with the required technical qualifications, except in aviation and signals, to meet the needs of any force that might conceivably have to be raised on short notice.[32] In maintaining that scientifically educated civilians and successful businessmen could master the modern technological battlefield better than military professionals, McNaughton manifested a not uncommon postwar perception. Ironically, it was also fundamentally the view of that quintessential militiaman, Sir Sam Hughes.[33]

Convinced that the next war would be won by the side whose officers had received the soundest scientific education, and hence understood modern weapons and techniques, McNaughton substantially increased the technical emphasis already pronounced within the militia since the Great War. In the postwar reorganization, for example, officers of artillery, engineer, and signals affiliations handily outnumbered their infantry and cavalry colleagues; by 1922 nearly 50 percent of the general officers came from technically oriented branches or corps. Under McNaughton this trend was accelerated, and it became policy to send the technically competent to the Imperial Defence College (IDC) to broaden their strategic scope. Of 13 senior officers who attended between 1927 and the outbreak of war, McNaughton being the first, five were artillery, three air force, and three engineers. Only two were infantry, one before and one after McNaughton's term as CGS, which appointment approved such selections.

McNaughton further ensured the predominance of engineering and scientific specialization over general education in junior officer training by appointing a nongraduate, Brigadier H.H. Matthews, commandant of the Royal Military College (RMC) in Kingston. As the RMC already offered highly technical training, the implications of this action were considerable. Significantly, on the appointment list for the overseas force drawn up in 1936, only one of six infantry brigades was slated to be commanded by a serving regular infantry officer, and out of 19 senior staff positions 14 were given to engineers and gunners. Of 17 top militia command appointments in January 1939, the artillery occupied five, the engineers six, the cavalry two, the infantry three, and the RCAF one. Of these, no less than 12 were held by RMC graduates, the great majority of them gunners and engineers.[34]

Not everyone, least of all the indomitable Sutherland Brown, was content with McNaughton's professional philosophy. The "drastic reduction of the Canadian infantry and Canadian cavalry," wrote the former in 1933, "appears to . . . be an intrigue by the Artillery Association which has been running the Department, or trying to, for a good many years."[35] Indeed, if the aim of the proposed 1931 militia reorganization had been to trim the fat to save the lean, the infantry and cavalry "troop leading" arms might have thought themselves in the first category. The overwhelming predominance of gunners and sappers on the Canadian General Staff by 1932 nonetheless presents the strongest evidence that Sutherland Brown's criticisms were rooted in some reality at least. McNaughton may have felt that he was selecting the best and the brightest, but to Sutherland Brown they were the lackeys of a CGS too inclined to harken to the right political tune with which to fall in step. As Brown described McNaughton in 1932:

> the C.G.S. is a super-engineer and college professor by profession. He is a gunner in the Canadian Militia and, technically, he is a good one. He is cold, calculating, touchy, and determined to pursue his own schemes, inclined to do everything himself, and will not take advice.[36]

Given the studied way in which McNaughton ignored infantry and cavalry officers, there were few eligible for senior commands in 1939. Simply put, he expected that officers of the technical arms—artillery, engineers, and signals—would adapt easier to the challenges of high command in modern war. Yet, McNaughton's principal focus as CGS was not on war or training for it. The emphasis he placed on the political visibility of the military and on the IDC as a virtual prerequisite for high command ensured that peacetime routine in headquarters, maintenance of military properties, and higher strategic issues eclipsed operations in relative importance. The senior officers of the militia, those paid well in peace to command during hostilities, were as a consequence better trained in the "great issues of peace and war, not [for] the battlefield." As McNaughton himself was destined to show, scant attention was devoted to developing higher commanders capable of managing a battle. Indeed, by tending "to treat military experience as something to be absorbed along the way like osmosis,"[37] McNaughton essentially denied the existence of a profession of arms that, akin to an academic discipline, called for the detailed and concentrated study of what Clausewitz termed "fighting proper."

At the lower levels, on the other hand, the Canadian military scene was not quite the professional wasteland that some have portrayed. A good glimpse of the level of Canadian military thought during this period can be gleaned from the *CDQ*. Published from 1923 at the expense of the Cavalry, Artillery, and Infantry Associations, this impressive professional journal endeavored "to reflect military thought, examine critically the direction of military development, and study in some degree the trend of world movements." By 1928 under the editorship of Lieutenant-Colonel K. Stuart, it had "hit its stride."[38] In a 1929 article that stressed the value of Fuller's principles of war, Major-General W. A. Griesbach argued that "since wars cannot be arranged to order merely to train officers, it follows that, after a long period of peace, the officers of an army must get their military education from reading and study." Concerned that "observance of rigid rules of trench warfare had carried... [many officers] forward to responsible command without requiring of them any deep knowledge of the principles, or the history of war," he warned that only "intellectual leadership" could be expected to penetrate with any hope of success the dual conditions of the "fog" and "friction of war."[39]

Through a series of prize essay competitions, the *CDQ* also managed to inspire topical submissions such as Lieutenant-Colonel H. F. G. Letson's 1933 article, "The Influence of Mechanization and Motorization on the Organization and Tactics of the Non Permanent Active Militia." His recommendations, not surprisingly "in accord with the example of the British Army", were to convert cavalry units in the larger centers into armored car organizations, encourage the use of motor transport in artillery training, and motorize a "fair proportion" of infantry battalions with which the reserve force was "top-heavy," some of them in "comatose" condition. Since mechanization appeared out of the question due to expense, Major E. L. M. Burns in 1935 proposed using less costly "motor-cars" in lieu of unaffordable tanks. Significantly, the editor had earlier advocated the light two-man Carden-Loyd armored machine-gun carrier, which had been issued to regular force units in small number, as the solution to dealing with enemy machine guns.[40]

The most interesting tactical polemic vented within the pages of the *CDQ* was that sparked by Lieutenant-Colonel Burns's article, "A Division That Can Attack," which proposed integrating "the medium tank as the principal engine of assault." Aware that commanders in annual British maneuvers failed habitually to drive home the attack, Burns advocated replacing one of the three infantry brigades in the restructured 1936 British "line of battle" division with a mixed armored brigade of two medium and two light tank battalions. Maintaining that there was more to the assault than "closing with the enemy," he argued that fast medium tanks possessed more capacity for breaking through to a defender's artillery zone than infantry supported by heavy "infantry tanks" plodding along at a pedestrian pace.[41] Almost immediately, these views came under fire from gunner Captain G. G. Simonds who forcefully challenged them in a subsequent *CDQ* article entitled, "An Army that Can Attack—A Division that Can Defend."

In Simonds's opinion, Burns in designing his "unwanted brain-child" had overlooked the practical limitations of British industrial capacity and the heavy coincident demands made upon it by sister services. Given a likely paucity of "offensive material," Simonds did not consider it "logical to design the basic formation of the British Army as a whole for offensive action." As many "holding tasks" would be required even of a side possessing the initiative, he determined that the "minimum strength for a basic formation must be a 'division that . . . [could] hold'." The "bulk of . . . hitting power," Simonds maintained, "should be at the disposal of the highest commander who . . . [could] control the battle—not arbitrarily divided between divisions in 'penny packets'." If circumstances like "the approach march or broken battle" necessitated decentralization, offensive resources could be allocated as required.[42]

In a kindly rebuttal entitled "Where Do the Tanks Belong?," Burns expressed his doubts that "any reasonable person would recommend a 'one purpose' or holding division," but added that there was unquestionably room for compromise as to where the main reserve of offensive power should be held.[43] The last shot was appropriately fired by Simonds who enjoined that in an "age of 'totalitarian war' the 'Army' . . . [had] replaced the 'division'," which was only capable of "pinpricks"; Burn's "unbalanced division . . . [would] still be unable to attack" for lack of organic artillery support.[44] While too much significance should probably not be accorded the foregoing debate, it does, even in its junior-senior interaction, serve to illustrate the heights to which regular force professionalism was capable of rising. The articles by the prolific Burns and Simonds were by any standard highly reputable works that reflected credit on an already respectable journal.

As graduates of the RMC, "the cornerstone of the Canadian Militia," which along with Canadian Officer Training Corps (COTC) contingents at civilian universities provided mainstream officers for militia service, Burns and Simonds had both benefited from a solid grounding in their professional education.[45] The four-year RMC course reinstated after the war unquestionably furnished the subaltern officer with a sound, if highly technical, military foundation upon which to build. In addition to academic instruction, cadets received theoretical and practical training in musketry and weapon handling, military topography (field sketching and map and air photo reading), imperial military geography, imperial and international affairs, campaign military history, and military organization, administration, and law. Equitation, horsemastership, and cavalry drill were also taught, no doubt the macho equivalent of parachuting today.

A formally established Tactics Department additionally provided detailed instruction in *Field Service Regulations*, the chief doctrinal manual for the conduct of field operations. Subject areas taught included the principles of war, the characteristics of fighting troops, the intricacies of attack, defense, pursuit, and retreat operations, reconnaissance, interarm cooperation, and intercommunication, including the drafting of appreciations, messages, and orders. Tactical training up to infantry company level was also accomplished through map studies, the use of sand table models, and more advanced tactical exercises without troops (TEWTs). In the associated area of military engineering, the elementary principles of field works, obstacle construction, advanced demolitions, and bridging were covered. To graduate, cadets had to pass written examinations in each of the foregoing fields.[46]

Within the all-arms training conducted at the RMC, however, technical and artillery aspects received special attention. In addition to the Tactics Department, there existed a separate Artillery Department that provided advanced gunnery instruction identical to that carried out at the Royal Military Academy, Woolwich, with the exception of siege artillery. A gentleman cadet upon graduation was thus qualified and competent to take charge of a section of field artillery. He also possessed a good grasp of the tactics and training of a battery.[47] The observation that the cadet "likes but to have practical, concrete facts thrown at him, not theories"[48] seems to have stemmed from this period. It was not until 1937 that the "technical subjects of artillery and military engineering . . . [were] reduced to an 'all arms' basis . . . [with] Cadets taking commissions in . . . these corps . . . [being] given special courses in their final year."[49]

Given RMC domination of the military establishment between the wars and the influence of other stream gunner commanders, it is additionally likely that militia doctrinal inclination at large was to embrace the artillery approach. To be sure, comments emanated from some reserve force quarters in 1931 that claimed "the infantry does not count now . . . it must be all artillery."[50] McNaughton, it must further be stated, regularly drew attention to artillery performance in the Great War. Unlike Burns and Simonds though, his published articles on Great War artillery, counterbattery, survey, and DND activities tended to reflect first-hand personal involvement, not conceptual thinking about tactics and operations. It could be that the technically proficient McNaughton fell into the trap of believing that the only experience that counts is one's own. In any event, he continued to preach the doctrine of shooting the "ultimate round," since "the price paid in casualties was inversely proportional to the ammunition which was expended."[51]

For the most part, however, Canadian doctrine reflected that promulgated by the British War Office. At the Colonial Conference of 1907 and subsequent Imperial (Defence) Conference of 1909, uniform standards of organization, training, equipment, and stores had been agreed and accepted within the Empire. In keeping with the idea of an Imperial General Staff,

Canadian officers were also nominated to attend the British Army Staff College at Camberley and the Indian Army Staff College at Quetta. Officer exchanges between dominion and imperial forces were also instituted. The Great War, in which the dominions mobilized almost a million of the nearly six million men raised within the Empire, resulted in an even closer association of Canadian and British forces at the working level. As the key factor in maintaining uniformity of doctrine following the war was considered to be staff college training, Canadian militia headquarters "fought . . . against setting up separate establishments for the study of higher command, military affairs and staff duties."[52]

The Canadian regular officer, in short, was an imperial animal. Following successful completion of an RMC preparatory course and entrance examinations, he continued to attend Camberley or Quetta as well as the Senior Officers' School (SOS) at Sheerness. In fact, because "the practical assimilation of the Military Forces of the Empire" was viewed as desirable, the Canadian regular officer received training identical to that given to his British Army counterpart. Both were expected to pass the same examinations, which anyone familiar with them would admit were tough and comprehensive. Candidates had first to pass "practical" portions before attempting associated written examinations in tactical problems set for company and battalion commander level. Other subjects covered were military organization and administration, military law, imperial geography, military history, military geography and tactics, administration in the field, map reading, and field works. Promotion examinations were set by the War Office to ensure uniformity, though allowance was made for Canadian differences in pay and peacetime administration. Promotion to lieutenant-colonel in both armies was dependent upon passing out of the SOS.[53]

Admittedly, a serious deficiency in the professional development of the Canadian regular officer, and NCO for that matter, was the absence of any worthwhile collective field training.[54] In this respect, however, they were hardly more handicapped than many British regular officers who often spent up to six years on isolated overseas garrison duty "without seeing any of the latest developments, and . . . rarely . . . [hearing] a lecture on a subject of first-rate importance." According to Ironside, after three to four years internal security duty in India, which put a premium on turn-out, barrack inspections, and cookhouse sanitation, a battalion was almost utterly useless as a military force.[55] Indeed, peacekeeping then as peacekeeping today in no way enhanced the capability of a professional army to wage war effectively against a first-class enemy.

On the Canadian scene, scarce funds as well as geographic isolation put a damper on officially authorized training. While in normal years militiamen trained for about 12 days at camp or local headquarters, during 1923 and 1924 they trained on average for but eight or nine days. Due to a higher training priority, officers, NCOs, and specialists in 1924 managed 16 days, chiefly at camp schools; the reserve force artillery in the same year conducted no firing practices. Lack of top leadership between 1924 and 1927 appears to have exacerbated the situation. Due to an inadequate performance the year before, field training exercises for 1927 were cancelled.[56] Increased funds plus volunteer contributions briefly rejuvenated central camp training between 1928 and 1930. As reported by several observers, however, regular force collective training in 1928 merely demonstrated that the maneuvers attempted had been too ambitious.

Attention in 1929 accordingly fixed on "fundamentals" in order to prepare regular officers and NCOs for their primary purpose: the instruction of reserve force personnel. Emphasis in tactical exercises focused upon "a small force of all arms" acting on advanced, rear, and flank guard duties, outpost duty, and defense in mobile warfare, including counterattack.[57] Training policy for the year 1930–31 stressed unit and subunit (section, platoon, and company) tactics and individual weapon handling. Two regular force units also concentrated at Camp Sarcee in Alberta. During the financial year 1931–32, however, the impact of the Great Depression practically eliminated reserve force training at camp; although in British Columbia in July 1932, a low-level "combined operations" exercise was conducted for the fourth time by the redoubtable Sutherland Brown. No regular force collective training in central camps was authorized for 1934–1935, the heyday of Royal Twenty Centres and the period in which the Canadian militia reached its nadir of neglect.[58] One could almost say, moreover, that with respect to training, it was a case of the blind leading the blind.

Although the "Memorandum on Training of the Militia (1934)" decreed the normal scope of training was limited to the infantry brigade with attached troops, the shortness and irregularity of summer concentrations precluded even the conduct of satisfactory reserve unit training. Some argued, in fact, that it was not advisable to attempt more than company level training. Still others, less visionary, maintained the widespread perception that it was "useless to . . . teach men . . . tactics . . . and . . . better to spend . . . time on close order drill." It was further contended that, in general, neither reserve force soldiers nor their officers were trained to the required standard, and certainly not to that of *trainer*, that would have enabled them to derive "value commensurate with effort" expended on larger scale exercises. A vicious circle thus developed as brigade and battalion schemes arrogated precious time from important subunit training, in many basic respects so necessary to the success of the former.[59]

One reserve officer even questioned in 1934 "whether the younger officers of the . . . [regular force], let alone the personnel of the . . . [reserves], have any accurate conception of what a full strength squadron, battery, or company looks like on parade, on the line of march or in action."[60] Though there were persistent cries from reserve force personnel for closer supervision that included demands for the attachment of regular force unit adjutants as in the British Territorial Army, the role of the regulars remained primarily to administer, guide, advise, and assist. Inevitably, the effect of such an approach was to permit the unproductive exercise of understrength, untrained units on far too many occasions solely for the purpose of letting less than qualified reserve force officers practice "their command." In light of the monotony and repetitiveness such training often entailed,[61] one reserve officer proposed as late as 1938 that summer camps be discontinued and replaced by major concentrations of all available regular and reserve force troops "for more extensive field training" every two or three years.[62]

Given such debilitating circumstances, it is perhaps not surprising that many militia officers began to cling ever more tightly to their colors, as if regimental loyalty and enthusiasm could compensate for lack of all-arms training. That this was an undesirable direction in which to advance had already in 1927 been noted by one Colonel T. A. Hunter who, in urging the cultivation of a brigade spirit, exhorted officers to

> divest yourselves of that parochial lone-wolfish jealousy that makes it so difficult to get Canadian battalions to fraternize. Also divest yourselves of that chronic hatred of staff officers. . . . Suspicion of other units and sullen dislike of the staff amount in the Canadian Militia to something like paranoia. Get cured.[63]

The Canadian militia, like the assortment of regiments known as the British Army, also tended to train but a collection of battalions.

While it is true that there were numerous officers and NCOs in the reserves who did not take their professional duties seriously and only attended courses of instruction as a means to retain their regimental sinecures, there were others who worked diligently toward higher training. Specialist and qualifying courses for reserve officers and NCOs were conducted through an elaborate system of Royal and Permanent Schools of Military Instruction, Camp Schools held during summer months, and Provisional Schools held during the winter months. Promotion to the rank of major was attained through a series of theoretical and practical courses of instruction and successful completion of promotion examinations in subjects similar to those studied by their regular force colleagues.[64] The most advanced course of instruction open to officers of the reserves was the Militia Staff Course, which required candidates to hold a captain's appointment and was reputedly "the finest investment . . . ever . . . made with training funds."[65]

Given the opportunities available then, it was possible for determined reserve officers to attain, on the *individual* level, a degree of professional excellence. As one RMC graduate and Great War veteran who served with distinction at a high level in the Second World War put it:

> there is no fear in battle equal to the fear of a commander—of whatever rank—who has the responsibility to make decisions, but is ignorant of the technical

knowledge necessary to reach a sound and proper conclusion in the circumstance. I made up my mind, that if I was to be a gunner, I would endeavour to make the science of Gunnery, and all that was related to it, my own. Books and courses were available for study, and I took every available opportunity to learn all I could. . . . Later I was to be forever grateful for the years given to me in which to learn.[66]

In the 1930s much of his training was accomplished on his own time in an armory on an improvised miniature artillery range called a "puff" table.

That a good reserve force officer could rise to command of his regiment without having observed the field operations of other corps[67] nonetheless exacerbated the problem of combined-arms training. One is left with the impression, therefore, that a more sustained operational focus on the part of the CGS and General Staff would have yielded better training results. For a force top-heavy in officers, there were simply not enough imaginative and challenging TEWTs and war games, though the fine canvas model or sand table demonstrations published by the *CDQ*, which reflected current doctrine, were a modest initiative in this direction.[68] The 1937 *CDQ* publication of Brigadier Montgomery's enlightened work on "The Problem of the Encounter Battle as Affected by Modern British War Establishment" would have also given the more alert officer a good insight into such higher level concepts as the "stage management of the battle," the need for advanced planning to ensure a good "start" in battle, and the notion of local "dog-fights."[69]

Not surprisingly, Simonds contributed the most comprehensive example of Canadian tactical thought in an article entitled, "The Attack." In it he addressed the problem of overcoming a first-class enemy once an "intact front, with interlocking fire" had, inevitably, formed. He logically assumed the enemy factor, more than time and space or even ground, to be the "crux of the problem in war" and rejected as "smug and dangerous" the contention that a volunteer army would necessarily be superior to a conscript one. To Simonds, any attack against a well-concealed enemy in a prepared defensive position would necessarily involve assault, "mopping up," and consolidation phases, the last two in particular being largely the province of infantry. He also saw that infantry with its unique ability to traverse almost any type of ground would be required for obstacle-breaching operations. Simonds nonetheless considered it a "useless waste of life" to let infantry attack without adequate fire support, since conditions of poor visibility and smoke had a greater degrading effect on antitank guns than machine guns, which could continue to fire along fixed lines.[70]

That enemy dispositions would never be well enough known to enable artillery to effectively suppress them beforehand convinced Simonds that "adequate fire support mean[t] a barrage." Since the occasional "short shell" was more likely to harm infantry than tanks, however, he went on to deduce that tanks could take better advantage of such covering fire than infantry. Simonds further reasoned that as it would be impossible for tanks to operate at high speed against prepared enemy defenses, the fundamental idea of the slower, heavily armored "I" tank remained tactically sound. Because tanks could also withstand enemy fire better than infantry, he asserted that where the ground permitted, they should fill the role of the main assaulting arm. Given the limited mobility and vulnerability of towed antitank guns, more-over, tanks would be more readily available to assist infantry in repelling enemy counterattacks during the consolidation phase. The obvious need for each arm to support the other led Simonds to conclude that attack "by infantry and tanks in cooperation should be the normal, not the abnormal, method." He ruefully noted nevertheless that this had been "almost an unexplored field since 1918."[71]

On a much higher plane, the reorganization of the reserve force along the lines proposed by McNaughton had been set in train in 1936, which year also marked the institution of a Canadian Defence Committee (later Defence Committee of the Cabinet) and the glimmerings of rearmament. Although a Canadian Tank School (redesignated the Canadian Armoured Fighting Vehicles School in 1938) was set up in that year, the recently elected government of Mackenzie King, like that of Chamberlain, continued to the last to dodge any possible form of European commitment. To make Defence Scheme No. 3 more palatable, therefore, the General Staff in March 1937 submitted a variation that provided for the deployment of a two-contingent "Mobile Force," totaling one cavalry and two infantry divisions, for operations in Canada as well as overseas. Sustained General Staff pressure in this area, which realistically aligned with the will of the Canadian people, eventually persuaded the government to mobilize this force on 1 September 1939 in general accordance with the provisions of Defence Scheme No. 3 (which also served as the basis of the 1941–1942 "Army [Expansion] Pro-gramme"). On 16 September it decided to dispatch a second CEF in the form of one division, and before the year was out there were almost 16,000 Canadian soldiers in Britain.[72]

Insofar as the primary purpose of a general staff is to prepare for war in peace, the Canadian General Staff can thus be said to have done its job reasonably well in a "capital staff"[73] sense. That is to say, it had a workable high-level war plan available for the military contingency at hand. Correctly anticipating that the Canadian public would so demand, it had for two decades planned to dispatch an expeditionary force that, after Dunkirk, was not to be denied. On the other hand, as a general staff in the sense of a "troop" staff, that is, one charged with training a field army for wartime operations in peace, it had done much less well. In fact, it had forsaken its Great War professional legacy and its true *raison d'être*. The regular force that deployed for collective training in the summer of 1938 was but a skeleton formation that exhibited many of the tactical shortcomings that were to plague Canadian arms five years later. Not surprisingly, interarm cooperation remained the major problem and, significantly, gunners and support services seem to have performed best. A few light tanks, armored cars, and modern antitank guns and artillery pieces were also employed for the first time.[74]

The primary focus of the general staff on defense planning and nonmilitary pursuits over the years contributed to this professional malaise because it detracted from training the militia as a fighting force. For this, McNaughton must largely bear responsibility. The lack or unsatisfactory nature of collective training further nudged the average reserve force officer toward a more traditional, regimental disposition and the regular officer toward higher staff work and the heady arena of imperial defense. To be sure, the path to career success for the latter definitely led through the IDC, which was generally recognized as the senior military institution. Yet, as established by Admiral Sir Herbert Richmond, the IDC aimed chiefly at improving interservice collaboration within a strategic context, giving due consideration to the diplomatic, economic, and political dimensions of an oceanic empire.[75] The strategic and regimental twin attractions, it must be concluded, ensured the general neglect of the operational and tactical sphere of war in militia training.

The dilettantish nature of the Canadian military establishment, increased by frequent officer transfers, further exerted an amateurish pull on those who chose simply to drift, buffeted by the system.[76] To one who broke out in the politico-strategic direction, the "Canadian military were not soldiers, though . . . many [were] experts on King's dress regulations . . . [who] . . . spent their time on hour-to-hour management and administration, not on matters of higher staff training or the like."[77] Fortunately for Canada, there were individual militia officers who, like Montgomery, withstood of their own volition professional compromise. The recent graduates of Camberley and Quetta staff colleges also generally fell into this category, protected by their very youth from fouling. The high command, on the other hand, was really incapable of training the militia for operations on the battlefield simply because, due to long neglect of this important area, it had little to teach.

NOTES

1. Carl von Clausewitz, *On War,* ed./trans. Michael Howard and Peter Paret (Princeton, N.J.: Princeton University Press, 1976), p. 127.

2. Brian Bond and Williamson Murray, "The British Armed Forces, 1918–39," *Military Effectiveness,* Vol. II: *The Interwar Period,* ed. Allan R. Millet and Williamson Murray (Boston: Allen and Unwin, 1988), p. 114.

3. Richard H. Gimblett, "Social Background as a Factor in Defence Policy Formulation: The General Officer Corps of the Canadian Militia 1923–1939" (un-

published M.A. thesis, Trent University, 1980), p. 28. On a national average, managerial salaries were in the order of $2,000 per year. DND salaries for roughly 184 people in 1932 ran to between $4,000 and $6,900 per annum [Donald Creighton, *The Forked Road: Canada 1939–1957* (Toronto: McClelland and Stewart, 1976), pp. 16–25; and James Eayrs, *In Defence of Canada: From the Great War to the Great Depression* (Toronto: University of Toronto Press, 1964), pp. 116–117.

4. Stephen John Harris, "Canadian Brass: The Growth of the Canadian Military Profession" (unpublished Ph.D. thesis, Duke University, 1979), p. 233; Col. C. P. Stacey, *Official History of the Canadian Army in the Second World War*, Vol. I: *Six Years of War: The Army in Canada, Britain and the Pacific* (Ottawa: Queen's Printer, 1966), pp. 4–5; Lt.-Col. D. J. Goodspeed, *The Armed Forces of Canada 1867–1967: A Century of Achievement* (Ottawa: Queen's Printer, 1967), pp. 91–93; and Eayrs, *Great War*, pp. 65–66, 302–306.

5. J. L. Granatstein, Irving M. Abella, David J. Bercuson, R. Craig Brown, and H. Blair Neatby, *Twentieth Century Canada*, 2d ed. (Toronto: McGraw-Hill Ryerson, 1986), pp. 184–237; Robert Craig Brown and Ramsay Cook, *Canada 1896–1921: A Nation Transformed* (Toronto: McClelland and Stewart, 1974), pp. 315–338; James Eayrs, *In Defence of Canada: Appeasement and Rearmament* (Toronto: University of Toronto Press, 1964), p. 56; Col. C. P. Stacey, *Arms, Men and Governments: The War Policies of Canada, 1939–1945* (Ottawa: Information Canada, 1974), pp. 1–2.

6. Eayrs, *Great War*, pp. 224–269, 274–287; National Defence Headquarters, Directorate of History (DHist) 82/468, Stephen Harris, "A Matter of Influence: The Canadian General Staff and the Higher Organization of Defence, 1919–1939," pp. 9–14; John Swettenham, *McNaughton* (Toronto: Ryerson, 1968), Vol. 1, pp. 241–244, 251–252, 300–304; Stacey, *Arms, Men and Governments*, pp. 67–68; and Stephen J. Harris, *Canadian Brass: The Making of a Professional Army 1860–1939* (Toronto: University Press, 1988), pp. 152–157, 196.

7. National Archives of Canada (NAC), McNaughton Papers (MP), Vol. 109, Otter Committee Papers.

8. Eayrs, *Great War*, pp. 62–67; and Capt. L. W. Bentley, "Aid of the Civil Power: Social and Political Aspects 1904–1924," *Canadian Defence Quarterly* (CDQ), 1 (Summer 1978): 47–49.

9. William C. Fuller, Jr., *Civil-Military Conflict in Imperial Russia, 1881–1914* (Princeton, N.J.: Princeton University Press, 1985), pp. 129, 137–144, 146–148, 157–158, 168–169, 262.

10. G. M. LeFresne, "The Royal Twenty Centers: The Department of National Defence and Federal Unemployment Relief 1932–1936" (unpublished B.A. thesis, Royal Military College, 1962), pp. 9–21, 32–39, 130–132, 142, 172, 182–193.

11. Swettenham, *McNaughton*, I, 276. He does not agree with Eayrs that "national security" was the main motivating factor behind the scheme; however, Roy R. Maddocks does build such a case in "A. G. L. McNaughton, R. B. Bennett and the Unemployment Relief Camps, 1932–1935," unpublished paper, 1973, DHist 74/795.

12. LeFresne, "Royal Twenty," pp. 54, 102–128, 193–197, 201–207; Swettenham, *McNaughton*, I, 269–285; Eayrs, *Great War*, pp. 124–136; and Goodspeed, *Armed Forces of Canada*, p. 95.

13. Reginald H. Roy, *For Most Conspicuous Bravery: A Biography of Major-General George R. Pearkes, V.C., Through Two World Wars* (Vancouver: University of British

Columbia Press, 1977), pp. 117–118, 122; and Richard H. Gimblett, " 'Buster' Brown: The Man and his Clash with 'Andy' McNaughton" (unpublished B.A. thesis, Royal Military College, 1979), pp. 64–65.

14. Roy, *Pearkes*, p. 116.

15. Norman Hillmer, "Notes of Interviews with Lieutenant-General Maurice Pope on 5, 27 July and 23 August 1977," DHist Biog P, p. 4.

16. Eayrs, *Great War*, pp. 257–258.

17. Maj. W. Alexander Morrison, "Major-General A. G. L. McNaughton, The Conference of Defence Associations, and the 1936 N.P.A.M. Re-organization: A Master Military Bureaucratic Politician at Work," Paper presented to the 1982 Annual Meeting of the Canadian Historical Association, DHist 82/470; and Hillmer, "Pope," p. 4. Airburst ranging was a technique for accurately and quickly engaging a difficult to observe target by bursting a shell over a known map location in the target vicinity and subsequently adjusting gunfire onto the target by correcting the fall of shot in relation to the observed burst over the known map location.

18. Tony Foster, *Meeting of Generals* (Toronto: Methuen, 1986), p. 165.

19. Swettenham, *McNaughton*, I, 213–24, 254–262, 292–297, 307; MP, Vol. 347, "Canada's Defence Forces and Their Place in the General Scheme of Our National Life," Address to the University Club of Ottawa 5 November 1931; and Maj.-Gen. A. G. L. McNaughton, "The Progress of Air Survey in Canada," *CDQ*, 3 (April 1937): 311–316. McNaughton would later help design the armor-piercing discarding sabot (APDS) tank round in the Second World War (Swettenham, *McNaughton*, II, 215–217).

20. Eayrs, *Great War*, p. 260.

21. MP, Vol. 109, Otter Committee Papers.

22. MP, Vol. 109, DCDS Memorandum to COS, 13 March 1923.

23. MP, Vol. 347, "Canada's Defence Forces and Their Place in the General Scheme of Our National Life", and "Address to Canadian Military Institute Toronto 15 December 1932"; and MP, Vol. 109, DCDS Memorandum to COS, 13 March 1923.

24. Stephen Harris, "Or There Would Be Chaos: The Legacy of Sam Hughes and Military Planning in Canada, 1919–1939," *Military Affairs*, 3 (October 1982): 121. Compare, for example, Eayrs, *Great War*, pp. 70–78 and Richard A. Preston, "Buster Brown Was Not Alone: American Plans for the Invasion of Canada, 1919–1939," *CDQ*, 4 (Spring 1974): 47–58.

25. MP, Vol. 109, DCDS Memorandum to COS, 13 March 1923.

26. Harris, "Chaos," p. 22. See also James Arthur Mowbray, "Militiaman: A Comparative Study of the Evolution of Organization in the Canadian and British Voluntary Citizen Military Forces 1896–1939" (unpublished Ph.D. thesis, Duke University, 1975) pp. 324–327.

27. Stacey, *Six Years*, pp. 6, 18–19, 29–30; Harris, "Chaos," pp. 121–123 and *Canadian Brass*, pp. 178–181; Morrison, "Military Bureaucratic Politician," pp. 3–4; "Service Notes," *CDQ*, 4 (July 1936): 468; and Maj. W. Alexander Morrison, *The Voice of Defence: The History of the Conference of Defence Associations, the First Fifty Years 1932–1982* (Ottawa: DND Canada, 1982), pp. 4–11, 45–57, 107.

28. Stacey, *Six Years*, p. 7.

29. Regular liaison channels existed between the Militia's Director of Military Operations and Intelligence (DMO and I) and the Imperial Defence College, the

War Office's DMO and I, Directorate of Staff Duties, and Master-General of Ordnance. The Deputy Chief of the Imperial General Staff and the CIGS also corresponded [General H.D.G. Crerar Papers (hereafter CP), MG 30, E157, Vol. 10]. See also Eayrs, *Great War*, pp. 91–92.

30. MP, Vol. 347, "Trend of Army Development," Address to Canadian Military Institute Toronto, 2 May 1929.

31. Ibid.

32. MP, Vol. 347, "Canada's Defence Forces," 5 November 1931.

33. Harris, *Canadian Brass*, p. 208.

34. Richard H. Gimblett, "Social Background as a Factor in Defence Policy Formulation: The General Officer Corps of the Canadian Militia 1923–1939" (unpublished M.A. thesis, Trent University, 1980), pp. 26–29, 34–39, 41–44, 46–47; and Harris, *Canadian Brass*, pp. 206–208.

35. Queen's University Archives (QUA), Brig. James Sutherland Brown Papers (SBP), Box 8, File 190, Sutherland Brown to Colonel H. F. H. Hertzberg, 5 January 1933.

36. Gimblett, " 'Buster' Brown," pp. 3–6, 48–61. As Gimblett points out, despite Brown being somewhat of a Yankee-hating "anachronism," his comments on McNaughton "provide us with what is very invaluable in historical analysis: two sides to the same story." It should also be borne in mind that Brown having lost the struggle within the militia to the "brilliant and good CGS," was subsequently portrayed, almost certainly unfairly, as a bigoted blockhead. There is evidence, however, that Brown was a popular officer, a good leader, more interested in the militia than McNaughton, and not necessarily alone without a following. He was the second Canadian officer to attend IDC (Ibid., pp. 9, 74–77). See also Charles Taylor, *Six Journeys: A Canadian Pattern* (Toronto: Anansi, 1977), pp. 3–38, for a more favorable view of Brown.

37. Harris, *Canadian Brass*, pp. 207–209.

38. Eayrs, *Great War*, pp. 95–102. For further evidence that this period was not the wasteland often painted, see James H. Lutz, "Canadian Military Thought, 1923–1939: A Profile Drawn from the Pages of the Old Canadian Defence Quarterly," *CDQ*, 2 (Autumn 1979): 40–48. *CDQ* circulation ran as high as 2,000.

39. Maj.-Gen. The Honourable W. A. Griesbach, "Military Study: Notes of a Lecture," *CDQ*, 1 (October 1929): 19–20, 26, 28.

40. Lt.-Col. H. F. G. Letson, "The Influence of Mechanization and Motorization on the Organization and Training of the Non Permanent Active Militia," *CDQ*, 1 (October 1933): 27, 29–30; Maj. E. L. M. Burns, "A Step Towards Mechanization," *CDQ*, 3 (April 1935): 305; Lutz, "Canadian Military Thought," pp. 42–43; and "Military Notes," *CDQ*, 1 (October 1931): 128.

41. Lt.-Col. E. L. M. Burns, "A Division That Can Attack," *CDQ*, 3 (April 1938): 282–298.

42. Capt. G. G. Simonds, "An Army that can Attack—A Division that can Defend," *CDQ*, 4 (July 1938): 413–417. Simonds also posed the question of what would happen if a large, highly trained, hard-hitting force met a small one.

43. Lt.-Col. E. L. M. Burns, "Where do the Tanks Belong?," *CDQ*, 1 (October 1938): 28–31.

44. Capt. G. G. Simonds, "What Price Assault without Support?," *CDQ*, 2 (January 1939): 142–147.

45. Eayrs, *Great War*, p. 86. On COTC, which dated from 1911 and was modeled on the 1908 British Officers' Training Corps, see Kathryn M. Bindon, *Queen's Men, Canada's Men: The Military History of Queen's University, Kingston* (Kingston: Trustees of the Queen's University Contingent, COTC, 1978), pp. 17–18, 59–60.

46. *The Royal Military College of Canada Syllabus of the Course of Instruction* (Ottawa: King's Printer, 1919), pp. 5–13. *Regulations and Calendar of the Royal Military College of Canada 1922* (Ottawa: King's Printer, 1923), pp. 28–62; *Calendar of the Royal Military College of Canada* (Ottawa: King's Printer, 1927), pp. 30–37: RMC Booklets "1933 Examinations," "1935 Examinations," "1936 Examinations," "1937 Examinations," and "1938 Examinations"; "The Royal Military College of Canada by 'Ex Cadet,' " *CDQ*, 3 (April 1925): 239–246; and Maj.-Gen. H. A. Panet, "The Royal Military College," *Canadian Geographic Journal*, 6 (June 1931): 441–454.

47. *RMC Calendar 1927*, pp. 30–31; and " 'Ex Cadet,' " 240–241.

48. W. R. P. Bridger, "Education and the Royal Military College of Canada," *CDQ*, 4 (July 1931): 451.

49. Lt.-Col. K. Stuart, "Educational Changes at the Royal Military College," *CDQ*, 1 (October 1937): 38; and *Royal Military College of Canada Calendar 1939–40* (Ottawa: King's Printer, 1939), pp. 34–39.

50. Eayrs, *Great War*, pp. 86, 309, 312.

51. Maj.-Gen. A. G. L. McNaughton, "The Development of Artillery in the Great War," *CDQ*, 2 (January 1929): 168; and MP, Vol. 347, "Cooperation of All Arms," Lecture to Special Instructors Course, 16 October 1928. McNaughton seems to have preferred such topics as "Some Aspects of the Work of the Department of National Defence," *CDQ*, 2 (January 1927): 143–149.

52. Lt.-Col. H. D. G. Crerar, "The Development of Closer Relations Between the Military Forces of the Empire," *Journal of the Royal United Service Institution (JRUSI)*, 483 (August 1926): 443–446, 449–452.

53. Lt.-Gen. Maurice A. Pope, *Soldiers and Politicians* (Toronto: University Press, 1962), pp. 52–55; Col. T. V. Anderson, "Qualifying for Promotion in the Permanent Force," *CDQ*, 4 (July 1925): 327–330; Richard A. Preston, *Canada and 'Imperial Defence': A Study of the British Commonwealth's Defence Organization* (Toronto: University of Toronto Press, 1967), pp. 353–362, 370–378, 401–413; and MP, Vol. 347, "Canada's Defence Forces."

54. Staff Sgt. J. W. A. Wallace, "Training of N.C.O.'s of the Permanent Active Militia in Peace Time," *CDQ*, 4 (July 1926): 474–476.

55. Capt. H. C. Westmorland, "The Training of an Army Officer," *JRUSI*, 499 (August 1930): 583; and Brian Bond, *British Military Policy Between the Two World Wars* (Oxford, U.K.: Clarendon Press, 1980), p. 105.

56. Eayrs, *Great War*, pp. 305, 309, 315; Harris, *Canadian Brass*, pp. 196–197; Brig. J. Sutherland Brown, "The Canadian Defence Forces," *JRUSI*, 497 (February 1930): 21; George F. G. Stanley, *Canada's Soldiers: The Military History of an Unmilitary People* (Toronto: Macmillan, 1974), pp. 341–343; and MP, Vol. 347, "Canada's Defence Forces."

57. MP, Vol. 347, Address to the Officers of the Permanent Active Militia, Petawawa, 26 July 1929; SBP, Box 9, File 194, DMT and SD to Camp Commandants, P.F. Collective Training, Camps Petawawa and Sarcee, 9th July, 1929; Harris, *Canadian Brass*, pp. 197–198 and "Canadian Brass," pp. 253–254.

58. SBP, Box 9, File 195, CGS Policy of Training, Active Militia 1930–31, 25

March 1930, and File 197, CGS Policy of Training 1933–34; SBP, Box 8, File 161, Report on Combined Operations M.D. No. 11, 30–6–32 to 3–7–32; and Eayrs, *Great War*, pp. 309, 315–316, and *Appeasement*, p. 134.

59. Lt.-Col. H. Wyatt Johnston, "From Civilians to Colonels," *CDQ*, 3 (April 1935): 262–263, 267; "How to Train Militia by A.B.C.," *CDQ*, 2 (January 1939): 148–154; and Capt. L. M. Chesley, "Notes on the Training of the Volunteer Infantry Militiamen [*sic*]," *CDQ*, 2 (January 1937): 183, 190.

60. Johnston, "From Civilians," p. 267.

61. "A.B.C.," pp. 148–149, 154; and MP, Vol. 347, Address to the Officers of the Permanent Active Militia, Petawawa, 26 July 1929.

62. Maj. A. A. Bell, "N.P.A.M. Training," *CDQ*, 1 (October 1938): 84–85.

63. Col. T. A. Hunter, "The Necessity of Cultivating Brigade Spirit in Peace Time," *CDQ*, 1 (October 1927): 22–23.

64. SBP, Box 9, File 194, G. R. Pearkes to Rowley September 1929; Chesley, "Notes on Training," pp. 184, 191; Maj. E. Lisle, "The Efficiency of an Army Depends upon the Efficiency of its Leaders," *CDQ*, 2 (January 1935): 163, 151–155; Johnston, "From Civilians," pp. 264–266, 269–273, 275–277; and SBP, Box 9, File 197, CGS Policy of Training 1933–34.

65. Letson, "Influence of Mechanization," p. 36.

66. *As You Were! Ex-Cadets Remember* (Kingston: The R.M.C. Club of Canada, 1984), II, 41. The officer was Brigadier P. A. S. Todd, who commanded divisional and corps artilleries in northwest Europe.

67. Bell, "N.P.A.M. Training," p. 85.

68. "A.B.C.," pp. 154, 156; T. C. Willett, *A Heritage at Risk: The Canadian Militia as a Social Institution* (Boulder, Colo.: Westview, 1987), p. 70; "The Brigade, Battalion, Company and Supporting Arms in Defence and Withdrawal," *CDQ*, 2 (January 1937): 158–174; and "The Brigade, Battalion, Company and Supporting Arms in the Attack," *CDQ*, 1 (October 1936): 49–70.

69. Brig. B. L. Montgomery, "The Problem of the Encounter Battle as Affected by Modern British War Establishment," *CDQ*, 1 (October 1937): 13, 16, 23. The editor described it as "the most thoughtful and valuable tactical discussion that has appeared in any British service journal for some considerable time" (Ibid., p. 1).

70. Capt. G. G. Simonds, "The Attack," *CDQ*, 4 (July 1939): 379–390.

71. Ibid.

72. Harris, "Chaos," 124–126; Stacey, *Arms, Men and Governments*, pp. 67–69, 108–109, 113; and *Six Years*, pp. 9, 19, 34, 58–61; and Mowbray, "Militiaman," pp. 345, 349–350. Harris has done some considerably impressive research in this area; see his *Canadian Brass*, pp. 181–191.

73. Dallas D. Irvine, "The Origins of Capital Staffs," *The Journal of Modern History*, 2 (June 1938): 161–179. To "devote constant and thorough attention in time of peace to plans for war" was the purpose of a General Staff, but Irving makes a clever distinction between "a central military organ assisting the supreme military authority of the state . . . and particularly in determining and implementing intellectually the higher directives which are to govern military activity," and an army staff in the field. In Prussia, he points out, the former function was first fully developed in the Great General Staff (*Grosser Generalstab*) of Moltke in distinction from the "General Staff with Troops" (*Truppen Generalstab*). In Tsarist Russia the

former was called the "Capital Staff" (*glavny shtab*), which term Irvine adopted (Ibid., pp. 162–163, 178).

74. Harris, *Canadian Brass*, pp. 191, 198–203; Brereton Greenhous, *Dragoon: The Centennial History of the Royal Canadian Dragoons, 1883–1983* (Ottawa: Guild of the Royal Canadian Dragoons, 1983), pp. 288–293; and DHist 114.1 (075) CGS Training Policy 1939–1940, 20 April 1939.

75. MP, Vol. 347, Letter H. W. Richmond to McNaughton, undated; and Barry D. Hunt, *Sailor-Scholar: Admiral Sir Herbert Richmond 1871–1946* (Waterloo, Ont.: Wilfred Laurier University Press, 1982), pp. 149–166.

76. It still does today. "It is a feature of peacetime armies," writes Hew Strachan, "that the maintenance of the flow of promotion and the prevention of boredom by a wide range of duties become predominant preoccupations. But despite proud claims of being 'a professional army' . . . emphasis on rotation between jobs makes for amateurism" [Hew Strachan, "The British Army and the Study of War—A Personal View," *The Army Quarterly and Defence Journal*, 2 (April 1981): 138].

77. Hillmer, "Pope," p. 2.

Chapter 3

Shaping an Expeditionary Force

The Canadian Corps is a dagger pointed at the heart of Berlin—make
no mistake about this.

Major-General A. G. L. McNaughton, 1941.[1]

The Canadian field force sent overseas during the Second World War was
in several respects one of the most remarkable in history. Though many of
its soldiers never saw Canada for over five years and suspected they were
forgotten on the home front, it never cracked or went to pieces in the field.
That the white cliffs of Dover supplanted the Rocky Mountains in some
Canadian hearts in no way diminishes the pride of place they so richly
earned in Canadian history. Canada possibly never deserved such an army,
the likes of which it will probably never see again. In point of fact, the
creation of the highly complex fighting formation that became the First
Canadian Army was not by any means an entirely national accomplishment.
In the areas of equipment, manning, training, and even organization, which
the following chapter will address, Canada always required substantial assistance. As noted by the CGS in late 1940, a further complicating factor
was the definite tendency "on the part of the Government in general, and
. . . [DND] in particular, to go in all directions at highest possible speed."[2]
Uncritical acceptance of air power as a cheaper military means of decision
especially heightened the intensity of RCAF competition with army expansion programs.

The day Great Britain declared war on the Third Reich, the prime minister
of Canada sent a message to the prime minister of the United Kingdom
asking how the Dominion might possibly lend assistance. Three days later

on 6 September 1939, the British government outlined its requirements, requesting Canada to consider providing a token expeditionary force and technical units and personnel for attachment to British formations. Sixteen days after Canada declared war, however, Prime Minister Chamberlain made an additional appeal for Canada to participate in the British Commonwealth Air Training Plan (BCATP), a grand air training scheme intended to annually qualify 20,000 British, Canadian, Australian, and New Zealand air crews for service with the RAF. Though Prime Minister Mackenzie King expressed regret that this overture had not been made earlier "so that [Canadian] . . . war effort would have been framed on these lines instead of having to head so strongly into expeditionary forces at the start,"[3] he cabled his approval in principle two days later.

That Mackenzie King personally favored such a limited liability air contribution is undoubted; indeed, RCAF prewar appropriations for 1939–1940 constituted nearly half the total allocation for all three services and exceeded those of the militia by eight million dollars. The prime minister pressed, moreover, for public British acknowledgment that Canadian participation in the BCATP "would provide for more effective assistance toward ultimate victory than any other form of military cooperation which Canada . . . [could] give."[4] His parsimonious refusal to provide Canadian ground crews, of course, complicated the matter of the formation of Canadian squadrons and virtually ensured that for the rest of the war the RCAF would fight as much less a national entity than the army. Originally, Mackenzie King had also intended to proclaim the signing of the BCATP before announcing the landing of the 1st Canadian Infantry Division in Britain. Much to his chagrin, however, an ebullient Winston Churchill immediately broadcast the division's safe arrival, thereby confirming continued British interest in a Canadian expeditionary force.[5]

Ironically, when the BCATP was signed on 17 December 1939, Mackenzie King's birthday, the leading elements of the 1st Division disembarked in Scotland. The division was commanded by Major-General McNaughton who, though retired and President of the National Research Council from 1935, had been personally called back by the politically astute prime minister to head the overseas army. The 1st Division was to remain in Britain until it sailed for the Mediterranean theater in July 1943. In the meantime, the second CEF swelled in strength beyond division, beyond corps, to army formation size. By the end of the war, the First Canadian Army comprised two national corps composed of three infantry divisions (each of three infantry brigades), two armored divisions (each of an armored and an infantry brigade), two independent armored brigades, and ancillary troops. Expressed another way, in terms of combat arms, it fielded six reconnaissance regiments, 12 armored regiments, 42 infantry battalions, 45 field batteries, 12 medium batteries, 28 antitank batteries, and 21 antiaircraft batteries.[6] Although not the largest of armies, it was the first and last such formation that Canada fielded.

Despite the government's initial decision on 16 September not to dispatch an expeditionary force larger than one division, it was almost a foregone conclusion that a corps would ultimately be required. The reason was ancillary troops. As previously mentioned, Defence Scheme No. 3 had called for raising a two-division corps with supporting or ancillary troops. The CGS naturally recommended precisely this size of force as the minimum Canada should aim to field, with the possibility of later increasing it to one cavalry and six infantry divisions plus ancillary units. On 19 September the government announced that a second division would be formed as an additional measure of preparedness. Ten days later it signaled its further willingness to send up to 6,000 all ranks in technical units (signals, engineers, ordnance, transportation, medical, and others) to be selected from a list provided by the British and equipped at their expense. The reasonable chance of the second division joining the first overseas, however, prompted Canadian authorities to advocate revision of this list so that such "nondivisional" units could eventually be used as ancillary troops within a Canadian corps.

The British accordingly promulgated a new list that included a requirement for a regiment of medium artillery and two army field artillery regiments.[7] McNaughton had judged this to be "the minimum additional artillery support required by the 1st Canadian Division in ordinary operations" and "a most important nucleus upon which to build up further artillery support provided from British resources."[8] While the British agreed that Canadian ancillary units would normally be employed in support of the 1st Division, the very nature of higher formation organization militated against such inefficient dedication of corps and army support resources to a single division. This was particularly true of artillery, the fire of which though planned in detail and controlled at the grass roots, is best commanded and coordinated at the highest level to ensure the most effective distribution of concentrated fire in time.

During the seven-month lull or "phoney war" that characterized the Western Front after the destruction of Poland in September 1939, the matter of equipping and financing ancillary troops for a "war lasting . . . three years" developed into a contentious issue. While Canada maintained that Britain should continue to finance ancillary units until such time as they came under Canadian higher command, the War Office countered that persistent Canadian involvement in their selection and administration already placed them under Canadian command, thus relieving Britain of further responsibility. This issue probably accelerated the formation of a Canadian Corps, for "it was fully recognized that negotiations with the United Kingdom . . . respecting the financial arrangements for . . . Ancillary

Figure 3.1
First Canadian Army[1]

25th Armoured Delivery Regiment (The Elgin Regiment)

1st Armoured Personnel Carrier Regiment[2]

1st Army Group, Royal Canadian Artillery (1 Canadian AGRA):
  11th Army Field Regiment
  1st Medium Regiment
  2nd Medium Regiment
  5th Medium Regiment

2nd Army Group, Royal Canadian Artillery (2 Canadian AGRA):
  19th Army Field Regiment
  3rd Medium Regiment
  4th Medium Regiment
  7th Medium Regiment
  2nd Heavy Anti–Aircraft Regiment (Mobile)

1st Rocket Battery

1st Radar Battery

1st Canadian Army Troops Engineers
  10th Field Park Company
  5th Field Company
  20th Field Company
  23rd Field Company

2nd Canadian Army Troops Engineers
  11th Field Park Company
  32nd Field Company
  33rd Field Company
  34th Field Company

No. 1 Workshop and Park Company
1st Field (Air) Survey Company
2nd Field Survey Company
3rd Field (Reproduction) Survey Company

First Army Signals

First Canadian Army Headquarters Defence Battalion (Royal Montreal Regiment)

No. 1 Army Headquarters Car Company

No. 35 Army Troops Composite Company

No. 36 Army Troops Composite Company

No. 81 Artillery Company

No. 82 Artillery Company

No. 41 Army Transport Company

No. 45 Army Transport Company

No. 47 Army Transport Company

No. 63 Army Transport Company

No. 64 Army Transport Company

No. 1 Motor Ambulance Convoy

No. 2 Motor Ambulance Convoy

No. 2 Casualty Clearing Station

No. 3 Casualty Clearing Station

No. 4 Casualty Clearing Station

No. 5 Casualty Clearing Station

No. 6 Casualty Clearing Station

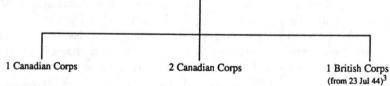

1 Canadian Corps   2 Canadian Corps   1 British Corps
                                                            (from 23 Jul 44)[3]

NOTES:

1. Not listed are elements of the Canadian Dental Corps, Royal Canadian Ordnance Corps, Royal Canadian Electrical and Mechanical Engineers, Canadian Postal Corps, and Canadian Provost Corps.

2. 1st Armoured Personnel Carrier Regiment operated under 79th British Armoured Division.

3. Including from 13 August 1944 the Royal Netherlands Brigade (Princess Irene's) and the 1st Belgian Infantry Brigade. On 9 October the 1st Czechoslovak Independent Armoured Brigade Group also came under First Canadian Army.

troops . . . would be facilitated by an understanding . . . that a Canadian Corps would be formed at some future date." On 19 April 1940, the Canadian Minister of National Defence, Norman Rogers, in a meeting with British Secretary of State for Dominion Affairs, Anthony Eden, expressed the opinion that "Canadian higher command" in respect of ancillary troops "meant the formation of a Canadian Corps."[9]

The next day Rogers and McNaughton considered the conditions under which ancillary troops would either be combined with the 1st Division in a self-contained formation under British General Headquarters (GHQ) or, with British support, be included with 1st and 2nd Divisions in a Canadian Corps in France. In McNaughton's view, placing Canadian nondivisional troops under British command risked unnecessary administrative complications and the undesired dispersal of Canadian overseas land forces. As he saw it, "a corps was probably the smallest organization through which the Canadian forces in the field could be effectively administered and fought." The minister, while pointing out that financial obligations assumed under the BCATP had "aggravated this aspect of the situation," suggested that if "a Canadian corps could be formed with very little additional cost to present military commitments, this might be acceptable" to the Cabinet.[10] The key was whether arrangements could be worked out "with the War Office under which the United Kingdom would provide as many as possible of the units required for a completion of the Corps over and above two Canadian Divisions and the Ancillary troops . . . in England." The first "rule . . . [to] be observed" suggested by Rogers was that "in general, Canadian organization should conform to the British."[11]

The British, not surprisingly, encouraged the formation of a Canadian Corps. They had already agreed not to send the 1st Division to France as part of 4 British Corps, but instead to employ it with Canadian ancillary units as an independent reserve formation styled "Canadian Force" under direct control of GHQ. It took the cataclysmic fall of France and the near destruction of the BEF, however, to shake Canada free from her Depression-driven preoccupation with finances. On 17 May, the War Committee of the Canadian Cabinet decided to form a Canadian Corps overseas and to raise a third division. On the day of the Dunkirk evacuation, the government announced that a fourth division would also be recruited. In July 1940, at War Office instigation, Canadian Force was augmented with British and New Zealand formations to form 7 Corps, commanded by Lieutenant-General McNaughton with Brigadier M. C. Dempsey as BGS (Operations). Canada now accepted financial responsibility for Canadian ancillary troops from 1 September. With the arrival of the bulk of the 2nd Canadian Infantry Division, by way of Iceland occupation duties, 7 Corps began to take on an even more pronounced Canadian character. On Christmas Day 1940, it was officially redesignated the Canadian Corps with the British 1st Armoured Division, 1st Army Tank Brigade, 53rd Light Antiaircraft Regiment, and ancillary units remaining momentarily under command.[12]

The Canadian Army Programme for 1941 (which reflected the demise of militia as a wartime title) anticipated a Canadian Corps of three divisions plus an independent armored brigade. A Canadian Armoured Corps was accordingly authorized on 13 August and the 1st Canadian Armoured Brigade formed. Shortly thereafter, the War Office announced its intention to form five armored divisions plus the equivalent of three more in armored brigades. At the same time it requested Canada and Australia each to provide one armored division. Unable to compete with the enemy in manpower, the British evidently reasoned that compensation might be found in armored fighting vehicles, which were given the highest priority. It was agreed subsequently that the Canadian Corps would by the end of 1941 comprise in addition to three infantry divisions and ancillary troops, an armored division equipped with "cruiser" (cavalry role) tanks and an army tank brigade of three tank regiments equipped with "I" tanks for infantry support.

To create the 1st Canadian Armoured Division, personnel were taken from the 4th Infantry Division which, in the wake of British victories over the Italians, had been allowed to run down. Following subsequent defeat in North Africa and Greece at the hand of the Germans, however, the 4th was reconstituted and plans were made to mobilize a sixth division for home defense. The 1st Armoured Division was in the meantime formed in accordance with a war establishment that called for two armored brigades, each of three tank regiments and a motor battalion of infantry, a field artillery regiment, an antiaircraft regiment, an antitank regiment, and one infantry battalion. Two experienced British officers were also taken on strength to fill the key staff appointments of GSO 1 and Assistant Adjutant and Quartermaster General (AA&QMG). Redesignated the 5th Canadian Armoured Division, this formation followed the 1st Canadian Army Tank Brigade and the 3rd Canadian Infantry Division to the United Kingdom in November 1941. By the end of that year the Canadian Army overseas totaled 124,472 all ranks.[13]

The opinion of the new CIGS, General Sir Alan Brooke, was that further expansion would leave too large a force for a corps commander to command and still perform his operational and training role. This view was shared by the Commander-in-Chief Home Forces, General Sir Bernard Paget, who with his superior recommended that consideration be given to creating an army headquarters. Significantly, the Canadian CGS, Major-General H.D.G. "Harry" Crerar, had on 11 August 1941 estimated that there existed sufficient manpower for Canada to field an overseas "army" of two corps, each of one armored and two infantry divisions, for a war period of over six years. In the event, the Overseas Army Programme for 1941–42 called for conversion of the 4th Infantry Division to armor and the creation of an overseas field army headquarters to command and administer a Canadian Corps of three divisions and a Canadian Armoured Corps of two divisions.

Headquarters First Canadian Army thus came into existence on Easter Monday 6 April 1942, with McNaughton named General Officer Commanding-in-Chief (GOC-in-C). The 4th Canadian Armoured Division proceeded overseas that summer. The 2nd Canadian Army Tank Brigade, organized the same year, shipped to Britain in June 1943, five months after the establishment of Headquarters 2 Canadian Corps. Again in the complex matter of fielding large fighting formations, the major problem encountered was that of ancillary troops. They actually represented a larger manpower commitment than the fighting formations. The result was that with an RCN and RCAF destined to grow to 92,000 and 215,000, respectively, the First Canadian Army could not, and was never able to, operate entirely as a Canadian field force. The War Office responded by contributing upwards of 9,000 men per division as a permanent commitment to complete its rearward support services. By the end of 1943, the year in which the 1st Division and the 1st Canadian Army Tank Brigade left for Sicily, the Canadian Army overseas reached its peak development as a force of over a quarter of a million men. Though smaller than the first CEF, which from January 1917 was in excess of 300,000 all ranks, it was still a sizable body."[14]

The "days of great expeditionary forces of infantry crossing the oceans," which Prime Minister Mackenzie King confidently ventured on 30 March 1939 were unlikely to recur, had thus returned like some unwelcome premonition. To fill the ranks of this growing overseas commitment, the Canadian government from the beginning appealed to the patriotic zeal of its citizenry. The initial lack of key munitions industries and high unemployment nicely complemented the volunteer spirit in 1939,[15] to the extent that men of the 1st Canadian Infantry Division were uncharitably dubbed "breadliners" by those who followed.[16] Since the Militia Act stipulated that no soldier could be compelled to serve continuously in the field for more than a year, volunteers were encouraged to enlist for the duration of the war on general service (GS) in the newly created Canadian Active Service Force (CASF), which for legal and administrative reasons also incorporated activated reserve units alongside those of the smaller regular force. About half of the 58,337 volunteers who joined the CASF in September 1939 were former or serving members of either the regulars or reserves. In December 1939, regulations were even altered to permit the enlistment of resident aliens, which enabled U.S. citizens to join.

With the Dunkirk-prompted passage of the National Resources Mobilization Act (NRMA) in June 1940, however, two classes of soldier were officially embraced within the Canadian land forces. The NRMA imposed conscription not for GS that included service overseas, but for home defense duty in Canada only. Initially, only unmarried or widowed men without children between the ages of 21 and 24 were called up for 30-days training, all that was considered manageable given existing equipment and weapon shortages. Later, compulsory training for NRMA soldiers was extended to four months, which from 20 March 1941 was conducted with GS recruits in accordance with a common program. Following this training, NRMA men were posted to home defense formations or placed on reserve unit rolls until required. On 23 April 1941, authority was obtained to have them replace for the duration of the war GS soldiers on coast or home defense duty, thereby releasing the latter for service overseas. After Pearl Harbor, in the face of mounting public pressure, the government announced its intention on 22 January 1942 of seeking through a national referendum a release from its commitment to not conscript for service overseas.[17]

The decision to train NRMA conscripts or "R" recruits together with GS or "A" recruits naturally simplified the military pedagogical system. Whereas before, conscripts received instruction at reserve force NPAM Training Centres, both R and A recruits from all arms and branches now underwent eight weeks basic infantry or "common-to-all-arms" training at Basic Training Centres (BTC). During 1942 the number of BTCs grew from 28 to 39, which permitted an eventually excessive annual output of close to 190,000 recruits. After successfully completing the BTC stage, recruits passed on to Advanced Training Centres (ATC) where they underwent an additional two to five months training peculiar to their respective arms or services. Upon conclusion of training at an ATC, which also ran special courses for officers and NCOs, the soldier was available for reinforcing purposes. All told, 33 ATCs were established, among them nine infantry, five artillery, two engineer, and two armored, including reconnaissance. In order to lessen administrative overhead and increase training efficiency, most BTCs and ATCs were linked on a corps or branch basis in August 1943. This move resulted in the closure of 13 BTCs and reductions in the size of others.[18]

In the meantime, initially because of instructor deficiencies and officer shortages, the army in England established its own Canadian Training School (CTS) in August 1941. By mid–1942, the CTS consisted of six wings responsible for training as follows: Number 1 Wing, officer cadets; Number 2, driver maintenance and junior NCOs; Number 3, range work and weapons; Number 4, unit tactics; Number 5, battle drill; and Number 6, chemical warfare.[19] Given the proliferation of British Army courses that were also open to Canadians, it is not surprising that some training overlap occurred. Indeed, according to one 1942 report, the training "confusion and repetition between Canada and England result[ed] in a tremendous loss of time"; the "constant retesting" that officers and men had to undergo furthermore produced a corresponding "loss of morale."[20]

The armored corps had a particular problem in this respect as troops who received driver and gunnery training on the Canadian Ram tank had overseas to convert to Shermans. Also, complaints about the unsatisfactory training state of reinforcements arriving from Canada arose in 1943 and continued into 1944. Of armored reinforcements, only 30 percent on average were capable of passing tests on elementary training (TOETs); many had never fired a rifle or light machine gun. Infantry reinforcements in the fall of 1944 were found to have little "fieldcraft sense" and less training on grenades, the submachine gun, and PIAT (projector, infantry, antitank). While BTC and ATC linking was intended to alleviate this problem, the Number 1 Training Brigade Group was also established at Debert, Nova Scotia, in October 1943. Designed to give reinforcements four weeks of individual and collective training before proceeding overseas, it unfortunately lacked armored elements.[21]

While detailed treatment of individual training is beyond the scope of this work, though it begs further research and analysis, a brief word on officer training is in order. As of April 1941 all candidates for nonspecialist commissioning in the Canadian Army had first to serve in the ranks, either with an active or reserve unit, prior to undergoing training as a reinforcement officer. A further stipulation was that 25 percent of junior officer requirements were to be provided from the ranks of overseas formations, via the CTS officer cadet wing or training unit (OCTU); the remaining 75 percent were to be provided from Canada. Two Officer Training Centres (OTC) accordingly opened in 1941, one at Brockville, Ontario, with a capacity of 1,200 candidates, and one at Gordon Head near Victoria, British Columbia, with a capacity of 800. At these OTCs, candidates were trained over three months to infantry platoon commander standard, after which they were appointed second lieutenants and sent to ATCs for two to five months corps or branch training before being posted as officer reinforcements. The RMC, its four-year course shortened to two in 1939, graduated its last officer cadet class in 1942. By September 1943, however, an officer surplus had been identified and only the Brockville OTC remained open in Canada.[22]

The OCTU, except for its basic course, was also briefly closed in 1942, though loss of time in travel to Canada and the proximity of better training facilities in Britain soon prompted its reopening in September. Of all the arms, only the infantry continued to send officer candidates to Canadian OTCs. That the standard of OTCs may have been lower, however, is indicated by the report of the CTS Commandant in September 1943 that "something seemed wrong" with the Brockville establishment and "cadets from overseas who were spoken to felt that most of their time . . . [there] was wasted."[23] This opinion was corroborated by the Director of Military Training who admitted that "for some considerable time . . . the tr[ainin]g itself and direction of tr[ainin]g ha[d] not been up to requirements." The matter of replacing the Brockville commandant, he added, was "under active consideration."[24]

It would appear that similar teething problems were experienced in senior officer training. One RMC Company Commanders Course reported a failure rate of 37 percent, which "as in the case of the first" was attributed to a low standard of professional and educational knowledge. According to a CTS report on a 1942 Senior Officers Course, "A short run of some 200 to 300 yards completely winded the majority [of candidates], and in some cases was not even attempted." In 1943 the Company Commanders Course and Senior Officers Course were merged into one 11-week Field Officers Course. This course, after being conducted twice, was discontinued in December to make room at the RMC for the Canadian Civil Affairs Staff Course. The purpose of the last course was to train officers in the civil administration of areas liberated by the Canadian Army overseas.[25]

Within the army at large meanwhile, unit morale reports for June 1943 indicated that "NRMA personnel and policy" in 31 percent of cases represented, after "training difficulties" at 34 percent, the second principal factor detrimental to army morale.[26] Though "mixed in huts and shar[ing] . . . duties and pleasures," the very existence of two official factions invited comparison and criticism that inevitably translated into outright antagonism. For every unit that described improvement in relations between NRMA and GS soldiers, there were two that described deterioration. Exhorting "R" recruits to "go active" through cajolery and sustained pressure doubtless contributed to this military schism, as most certainly did the waxing tempo of the land war with its dual implications of heavy casualties and a quick end to fighting. The perception of NRMA men as a privileged class had some basis, in fact, since many tended to use their status to bargain for occupational leave to work as wage earners on farms and construction projects.

As GS NCOs proceeding overseas usually had to revert in rank, moreover, NRMA men often leapt at the chance to fill such vacancies. This naturally further aggravated the situation as GS soldiers intensely disliked serving under NRMA NCOs who, in turn, experienced great difficulty in dealing with GS subordinates.[27] The perception that the public did not distinguish between GS volunteers and NRMA "zombies," plus the education campaign this prompted, served to accentuate differences that were now made visible on the uniform of the soldier.[28] An Adjutant-General Branch survey of 1,300 NRMA and 1,800 GS soldiers, conducted in August 1944, concluded that it was more difficult to recruit volunteers within the army than without.[29] By March 1945 the NRMA reinforcement situation was reported overwhelmingly by units to be "the most widespread morale obstacle in Canada" and "the foremost cause of lowered morale" in Corps Training Centres.[30] Aside from the debilitation wrought by poor morale, the sheer administration of problems related to NRMA could not but have dissipated the effectiveness of training.

Given that training centers are the heart of any army, moreover, it is difficult to believe that discordance within them would not have echoed overseas. The problem would not have arisen before 20 March 1941, by which time both the 1st and 2nd Divisions were already overseas, but it most certainly would have affected following formations and individual reinforcements. Indeed, this may even explain why in the national plebiscite (of 27 April 1942), 72 percent of military voters abroad agreed to release the government from its original pledge not to introduce compulsory overseas service. True, the 84 percent military approval vote at home was 12 percent higher, a discrepancy long interpreted by some as an indication that the all-volunteer army in Britain preferred to remain that way.[31] Compared to the Canadian national approval vote of 64 percent, however, the 72 percent overseas approval stands as an overwhelmingly positive statement. It also remains to be seen whether the "de-Canadianization" phenomenon, the outright antagonism of many troops toward Canadian policy and Canadians at home, can be linked to the 12 percent difference. If interest in the NRMA question was later found to have been slight overseas, it should further be noted that the "only consistent and pervasive object of Canadian interest to the majority of . . . personnel . . . overseas was their families."[32]

Recognition of the depth to which such concern could run no doubt prompted Keegan to observe in his masterly work *The Face of Battle* that "one of the most insidious cruelties that the Second World War inflicted" on society was that of not granting home leave to soldiers. While he was specifically referring to the impact of Red Army policy between 1941 and 1945 on the Russian people,[33] it is sobering to reflect that until the autumn of 1944 there was no system of rotational leave for the Canadian soldier overseas. When it did come into effect, eligibility was restricted to those with "five years satisfactory continuous service overseas."[34] There is also good reason to believe that thrice-wounded soldiers were sent back into the line. On the home front, in the meantime, NRMA men engaged to "save the tobacco crop" earned six to seven dollars over and above their $1.25 daily soldier's pay.[35]

While a good sociological treatment of Canada's army in the Second World War needs yet to be done, an occupational profile can be discerned from several extensive surveys conducted by the Adjutant-General's Branch in late 1944 and the autumn of 1945. Special Report No. 180 prepared by the Research and Information Section was based on a rehabilitation canvass of some 12,000 army personnel who constituted a 2.4 percent cross section of the Canadian Army as a whole. Similar surveys considered to be equally representative and statistically valid were conducted during the first 12 days of August, September, and October 1945 among 3,629 officers and men awaiting discharge in depots. A high degree of internal consistency was noted among the August, September, and October samples and the total was further considered to be consistent with the findings recorded in Special Report No. 180. Of those asked to describe their regular pre-enlistment employment, between 82 and 87 percent responded positively. In all instances occupations reported on questionnaires were those "regarded by the individual as his regular job."

Classified in terms of the "Dictionary of Occupational Titles" and taking into account some probable inflation due to individual desire for prestige, the categories below were identified in the percentages indicated:

Professional and managerial	7.4–8.6%
Clerical	7.4–8.8
Sales Persons	4.0–4.9
Agricultural	14.1
Skilled Industrial	19.9–20.2
Semi-skilled Industrial	14.9–16.9
Unskilled Industrial	7.2–8.7
Other (including service, fishing, and forestry)	4.7
Student	5.0–7.3
Insufficient/No information	9.5–9.7[36]

Pre-enlistment residence as reported on questionnaires provided an additional persepctive on the general composition of the Canadian Army:

Farm residents	15.2%
Rural but not farm	6.1
Villages under 5,000	21.8
Cities over 5,000	53.9[37]

Given the importance of agriculture to the war effort, of course, only one-sixth of farmers as compared to one-fifth of skilled industrial workers were deemed eligible for service.[38] These statistics suggest that the Canadian Army was less ruggedly rural in character than has sometimes been assumed. As the image of the Australians in the Great War as "leathery men from the Outback" has been shown to be false, so the military perception of Canadians in the Second World War as hardy frontiersmen must be rejected.[39] "Like their fathers before them, they shivered in the damp cold of the English climate, and, although provisioned with a more generous allocation of heating coal than British troops, chopped up park and bus stop benches to gain extra warmth."[40]

The formation structure of the Canadian Army, while not "slavishly follow[ing] the model of any other country, however efficient," was based on an existing regimental system of units.[41] Under Defence Scheme No. 3 the composition of expeditionary force divisions had been prede-termined so as to give proportional representation to the major territorial regions of Canada. Thus, within the 1st Canadian Infantry Division, units from Ontario made up the 1st Brigade, units from the West the 2nd, and units from Quebec and the Maritimes the 3rd. Similarly, in the 2nd Division, Ontario units made up the 4th Brigade, Quebec units the 5th, and Western units the 6th. The French-speaking complexion of the 5th Brigade was compromised, however, when the Royal 22nd Regiment was transferred with other regular force battalions originally earmarked for the 2nd Division to the overseas bound 1st Division. The dispatch of Les Fusiliers Mont-Royal to Iceland and their replacement by the Calgary Highlanders in the summer of 1940 was followed by a recommendation from the francophone commander of the 5th Brigade that, due to a criti-cal shortage of qualified staff officers and commanders, it cease to be a French-speaking formation.[42] Viewing the matter from another perspec-tive, McNaughton considered it "unwise to re-group [French-speaking units] . . . owing to the political difficulties that might arise if there were a heavy incidence of casualties in the French-Canadian B[attalio]ns due to their grouping in one formation."[43]

While the Canadian Army was if anything more urban than rural in its regional roots, it was also a virtually untrained citizen force of limited corporate military proficiency. Raw recruits who required individual train-ing made up more than half the 1st Canadian Infantry Division upon its arrival in the United Kingdom. As it transpired, the 1st Division had more than three years in which to overcome this deficiency before being com-mitted to Sicily in June 1943. The less fortunate 2nd Canadian Infantry Division passed little more than 22 months in Britain before its decimation on the beaches of Dieppe in August 1942; thereafter it enjoyed an equivalent period in which to recover for battle in Normandy. The 1st Canadian Army Tank Brigade and the 3rd Canadian Infantry Division both had more than two and a half years in which to prepare. The 5th Canadian Armoured Division trained for roughly 18 months in England before departure for the Italian theatre, while the 4th Canadian Armoured Division passed a similar period in Britain prior to taking part in the Normandy campaign. The 2nd Canadian Army Tank Brigade arrived overseas but ten months before its commitment to battle.[44]

This expansion of the Canadian field force was accompanied by the growth of a relatively large and elaborate supporting artillery infrastructure. By autumn 1942, the British had begun to form army-level artillery brigades or groups that, on rejection of the potentially risible appellation Royal Artillery Group for its acronym RAG, were called Army Groups Royal Artillery (AGRAs). Headquarters Medium Artillery, 1 Canadian Corps subsequently emerged in October as Headquarters 1st Canadian Army

Group R.C.A., a designation later changed to 1 Canadian AGRA. In November 1942, 2 Canadian AGRA was formed, eventually to comprise three medium regiments, one field regiment, a heavy antiaircraft regiment, and a rocket and a radar battery. Again, as the Canadian Army possessed no heavy artillery, these formations usually had British regiments attached.[45]

The magnitude of the training problem naturally increased with the rapid growth of the army. As Clausewitz so wisely pointed out, "the nature of military activity in general should not be taken as applying equally at all levels"; indeed, the lower the level the more physical the activity, the higher the level the more intellectual the activity.[46] It was one thing to train an infantry division, another to synchronize the fighting functions of three infantry and two armored divisions, two independent tank brigades, and two AGRA. The customary approach toward this end was to conduct training in three sequential stages: individual, unit (single-arm) collective, and formation (all-arms) collective. In the case of the inadequately trained 1st Division, for example, it was intended to complete individual training by the end of February 1940. After this, unit training was to commence until completed by April, when brigade and divisional collective exercises were to be undertaken.

Even before being upset by the exigencies of war, this ambitious program had to be extended somewhat due to an exceedingly bitter winter, lack of transport and clothing (a second pair of boots and a second set of battle dress were not issued until February and March), and the invidious pull of ceremonial parades. On 18 April, the rifle strengths of two battalions of the 2nd Brigade, approximately 1,300 men, were deployed to Scotland for a proposed raid on Trondheim, Norway. In response to the *Blitzkrieg* of May 1940, a small divisional headquarters and reinforced 1st Brigade were also placed on standby for possible action in support of the Dunkirk perimeter. Fortunately, neither operation was carried out, though the 1st Brigade was eventually dispatched to Brest on 13 June in an abortive last-minute attempt to shore up a rapidly collapsing French army.[47]

It is most evident that up to this point many Canadian as well as British senior commanders expected to fight a protracted struggle marked by an initial trench warfare phase, which would have permitted the gradual development of an offensive capacity. McNaughton even studied the possibility of retaking Maginot Line defenses by employing Canadian Tunnelling Company diamond drillers in countermining operations.[48] From the beginning of April 1940, 1st Canadian Infantry Division units each spent an overnight period in a model trench system especially constructed at Pirbright for training in trench relief, routine, patrolling, and raiding.[49] 1st Canadian Division Training Instruction No. 3 of 27 April 1940 further warned infantry brigade groups for attendance at the Trench Warfare Training and Experimental Centre (TWTEC), Imber. As detailed in an instruction of 2 May 1940, they were each to undergo training in trench warfare for eight to ten days between 11 May and 2 June.[50]

The comprehensive program called for units to entrench opposite one another and practice, in addition to trench routine and repair, mounting patrols, night raids, and dawn assaults against one another. Tanks, when available, participated in attacks on trench lines. Trials were also conducted to assess the effect of supporting smoke on direct and indirect friendly fire. Efforts were additionally made to determine practical procedures for laying minefields and clearing gaps in them for the passage of tracked vehicles. The army trained, in short, for a repetition of the middle years of the Great War. Ironically, on the very day units of the 1st Canadian Infantry Brigade Group were patrolling and practicing dawn trench attacks supported by smoke, *Panzergruppe Kleist* slashed through the French front west of the River Meuse and set out on its drive to the English Channel.[51]

Reaction to the invasion scare in the summer of 1940 did little to further the collective training of the 1st Division, though it was by then, comparatively, one of the best equipped and manned formations in the British order of battle. With the reconstitution of Canadian Force in June, emphasis was again placed upon training battalion mobile columns in rapid motor transport movement by day and night for possible action against German diversionary or paratroop assaults. British coastal forces were also to be rapidly reinforced in event of a major enemy seaborne landing. As in the previous month, McNaughton split the division into nine battalion groups, which involved allotting field as well as antitank artillery troops "*under command* of Battalions." All units subsequently completed "dawn attack exercises" with limited armored and air cooperation, but there was scant opportunity for divisional exercises. Indeed, it was not until late September that decentralized artillery regiments reverted to divisional command.[52]

The impression is nonetheless gained that during this period of much fervent dashing about, unbounded enthusiasm and misdirected energy often substituted for calm and collected reason. Instead of taking pains to devise and conduct worthwhile tactical training, the tendency was to shoot off at high speed, occasionally into orbit. Not for its role alone does Canadian Force seem to have earned the sobriquet "McNaughton's Flying Circus."[53] Neither did the creation of 7 Corps solve the higher level collective training problem to any substantial degree. The new GOC 1st Division, Major-General George Pearkes, noting that one regiment had fired its two-inch mortars for the first time in June, considered his formation still only partially trained. He also found it difficult to train beyond battalion, let alone brigade level, with tank-infantry exercises in conjunction with the 1st British Armoured Division simply out of the question. At the same time, he detected "too much of the 'militia camp' attitude" toward training.[54]

Unquestionably, equipment shortages also continued to retard the progressive pace of training. For Canada's lack of "practically all . . . modern equipment other than personal equipment of the soldier, including his rifle, . . . [and] Vickers machine guns,"[55] the 1st Canadian Infantry Division had to be "very largely equipped from United Kingdom stocks."[56] With Bren light machine guns in critically short supply, Canadian units overseas were until early 1940 armed with Great War-vintage Lewis guns; these were gradually replaced during 1940–41, the first Canadian-manufactured Brens arriving overseas in November 1940. It was not until the following summer that the issue of Canadian-made two- and three-inch mortars commenced, which meant that for its planned raid on the Norwegian coast the 2nd Brigade had to borrow three-inch mortar stores from the 1st Brigade. The two-pounder antitank gun remained in short supply as production priority went to tank armament.

Critical equipment shortages continued to exist throughout 1941. Most glaringly, 40-mm Bofors were simply unavailable to light antiaircraft regiments. As late as 31 January 1942, there were only 58 Bofors within an authorized establishment of 280 for the Canadian Army Overseas. The tank situation, though less serious, was complicated by technological considerations. The 1st Canadian Army Tank Brigade received tanks on a training scale during July 1941 and by the New Year had taken 157 Churchill "I" tanks on establishment. The 5th Canadian Armoured Division had to wait a longer period for its cruiser tanks, only a few U.S. Lees being delivered before the end of the year, with the result that it did not come under command of the First Canadian Army until 25 June 1942. By that time it had received 112 tanks, including light and obsolescent models, of which only 34 were Rams now coming from Canada. The 4th Canadian Armoured Division had, in the meantime, commenced training on Rams in Canada,[57] a development that but for the introduction of the better Sherman would have eliminated the need for conversion training overseas.

A similarly dismal situation confronted artillery field regiments, which in December 1939 were initially armed with 18/25-pounder guns (18-pounders rebored to take the improved 25-pounder shell) on a limited scale of four per regiment. It should be noted, however, that on receiving its full quota of 72 such weapons in the summer of 1940, the 1st Canadian Division was the only formation in Britain after Dunkirk so equipped. The remarkable 25-pounder gun-howitzer, "which proved to be among the war-winning weapons of the Second World War," though in production, was not issued to a Canadian unit until December 1940. It was not until early 1942 that the first field regiment in Canada received 25-pounders; 2nd Division artillery, for example, could only train on 18-pounders and 4.5-inch howitzers before proceeding overseas.[58]

To make matters worse, the 2nd Division's three field regiments were issued but 28 obsolete 75-mm guns during November 1940; it was not until September 1941 that they received their full complement of 25-pounders, which from July of that year were beginning to be supplied through Canadian sources. The 3rd Canadian Infantry Division, which arrived in the United Kingdom much better equipped and trained than the 2nd, received its complete establishment of 25-pounders by November 1941.[59] Fortunately, Canadian gunners from the beginning took fullest advantage of British facilities at the School of Artillery at Larkhill, to the point that it was claimed "so far as the school was concerned there were not two armies, British and Canadian, but one."[60]

It is, of course, a matter of record that McNaughton on 8 June 1940 advised the prime minister of Canada by cable that it was his "privilege to inform His Majesty today that . . . [he] now considered the Canadian Force to be battle worthy."[61] By September, having pronounced the troops "highly trained," he was of the opinion that "further intensive military training during the winter . . . would make . . . [them] stale." Educational training that would be of benefit upon cessation of hostilities was accordingly introduced to occupy over the winter months minds grown *"blasé* about training."[62] Such concern for troop welfare no doubt explains why McNaughton, like General George McClellan of the Union Army during the U.S. Civil War, never lost the affection of his soldiers. It may also bespeak a confidence borne of the fact that McNaughton, built up into a major national figure by a publicity drive from the start of the war, had by this time begun to enjoy a greater popularity than any other general. Hailed by the press as a "soldier scientist," he even appeared in the darkness of defeat to be the natural choice to lead the Allied invasion of the Continent. In his own mind, McNaughton clearly envisioned the Canadian Army spearheading the assault on Berlin.[63]

It seems perfectly clear, however, that McNaughton's force had not yet mastered the critically important technique of formation road movement. To maneuver large bodies of troops efficiently by day and night over winding English lanes, most of which were unsigned as an anti-invasion measure, required good staff work and a high individual standard of driving and map using. During the first divisional-scale anti-invasion scheme of 1941, Exercise "Fox" held in February, problems with motor vehicle movement "managed to tie everyone in knots from a platoon to a corps level." Directed by McNaughton's own corps headquarters, "Fox" was designed to practice the 1st Division in a vehicular move to a concentration area, an advance to contact with a simulated enemy, and battle procedure and deployment for attack. Unfortunately, poor staff planning at the corps level, inadequate traffic control, and an excessive number of vehicles all contributed to the creation of monumental road congestion. This not only prevented artillery from getting forward to support infantry attacks, but turned the entire exercise itself into a fiasco. At the end, McNaughton remarked that the exercise had "shaken the complacency of everyone participating, from the Corps Commander to the lowest private soldier."[64]

Large-scale exercises were to remain a feature of Canadian training overseas from 1941 onwards. Exercise "Waterloo," directed by Headquarters South Eastern Command during the period 14–16 June, was the first major scheme in which the entire Canadian Corps participated under McNaughton's command. Like "Fox," it practiced the formation in a mobile counterattack role within an anti-invasion scenario. Again, certain shortcomings were revealed, among which the observation by General Paget that too many conferences were held in lieu of issuing brief directives and verbal orders.[65] Between 29 September and 3 October, the Canadian Corps took part in Exercise "Bumper," the largest and perhaps most portentous maneuvers ever to be held in the United Kingdom. Involving two armies of four corps of 12 divisions, three of them armored, plus two army tank brigades and ancillary troops, "Bumper" practiced the field army in Britain in the anti-invasion role. Significantly, the Chief Umpire for "Bumper" was Lieutenant-General Montgomery who on 17 November 1941 assumed the appointment of G.O.C.-in-C. South Eastern Command. On the same day, Canadian Corps headquarters took over the 4 British Corps defensive sector on the Sussex coast, which placed it directly under his operational control.

Though the Canadian role was now more positional than mobile, the invasion of the Soviet Union on 22 June greatly lessened the likelihood of a German attack on Great Britain. As a result, the emphasis in training throughout the field army assumed a more offensive orientation. The two-sided exercises "Beaver III" and "Beaver IV," conducted under Canadian Corps direction from 22–24 April and 10–13 May 1942, respectively, saw participating divisions attacking and defending in turn. The last and most famous exercise conducted by Montgomery before he left to take command of the Eighth Army in North Africa had nothing to do with invasion. Exercise "Tiger," as it was labeled, pitted the 12 British Corps and the 1 Canadian Corps against each other in an 11-day encounter battle that tested fighting organization, doctrine, and troop capabilities to the limit.[66] It also provided, as will be shown, a reasonably accurate measure of the state of Canadian Army training at that juncture.

NOTES

1. R. C. Coleman, "General McNaughton and the Command and Control of the Canadian Army 1939–1943" (unpublished BA thesis, Royal Military College, 1967), p. 50.

2. General H. D. G. Crerar Papers (CP) Vol.1, Crerar to McNaughton, 8 August 1940.

3. J. W. Pickersgill, *The Mackenzie King Record*, Vol. I: *1939–1944* (Toronto: University of Toronto Press, 1960) pp. 40–41. See also Col. C. P. Stacey, *Official History of the Canadian Army in the Second World War*, Vol. I: *Six Years of War: The Army in Canada, Britain and the Pacific* (Ottawa: Queen's Printer, 1966), pp. 58–61,

65; and Col. C. P. Stacey, *Arms, Men and Governments: The War Policies of Canada, 1939–1945* (Ottawa: Information Canada, 1974), pp. 17–30, 43, 201; and Desmond Morton, *Military History of Canada* (Edmonton, Alberta: Hurtig, 1985), p. 180.

4. Pickersgill, *Mackenzie King Record*, I, 30, 59. See also Stacey, *Six Years*, pp. 13, 36, 65.

5. Pickersgill, *Mackenzie King Record*, I, 39–59; and Donald Creighton, *The Forked Road: Canada 1939–1957* (Toronto: McClelland and Stewart, 1976), pp. 3–7.

6. Pickersgill, *Mackenzie King Record*, I, 38–39; DHist 508.045 (D1), HQS 8350–21 FD 4 Dated 15 Mar 45, Home Stations—Canadian Army Overseas 1939–1945; *Report of the Department of National Defence* (Ottawa: King's Printer, 1944), p. 22; and Honourable J. L. Ralston, *The Extent of Canada's War Effort: Speech Delivered in the House of Commons February 10, 1942* (Ottawa: King's Printer, 1942), p. 12.

7. Stacey, *Six Years*, pp. 60–68.

8. Royal Military College of Canada Massey Library (hereafter RMC), Maj.-Gen. W. H. P. Elkins Papers (hereafter EP), Notes on Conference held in room [sic] of High Commissioner for Canada 1030 hours, 20 April 1940. Elkins was Master-General of Ordnance.

9. Queen's University Archives (QUA), the Honourable Norman McLeod Rogers Papers (hereafter RP), Box 8, File 2125a, Record of a Visit to United Kingdom of Canadian Minister of National Defence (Mr. Norman McL. Rogers), 18 April to 9 May, 1940; EP, Notes on Conference held in the office [sic] of the Secretary of State for War 1900 hours, 3 May 1940; Notes of an Informal Meeting Between Representatives of the United Kingdom and Canada held at Treasury Chambers S.W.1, on Friday, 26 April 1940 at 3:00 P.M.; and Stacey, *Six Years*, pp. 67–68.

10. EP, Notes on Conference held in room of High Commissioner for Canada 1030 hours, 20 April 1940, and Notes of an Informal Meeting Between Representatives of the United Kingdom and Canada held at Treasury Chambers S.W.1, on Friday, 26 April 1940 at 3:00 P.M.

11. RP, Box 8, File 2125a, Record of a Visit to United Kingdom of Canadian Minister of National Defence (Mr. Norman McL. Rogers), 18 April to 9 May 1940; and EP, Notes on Discussion between the Minister of National Defence, and Maj.-Gen. Crerar, Senior Officer, Canadian Military Headquarters, morning of 26 April 1940 at Canadian Military Headquarters. Maj.-Gen. H. D. G. Crerar was granted permission on 7 May to furnish the War Office with lists of units it was hoped Britain could lend for a time. EP, Memorandum on Decisions made by the Minister of National Defence at a Conference at 2100 hours on 7 May 1940.

12. Stacey, *Six Years*, pp. 68, 74–78, 86, 273–274, 287–289; and RP, Box 5, File 2125c, Address by the Honourable Norman McL. Rogers at the Annual Convention of the British Empire Service League, Montreal, 29 May 1940. As Stacey points out, financial limitations had ceased to be applied by Britain on declaration of war, whereas Canada persisted with restrictions until Dunkirk (*Six Years*, p. 69). 7 Corps also had a BGS (Canadian) who handled national organization; the chief administrative staff officer in the corps, the Deputy Adjutant and Quartermaster General (DA&QMG), was British. Canada agreed to pay for ancillary troops from 1 September, a date selected to "split the difference" between British and Canadian positions on accepting responsibility [EP, Memorandum from Master-General of

the Ordnance (Elkins) to Mr. Dyde, Special Assistant to the Minister of National Defence, 2 May 1940 covering paper "The Canadian Corps Question"].

13. Stacey, *Six Years*, pp. 87–93; *Report of the Department of National Defence* (Ottawa: King's Printer, 1941), pp. 15–19; and DHist 723.012 (D10), Canmilitry to Defensor from Ralston to Prime Minister and Power 5 January, 1941. Crerar complained that PAM was "an awful mouthful" and "a horribly unwieldy and unattractive title" (CP, Vol. 14, Crerar to Stuart, 8 July 1939).

14. Ralston, *Canada's War Effort*, pp. 11–14; *Report of the Department of National Defence* (Ottawa: King's Printer, 1942), pp. 10–16 and (1943), pp. 37–38; Stacey, *Six Years*, pp. 94–104, 108–109, 190; and *Arms, Men and Government*, pp. 44–45. Defence Scheme No. 3 as approved in 1932 anticipated an eventual force of seven divisions, the size of that contemplated in 1919. There were over 190,000 Canadian soldiers abroad on 31 March 1943. The manpower ceiling of the Canadian Army overseas to 1 September 1943 was 232,100; in August 1944 the total was fixed at 234,500 all ranks (Stacey, *Six Years*, pp. 31, 103). Canada's field force at the end of the Second World War was roughly 170,000 strong. Currie commanded 110,000 of the 150,000 Canadian troops in France and Belgium during the Great War; the total strength of the CEF in December 1918 was 342,648 [Col. C. P. Stacey, *Official History of the Canadian Army in the Second World War*, Vol. III: *The Victory Campaign: The Operations in North-West Europe, 1944–1945* (Ottawa: Queen's Printer, 1966), p. 641 and Col. G. W. L. Nicholson, *Official History of the Canadian Army in the First World War: Canadian Expeditionary Force 1914–1919* (Ottawa: Queen's Printer, 1962), pp. 485, 546–547]. As of 31 December 1944, the net drain of armed forces on manpower was 801,000; with 1,250,000 men and women engaged in war production, this amounted to 17.2 percent of the total population [DHist 112.3S2009 (D118) HQS 9011–0 FD 4 (DSD3) memo DCD to DCGS (A) on Manpower Services in Canada, 31 December, 44].

15. Stacey, *Six Years*, pp. 111–112.

16. W. A. B. Douglas and Brereton Greenhous, *Out of the Shadows: Canada in the Second World War* (Toronto: Oxford University Press, 1977), p. 36.

17. Stacey, *Six Years*, pp. 43, 49–50, 63, 82, 113, 115, 118–123, 134. The Cabinet decision to use the euphemistic CASF, later redesignated the Canadian Army (Active) or CA(A), proved costly as it replaced the term "Canadian Field Force" on all previously prepared mobilization documentation.

18. National Archives of Canada (NAC), Record Group (hereafter RG) 24: National Defence, 1870–1981, Vol.13, 240, Military Training in Canada 1942 by DMT, 2 December 1942; RG 24, Vol. 9887, Training of Reinforcements in Canada by Brig. K. Stuart, V.C.G.S., 17 July 1941; and Stacey, *Six Years*, pp. 121, 134–135, 530–533. Enrollment in the reserve force, officially redesignated in November 1940 the Canadian Army (Reserve) or CA(R), was during 1942 restricted to men not eligible by age or medical category for military service under the NRMA.

19. RG 24, Vol. 9841, CTS Monthly Training Report, September 1942; McNaughton Papers (MP), Vol. 157, Col. T. E. Snow to Trg C.M.H.Q., 23 July 1943; RG 24, Vol. 9802, OC #5 (Battle) Wing to H.Q. CTS, 20 November 1943; and Stacey, *Six Years*, pp. 236–237, 240, 247. Wing Numbers 1 to 3 were located at Bordon, Number 4 at Lavington House, Number 5 at Windlesham House School, and Number 6 at Shillinglee Park (RG 24, Vol. 9887, memo Brig. M. H. S. Penhale to 1 Cdn Corps, 27 August 1942).

20. RG 24, Vol. 13,240, Memorandum of discussion and joint report submitted to the D.M.T. by Commandants of A–1, A–2, and A–4 T.C.s . . . on their return from England, 11 December 1942; and DHist 112.3H1.005 (D28) C.M.H.Q. Courses. The term "morale" replaced the phrase "spirit of the troops" during the Great War. Rooted in the French word *moral*, state of discipline or spirit in armies, there was argument over whether it should take a terminal "e" [Maj.-Gen. A. C. Duff, *Sword and Pen* (Aldershot, U.K.: Gale and Polden, 1950), pp. 77–78].

21. RG 24, Vol. 9901, memo DCGS to HQ CRU, 22 November 1944, memo SD&T to DCGS, 8 September 1944, and letter SO, CMHQ, to Secty DND, 27 August 1943; *Report of the Department of National Defence* (Ottawa: King's Printer, 1944), p. 24; and Stacey, *Six Years*, pp. 135. Corps Reinforcement Units (CRU) were supposed to bridge the gap between training in Canada and the field, but as admitted in memo HQ CRU to DCGS, 27 November 1944, this was impossible without Canadian syllabi!

22. CP, Vol. 1, Crerar to McNaughton, 4 March 1941; RG 24, Vol. 9887, Training of Reinforcements in Canada by Brig. K. Stuart, V.C.G.S., 17 July 1941; RG 24, Vol. 13,240, Military Training in Canada 1942 by DMT, 2 December 1942; DHist. CMHQ Historical Reports No. 21, 24 April 1941, and No. 156, 31 July 1946; and Stacey, *Six Years*, pp. 128–132, 138–141. A temporary OTC was established at Three Rivers, Quebec, and francophones were inducted through a facility at St. Jérome. From 1 April 1941 to the end of the war, nearly two-thirds of army officer vacancies were filled by men who had served in the ranks. British policy from September 1939 decreed that all candidates for commissions, save in certain technical and medical services, had to pass some time in the ranks. The British established 35 OCTUs [Gen. Sir David Fraser, *And We Shall Shock Them: The British Army in the Second World War* (London: Hodder and Stoughton, 1988), p. 101].

23. RG 24, Vol. 9841, Commandant C.T.S. Overseas Visit to Training Establishments, 30 September 1943.

24. Report of Visit to Special Trg Ests by Col. J. G. K. Strathy to Col. T. E. Snow, Comd, C.T.S., 4 October 1943. The Commandant in question was Col. K. R. Mitchell, who replaced Brig. M. F. Gregg in April 1943.

25. RG 24, Vol. 13,239, CGS Circular HQ 54–27–35–128 (Trng 1), 3 February 1942; RG 24, Vol. 9841, CTS Monthly Training Report, August 1942, by Maj. J. Campbell; DHist 171.009 (D268) Field Officers Course General Directive, October/December, 1943; and Stacey, *Six Years*, pp. 140–141. Two more Field Officers Courses were conducted at Brockville for reserve officers [*Report of the Department of National Defence* (Ottawa: King's Printer, 1944), p. 27].

26. "What the Canadian Serviceman Thinks," DHist. 113.3R4003 (D1) Research and Information Section. Vol. I, "Special Reports," H.Q.C. 8917, 15 September 1943.

27. DHist 113.3R4003 (D1) Research and Information Section, Adjutant-General Branch, Vol. VII, "Trends in the Thinking of Army Units Feb 44–Dec 44," Volume III, Number VI, June 1944, and Volume III, Number IV, April 1944; and "Why Do N.R.M.A. Soldiers at Depots Not Volunteer," DHist 113.3R4003 (D1) Research and Information Section, Vol. II, "Special Reports," Special Report No. 10, 3 January 1944. The problem of NCO reversion in rank was a major factor in the growing "spirit of dissension." [EP, Letter GOC-in-C Atlantic Command (Elkins) to Maj.-Gen. R. O. Alexander, GOC-in-C Pacific Command, 7 January 1942 and

letter GOC-in-C Pacific Command to the Secretary, Department of National Defence, 19 January 1942.

28. DHist 113.3R4003 (D1) Research and Information Section, Vol. VII, "Trends in the Thinking of Army Units," Volume III, Number X, October 1944, and Volume III, Number VII, July 1944.

29. DHist 113.3R4003 (D1) Research and Information Section, Vol. VII, "Trends in the Thinking of Army Units," Volume III, Number VIII, August 1944.

30. DHist 113.3R4003 (D1) Research and Information Section, Vol. VIII, "Trends in the Thinking of Army Units Jan-Mar 45," "Some Factors in Maintaining Morale," Volume IV, Number 2, March 1945.

31. J. L. Granatstein, *Broken Promises: A History of Conscription in Canada* (Toronto: Oxford University Press, 1977), p. 171.

32. "Attitudes of Army Personnel Recently Returned from Overseas," DHist 113.3R4003 (D1) Research and Information Section, Vol. III, "Special Reports," Special Report No. 161, 20 November 1944; and "Trends in Thinking of Army Units," Volume III, Number XII, December 1944.

33. John Keegan, *The Face of Battle*, (New York: Viking, 1976), pp. 303–304.

34. Stacey, *Six Years*, pp. 428–431. One month of service completed in an active theater like the Mediterranean or northwest Europe counted as two for purposes of home leave (Ibid., p. 430). British home leave was not granted until September 1944. Until then a regular might have served up to nine years abroad and a conscript four (Fraser, *And We Shall Shock Them*, p. 105).

35. DHist 111.13 (D9) Canmilitry MGA 77 to Defensor 121510A Mar 45; and J. W Pickersgill and D. F. Forster, *The Mackenzie King Record,* Volume 2: *1944–1945* (Toronto: University of Toronto Press, 1968), pp. 202–203. King observed, "I did not notice anyone in the Cabinet [on 3 November 1944] who had said that he had knowledge of men receiving extra money. They had understood employers were to pay for labour at the price that other labour would receive, but that whatever was in excess of the pay which the NRMA men were receiving would go to the state. . . . Mitchell [Minister of Labour] said there had not been such an agreement. Ilsley [Minister of Finance] and others thought there had been." McNaughton, by this point Minister of National Defence, put a stop to this practice, stating, "If they were to be an army they should be an army of soldiers doing work as soldiers and not as wage earners" (Ibid.).

36. "Rehabilitation 1945: A Survey of Opinions in the Canadian Army," DHist 113.3R4003 (D1) Research and Information Section, Adjutant-General Branch, Vol. V, "Rehabilitation Reports," Special Report No. 180, pp. 5–6, 10–12, 34; A. G. Coord 2 Adjutant-General Branch, "Rehabilitation: A Survey of Opinions among Army Personnel Awaiting Discharge," (October 1945), p. 3–4, 8, 10–13; (September 1945), pp. 8–11; and (August 1945), pp. 6–9.

37. A.G. Coord 2 Adjutant-General Branch, "Rehabilitation: A Survey of Opinions Among Army Personnel Awaiting Discharge," (October 1945), p. 38.

38. DHist 112.3S2009 (D 118), Manpower Requirements, Vol. 2, Memorandum on Manpower, 25 June 1942. Farm and unskilled industrial workers were considered equally eligible for service. The argicultural occupational group accounted for slightly more than 25 percent of the Canadian labor force in 1941 and blue-collar workers about one-third [John Porter, *Canadian Social Structure: A Statistical Profile*

(Toronto: McClelland and Stewart, 1967), p. 93; and M. C. Urquhart and K. A. H. Buckley (eds.), *Historical Statistics of Canada* (Toronto: Macmillan, 1965), p. 59].

39. Dominick Graham, "Sans Doctrine: British Army Tactics in the First World War," *Men at War: Politics, Technology and Innovation in the Twentieth Century*, ed. Timothy Travers and Criston Archer (Chicago: Precedent, 1982), p. 89. The Australian Imperial Force was predominantly from the cities. As Gimblett has already shown, more than 60 percent of the Canadian general officer corps in the post-Great War era had urban roots; this was in contrast to the U.S. Army officer corps, which Morris Janowitz found to be 77 percent rural in 1920. The largely aristocratic British officer corps was probably also more rural [Richard H. Gimblett, "Social Background as a Factor in Defence Policy Formulation: The General Officer Corps after the Canadian Militia 1923–1939," (unpublished M.A. thesis, Trent University, 1980), pp. 16–18].

40. C. P. Stacey and Barbara M. Wilson, *The Half-Million: The Canadians in Britain, 1939–1946* (Toronto: University of Toronto Press, 1987), p. 36; and Stacey, *Six Years*, pp. 231, 419.

41. CP, Vol. 7, Speech by General McNaughton at the Opening of the ABCA Course for Canadian Officers, Chiefly OsC. and 2sI/C at Chatam House, on Friday, 12 February 1943 at 1415 hrs. Years earlier, a young Lester B. Pearson had ventured that "modelling the [Canadian] army on British lines" was akin to adopting British judicial institutions (CP, Vol. 10, Pearson to Crerar 14 January 1938).

42. Stacey, *Six Years*, pp. 32, 43–45. The reinforcement of French-Canadian units was perceived as a particularly knotty problem in 1944, when it was thought it might be necessary to "cannibalize" one of four French-Canadian battalions in order to maintain the remaining three at requisite strength. Another option entertained was to simply reinforce them with English-speaking companies. CP, Vol. 8, Memoranda GOC-in-C First Canadian Army to Chief of Staff, Canadian Military Headquarters (CMHQ), 21 May 1944 and 4 June 1944; and DHist 111.13 (D16) Most Immediate Message A.9249 COS, CMHQ, to Lt.-Gen. J. C. Murchie, CGS, 151005 November 1944. By 8 September 1944, the COS, CMHQ, referred to an additional facet of "our old friend the French-Canadian problem," namely, "to get a French-Canadian brigadier in the field in 21 Army Group" so as to assuage "the usual complaint[s] . . . from the French-Canadian press" (CP, Vol. 8, letter COS, CMHQ, to Commander First Canadian Army 8 September 1944.

43. NAC, Maj.-Gen. V. W. Odlum Papers (hereafter OP), MG 30, E300, Vol. 26, Memorandum on a meeting held at H.Q. 7 Corps at 1200 hrs, 8 August 1940.

44. Stacey and Wilson, *Half-Million*, pp. 5, 13–14; and Stacey, *Six Years*, p. 191.

45. Col. G. W. L. Nicholson, *The Gunners of Canada: A History of the Royal Regiment of Canadian Artillery*, Vol. II: *1919–1967* (Toronto: McClelland and Stewart, 1972), p. 111.

46. Carl von Clausewitz, *On War*, ed./trans. Michael Howard and Peter Paret (Princeton, N.J.: Princeton University Press, 1976), p. 140.

47. Stacey, *Six Years*, pp. 231–234, 257–285; RP, Box 8, File 2125a, Record of a Visit To United Kingdom of Canadian Minister of National Defence (Mr. Norman McL. Rogers) April 18 to May 9, 1940, pp. 1–3, 10, 15–16; and G. R. Stevens, *Princess Patricia's Canadian Light Infantry 1919–1957*, Vol. III (Griesbach, Alberta: Historical Committee of the Regiment, undated), pp. 28–34.

48. John Swettenham, *McNaughton* (Toronto: Ryerson, 1968), Vol. II, pp. 15–

16, 41; EP, Memorandum of Conference Held at C.M.H.Q., London, at 0945 hours, 2 May 1940, to Discuss Matters Pertaining to the Organization, etc., of Canadian Forces Overseas; and MP, Vol. 170, cipher Ralston to Power 28 December 1940, McNaughton to Paget 9 October 1942, and 2/CCTE/5–1–2 Lt. Col. Colin A. Campbell CRCE 2 Cdn Corps Tp to CE 1st Cdn Army 28 September 1942.

49. Stacey, *Six Years*, p. 233; Strome Galloway, *A Regiment at War: The Story of the Royal Canadian Regiment 1939–1945* (London: Regimental Headquarters, 1979), pp. 28–29; and RG 24, Vol 13,722, War Diary (hereafter WD) 1st Canadian Infantry Division (hereafter 1 CID), Training Progress Report for Week Ending 27 April 1940.

50. RG 24, Vol. 13,722, 1 CD/4–0–2 Vol. 2, 1 Canadian Division Training Instruction No. 3, 27 April 1940 (signed by Maj. G. G. Simonds for Lt.-Col. G. R. Turner, GS), 1 CD/GS 4–0 H.Q. 1 Cdn Div., Imber Trench Warfare Training and Experimental Centre (TWTEC), 2 May 1940, and Security G. 300, letter from Commandant of Trench Warfare Training and Experimental Centre to GOC 1st Canadian Division, 30 April 1940; and RG 24, Vol. 13,723, WD 1 CID, Canadian Force Notes for Conference at 4 Corps Headquarters. One brigade had to cut its tour to three days due to the move of Canadian Force to the Northampton area.

51. Ibid.; and Maj.-Gen. F. W. von Mellenthin, *Panzer Battles: A Study of the Employment of Armor in the Second World War*, trans. H. Betzler, ed. L. C. F. Turner (Norman Okla.: University of Oklahoma Press, 1983), pp. 11–16.

52. RG 24, Vol. 13,723 WD 1 CID, Minutes of Conference at 1100 hours on 20 June 1940, held at Pinewood, Farnborough; Stacey, *Six Years*, pp. 234–235, 273, 287; and Reginald H. Roy, *For Most Conspicious Bravery: A Biography of Major-General George R. Pearkes, V. C., Through Two World Wars.* (Vancouver: University of British Columbia Press, 1977), *Pearkes*, p. 160. Italics added.

53. Col. G. W. L. Nicholson, *The Gunners of Canada: A History of the Royal Regiment of Canadian Artillery*, Vol. II: *1919–1967* (Toronto: McClelland and Stewart, 1972), p. 72.

54. Roy, *Pearkes*, pp. 153–155, 158, 160.

55. EP, Memorandum MGO to the Minister, 22 September 1939.

56. EP, Notes on a Conference held at Treasury, Whitehall 1500 hours, 26 April 1940; and Notes of an Informal Meeting Between Representatives of the United Kingdom and Canada held at Treasury Chambers S.W.1, on Friday, 26 April 1940 at 3:00 P.M

57. Stacey, *Six Years*, pp. 99, 231, 234, 242, 245, 544, 546 and his DHist, CMHQ Historical Section Report 46, 19 September 1941, The Problem of Equipment. Elkins drew the Minister's attention to cables from the Canadian High Commissioner in Britain that warned of a "great shortage of equipment in England for Army Tank battalions and urge[d] Canadian production of tanks for use by Canadian Tank units" (EP, Memorandum MGO to The Minister 7 February 1940). As to the type of tank to be produced, Elkins opined "British and French design leads the world. . . . We have no information to indicate that any U.S. design has been satisfactory" (Memorandum MGO to The Minister, June 1940). The Ram has been described as a "disaster . . . underpowered and undergunned;" it also "was considered unacceptable by the Canadian armoured forces" [James Alan Roberts, *The Canadian Summer* (Toronto: Oxford University Press, 1981), p. 67].

58. Nicholson, *Gunners*, II, 55, 85, 94, 101.

59. Stacey, *Six Years*, pp. 234, 242, 545; and CP, Vol. 1, Crerar to McNaughton, 26 June 1941.

60. Nicholson, *Gunners*, II, 57. The Canadian School of Artillery Overseas was established in November 1942 at Pinewood, Whitehall, Hampshire. It was moved in August 1943 to Seaford, Sussex ["Canadian School of Artillery Overseas (o) 1942–45," *Quadrant*, 1 (June 1982): 7].

61. RG 24, Vol. 13,723, Cablegram 1CD/GS 4–8 Canmilitry to Defensor, 8 June 1940.

62. Swettenham, *McNaughton*, II, 150–151; and Stacey, *Six Years*, p. 420.

63. Coleman, "McNaughton," pp. 46–50; Swettenham, *McNaughton*, II, 153–154; and "Commander of the Canadians," *Life*, 18 December 1939, p. 9. (McNaughton made the cover.)

64. Galloway, *Regiment at War*, p. 44; and Roy, *Pearkes*, pp. 161–163.

65. Stacey, *Six Years*, p. 238. Similar problems were encountered in the 2nd Division during Exercise "Dog" in March. The 1st Division and corps troops were again practiced in road movement between 9–11 April in Exercise "Hare" and the 2nd during 16–19 April in "Benito" (Ibid.).

66. Ibid., pp. 238–240, 243–244, 297–298; and Nigel Hamilton, *Monty, vol. I: The Making of a General 1887–1942* (Sevenoaks, U.K: Hodder and Stoughton, 1984), pp. 469–470, 498–513.

Chapter 4

The Staff Caste

The . . . General Staff [acts] as a nervous system animating the lumbering body of the army, making possible that articulation and flexibility which alone render . . . it an effective military force.

Michael Howard, *The Franco-Prussian War*[1]

In order to gain a better insight into the operational functioning of a modern army, it is first necessary to acquire a knowledge of staff organization and training. The staff converts the ideas of a commander into orders and by working out all details related to their execution frees his mind to deal with other, more important, matters. At the other end of the spectrum, the staff remains responsible for watching over the fighting condition and material welfare of the troops.[2] Thus, if the chain of command can be said to drive the fighting arms and their supporting services, then the staff can be considered its lubricant. As John Masters has so succinctly put it, the staff solves problems related to people, things, and fighting. Working on behalf of a commander and his troops, it coordinates the activities of the whole through meticulous planning and detailed direction so as to avoid sending ammunition and "rations to Rome if the . . . [army is] attacking Paris."[3]

Since a staff also serves an educational function and provides the primary avenue by which an army can prepare for war in peace, one might expect it to be a more studied subject in its own right. Surprisingly, however, not all that much has been written about staff, which in the Canadian case is still largely an unexplored field. This chapter thus represents an attempt to delve deeper into the staff experience of Canada's Second World War army.

Here of course the conduct of training at the staff college level remains central, for just as in other armies it was unquestionably the most important thread in the operational fabric of field forces. While the Canadian Army grew to almost half a million during the Second World War, it could boast at the outbreak only 45 regular staff officers who had passed through Quetta or Camberley, described by Winston Churchill as "the most exclusive institution in the world."[4] By way of comparison, the 1939 German army, which swelled to over six million in the course of the war, fielded 415 fully trained staff officers, 93 recalled or transferred to the General Staff, and 303 candidates undergoing training, for a grand total of 811.[5]

Ever since the reforms of Prussian General Gerhard von Scharnhorst, it was accepted that a good staff could often save even the most incompetent commander, but given the increased complexity of modern warfare, a commander was no longer likely to prevail without a competent staff. Indeed, Scharnhorst's greatest contribution was to introduce the concept of the "general staff with troops," by which means he and his fellow reformers sought to compensate for the absence of military ability among aristocratic commanders. Specifically, the system sought to institutionalize military effectiveness by ensuring through a common doctrine that different officers would in most situations react roughly similarly, making the best use of available resources. In 1821 the *Truppen Generalstab* (Troop General Staff) combined with what became the *Grosser Generalstab* (Great General Staff), the central military organ of the state or "capital staff" from which it was distinguished, to attract the best and brightest military minds. This powerful caste of nonregimental officers, later identifiable by their distinctive carmine trouser stripes, constituted the corporate brain of the German army. Within the *Truppen Generalstab*, formally up to 1938 and informally thereafter, it was accepted practice for chiefs of staff to share responsibility for operational decision making with their respective formation commanders. This notion of having a junior partner in command apparently first proved its worth in the Waterloo campaign.[6]

Naturally, as battlefield success increasingly came to depend upon mass troop movements by rail and road, heavy ammunition dumping programs, and longer lines of communication within wider deployments, the greater requirement there was for detailed staff calculation. To ensure that enough officers were capable of performing the staff functions of planning, coordination, and supervision, the Prussians established a special school for officers called from 1859 the *Kriegsakademie*. Entrance to this "nursery" of the elite general staff was by competitive examination and the course was of three years duration. Gone were the days when a commander astride a white horse on a hill could pretend to control forces within his purview through the dispatch of gallopers. War had become professionalized and, in a large sense, "an art to be pursued upon a map."[7] Staff colleges thus replaced cadet academies like West Point, whose graduates dominated the Civil War, as the principal institutions of military learning.

In 1890 Spenser Wilkinson published a popular and influential account of the German General Staff entitled *The Brain of an Army*, which called upon Britain to adopt a similar organization. Only after the British Army's lackluster performance in the South African War, however, was concrete action taken in this direction. In 1904 the War Office (Reconstitution) Committee headed by Viscount Reginald Esher recommended the abolition of the traditional post of Commander-in-Chief and the institution of an Army Council in its place. Arguing that the British Empire was preeminently a naval, Indian, and colonial power, it further proposed the creation of a civil-military cabinet Committee of Imperial Defence (CID) to ensure in peace that national effort would be correctly coordinated in war. In order to maintain military focus on war preparation as opposed to peacetime administration, the committee additionally advocated the institution of an elitist "blue ribbon" general staff to be recruited mainly from the Staff College, Camberley, which had been in existence since 1857. The hope was that, given a permanent nucleus, the CID could become the "Great General Staff" of Empire providing advice on broad military policy. In the event, the CID received but a small secretariat and the army General Staff, established on a firm basis 12 September 1906, bore small resemblance to the German model.

Chaired by the Secretary of State for War, the Army Council comprised civil, financial, and four military members, each responsible for their own staff branch. The first military member was the CGS, from 1909 CIGS, who as *primus inter pares* assumed responsibility for staff coordination as well as "G" or operational matters including intelligence, training, and doctrine; the second, the Adjutant-General (AG), looked after "A" or administrative matters concerning individual persons, which included mobilization and army schools; the third, the Quartermaster-General (QMG), took care of "Q" facets pertaining to material needs such as supply, quartering, and movement; and the fourth, the Master-General of Ordnance (MGO), was responsible for armament, fortification, and procurement.[8] As Major-General Fuller so correctly pointed out, the CIGS was neither "general" nor "imperial," for he headed little more than an operational staff.[9] The British General Staff, unlike the German, was but one part of the whole.

Staff representation on the Army Council projected throughout the field army, with the exception of the MGO Branch, whose responsibilities were discharged by Q. By 1913, however, staff officers were appointed to A and Q branches conjointly, rather than separately, thus enabling senior administrative or AQ appointments to supervise the work of both, "distributing it among the several 'AQ' staff officers as was most convenient." The nomenclature of designated G appointments had in the meantime been changed from the traditional administrative titling to reflect General Staff Officer (GSO) grades 1, 2, and 3. Thus, at the divisional level in 1909, the senior G staff officer was a GSO 1 in the rank of lieutenant-colonel, with his assistants graded GSO 2 and GSO 3 in the ranks of major and captain, respectively. The senior AQ officer was the Assistant-Adjutant and Quartermaster-General (AA&QMG).

The divisional AA&QMG had as assistants a Deputy Assistant Quartermaster-General (DAQMG) and a Deputy Assistant Adjutant and Quartermaster-General (DAA&QMG). When the latter designation came eventually to identify the senior AQ officer at the brigade level, the divisional appointment changed to Deputy Assistant Adjutant-General (DAAG). The chief operations officer at brigade retained the title of Brigade Major (BM) rather than GSO 2 and, from 1914, was assisted by a Staff Captain. At corps headquarters, the senior G appointment was the Brigadier-General, General Staff (BGGS) who had as his chief assistant a GSO 1; the senior AQ officer was the Deputy Adjutant and Quartermaster-General (DA&QMG), also in the rank of brigadier, who was assisted by administrative staff officers exclusively responsible for A and Q matters. By virtue of its coordinating responsibility, the G Branch at all command levels tended to predominate.[10]

The Canadian government embraced the British staff system in November 1904 with the institution of an advisory Militia Council. Like the Army Council, it was presided over by the Minister of Militia and Defence and composed of the Deputy Minister as civil member, a financial member, and four military members: CGS, AG, QMG, and MGO. From 1903, selected Canadian regular officers also began to attend the Staff College, Camberley. When war broke out in August 1914, a total of 12 had graduated from the two-year course and three were undergoing training. The failure of two candidates to pass entrance examinations for the 1906–07 course and the continued difficulties initially experienced by those selected had in the meantime prompted the introduction of a short preparatory staff course at the Royal Military College of Canada. In 1908 a Militia Staff Course consisting of theoretical and practical portions, each punctuated by examinations, was also reinstituted to train members of the reserves in administrative and general staff duties. By 1914 there were 124 successful graduates of this course, which, though inadequate by Camberley standards, served to alleviate the shortage of staff officers within the Canadian General Staff.[11]

In keeping with British General Staff practice, however, only staff college graduates were considered truly qualified to fill field staff positions during war. Not even graduates of the independent Canadian staff course established in Britain by defense minister Sam Hughes, whose mistrust of "staff college paternalism" was legendary, were to wear the scarlet gorget patches of the staff officer. Indeed, the course was closed down in December 1916,

those officers who completed it being judged unfit for either staff employment or appointment to the position of second-in-command of an infantry
battalion.[12] Fortunately, the Canadians continued to be supported by high-
caliber British regular staff officers who "in some cases were reputed to be
the real commanders." Three rose to become CIGS. Because these officers
were understudied by Canadians in the same grades, a double staff establishment also developed within the Canadian Corps; in other words, when
the British staff officer was eventually replaced by a competent Canadian
understudy, the latter's position was not deleted. Thus, while in a British
divisional headquarters the GSO 1 had under him one GSO 2 and one GSO
3, Canadian divisions had two each. At brigade level the story was the
same; whereas only one staff captain was on British establishment, Canadian
brigades had two, one for A&Q and one for intelligence.[13]

Staff officer deficiencies that afflicted the CEF were little less pronounced
within the British Army at large. The Staff College was simply too small
to have produced more than a portion of the trained staff officers required
when the army expanded beyond its initial six division size. Out of the 447
British officers in 1914 who were graduates of Camberley or Quetta, moreover, a fraction less than 50 percent were killed during the war. The Staff
College was nonetheless closed shortly after the outbreak of hostilities on
the erroneous assumption that they would be "over by Christmas." To
replace staff casualties, British and Canadian commanders resorted to attaching officers as "learners" to their headquarters where they could understudy key staff appointments. Later, General Headquarters and army-
level schools were established, and, in what marked the first comprehensive
attempt to train staff officers in France, junior and senior staff schools were
established at Hesdin. It was not until April 1916, however, that the War
Office set up staff schools in Britain and introduced a uniform system for
staff training.

By 1917 satisfactory attachment as a "learner" qualified an officer for a
. GSO 3 appointment; for GSO 1 and GSO 2 positions, respective qualification at a Senior and Junior Staff Course at Camberley, Cambridge, or
elsewhere was required. In resorting to such expedients, of course, it was
implicitly admitted that a first-class staff officer could not be hurriedly
trained in a matter of a few weeks. One can only surmise that the hasty
improvisation of formation staffs necessarily wrought by shortages of qualified staff officers must have adversely affected the outcome of certain operations. In any event, possibly for this reason among others, the red tabs
of the staff officer came to have the same effect upon front-line soldiers as
the proverbial red flag before a bull.[14] Oddly, this does not seem to have
been the case with the elitist German General Staff, which apparently retained the respect of the *frontschwein* to the very end.[15]

In January 1919 a special committee convened under Lieutenant-General
Sir Walter Braithwaite to report on British field staff organization during

the Great War. Examining 84 witnesses representing every grade and branch, it asserted that the system was essentially sound. The "keynote of . . . Staff organization" was determined to be "the unity of the Staff, although its work . . . divided into three main branches." The committee accordingly recommended the interchange of staff officers among branches and proscribed the maintenance of separate G, Q, and A messes. Not everyone agreed, however, that the inherent weakness of the British staff system could be so easily overcome; the very idea of separate branches controlling their own appointments seemed fundamentally faulty. Administrative branch heads, who were often senior, invariably resented General Staff primacy, which they perceived as emanating from the sunnier side of an artificial barrier. The British General Staff was neither in theory nor practice a "staff in general."[16]

Whereas German staff branches were headed by General Staff officers and unified under the direction of a single COS or operations officer at every level, British branches were separately expected to cooperate. The greater efficiency of the German staff structure, it is worth interjecting, was fully recognized by Montgomery as early as 1918, and he thereafter regularly employed what he termed the " 'COS' Principle" within all his commands. Formally introduced in the staff organizations of corps and armies operating under the 21st Army Group, which included the First Canadian Army, the COS principle was described as a "variation from FSR [*Field Service Regulations*] Vol I." Also touted as "in effect, analogous to the continental staff system," its stated purpose was to relieve the commander from the necessity of coordinating the work of the staff so that he could devote his full attention to prosecution of operations. The staff coordinating function became instead the province of the COS who had "to have the necessary authority and confidence to make all decisions" implementing a commander's policy.[17]

Between the wars, however, the British staff system remained essentially unchanged, apart, that is, from restricting wear of scarlet gorget patches and red-banded hats to officers of the rank of colonel and above. Camberley reopened in 1919, the first two postwar courses conducted each being a year long. In 1921 the reintroduction of competitive entry examinations, which ushered in a two-year curriculum, required prospective candidates to master the compulsory fields of training for war, including military history; organization and administration, including military law; and imperial organization, which covered systems of government, geography, and foreign affairs. Passes were also expected in three optional subjects, one of which had to be a language (French, German, or Russian), selected from a list that embraced history, chemistry, physics, mathematics, business administration, political economy, and movement. At the discretion of the Army Council, however, an officer could be "nominated" to attend staff college provided he had good service in the field, served as an adjutant for three years, and performed well on staff or as an instructor for two years.[18]

Up until 1938 Camberley annually graduated 60 staff-trained British and imperial officers, usually captains or junior majors of about 33 years of age. When Fuller went there as a chief instructor in 1923, he introduced a new approach to learning based on students and instructors teaching each other.[19] Essentially Socratic, the staff college method incorporated a tutorial system of ten-man "syndicate" round table discussions and exercises, each "directed" by a member of the Directing Staff (DS). Prior to participation, students read the pertinent précis and manuals and listened to the relevant lecture-demonstrations. Indoor demonstrations on cloth or sand models were followed as appropriate by outdoor demonstrations of equipment, troops, and field organizations. As training progressed, students assumed staff and command roles in signals exercises, telephone battles, and TEWTs on the ground. Every six to eight weeks, syndicates were reshuffled, in theory for greater exposure to the knowledge of others, but also for assessment purposes. Significantly, this feature was absent in German staff training, which saw students tutored throughout by one dedicated DS who took full responsibility for them.[20]

The Camberley curriculum in the first year or junior division primarily covered staff duties within a division, which encompassed among other things preparing written correspondence, organizing headquarters to run efficiently, and disseminating information and direction. Techniques selected for their universal applicability and effectiveness also received emphasis as they facilitated the ease with which operations could be coordinated among different headquarters and formations, especially during periods of strain or great pressure. Naturally, both discussion and written work stressed extreme thoroughness and attention to detail, since the broad brush approach was of small worth in arranging the ordered deployment, movement, and administration of such a large formation. Command and staff outdoor exercises or "tours" that called for drafting orders and instructions in the field also consumed a great deal of time. During the second year or senior division, candidates studied corps and army formations as well as interservice combined operations, industrial mobilization, imperial defense, and grand strategy. Significantly, many considered second year work to be the "more interesting."[21]

Why this should be so, while not exactly surprising, is the more intriguing for it was thorough mastery of junior division subject matter that made Montgomery so exceptionally field competent. To Brigadier C.N. Barclay, who entered Camberley in 1930, "the work in . . . [the] second year was on too high a level," with captains learning "to be higher . . . commanders . . . some twelve years before even a select few could possibly attain such heights."[22] As explained by former commandant Major-General Ironside, however, "the Staff College exist[ed] for giving an officer, firstly, training in the higher art of war, and secondly, in the duties of the Staff—in that order." The object was not to produce a "special breed of Staff Officer," but to take the best regimental officers and staff train them to "the highest point." Camberley and Quetta were thus "not really Staff College[s] but . . . War College[s]," which trained not only "higher Staff officers [but] . . . also Commanders." This, in his view, made them "rather different from Staff Colleges which exist[ed] on the Continent."[23]

It was simply untrue to imply, of course, that German General Staff officers did only staff work. Like their British counterparts, they also rotated through line command appointments and trained to assume positions one or two ranks higher on mobilization. Actually, the greatest difference in approach appears to have had less to do with command per se than the fact that the German staff course, cut from three to two years between 1933 and 1937, concentrated more heavily upon purely military subjects. Primarily aimed at training general staff officers as advisers and assistants to field commanders or members of the central command cell of the *Oberkommando des Heeres* (Army High Command), the course was not designed to train future senior commanders or staff officers for ministerial appointments. General Ludwig Beck, Chief of the General Staff 1933–1938, further restricted training to the framework of the division. Since this prevented students from studying "operational" in supradistinction to "tactical" or divisional level deployments, Beck's decision drew criticism from many German officers. In his defense, however, he appears to have been especially anxious to establish basic formations on a firm tactical footing within a rapidly expanding army. In any case, the reinstitution of the third year of staff training in 1937 allayed this operational concern.[24]

While British doctrine did not recognize the *operativ* level between tactics and strategy, it did possess an imperial dimension that was truly unique. Indeed, one might say that British military thought skipped the operational level, proceeding directly from the tactical to the grand strategical realm of the Empire. Evidence of this can be found not only in the senior division curriculum of the Staff College, but in the 1926 establishment of the IDC. The original purpose of this "Joint College," placed under the supervision of the Chiefs of Staff Sub-Committee of the CID, was "to create a common doctrine in regard to defence policy and to produce . . . officers trained to look at the problem of war as a whole." As viewed by its first commandant and founder, Admiral Richmond, the IDC was not merely a joint version of a single service staff college, but a "combined War College" and "centre of higher studies" superimposed on existing staff training systems. Politico-military in both focus and student body, its function was described as "training . . . a body of officers and civilian officials in the broadest aspects of Imperial Strategy."[25] Invaluable as it was for the oceanic empire it served, however, the IDC was clearly not geared to produce battlefield commanders capable of handling sizable formations in combat.

It is nonetheless equally clear that many army officers considered the IDC the most desirable defense college to attend for career and "professional" advancement. McNaughton, for example, attended the first course in January 1927, Crerar the eighth in 1934, and Pearkes the one in 1937. Yet, while the IDC became a stepping stone to high command and produced students more or less expert in imperial defence and constitutional issues, it hardly enhanced their field generalship.[26] The attraction of the grand strategic sphere, in short, led many senior officers of the British and Canadian armies, most especially McNaughton, to neglect the operational field. The "initial division of staff duties" into "two classes"—the "first [in the field] . . . with troops, and the second . . . at the War Office"—[27] further exacerbated the situation as, once again, it proved more career-beneficial to serve with "the Staff not in the field." Activities associated with "preparation" for war, like equipment and weapons procurement, thus received greater attention than those more directly related to "fighting proper." The "art of using . . . given means in combat," to quote Clausewitz, suffered accordingly.[28]

No institution like the U.S. Army War College, which educated officers specifically for higher field command,[29] existed for redressing this imbalance in focus. Only a few dedicated individuals like Montgomery, who was considered eccentric and consequently passed over, seem even to have attempted it. At Quetta, against a "background of polo-playing . . . regimental parties . . . and abundant drink," he nonetheless warned his students that they would "neglect the study of . . . [their] profession at . . . [their] peril."[30] The truth was, though the "junior" staff colleges rather than the IDC remained the principal avenues by which regular army officers could expand their knowledge of land operations, to most they represented but lesser steps in their career progression. Despite the charge that the "staff colleges in the 1920s taught . . . [trench warfare] and nothing else,"[31] it is clear that they were the only institutions concerned with fighting large-scale war on land. Like the *Kriegsakademie*, they may also have compensated for backwardness in tactical teaching by producing officers skilled in map reading and terrain appreciation, both vital to the application of tactics, and capable of producing clear, concise orders and correct responses in rapid, accurate fashion.[32]

Canada resumed sending two officers per year to Camberley in 1920 and one annually to Quetta from 1924. A five-month Staff College Preparatory Course through which all candidates had to pass was also reinstituted at the RMC in 1921. These actions were in keeping with the view that staff college training remained a key factor in maintaining uniformity of doctrine, which ever since the Colonial Conference of 1907 and subsequent Imperial (Defence) Conference of 1909 had reflected that promulgated by the British War Office. There was never any serious attempt between wars to establish an army staff college in Canada. Indeed, Crerar had even stated that he could "personally . . . imagine no worse blow to the practical assimilation of the Military Forces of the Empire than that each Dominion should have its own Staff College." If the dominions were to "march in step," he concluded, they "must absorb the same doctrine—the same learning."[33]

The year 1922 witnessed, nonetheless, the revival of the venerable Militia Staff Course designed to qualify "selected officers of the [reserve] Non-Permanent Active Militia for appointment to the staff of formations in the field." Also a qualification for field rank (major), it again comprised theoretical and practical portions. The first, conducted at convenient centers within military districts or by correspondence during the winter months from October to April, terminated with an examination. Subject material covered included two précis on strategy, seven on combatant arms, six on tactics, two on map reading and field sketching, and, respectively, nine, eight, and five on G, A, and Q staff duties. The practical portion, usually held during two weeks in July at a central camp, kicked off with a two-hour equitation course for candidates on their allocated horses. Thereafter they tackled tactical problems based on the theoretical portion in both command and staff dimensions, from section to brigade level in the former case, and from staff captain to divisional staff in the latter.

Though a brave attempt to conduct training for war, the Militia Staff Course suffered from obvious limitations. The question of how to maintain the proficiency of successful candidates posed an additional problem. The inauguration of the Advanced Militia Course in 1935 consequently aimed at giving further training to graduates under age 45. By the time the Militia Staff Course terminated in 1939, over 400 officers possessed the "msc" qualification and another 29 the advanced MSC certificate. On the surface this represented a substantial adjunct to the 45 regular officers who qualified "psc" by virtue of having passed through either Camberley or Quetta. As most Militia Staff Course graduates could not handle more than garrison staff appointments,[34] however, they actually added little depth to the Canadian staff situation on the outbreak of war.

By April 1940 the provision of competent trained staff officers had become a matter of serious concern to the Canadian field force overseas. Though the British Army had started conducting 17-week junior war staff courses at Camberley for more than 100 students at a time from 15 September 1939, only a few Canadian vacancies were allocated on each. While of great value, these were clearly not enough to satisfy the growing demand for staff officers bought on by increased diversity in weapons, equipment, and techniques of war. The British brigade staff, for example, had expanded threefold over what it was in the Great War. As a first step toward meeting this shortcoming, McNaughton established the Canadian Junior War Staff Course (CJWSC) at Ford Manor, Lingfield, Surrey, in the fall of 1940. Sixty-one officers attended the first course conducted from 2 January to 12 April 1941. The directing staff consisted of a Commandant/GSO 1, Lieutenant-Colonel Simonds, and ten GSO 2 instructors; of the latter, three were British combat arms officers with recent battle experience, nine were staff qualified, and another nine had held staff appointments with field formation headquarters.[35]

As Simonds reported, organizing a training program in the space of four weeks did not give rise to the "question of what a war staff course should include in absolute terms." Determining the scope of the course became principally a matter of deciding what could be covered with reasonable thoroughness in a period of about three months. The syllabus, restricted to "staff work in the field, mainly on the Grade 3 and Grade 2 level," largely reflected that of the Junior War Staff Course conducted at Camberley. Some modifications proved necessary, however, since Canadian officers attending CJWSC had on average little more than a year's service with their units and practically no experience with arms other than their own. The great majority of British candidates at Camberley, on the other hand, were regulars "with ten or more years continuous regimental experience . . . [many of whom] had qualified for entrance to the Staff College before the outbreak of War." Special emphasis was thus accorded to giving less experienced Canadian candidates "thorough grounding in the organization and characteristics of the arms and services and in elementary staff duties."[36]

Naturally, the CJWSC benefitted from its near proximity to Camberley and large-field formations like the 1st Canadian and 1st Armoured divisions, which were capable of staging outdoor demonstrations of actual troop deployments on selected ground. This was particularly fortunate, since in Simonds's view the tactical knowledge of Canadian candidates joining the course appeared "definitely below what the average should [have] be[en] for officers training for the General Staff."[37] Progress was often retarded, moreover, by the frequent requirement during exercises to deal with details of minor tactics with which officers should have been familiar. Another very pronounced and general failing, deemed by Simonds to be the result of a flaw in the Canadian educational system was the "inability . . . of most student officers to express themselves clearly and concisely on paper." Much instruction during the first month consequently concentrated on writing orders and preparing correspondence. Each student during the course had also to submit three written papers.[38]

Significantly, of the 59 students who completed the first course, only 36 received a clear staff qualification (SC). Of the remainder, seven obtained conditional passes and 16 failed to qualify, including 14 not recommended for staff employment in any capacity. Simonds bluntly depicted this unsatisfactory performance as "the inevitable result of the rapid expansion of a force in which a meager peacetime training depended solely upon good will." Rapid officer turnover, unit focus on administrative problems, and frequent interruption of training since mobilization had, in his estimation, further ensured a generally "low standard of individual tactical training in the corps of officers." Simonds also expressed concern that the proportional representation of the various arms and services had been given too much precedence over individual ability as a criterion for selection. Thus, although course candidates as a group represented "selected officers specially recommended for staff training," few of them had even read widely circulated "Army Training Memoranda" in their units. As Simonds warned, however, the real danger lay in the "failure to recognize frankly that this situation exist[ed]."[39]

Prior to the termination of the first course, Crerar, then CGS, confirmed his intention to transfer the CJWSC to the RMC, Kingston. The second CJWSC with 40 students between the ages of 22 and 35 commenced on 24 July 1941 and lasted for 16 weeks. Four GSOs 2 from Ford Manor, one of whom became Commandant/GSO 1, returned to Canada to form the nucleus of the instructional staff for the second course. Instead of observing operational field formation headquarters and demonstrations, however, this course visited Canadian military installations to observe how training problems in Canada were being handled. Again, with four failures and nine provisional passes recorded, the success rate on the course was low. A similar number failed to meet the standard on the third course attended by 48 officers. Only two candidates failed the fourth course, but the award of 36 "B" gradings within 54 passes attested to a less stringent assessment standard. Three more courses for 192 students followed in 1942, and on 1 December the CJWSC was redesignated the Canadian War Staff Course (CWSC).[40]

In the same year the British sensibly split the Staff College into three wings: a 16-week Senior Staff Course at Minley Manor designed to train officers, including Canadians, for senior staff appointments; a 16-week Intermediate Staff Course at Camberley designed to train officers for second-grade staff appointments in field formations; and a 12-week Junior Staff Course at Sandhurst designed to train officers to fill second-grade appointments at headquarters other than those of field forces. In 1943 the CWSC wisely followed suit, reorganizing along similar lines into an Intermediate "A" Wing for field staff and a Junior "B" Wing for static headquarters staff, the first course of which commenced in October 1943. Significantly, the courses tended to get longer; in the final year of the war, the A Wing course expanded beyond seven months and the B Wing to four. By 31 December 1945, a total of 772 officers had graduated from the CWSC (Intermediate Wing) and 238 from the CWSC (Junior Wing).[41]

While it is difficult at any time to gauge precisely the effectiveness of staff work let alone staff training, certain observations are possible. The first is that in aim and content the shortened British and Canadian war courses sought only to scratch the surface of higher military knowledge. Whatever woefully little depth the Canadian Army possessed in this area also continued to be eroded as the most successful staff candidates proceeded to assume the highest command appointments. As war staff course syllabi allocated few periods to training methodology, moreover, the policy of employing better students as instructors tended to yield diminishing returns. In one instance, a major who received an average grading on the second course returned as a DS member to instruct on the fifth and sixth courses.[42] Predictably, British Army staff training suffered a similar erosion, but with the difference that it was quality of candidate rather than quality of instructor that caused the deterioration.

In the estimation of General Sir David Fraser, the standard of British DS, many of whom had generally proven themselves in action, remained high throughout the war.[43] That this was not the case in Canada is evident from the August 1942 complaint of the CJWSC Commandant, Lieutenant-Colonel C. Sanford, that by the fourth course none of the GSOs 2 held the qualification of "psc." According to one battle-experienced and respected member of the DS, Major P. H. LaBouchere, Canadian instructors often had "to go through their material many times" as compared with their Camberley "regular officer" counterparts who "with a very broad training background . . . [could] frequently gain sufficient additional knowledge of the subject to instruct . . . by reading through the latest précis . . . once."[44] The requirement to keep up with doctrinal changes also proved more difficult in Canada. Indeed, one cannot escape the conclusion that the transfer of the course from Ford Manor to Kingston neither enhanced staff training nor improved instructional standards.

Rapid changes in appointments brought on by expansion continued to plague the Canadian Army up to January 1944. Hardly had an officer learned his job than he was posted, usually with a promotion.[45] A shortage of trained staff officers delayed the establishment of 2 Corps headquarters, originally planned for 1 July 1942, until 14 January 1943. The basic nature of the staff training conducted also meant that the handling of large formations had to be learned on British courses, exercises, or in actual operations. There were nonetheless those, like Major-General B. M. Hoffmeister, GOC 5th Canadian Armoured Division from 20 March 1944, who claimed that they commanded better battalions for having had basic staff training.[46] The harsh reality remained, however, that the primary function of war staff courses was to impart doctrine rather than consider the conduct of operations objectively. They were no longer capable, to paraphrase Fraser, of offering "military education in any but the most shallow sense."[47]

Recognition of this subtle difference no doubt explains why professional soldiers have traditionally insisted that a good staff officer cannot be trained in less than a year. In the opinion of many scholars, the analytical studies carried out during the three-year *Kriegsakademie* course lay at the root of German tactical and operational excellence.[48] This is partly borne out by the conclusion of others that in the first half of the twentieth century, "those who trained most ruthlessly and honestly in peacetime have done best on the battlefield.[49] The link between training and performance having thus been established, it follows naturally that the Canadian Army could scarcely have become operational without British assistance and the existence of its small caste of prewar staff-trained officers. Again, the greatest value of a general staff, that it permits an army and its officers to train for war in periods of peace, seems to be confirmed. That this should be is simply because there is rarely enough time in war to train a really good field staff.

NOTES

1. Michael Howard, *The Franco-Prussian War: The German Invasion of France, 1870–1871* (New York: Methuen, 1981), p. 24.

2. Maj.-Gen. Bronsart von Schellendorf, *The Duties of The General Staff*, trans. W. A. H. Hare (London: Kegan Paul, 1877), p. 4.

3. John Masters, *The Road Past Mandalay: A Personal Narrative* (New York: Bantam, 1979), pp. 86–88.

4. W. E. J. Hutchinson, "Test of a Corps Commander: Lieutenant-General Guy Granville Simonds, Normandy 1944" (unpublished M.A. thesis, University of Victoria, 1982), p. 71. According to U.S. Gen. J. Lawton Collins, "for the Army as a whole, the courses at the Command and General Staff School were probably the most important in the entire system of military education, and were to prove invaluable in World War II" [Robert H. Berlin, "United States Army World War II Corps Commanders: A Composite Biography," *The Journal of Military History*, 2 (April 1989), p. 156].

5. Col. C. P. Stacey, *Official History of the Canadian Army in the Second World War*, Vol. I: *Six Years of War: The Army in Canada, Britain and the Pacific* (Ottawa: Queen's Printer, 1966), p. 414; and Barry Leach, *German General Staff* (New York: Ballantine, 1973), pp. 48, 99.

6. Dallas D. Irvine, "The Origin of Capital Staffs," *The Journal of Modern History*, 2 (June 1938): 162–165, 168–170; David N. Spires, *Image and Reality: The Making of the German Officer, 1921–1933* (Westport, Conn.: Greenwood, 1984), pp. 30–31, 41; Maj.-Gen. F. W. von Mellenthin, *German Generals of World War II* (Norman, Okla.: University of Oklahoma Press, 1977), p. 275; Gunther E. Rothenberg, "Moltke, Schlieffen, and the Doctrine of Strategic Envelopment," *Makers of Modern Strategy*, ed. Peter Paret (Princeton, N.J.: Princeton University Press, 1986), pp. 301–302; Col. T. N. Dupuy, *A Genius for War: The German Army and General Staff, 1807–1945* (London: Macdonald and Jane's, 1977), pp. 28, 30, 34, 38–39, 46–48; Philip A. Bayer, *The Evolution of the Soviet General Staff, 1917–1941* (New York: Garland, 1987), pp. 4–11; and Brian Bond, *The Victorian Army and the Staff College 1854–1914* (London: Eyre Methuen, 1972), pp. 12, 19, 30–39. Hitler abolished the COS's coresponsibility for operational decision making. Mellenthin, *German Generals*, p. 276.

7. Irvine, "The Origin of Capital Staffs," p. 173; Schellendorf, *Duties of The General Staff*, pp. 4–49; Lt. Col. Vernon (ed.), "Project #6 German General Staff," Vol. III. "Training and Development of German General Staff Officers," trans. G. C. Vanderstadt, Historical Division, U.S. European Command, 21 June 1951; and Leach, *German General Staff*, pp. 28–29.

8. Bond, *Staff College*, pp. 73, 143–146, 192–194, 215–243; Jay Luvaas, *The*

Education of an Army: British Military Thought, 1815–1940 (Chicago: University Press, 1964), pp. 259–264; Capt. M. V. Bezeau, "The Role and Organization of Canadian Military Staffs 1904–1945" (unpublished M.A. thesis, Royal Military College, 1978), pp. 11–16; Brian Bradshaw-Ellis, "Seven Lean Years: The Organization and Administration of the Imperial General Staff, 1926–1933" (unpublished M.A. thesis, University of New Brunswick, 1976), pp. 38–39, 88–89, 123–127, 150–151; Maj.-Gen. E. K. G. Sixsmith, *British Generalship in the Twentieth Century* (London: Arms and Armour, 1970), pp. 31–32; and John Gooch, "The Creation of the British General Staff 1904–1914," *Journal of the Royal United Services Institute (JRUSI)*, 662 (June 1971): 50–53. The Elgin Commission issued a monumental report on the South African War in 1903. The reforms of the Esher Committee were to an extent the fruits of the 1890 Hartington Committee, which proposed replacing the Commander-in-Chief with a Chief of the General Staff and setting up a War Office Council. Bond argues that had there been a British version of von Moltke, the General Staff could have become an even more effective army elite and "brain" capable of forming a "school of thought" than it did. In his estimation, the nearest approximation turned out to be Maurice Hankey, the secretary of the CID. On the CID, see Nicholas D'Ombrain, *War Machinery and High Policy: Defence Administration in Peacetime Britain 1902–1914* (London: Oxford, 1973).

9. Maj.-Gen. F. C. Fuller, *The Army in My Time* (London: Rich and Cowan, 1935), pp. 107–110, 117. In 1909 the General Staff expanded into an Imperial General Staff to give unity "to the training, education and war organization of the forces of the Crown in every part of the Empire" (Luvaas, *Education of an Army*, p. 309).

10. Bezeau, "Military Staffs," pp. 16–18; and WO 2923 *Field Service Pocket Book. 1914. (Reprinted with Amendments, 1916)* (London: H.M. Stationery Office, 1916), p. 7. The "AQ" grading in descending order of precedence was Deputy, Assistant, Deputy Assistant, and Staff Captain [J. Mackay Hitsman, "The Staff That Was," *Canadian Army Journal (CAJ)*, 3 (1964): 33–38; and Maj. G. R. N. Collins, *Military Organization and Administration* (London: Hugh Rees, 1918), pp. 61–62].

11. Col. G. W. L. Nicholson, *Official History of the Canadian Army in the First World War: Canadian Expeditonary Force 1914–1919* (Ottawa: Queen's Printer, 1962), pp. 8–9; Kenneth Charles Eyre, "Staff and Command in the Canadian Corps: The Canadian Militia as a Source of Senior Officers" (unpublished M.A. thesis, Duke University, 1967), pp. 43–46, 55, 71–72, 77–78, 92–96, 113–114, 129–130, 163; Bezeau, "Military Staffs," pp. 32, 38, 49; and Stephen John Harris, "Canadian Brass: The Growth of the Canadian Military Profession" (unpublished Ph.D. thesis, Duke University, 1979), pp. 131–133, 209–211. The first Militia Staff Course had been introduced in 1898, but "died a natural death . . . [in 1903] the victim of its reputation for asking the impossible of part-time citizen soldiers" (Harris, "Canadian Brass," pp. 129–130).

12. Harris, "Canadian Brass," p. 210.

13. Lt.-Gen. E. L. M. Burns, *General Mud: Memoirs of Two World Wars* (Toronto: Clarke, Irwin, 1970), pp. 75–76.

14. Bond, *Staff College*, pp. 303–309, 323–328; and Maj. A. R. Godwin-Austin, *The Staff and the Staff College* (London: Constable, 1927), pp. 263–265.

15. Introduction by Barrie Pitt to Leach, *German General Staff*, pp. 6–7. The Germans also closed the *Kriegsakademie* on the outbreak of war. The staff replacement system encouraged officers to sit general staff examinations, after which they were

scrutinized by higher staff officers and served a nine-month apprenticeship. Preference was accorded to those who had gained entry to the *Kriegsakademie*; of those who applied, only one-half gained admission to the general staff corps. From July 1917 to September 1918, 13 three-week courses were conducted and 500 officers qualified (Dupuy, *Genius*, pp. 186–187).

16. Godwin-Austin, *Staff College*, pp. 269–270; Bond, *Staff College*, pp. 328–329; and Maj. E. W. O. Perry, "The General Staff System, The Rise of the British Imperial General Staff: Part 2," *CAJ*, 6 (September 1949): 27–29.

17. Royal Military College of Canada Massey Library (RMC) and Gen. H. D. G. Crerar Papers (CP), Vol. 9, Memorandum on the Organization of Command, the Functioning of the Staff, Services, Miscellaneous Appointments at HQ First Cdn Army, and Certain Other Organizations which Operate in Close Liaison with this HQ, Second Edition, 1 February 1945; and Record Group (RG) 24, Vol. 13, 711, Minutes of a Conference Held by General Montgomery HQ 21 Army Group 0930 hrs, 13 January 1944. See also Nigel Hamilton, *Monty*, Vol. I: *The Making of a General 1887–1942* (Sevenoaks, U.K.: Hodder and Stoughton, 1984) pp. 127, 326–327, 460; and Maj. E. J. Perkins, "The Military Staff," *CAJ*, 1 (April 1953): 33. In the German field general staff system, the "Ia" looked after operational and training matters, the "Ic" reconnaissance and intelligence, and the "Ib" logistics. Corps, army, and army group levels were served by a COS. Montgomery used a COS at division.

18. Godwin-Austin, *Staff College*, pp. 270–274, 279. In 1922 there were only 32 places open for competition, which meant there were likely close to that number nominated. In the view of the Commandant at the time, Maj.-Gen. W. E. Ironside, "nominations by no means produced the best staff officers" (Maj.-Gen. Sir W. E. Ironside, "The Modern Staff Officer," *JRUSI*, 491 (August 1928): 441–442).

19. Luvaas, *Education of an Army*, pp. 345–346; and Lt.-Col. F. W. Young, *The Story of the Staff College 1858–1958* (Camberley: Staff College, 1958), p. 4. Fuller wrote in 1926 that, "The Staff College was run like a school (absurd)," but that he changed his division "into a university." Brian Holden Reid, *J. F. C. Fuller: Military Thinker* (London: Macmillan, 1987), p. 83.

20. Lt.-Gen. Maurice A. Pope, *Soldiers and Politicians* (Toronto: University of Toronto Press, 1962), pp. 52–63; Robert Speaight, *Vanier: Soldier, Diplomat and Governor General* (Toronto: Collins, 1970), pp. 98–99; and DHist CMHQ Historical Officer Report No. 14 dated 10 March 1941; and CP, Vol. 3, First Canadian Army Intelligence Periodical Number 4. The title "Directing Staff" was introduced in 1906 in place of "Professors" for members of the faculty (Young, *Staff College*, p. 3).

21. Godwin-Austin, *Staff College*, pp. 287–291; and Maj. R. G. Jessel, *G, A, and Q: An Introduction to the Staff* (Aldershot: Gale and Polden, 1947), pp. 30–31.

22. Brig. C. N. Barclay, "Four Generations of Staff College Students—1896 to 1952," *The Army Quarterly*, 1 (October 1952): 49–50.

23. Ironside, "The Modern Staff Officer," pp. 441–442. Ironside thought "the dissipation of the German Staff [after Versailles] ha[d] destroyed German military power more than anything" (Ibid., p. 445).

24. Leach, *German General Staff*, pp. 28–29, 44; Spires, *Image and Reality*, pp. 45, 56–67, 176–178; and CP, Vol. 3, First Canadian Army Intelligence Periodical Number 4, dated 5 June 1943. Beck's intention was to leave higher staff training to senior

officers courses. He was also criticized for stopping the practice of allowing students rather than their instructors set tactical problems for their comrades.

25. Barry D. Hunt, *Sailor-Scholar: Admiral Sir Herbert Richmond 1871–1946* (Waterloo, Ont: Wilfred Laurier University Press, 1982), pp. 149–166.

26. The bulk of work at the IDC consisted of "written exercises on major war problems," conferences, and lectures (CP, Vol. 10, Lecture on 1934 Course to Cdn Arty Assoc, Ottawa 9 February 1935.

27. Ironside, "The Modern Staff Officer," pp. 436, 438.

28. Carl von Clausewitz, *On War*, ed./trans. Michael Howard and Peter Paret (Princeton, N.J.: Princeton University Press, 1976), p. 127. It has been suggested that "political-strategic wisdom is far more important to national military effectiveness than tactical and operational performance on the battlefield" [Alan R. Millett and Williamson Murray, "Lessons of War," *The National Interest*, 14 (Winter 1988), p. 93]. That the Second World War was won principally, and operationally, on the Eastern Front would seem to defy this conclusion however.

29. Berlin, "United States Army World War II Corps Commanders," p. 156.

30. Hamilton, *Monty*, I, 227–228, 236–237.

31. Lt.-Gen. Sir Francis Tuker, *The Pattern of War* (London: Cassell, 1948), p. 47.

32. Leach, *German General Staff*, p. 46.

33. Lt.-Col. H. D. G. Crerar, "The Development of Closer Relations Between the Military Forces of the Empire," *JRUSI*, 483 (August 1926): 452.

34. Lt.-Col. A. C. Garner, "Impressions of the Militia Staff Course Western Canada, 1928–1929," *Canadian Defense Quantity* (*CDQ*), 3 (April 1930): 376–382; Capt. W. E. Baxter, "The M.S.C.—and After," *CDQ*, 1 (October 1937): 67; DHist 114.1 (D75), CGS Policy of Training, 1939–40; Brig. James Sutherland Brown Papers (SBP), Box 8, File 179, Militia Orders No. 418–424 dated 28 September, 1932, and Brown to Rowley, September, 1929; Lt. Gen. Howard Graham, *Citizen and Soldier*, (Toronto: McClelland and Stewart, 1987), pp. 100–105; Maj. Barry M. Watson, "The Advanced Militia Staff Course," *CDQ*, 1 (October 1938): 68–69; and Bezeau, "Military Staffs," pp. 101–102, 111–112, 134, 161.

35. Maj.-Gen. W. H. P. Elkins Papers (EP), Elkins to the Minister, 25 April 1940; McNaughton Papers (MP), Vol. 222, memorandum of discussion on institution of a junior C.S.C. with Major-General Collins and Colonel Evelegh, Commandant and G.S.O.1, Junior Wing [Camberley] respectively by B.G.S. (Cdn) 7 Corps, 17 September 1940; MP, Vol. 347, article *Montreal Standard* 10 May 1941; J.H.L., "Canadian Junior War Staff Course," *RMC Review*, 22 (December 1941): 21; DHist CMHQ Historical Officer Report No. 22, dated 24 April 1941; Maj.-Gen. A. C. Duff, *Sword and Pen*, (Aldershot, U.K: Gale and Polden, 1950), pp. 43–44; and Stacey, *Six Years*, p. 237. Some 4,000 students were trained at Camberley during the war (Young, *Staff College*, p. 4).

36. RG 24, Vol. 9874, Report on the First Canadian Junior War Staff Course, 20 April 1941.

37. Ibid.

38. Ibid.; and DHist CMHQ Historical Officer Report No. 14 dated 10 March 1941.

39. Ibid.; and MP, Vol. 347, article *Montreal Standard* 10 May 1941. Simonds claimed that too many candidates expected "spoon feeding" (DHist CMHQ Historical Officer Report No. 22, dated 24 April 1941).

40. J. H. L., "Canadian Junior War Staff Course," pp. 21–22; RG 24, Vol. 13,240, Military Training in Canada 1942, DMT paper, dated 2 December 1942; RG 24, Vol. 9873, G.S.O. 1's Report on Fourth Canadian Junior War Staff Course 22 August 1942; RG 24, Vol. 186, Individual Grading Reports from CJWSC Numbers 2 and 3; and RMC Kingston WD, 31 December 1945.

41. RG 24, Vol. 13,243, NDHQ Trg Ln Letter No. 19, dated 14 February 1945; CP, Vol. 2, Matters for Discussion with GOC, 1 Cdn Corps and Sr Offr, CMHQ 13–6–42 by AAG (MS) First Cdn Army; Stacey, *Six Years*, p. 140. By A.C.I. 2432 of 1942, Staff College Camberley was organized in three wings (RG 24, Vol. 9874). Seventeen-week courses designed to train second-grade staff officers for field army headquarters (awarding an "sc" qualification) were conducted at Camberley and Haifa staff colleges. Ten to 13-week junior staff courses designed to train staff officers for non-field grade two positions (with the qualification "jsc") were conducted at Sandhurst, Sarafand, and Quetta. An 18-week "sc" course was also run at Quetta [RG 24, Vol. 9874, WO DMT 43/SC/S662 (MT1), 16 April 1944 and File 2/Staff/7–2 memo 2/Staff/7/2 (SD&T) SD&T, CMHQ to D.C.G.S., 14 September 1944].

42. This was Maj. J. V. Allard whose course report read: "His mental process is rather slow, but he shows sound sense and a good judgement." He was assessed as competent to perform "in a third grade appointment" [RG 24, Vol. 186, Third (and final) report on Maj. J. V. Allard, 12 Army Tk Bn (TRR)]. See also *The Memoirs of General Jean V. Allard*, written in cooperation with Serge Bernier (Vancouver: University of British Columbia Press, 1988), pp. 36–37, 44–45. Allard went on to head Canada's peacetime forces in the intoxicating days of unification and latter stages of Quebec's "Quiet Revolution."

43. Gen. Sir David Fraser, *And We Shall Shock Them: The British Army in the Second World War* (London: Hodder and Stoughton, 1988), p. 103. The general reluctance of officers to leave the regimental family chiefly accounted for the lowering of British staff candidate quality. Canadian staff training suffered similarly.

44. RG 24, Vol. 9873, Memorandum "Canadian War Staff Course" GSO 2 (S.D.1) minute added by Col. J. F. A. Lister to B.G.S., 20 December 1942; and GSO 1's Report on Fourth Canadian Junior War Staff Course, 22 August 1942. LaBouchere made his remarks, of course, while attempting to right the "perfect murder" of an obviously overworked, and correspondingly less efficient, Directing Staff cadre.

45. Burns, *General Mud*, p. 105.

46. Hoffmeister, Canadian Land Forces Command and Staff College (hereafter CLFCSC) SC 1450–2027 "The Influence of Staff College Major-General B. M. Hoffmeister," 20 September 1985. Hoffmeister attended the course when LaBouchere was a member of the Directing Staff. He was described by Hoffmeister as "fresh from the desert, and . . . knowledgeable."

47. Fraser, *And We Shall Shock Them*, p. 103.

48. Martin van Creveld, "On Learning From the Wehrmacht and Other Things," *Military Review*, 1 (January 1988): 67; and Lt.-Gen. John H. Cushman, "Challenge and Response at the Operational and Tactical Levels, 1914–45," *Military Effectiveness*, ed. Allan R. Millett and Williamson Murray (Boston: Allen and Unwin, 1988), Vol. III, pp. 321, 329–330.

49. Millett and Murray, "Lessons of War," p. 94.

Chapter 5

Battle Drill Die

Early in '42 the Canadian Army in England went Battle Drill mad. Assault courses, live ammunition exercises and speed marches dominated the lives of all infantrymen and impinged on those in other corps. Training had become boring. For two years, in the case of some of us, barrack square routine and large scale manoeuvres... had started to turn us into a fed-up, browned-off, disillusioned band of volunteer warriors. We were getting to the point where we couldn't have fought our way out of a paper bag.

Strome Galloway, *The General Who Never Was*[1]

At several removes from staff organization and functioning, the Anglo-Canadian training phenomenon known as battle drill merits attention for at least two reasons. First, because it encapsulated the general thrust, pulse, and hence effectiveness of Canadian Army training at the lower level, and secondly, because it may have been a pedagogical dead end. The speed and enthusiasm with which Canadians embraced battle drill, of course, seems more reminiscent of a fad than any deliberate direction on the part of their high command. One can only speculate that Canadians as a group may have too eagerly seized upon new methods merely to escape having to learn older, proven ways with which they were largely unfamiliar. It thus remains to be determined to what extent, if any, battle drill was actually the result of high command initiative. Whatever the determination, the far greater question arises as to whether battle drill detracted from other more worthwhile training pursuits. If it did, and in effect became a dead end in itself, high command cannot be absolved of blame.

Since battle drill initially possessed artillery and armored as well as infantry dimensions, it affords an excellent vehicle by which to ascertain the direction and progress of Canadian combat arms training. As the way an army trains usually determines the way it will fight, moreover, the state of Canadian Army troop training in Britain deserves as much scrutiny as the staff training of officers. To understand an army from the standpoint of command and staff is one thing, but to discover the essence of its fighting ability one has to look at the lower levels. Without a conditioned body, the brain of an army is of little consequence, for battles are in the end fought and won by small groups of soldiers at the front. Yet how a high command ensures their training remains of the utmost importance. Fortunately, within this extremely complex and variegated field, battle drill provides an apposite avenue that can be profitably explored in this respect. It is, after all, not how long, but how well an army trains that counts.

That the Canadian volunteer soldier was excellent raw material of unmatched willingness can hardly be doubted. He simply manifested a burning desire to get into action. Military authorities in Canada, at the beginning of December 1941, attributed "the . . . 'inferiority complex' suffered by the soldier in comparison with the Air Force," to the fact that "he [wa]s not doing any fighting."[2] Barely two days later, however, Canadian soldiers in the Hong Kong garrison found themselves in the thick of an impossible struggle. They nonetheless held out with their imperial comrades for 17 days, proving that regardless of their state of training, Canadian troops were prepared to fight tenaciously and die hard. Of 1,975 soldiers, 557 never saw their homeland again. In no small way, Canada's earlier insistence on British abrogation of the Anglo-Japanese Alliance had ensured that they, along with the defenders of Singapore, "paid the final installment on the Washington Treaty."[3]

In Britain about the same time, their countrymen embraced battle drill just as Montgomery began to exert his unique professional stamp on Canadian training. Like their personal acquaintance with Montgomery, however, Canadians came into contact with battle drill more through accident than design. During July and August 1941, the 2nd Canadian Infantry Division relieved the 55th Division within 4 British Corps on the Sussex coast, thus opening a close association with the 47th (London) Division, a British Territorial Army formation commanded by Major-General J. E. Utterson-Kelso. Unique among 4 Corps formations, the 47th Division had a battle drill school in full operation when the first Canadians to see it, the Calgary Highlanders, arrived. General Utterson-Kelso had served in the 1st Division BEF under Major-General H. R. L. G. Alexander whom, it would appear, first suggested the idea of battle drill on observing the actions of German troops. Interested in basic tactical problems such as how to defend a bridge or clear a woods of enemy, Alexander was also supposedly forever illustrating suggested solutions through field sketches.

Upon Alexander's appointment to command 1 British Corps after Dunkirk, his BGS had certain of his annotated infantry training sketches published in a pamphlet entitled, "1st Corps Tactical Notes." In the introduction Alexander likened battle to a "supreme sport" that required previously worked-out team plays. "Surely," he argued, "a soldier on the battlefield, beset by fear and doubt, is far more in need of a guide to action than any games player at Lord's or Wimbledon." Suggesting that it was preferable "to know instinctively some orthodox line of conduct than . . . be paralyzed by . . . uncertainty of what to do," he recommended drawing up "lines of conduct—simple guides for simple soldiers" so that men when faced with battlefield problems would have answers to them. In all, about eight to ten operations such as village clearing and how to attack a strongpoint were presented. A corps training school was subsequently established through which every subaltern in the 1st and 2nd British Divisions passed. Thirty thousand copies of "Tactical Notes" were produced, of which 5,000 went to Montgomery's corps.[4]

After the 1 Corps booklet attracted the attention of the CIGS, General Sir John Dill, the War Office had parts of it published in February 1941, though without any reference to "battle drill" per se. It was subsequently issued as a supplement to *Infantry Training, 1937* under the title "Tactical Notes for Platoon Commanders, 1941." Around roughly the same time, the 47th Division began developing battle drills based on *Training in Fieldcraft and Elementary Tactics*, a pamphlet published in March 1940 that advocated the exercise of greater imagination in teaching tactics. The divisional approach was to analyze each "movement and operation of war and . . . break it [*sic*] down to . . . bare essentials," work out an ideal plan for dealing with these under ideal conditions, and teach that plan as a drill with variations to ensure the latter did not become an end in itself. It assumed that the imaginative commander could work out an "adaption" that would "fit" the tactical circumstance; the unimaginative could "just carry out the drill woodenly—and still . . . [not] do too badly."

The 47th Division insisted on adding to this equation the highest possible standard of physical fitness. All training was performed at the double with ruthless application, paying strict attention to weapon handling. The next step saw the introduction of noise and live fire training. When Montgomery granted permission to practice with live ammunition, "battle inoculation" also became an integral element of battle drill training. Later, a series of lectures and précis were incorporated in a 169-page mimeographed publication entitled "Battle Drill."[5] This provided the basis for instruction at the divisional battle school run by a bright young Oxford graduate and officer from a territorial battalion of the Royal Fusiliers, Major L. Wigman. When queried as to the purpose of battle drill, he invariably replied with wry humour, "To make every man a general."[6]

On 31 December 1941, the C-in-C Home Forces announced that a central GHQ Battle School was in the process of formation at Barnard Castle on the Durham moor and that battle schools were to be established for each division. The objects of the latter were: to inculcate "battle discipline" by translating that of the parade square onto the battlefield; to study battle drill as a means of interpreting doctrine in a practical manner, especially in relation to fire and movement; to accustom officers through "battle inoculation" to think and act under the noise and strain of battle; to stimulate new and practical ideas among all ranks; and to train instructors in minor tactics to meet wastage in units. The purpose of the GHQ Battle School was to train instructors for divisional battle drill schools and other training establishments in the tactical handling of the infantry platoon in cooperation with Bren gun carrier sections, mortar detachments, and other arms.[7]

The first course at the GHQ Battle School commenced on 2 February 1942 and ran for three weeks. Of 102 officers attending, 17 percent were regular, 24 percent Territorial, and 21 percent had seen active service. Overall, their performance was disappointing. As weapon-handling tests showed, few of them knew how to fire the two-inch mortar, and some even attempted to put magazines on the Bren gun the wrong way round. The course further revealed that the majority of officers were quite physically unfit and largely unversed in basic fieldcraft skills. The widespread adoption of battle drill training nonetheless continued unabated. Until *The Instructors' Handbook on Fieldcraft and Battle Drill* was published in October 1942, of course, the 47th Division précis served as the basis for this training. In the meantime Major-General Utterson-Kelso, described as the "best platoon commander in the British army," became Major-General (Infantry) and Lieutenant-Colonel Wigman the Chief Instructor of the GHQ Battle School. The first army-wide Battle School Conference was held at the Horse Guards on 17 and 18 June 1942.[8]

It seems clear from a reading of the *Handbook* and précis that battle drill was a direct attempt to emulate the actions of German soldiers on the battlefield. In addition to calling attention to the relatively unknown development of *sturmtruppen* tactics and techniques in the Great War, battle drill advocates correctly noted that "in spite of the spectacular development of their Luftwaffe, and their Panzer Divisions and the successes which these . . . achieved, the Germans . . . owed much to some first-class infantry fighting at the right time and place." The most significant feature of the German method was also considered to be "the breaking up of the BIG battle into hundreds of LITTLE battles," in which circumstances small groups of well-trained energetic infantrymen performed a vital role. The British infantry's failure to see battle as a series of local actions, in short, had left it "the

Unskilled [*sic*] labour exchange of the rest of the Army . . . [and the] legitimate dumping ground for the lowest forms of military life." To "get on to higher training" became the ambition of the infantry officer as it "did not pay to think hard and long about . . . front-line fighting."

The Germans in contrast had determined that the basis of all infantry tactics was the rapid employment of fire,—that is, infantrymen using their own initiative and weapons to fight themselves forward. An infantry battalion supported by mortars, heavy machine guns, plus light and heavy infantry guns normally attacked on a narrow 600-meter front. The first step, *niederhalten*, involved "pinning down" the enemy and winning the fire fight (*feuerkampf*), which gained the attacker freedom to reconnoiter and maneuver further. The next action, *blinden*, aimed at stunning or "stupefying" the enemy with additional weight of smoke and explosive, thereby denying him observation and accurate counterfire, in order to aggressively deploy assault elements. Finally, during the *niederkampfen* or "beating down" stage the enemy was destroyed in detail through close combat. In a "war of little wars," such an approach provided substantial advantage to the Germans who, acting on minimal orders, became masters of small group fighting, termed "infiltration" by their opponents. As Alexander and Utterson-Kelso observed at Dunkirk, while some "willing and ignorant" British infantrymen were "psychologically outdone by the German dive bomber, screaming shell (or empty bottles) and window dressing," their coal-scuttle helmeted opposites performed magnificently.[9]

To say that the Calgary Highlanders seized upon battle drill as a panacea for the perceived ills of minor tactical practice, the state of which some at the time considered to be in the doldrums, would be a major understatement. They became its most fanatical disciples, proselytizing others with the fervor of evangelists. On first seeing a demonstration of battle drill by the 47th Division on 8 October 1941, the Highlanders's Commanding Officer, Lieutenant-Colonel J. F. Scott, arranged for three of his officers to attend the divisional battle drill school at Chelwood Gate. At the same time, he opened a battalion battle drill school at Burnt Wood near Bexhill, east Sussex. On 23 October a demonstration was even performed for the Minister of National Defence, Colonel The Honourable J. L. Ralston, and Generals McNaughton, Crerar, and V. W. Odlum, GOC 2nd Division. Eventually, the entire battalion passed through the school in a series of two-week courses, which were also regularly attended by NCOs from other 2nd Division units. When 1st Division personnel attempted to follow suit, however, they were stopped by their divisional headquarters, which chose instead to send candidates to the 47th Division.

Though War Office opposition temporarily forced the 47th Division to abandon its battle drill training on 27 November, the Calgary Highlander school continued to function and offer support. Stenciled copies of the 47th Division précis, now pronounced the "Battle Drill Bible," were surreptitiously produced in ever increasing quantities for sale as the regiment responded to a growing grass roots demand. The Toronto Scottish Regiment (MG) put their machine guns on the shelf to practice battle drill. By December 1941, all infantry units of the Canadian Corps were enthusiastically conducting their own battle drill training, which subject henceforth appeared over and over again on infantry training programs. On receipt of direction from C-in-C Home Forces, approval was given in April 1942 to form a Battle Drill Wing at the Canadian Training School, which as previously explained had been established in 1940 to train officers and instructors for units of the Canadian Army Overseas. No. 5 (Battle) Wing subsequently opened at Rowlands Castle, Hampshire, on 1 May 1942 under the command of Major J. Campbell, Calgary Highlanders. The first course, held 1–29 May, was attended by 96 officers and 96 NCOs.[10]

That battle drill training was taken seriously is evident from the fact that in August 1942 a number of Canadian battalion commanders were sent to attend the GHQ Battle School at Barnard Castle. That it took on an increasingly infantry, single-arm bent is a little less obvious, though no less true. The GHQ Battle School was eventually redesignated the GHQ Infantry School and, by 1943, reorganized as a central School of Infantry under the War Office. The Canadian Battle Drill School, established on 10 May 1942 under the command of Lieutenant-Colonel Scott at Courtenay, British Columbia, and subsequently moved to Vernon on 20 July, was also reorganized and incorporated into a Canadian School of Infantry on 31 August 1943. This visibly infantry orientation not only reflected a "new look" intended to show the "place of . . . infantrymen in the symphony of war," but, as well, confirmed the fact that battle drill was designed primarily by and for infantrymen. No doubt caught up in the enthusiasm of the moment, Scott had even seriously, though unsuccessfully, requested the use of the term "commando" to describe this training.[11]

As any review of the 47th Division précis reproduced by the Calgary Highlanders and the Canadian Battle Drill School will reveal, battle drill focus remained principally fixed upon minor tactics at section and platoon levels. Training, conducted under simulated combat conditions, emphasized specific practical drills related to: fieldcraft; observation; section and platoon movement; infiltration; embussing and debussing; woods clearing and attacks in large forests; village fighting, including house clearing; attacking enemy posts and pillboxes; night tank hunting and ambush; night patrolling; river crossing; antiaircraft; and defense of isolated and mutually supporting localities, river lines, villages, and houses.[12] Because platoon battle drills seemed suitably applicable to company infiltration operations, however, certain drills dealing with the attack, village and town fighting, and woods clearing came to be also taught at that level. In August 1943 the Canadian Battle Drill School course expanded from three weeks to 22 training days for the purpose of introducing such company battle drill, thereby bringing it into line with the CTS Battle Wing 26-day course.[13] The weight of evidence suggests, nonetheless, that there was never any intention to "teach ... tactical handling on a higher level than that of company."[14]

It is worthwhile noting, however, that the British reorganization of the infantry division to include an army tank brigade (replacing one of three infantry brigades) sparked greater interest in tank-infantry cooperation. To assist with such training, a Royal Armoured Corps Wing was opened at the GHQ Battle School in June 1942. Its stated purpose was to "train officers in a modified form of battle drill for army tanks in cooperation with infantry" and "standardize methods of battle inoculation for the personnel of Army Tank Brigades."[15] The CTS Battle Wing also conducted an exercise in which tanks firing blanks worked with infantry.[16] To gain a better understanding of what was entailed in such interarm cooperation, of course, it is revealing to review the battle scenarios and drills set forth in the 47th Division précis and the *Handbook on Fieldcraft and Battle Drill*, which were in this and other respects identical in detail. According to this doctrine, in circumstances where organized resistance was not likely to be overcome by infiltration, the "key to success [appeared] ... to be close cooperation between ... troops of tanks and ... platoons of infantry."

As described, the attack was foreseen as beginning with artillery concentrations and air strikes, to be followed immediately by teams of infantry and assault engineers breaching minefields and antitank ditches. A first echelon of tanks, massed for maximum effect, would then assault to achieve a break through by sheer speed and weight of numbers. Next would come a tank and infantry second echelon, the "Shepherding Wave," working at "infantry speed" to reduce pockets of resistance. A third echelon, also mixed, was slated to exploit success. Significantly, the "real scope for infantry-tank cooperation" was considered to lie in "second echelon work," for which a battle drill had been worked out. According to this drill, infantry were to move forward making best use of ground, preceding tanks that in the case of a platoon-troop were to be treated much like a bigger "Bren Group" for purposes of maneuver. On contact with an enemy, the tanks were to move forward to a position as nearly as possible right-angled to the infantry "fire line" to provide fire support for flanking or pincer movements by the latter.[17]

As a method for training infantry there was, and still is, much to be said for battle drill. The concept of every soldier having a part to play and ideas to impart was unquestionably a progressive pedagogical approach. Its introduction at a time when the war for many Canadians seemed to be "at a standstill" and others had "married and live[d] only ... [to] see their [British] wives,"[18] definitely heightened its appeal and attraction. The old military truism that the bigger the exercise, the less the challenge to the soldiery at large, had also been demonstrated once again; a fact particularly proven on "Bumper."[19] To some officers "the greatest danger" from the summer of 1941 was "that life was too easy and boredom, lack of discipline, and a lowering of morale would follow."[20] Battle drill that aimed to make every soldier exercise his initiative offered more exciting and challenging training. To many it seemed the antidote to boredom.

The problem was that when battle drill burst upon the scene it did so with a vengeance. If physical fitness had been a recognizable British fetish, battle drill appears to have become a Canadian virtue. By 1943, 2nd Division platoons practiced "all phases of battle drill . . . taught, at least once every three weeks, regardless of duties and leaves."[21] The assumption that German military performance was somehow attributable to fanaticism seemed furthermore to father the notion of cultivating and harnessing a like breed of fanatics who could be relied upon to "kill joyfully." Troops undergoing battle drill training were accordingly encouraged to shout mindless slogans such as "blood, blood, blood" and "kill, kill, kill."[22] Visits to slaughter houses to see animals destroyed and "hate" training that involved actual splashing of blood were consequently included in some of the earlier attempts to "inoculate" men for battle, much to the revulsion of leaders like Victoria Cross winner Major-General Pearkes, who had experienced firsthand the carnage of the Great War. In fact, all such measures were eventually deemed to be counterproductive to good training and were discontinued by direction of GHQ Home Forces in May 1942.[23] The rush of blood brought on by unbounded zeal and enthusiasm had been mainly to dizzy the head.

Initially, too, battle inoculation was carried to the extreme. The commendable aim of this training was to prepare soldiers "mentally and psychologically" to withstand the harsh realities of the battlefield; by "debunking," to attune them to endure the strain of screaming *Stuka* attack, artillery barrage, mortaring, assault by tanks, and enemy infiltration around flanks. In this respect it was different from field firing exercises designed to practice troops in tactical maneuvers using live fire. In trying to give the soldier experiences before battle that would sustain his morale in action, however, unbridled enthusiasm again reared its ugly head. Instead of conditioning men to battle noises and dangers, some school instructors set out either to impress the troops with exhibitions of their own toughness or frighten candidates beyond repair. Still others attempted both in what became little else than a test of nerves. Again, this approach was found to be defective; shocking erstwhile civilians mildly convinced of the horrors of war merely served to confirm their worst fears. What was required was the gradual application of battle effects progressing in severity up to battle conditions as near reality as possible. By such a process the average soldier could be accustomed to many of the noises and sights of war and persuaded that his innermost fears were at least manageable. In beleaguered Britain this was the equivalent of the Great War practice that placed untried troops in quiet sectors of the line for experience and gradual exposure to danger.[24]

To let men discover for themselves that noise was essentially harmless, they were subjected to two-pound charges exploded without warning from 20 to nine feet away. Tripod-mounted Brens were also used to fire ball and tracer in single shots and short bursts five feet above heads. More commonly, instructors used rifles and Tommy guns, a favorite of the British, to fire spontaneous, unrehearsed short bursts from 60 and 15 yards, respectively, to impact two to five yards away from troops. The main principle observed was that rounds were never put down on the "gunward side" between the firer and the man, and at least six feet overhead clearance was maintained at up to 60 yards. It was considered too impractical and dangerous to fire over men's heads at longer ranges. Another progressive feature of such training involved overrunning men in slit-trenches several times with tanks. For indirect fire effect, two-inch mortar smoke bombs were dropped 25 yards behind and forward of men; they then gradually crawled to within 300 yards of the fall of shot of 25-pounders firing overhead from 500 to 1,200 yards behind at a range of 1,500 yards.[25]

There remains a lingering suspicion, nonetheless, that battle inoculation and live fire training were neither as advanced nor as effective as they could have been in simulating the actual conditions of the battlefield. One is left to wonder, too, whether the less desirable aspects in the application of battle inoculation were ever entirely expunged. According to one veteran officer, better results may also have been obtained had more attention been paid to teaching soldiers to identify weapons and their locations through listening and observation. To recognize shells as either "coming" or "going" was tremendously important in his view, just as it was to know whether a Bren or *Spandau*, a Sten or *Schmeisser*, was firing. As he so sensibly put it: "I do not think that the type of battle inoculation in which you are shot at with the intention of being missed is of much consequence."[26]

It may be, in fact, that more time could have been devoted to such training had battle drill not been overly tied to the parade square. At some point the team play concept of Alexander, who was after all a Guardsman, was translated into "the modern equivalent of close order drill which 150 years ago was the way the soldier fought."[27] Starting battle "drill" (which the *Handbook* admitted was an "unfortunate" word) on a miniature nontactical scale, of course, did allow troops to quickly grasp their relative positions and duties within a team; it also enabled such training to be conducted in garrison where the parade square was naturally used. Theoretically, this was to be but one stage in a dynamic progression from lecture-demonstrations on "wrong" and "right" ways to the gradual application of the drill on increasingly difficult ground, finishing with live fire. Insistence that it was the "phase . . . most important of all," which "should not be left . . . until every student . . . [could] execute every movement *perfectly*," however, may have resulted in undue emphasis being given to whether soldiers were strictly at attention (simulating firing) or at ease (not firing).[28] Continual turnover of men also seemed to convince many believers of the necessity for repeating this particular portion.

Agreement was by no means unanimous, nonetheless, as to the worth of the parade square stage.[29] Some considered the prescribed nontactical drills too elaborate and stylized,[30] akin to teaching tactics by numbers. The 2nd Division in 1943 also noted a tendency in platoon orders "to accept the jargon laid down (as a guide) in Battle Drill pamphlets for orders, and apply it each time orders are given, whether it fits the case or not."[31] Still others judged battle drill itself "never really of great value, mainly because inexperienced junior commanders tended to regard it as an end in itself, a panacea for all ills, regardless of the ground or . . . other numerous factors which necessarily influence minor tactics in battle."[32] Here the reference to neglect of ground is difficult to dispute, for battle drill literature did assert that "ground must be subordinated to the plan, not the plan to the ground." Again, this was how the Germans were perceived to operate,[33] though the interpretation likely derived from their different, much subtler, concept that ground was something to be fought over, not for.

As there is a unity to tactics and operations that presumes what happens at the lower levels affects the top, and vice versa, it is instructive to note at this juncture how Montgomery, a relatively impartial and superlative trainer, viewed battle drill and the Canadian practice of it. In the first place, he unquestionably adhered to the view that "if . . . sub-unit [company, platoon, section] training is not good you fail in battle, however good your higher training."[34] During a visit to the 2nd Brigade in late February 1941, however, Montgomery found that with the company training period "nearly over . . . no company ha[d] done more than about two days really proper co[mpan]y training, i.e. complete company exercises, as a company." While a "good deal of Battle Drill training ha[d] been done," companies had not been "taught the art of war," specifically such aspects as how to fight the contact battle, the set-piece attack, reorganization, the counterattack, and the forcing of obstacles.[35] A similar situation obtained in the Calgary Highlanders where, because they chose to concentrate heavily upon battle drill during their company training period, "No proper co[mpan]y training ha[d] been done at all." It did "not seem to be understood," Montgomery counseled, "that Battle Drill [wa]s really [but] a procedure . . . [and a company had] still . . . to be taught how to carry out the various operations of war." In his professional judgement, the companies of the Calgary Highlanders had simply "not been trained to operate as companies in operations of war."[36]

To Montgomery, battle drill represented a "common line approach to the sub-unit battle problem" that speeded up deployment and ensured full cooperation despite casualties. He insisted, however, that it should be "servant and NOT . . . master." He further contended that battle drill "must not be regarded as peculiar to the infantry" (which likely meant it was) "or as applicable only to the sub-unit." At formation level the composition and disposition of reconnaissance parties and the like fell into the category of battle drill. As Montgomery elaborated, "Co-operation between the different arms [wa]s ensured very largely by good battle drill" and a "well trained armoured division [wa]s one where this battle drill, in which the correct positioning of... [commanders] is the most important factor, has reached a high standard. Every unit of every arm," Montgomery proclaimed, should "develop a battle drill suitable to its own special needs."[37] In spring of 1942 he nonetheless felt obliged to advise Crerar, acting commander of the Canadian Corps, that "*battle drill [was] not the whole art of making war.*"[38]

It appears, then, that battle drill often meant different things to different people. Montgomery clearly regarded it as pertaining to a higher level than that pressed by the Calgary Highlanders. In June 1942 he ordered the "utmost use... be made of the South Downs, and other similar training areas, to carry out Brigade exercises with live ammunition... to practice and demonstrate the co-operation of all arms in battle together with the co-operation of air forces."[39] The 8th Canadian Infantry Brigade with an army tank battalion and 3rd Canadian Division artillery in support conducted such a "battle shooting" exercise in Training Area No. 4 on the South Downs between 1–3 July. Apparently, the 3rd Division was the first Canadian division to do so. Exercise "Crump," as it was termed, called for an infantry-tank attack on a two-battalion front supported by timed and "on call" artillery high-explosive concentrations; the third battalion supported by a squadron of tanks had the task of passing through to maintain momentum. Impressive as it sounded, however, this live fire exercise was highly staged, involving a morning "dry" rehearsal by infantry battalions and a two-hour period of artillery registration of targets thereafter. Though the exercise aimed to practice infantrymen in fire and movement using live ammunition, under covering fire of supporting arms, the prescribed infantry rate of advance of "100 yds in four minutes"[40] seems not to have offered much scope for battle drill.

The case of "Crump" reinforces the suspicion that artillery planning at the formation level usually ran counter to the implementation of battle drill. Staff college teaching, of course, accorded greater emphasis to the importance of artillery fire. A brigade held up by enemy action, it suggested, could justifiably wait up to three hours if it meant doubling the size of artillery support available. Lack of definite information about an enemy's dispositions additionally made "the provision of a barrage obligatory."[41] Yet, following closely behind a barrage left little opportunity for battle drill or initiative on the part of lower level commanders. Whether Canadian senior commanders really comprehended the implications of this fundamental but terribly important dichotomy is questionable. Crerar appears simply to have been overwhelmed by the "tactical and psychological advantages" of what can only be described as a ground swell induced by Scott. On 17 August 1942 he directed that the emphasis placed on physical fitness and battle drill was to "be increased rather than diminished, for the adoption of the drill speed[ed] up deployment and enabl[ed] a unit or subunit to develop its maximum battle power quickly."[42]

By April 1943 training within 1 Canadian Corps invariably stressed the development of instinctive, immediate, and reasonably correct responses to battle situations through battle drills that provided a "habitual framework of action to typical situations" and a "realism in training . . . [that] simulat[ed] the varying conditions of battle."[43] Crerar stipulated like Montgomery, however, that battle drill could "never be more than a guide to action . . . a means, not an end . . . [that had] to be varied to a greater, or lesser, extent, in every battle action." Unlike Montgomery, he seems to have accepted them as "basic 'drills' of fire and movement, covering unit and sub-unit" that assisted in the execution "of the various operations of war."[44] In this respect, of course, some have argued that Maxse's system of teaching minor tactics set forth in *Platoon Training* (1919) was incomparably superior.[45]

Though still others attest to the value of battle drill,[46] one cannot escape the impression that it possessed distinctly faddist overtones. The perception that it somehow represented a new, inspired style of training innately superior to the older methods of the "rutted military mind" doubtless increased its appeal among a confident, even cocky, North American soldiery.[47] What seems to have been missed in adopting the battle drill expedient, however, is that training emphasis *reverted* from the formation level to individual training.[48] That the Canadian high command did not intervene to ensure a proper balance is obvious, and inexcusable. On the other hand, battle drill failed noticeably to supplant "smartening up" close order drill that continued to be conducted, with great regularity and questionable benefit, for companies and platoons on the parade square.[49] Ironically, and in keeping with the nature of a fad, the revised instructions promulgated for infantry corps training in August 1944 made no mention of battle drill.[50]

While Montgomery in February 1942 remarked on the "backwardness" of the 3rd Division, which he considered "behind the other Divisions in training and readiness for war," he did not blame the troops. That they had been issued no ammunition and were "thus living in a peace atmosphere,"[51] could only be ascribed to a lack of professionalism at the top. Montgomery's first-hand observations of Canadian battalions during Exercise "Tiger" between 19–30 May 1942 confirmed this impression. Though he found some of the men who had marched from 100 to over 150 miles "tired and unshaven," he encountered more who were "cheerful and marching well." The problem, as he saw it, was how to "put them into battle properly and with a good chance of success."[52] After "Beaver III" in April, he advocated further training in "offensive fighting in small self-contained groups of all arms" (rifle company-size with mortar detachment, carrier section, and "arm[oure]d O.P. [Observation Posts] from the artillery"); the object being to learn "to break the battle down, and to carry on the fight by the infiltration of hard hitting groups."[53] It is of course clear that Montgomery harbored more reservations about Canadian officers than their "fit and tough" troops. "The soldiery in the Canadian Corps," he recorded, "are probably the best material in any armies of the Empire."[54]

NOTES

1. Strome Galloway, *The General Who Never Was* (Belleville, Ont.: Mika, 1981), p. 72.

2. Maj.-Gen. W. H. P. Elkins Papers (EP) NDHQ letter to Maj.-Gen. W. H. P. Elkins, GOC-in-C Atlantic Command, 5 December 1941.

3. Correlli Barnett, *The Collapse of British Power*, (New York: William Morrow, 1972), p. 585; and Col. C.P. Stacey, *Official History of the Canadian Army in the Second World War*, Vol. I: *Six Years of War: The Army in Canada, Britain and the Pacific* (Ottawa: Queen's Printer, 1966), p. 489.

4. Gen. Sir William Morgan, "The Revival of Battle-Drill in World War 2," *Army Quarterly and Defence Journal*, 1 (October 1973): 57–60; and Stacey, *Six Years*, pp. 240–241, 297.

5. DHist 367.064 (D1), "Battle Drill," Canadian Battle Drill School Lectures and Précis, originally assembled by 47th London Division—and printed by Calgary Highlanders C.A.(O) in England for use in 47th Div., G.H.Q., and Calgary Highlanders Battle Drill Schools in England (October 1941). Revised and adapted to C.B.D.S., Coldstream Ranch, Vernon, B.C., for 9th Course 18 January–9 February 1943, pp. 16, 19–21; and DHist CMHQ Historical Officer Report No. 123, "Battle Drill Training," 31 August 1944, pp. 2–4.

6. Col. D. F. Spankie, "Get Cracking," unpublished article, DHist 87/110, undated, pp. 6–7.

7. DHist CMHQ Historical Officer Report No. 123, pp. 6–7; Record Group (RG) 24, Vol. 9764, G.H.Q. Battle School Joining Instructions; and RG 24, Vol 9764, Minutes of 1st Battle School Conference Held at the Horse Guards on 17 and 18 June 1942, G.H.Q. Home Forces, 5 July 1942.

8. DHist CMHQ Historical Officer Report No. 123, pp. 1, 3, 6–7; RG 24, Vol. 9868, Joining Instrs under covering letter HF. 16351/2/G. Trg G.H.Q. Home Forces to CMHQ 15 Sep 42; "Battle Drill" Précis, p. 16; Maj. Roy Farran, *The History of the Calgary Highlanders 1921–54* (Calgary, Alberta: Bryant, 1954), p. 98; DHist 322.009 (D472), letter Lt.-Col. J. F. Scott, Commandant S–10, C.B.D.S., Vernon, to Headquarters Pacific Command 18 May 1943; and RG 24, Vol 9764, Minutes of 1st Battle School Conference.

9. "Battle Drill" Précis, pp. 14–17, 20, 24, 61; and DHist 78/463 *The Instructors' Handbook on Fieldcraft and Battle Drill* (December 1942), p. 183.

10. Farran, *Calgary Highlanders*, pp. 95, 97–101, 106–107; DHist 322.009 (D472) Commandant A.31 Cdn B.D. Training Centre to Headquarters, Military District No. 11, 27 May 1942, and Commandant S–10 C.B.D.S. to Headquarters, Pacific

Command, 18 May 1943; Stacey, *Six Years*, pp. 241, 246; and DHist CMHQ Historical Officer Report No. 123, pp. 3, 5–8. Examples of training programs can be seen in RG 24, Vol. 13, 760, 3 Cdn Div Training Programme for week ending 10 January 1942, and Vol. 13,685, 1 Cdn Corps Training Report for week ending 14 May 1943.

11. DHist 693.038 (D1), Battle Drill in British Army Rec'd from C.A.H.L.O. 11 December 1952; DHist 322.009 (D590) Headquarters M.D. No. 11, Administrative Order No. 323, 14 July 1942; DHist CMHQ Historical Officer Report No. 123, p. 9; DHist 322.009 (D590), Report on Canadian Battle Drill School, Vernon, British Columbia, by Col. John K. Howard, AUS (under cover letter Howard to Brig. V. Hodson, Pacific Command Headquarters, 20 September 1943), p. 6; DHist 322.009 (D472) Headquarters, Pacific Command P.C.S. 504–25–A–31 (Trg), 22 June 1943, on subject of Doctrine, S.10 Battle Drill School, Vernon, letters Commandant A.31 Cdn. B.D. Training Centre to Headquarters, Military District No. 11 of 27 May and 4 September 1942, and memo BGS to GSO 1 Training, Pacific Command, 22 September 1942; "Battle Drill" Précis, p. 202; and Stacey, *Six Years*, pp. 136, 533.

12. "Battle Drill" Précis, pp. 21–23, 25–30, 181, 202, 209–210; and RG 24, Vol. 13, 750, GS 2 Cdn Inf Div General Notes on P1 Battle Drill 11 November 1943.

13. "Battle Drill" Précis, pp. 4–6, 17, 136–149; and DHist 322.009 (472) letters Commandant, S–10 C.B.D.S. to Headquarters, Pacific Command, 1 July 1943 and 13 August 1943, letter CGS (signed by Lt. Col. H. W. J. Paterson) to GOC-in-C Pacific Command 5 August 1943, and letter GOC-in-C Pacific Command to the Secretary DND 16 August 1943.

14. RG 24, Vol 9764, Minutes of 1st Battle School Conference.

15. Ibid.

16. RG 24, Vol. 9802, CTS/3 Wg/Canadian Training School, No. 3 (Battle) Wing, CI (Maj. E. G. Syme, Regina Rifles) to Senior Offr CMHQ, 27 October 1944. According to this report, it was the only exercise on the course during which tanks and artillery worked in cooperation with infantry. In this case, which included a walk-through, nine tanks, an infantry company, a battery of field artillery, and three medium guns participated. The tanks fired only blanks, though the artillery fired defensive fire tasks at the end for half an hour. By any scale, this was not an impressive live fire exercise.

17. "Battle Drill" Précis, pp. 195–197; and *Handbook*, pp. 90–95.

18. Farran, *Calgary Highlanders*, p. 103; and DHist CMHQ Historical Officer Report No. 123, p. 6

19. Farley Mowat, *The Regiment*, (Toronto: McClelland and Stewart, 1955), pp. 42–43. Mowat refers to Exercise "Bulldog" but possibly means "Bumper."

20. Lt.-Gen. Howard Graham, *Citizen and Soldier*, (Toronto: McClelland and Stewart, 1987), p. 128.

21. RG 24, Vol. 13,750, GS 2 Cdn Inf Div General Notes on Battle Drill, 8 October 1943.

22. "Battle Drill" Précis, pp. 25–26, 226, 243, 244. On British "fitness," see Lt.-Gen. E. L. M. Burns, *General Mud: Memoirs of Two World Wars*, (Toronto: Clarke, Irwin, 1970), pp. 108–109.

23. Reginald H. Roy, *For Most Conspicuous Bravery: A Biography of Major-General George R. Pearkes, V.C., Through Two World Wars* (Vancouver: University of British

Columbia Press, 1977), p. 170; Maj.-Gen. George Kitching, *Mud and Green Fields; The Memoirs of Major General George Kitching* (Langley, B.C.: Battleline, 1986), p. 135; Robert H. Ahrenfeldt, *Psychiatry in the British Army in the Second World War* (London: Routledge and Kegan Paul, 1958), pp. 197–201; and DHist 322.009 (D472), letter Lt.-Col. R. H. Keefler for Chief of the General Staff to GOC-in-C Pacific Command, 18 September 1942 covering Notes for Psychiatrists on Battle Inoculation. It was recommended that instead of taking men to slaughter houses, volunteers be allowed to visit hospital accident and operating rooms, provided they agreed to do it for "at least six times in succession" (Notes for Psychiatrists).

24. Notes for Psychiatrists; RG 24, Vol. 13,240, Memorandum D. M. T. to D. C. G. S. 20 June 1942, Training of Personnel Against War Noises; and RG 24, Vol. 9764, Minutes of 1st Battle School Conference.

25. Notes for Psychiatrists; DHist 322.009 (D472), Commandant S-10 C. B. D. S. to Secretary DND, Overhead Fire, 1 June 1943, and Safety Precautions during Battle Drill Training, 26 March 1943; and DHist 171.009 (D187), Special War Course—BD Trg, 24 August 1942/17 March 1943 Safety Precautions During Battle Drill Training. The effect of small-arms fire was supposedly the same whether it was five or 15 feet overhead. The two-inch mortar simulation does not appear to have been all that effective a measure for countering the shock of the German 81-mm mortar.

26. "Battle Impressions of a Platoon Commander," *Current Reports from Overseas* (hereafter *CRFO*), 71 (January 1945): 1; and DHist 322.009 (D472), Locating Enemy Practices, Commandant S-10 C. B. D. S. to Headquarters, Pacific Command, 13 September 1943.

27. "Battle Drill" Précis, p. 75; and *Handbook*, p. 62.

28. *Handbook*, p. 50; and "Battle Drill" Précis, pp. 28–30, 222.

29. RG 24, Vol. 9764, Minutes of the 1st Battle School Conference.

30. DHist 322.009 (D590), Notes on Battle Drill Training for Reserve Units by Maj. J. H. Horn, 5. 11. 42. The U.S. Army did not adopt formal parade ground tactical drills (Howard, "Report," p. 24).

31. RG 24, Vol. 13,750, GS 2 Cdn Inf Div General Notes on Battle Drill 8 October 1943.

32. Frederick Myatt, *The British Infantry 1660–1945: The Evolution of a Fighting Force* (Poole U. K.: Blandford, 1983), p. 211. Myatt also wrote *History of the Small Arms School* (Privately published, 1972).

33. "Battle Drill" Précis, p. 181; and DHist 322.009 (D472), Precis, Vernon, B.C. May 1942- September 1943, Battle Drill for Attack by W.W.M., 26 December 1941.

34. Gen. H. D. G. Crerar Papers (CP), Vol. 2, Notes on Inf. Bdes of Canadian Corps, No. 4, 27 February 1942, 4 Inf. Bde 28 February 1942.

35. CP, Vol. 2, Notes on Inf Bde of Canadian Corps, No. 5, 28 February 1942, 2 Innf [*sic*] Bde, 1 March 1942.

36. CP, Vol. 2, Notes on Inf Bdes. of Canadian Corps, No. 7, 3 March 1942, 5 Inf Bde, 4 March 1942.

37. Nigel Hamilton, *Monty*, Vol. I: *The Making of a General 1887–1942* (Sevenoaks, U.K.: Hodder and Stoughton, 1984), p. 678; and RG 24, Vol. 12,301, S.E. Army Exercise "Tiger" Final Conference, 4 June 1942. Remarks of Army Commander. Battle drills were worked out by 24 Armoured Brigade before Alamein

[McNoughton Papers (MP), Vol 156, GHQ Monthly Training Letter, April 1943, Some Lessons of El Alamein].

38. Author's italics. CP, Vol. 2, Montgomery's handwritten Points for Crerar, circa March 1942.

39. RG 24, Vol. 12,301, S.E. Army Exercise "Tiger" Final Conference, 4 June 1942. Remarks of Army Commander.

40. RG 24, Vols. 14,135 and 14,136, 8 Cdn Inf Bde Exercise "Crump" General Instructions 26 June 1942. The rehearsal was slated for 0800 hours, artillery registration between 1100–1300, and the live fire portion between 1500–1700. Forward observation officers (FOOs) with infantry companies were to call down "on call" targets, and smoke was employed to cover the movement of tanks. Only 15 rounds of .303 ammunition per rifleman and 90–120 rounds per Bren were allocated. See also Capt. T. J. Bell, *Into Action with the 12th Field 1940–1945* (Published by the Regiment, undated), p. 20.

41. DHist 000.7 (D9), Syllabus for Cdn Jr War Staff Crse No. 1 at RMC August 1941, Canadian Junior War Staff Course, Exercise No 8 Appreciation, D.S. Only.

42. Farran, *Calgary Highlanders*, pp. 106–107; and DHist CMHQ Historical Officer Report No. 123, pp. 9–10.

43. RG 24, Vol. 13,684, 1 Canadian Corps Training Instruction No. 22 of 18 April 1943; and RG 24, Vol. 13,750, 2 Cdn Inf Div Trg Instr No. 21 of 28 December 1943.

44. MP, Vol. 157, Memorandum by GOC, 1 Cdn Corps on Particular Training Requirements as Revealed by Exercise "Spartan," 18 April 1943. The specific applicability of battle drill to unit and subunit tactics is further stated in "Battle Technique or Battle Drill," *Canadian Army Training Memorandum* (hereafter *CATM*), 22 (January 1943), p. 25; and *CATM*, 40 (July 1944), pp. 33–34.

45. Maj. Gen. E. K. G. Sixsmith, *British Generalship in the Twentieth Century*, (London: Arms and Armour, 1970), p. 174.

46. According to Galloway, without battle drill the 1st Canadian Division could not have done the job it did in Sicily a year later. He adds, however, that it did little for the 2nd Division on the restrictive, deadly beaches of Dieppe (Galloway, *The General*, p. 73).

47. Kim Beattie, *Dileas: The History of the 48th Highlanders of Canada 1929–1956* (Toronto: Published by the Regiment, 1957), pp. 159–160.

48. G.R. Stevens, *Princess Patricia's Canadian Light Infantry 1919–1957* (Griesbach: Published by the Regiment, 1958), p. 54.

49. RG 24, Vol. 14,138, War Diary (hereafter WD) 8 Cdn Inf Bde (hereafter CIB) ALS/4–0 N Shore Regt, 22 October 1943, to 8 Cdn Inf Bde Trg Programme; and RG 24, Vol. 13,684, WD General Staff (hereafter GS) 1 Cdn Corps Weekly Progress Report Week Ending 2 April 1943, dated 3 April 1943.

50. RG 24, Vol. 9802, Appx "A" to WOM 43/Trg/3244 (MT2), 16 August 1944, General Instructions for Infantry Corps Training and 43/Training/3244 (MT2), 16 August 1944, to GHQ Home Forces and HQ No Ireland from DMT. Specific reference was made to battle inoculation however.

51. CP, Vol. 2, Notes on Inf. Bdes of Canadian Corps. 28 January: 6 Inf. bde. 3-2-42.

52. CP, Vol. 2, "Tiger" Observations, under Montgomery to Crerar 3-6-42; and RG 24, Vol. 12,301, S.E. Army Exercise "Tiger" Final Conference, 4 June

1942. Remarks of Army Commander. On hearing a regular CO, Lt.-Col. Bernatchez of the Royal 22nd Regiment, complain that blisters were occurring because boot leather was too hard, Montgomery noted that the boots had not been "dubbined." To his credit, Montgomery was greatly concerned about the weight (mainly equipment and food) the infantryman carried. Since overloading detracted from fighting performance, he recommended drastically limiting what was carried; he further suggested that Canadian soldiers had to learn how to live on their service rations alone. Montgomery considered it absurd that certain Canadian units allowed the soldier to carry both greatcoat and blanket, some "carrying greatcoats on their arms, as if out for a walk in the park." He consequently decreed that only one or the other should be taken and that "the infantry soldier should not be required to carry a greatcoat, or a blanket, into battle." To Montgomery, the "proper answer" was to conduct, "careful investigation . . . to determine what a man can carry without detracting from his proper fighting form. He should never carry one ounce more than this." In his view, 40 pounds was the ideal for which to strive and 50 pounds the absolute limit, as "there [wa]s no reason why *every* platoon should carry into *every* battle the whole of its . . . equipment on *every* occasion." Men had to be trained to go without either greatcoat or blanket for short periods, and he suggested that a dry vest, dry shirt, cardigan, and pair of dry socks would be "the minimum to keep him fit" (Ibid.; and CP, Vol. 2, Some Notes on the Broader Aspects of Beaver III, 23 April 1942; and handwritten letter Montgomery to Crerar, 17 May 1942).

53. CP, Vol. 2, Exercise "Tiger" Observations, under Montgomery to Crerar, 3–6–42; Some further Notes on Beaver III, 25 April 1942; and Notes on Beaver IV, Appendix 'A' Notes on Commander 3 Div. 13 May 1942.

54. CP, Vol. 2, Exercise "Conqueror" notes under Montgomery to Crerar, 16 April 1942. Montgomery was evidently less acerbic than Fuller, who on observing the disembarkation of the CEF in 1914 stated that Canadian soldiers would be good enough after six months training "if the officers could be all shot" [Anthony John Trythall, *'Boney' Fuller: Soldier, Strategist, and Writer 1878–1966* (New Brunswick, N.J.: Rutgers University Press, 1977), p. 33]. He would later advise, however, "that the proper way to get an American Army ready for battle is to teach *the Generals*. It is no good having Battle Schools [as Alexander urged] . . . If they know their stuff, they will teach the soldiers." Hamilton, *Monty,* Vol. II: *Master of the Battlefield 1942–1944* (Sevenoaks, U.K.: Hodder and Stoughton, 1987), Vol. II, p. 176.

Chapter 6

The Montgomery Measurement

Canadian troops (apart from Commandos in Norway and two battalions in Hong Kong) have not yet been in action. To judge from the experience of the world war, their fighting value is probably about the same as that of good English divisions. The command of Dominion troops has shown itself to be particularly inflexible and ponderous.

German *Manual of the British Army* 1942[1]

The Montgomery correspondence in the Crerar Papers at the National Archives of Canada provides an exceptionally revealing glimpse of the state of Canadian Army higher level training for most of 1942. As self-styled Commander of South Eastern "Army" from November 1941 until early August 1942, this monkish, ascetic, and overtly Germanophile general had ample opportunity to watch Canadians perform. He also stamped his mark indelibly upon them, for he was above all else a matchless military trainer. What has often been forgotten about Montgomery in the ink-spilling controversies that have raged round his name and memory is just how great a battlefield commander he really was; to U.S. soldier-historian D'Este "he was certainly a far greater commander than most Americans were willing to admit or to comprehend."[2] Even his critics have readily acknowledged his extraordinary organizational brilliance and outstanding professional skill in the management of battle. In the purely tactical realm he had few equals.

It is often forgotten that Montgomery grew up in Tasmania. Later, as a disenchanted veteran of the Great War and admirer of Australian General Sir John Monash, whom he rated "the best general on the Western front," Montgomery probably more than most manifested an abiding concern with avoiding unnecessary casualties. The almost magical rapport he managed to establish with the soldiers he commanded further reflected an inspired leadership only rarely realized. "Even Dwight D. Eisenhower with all his engaging ease," recorded General Omar Bradley, "could never stir American troops to the rapture with which Monty was welcomed by his." By 1944 dean of Allied field commanders and a living symbol of victory, Montgomery was by virtue of experience and knowledge the most suitable general officer in the Anglo-American array to command the cross-Channel assault.[3]

Unlike many others who rose to the top without having studied the art of war in any depth, Montgomery epitomized the professional in the truest sense of the word. He attended Camberley Staff College, where Broad was a member of the DS along with Lindsay and Paget in 1920, the same year he struck up a lasting if eventually strained intellectual association with Liddell Hart. Though by no means academic, Montgomery was widely read, studious, and possessed of sufficient common sense and ideas to have benefited from such contacts. Gifted with a talent for clear and logical exposition, he soon became an unsurpassed lecturer on tactics. He returned to Camberley as an instructor in January 1926, just after the departure of Fuller, who had been a chief instructor since January 1923. Montgomery remained on the directing staff of Camberley until 1929, "kn[owing] enough by then to realize that the teacher learns much more than his students." During this tour he also married Hobart's sister and became a protégé of then Colonel Alan Brooke, Director of Studies from 1925.

In 1934 Montgomery replaced Paget as chief instructor of the senior division at the Staff College, Quetta, where he was to direct second-year students in studying the broader issues of grand and imperial strategy. This appointment was almost immediately changed, however, and Montgomery took over as chief instructor of the junior division, which enabled him instead to teach first-year students the technique of battle command and staff duties. Here again he shone as a student of war, learning how to produce a simple plan from a mass of detail. By the time he left Quetta in May 1937, Montgomery was almost 50, but he went armed with a comprehensive and definite theory of tactics and training, important aspects of which he set forth in his articles on the "encounter battle."[4] His superb handling of the 3rd Division in France and the conduct of its fighting withdrawal to Dunkirk generally confirmed the soundness of his methods. It also gained him the one qualification that Helmuth von Moltke adjudged the critical measure of a great captain: in the very face of adversity to carry out a successful retreat.[5]

At the time Montgomery took over South Eastern Army, the Canadian field command was anything but in a stable state. According to Crerar, McNaughton suffered a "breakdown"[6] in November 1941 that resulted in his return to Canada for extended leave. The senior divisional commander,

Major-General Pearkes, assumed temporary command of the Canadian Corps. Although he had not commanded a battalion in peacetime, Pearkes had taken the 2nd Brigade overseas in 1939 and been promoted to command the 1st Division following McNaughton's appointment as 7 Corps commander in the summer of 1940. A graduate of Camberley Staff College, the SOS, and the IDC, Pearkes enjoyed a considerable reputation as the most experienced Canadian field commander; one enhanced by his having won the Victoria Cross in the Great War. When Pearkes took over as Acting Corps Commander on 14 November, McNaughton expressed the hope that the appointment would be made permanent upon formation of the First Canadian Army.[7] Yet, unknown to Pearkes, the former Senior Officer, Canadian Military Headquarters (CMHQ), London, and from July 1940 Canadian CGS in Ottawa, Major-General Crerar, had his eyes set on the same command.

A protégé of McNaughton, Crerar had taken over from him as Counter-Battery Staff Officer in the Great War, attended Camberley Staff College in 1924 and passed through the IDC in 1934. Though the same age as Pearkes, who was three months younger than Montgomery, Crerar had practically no experience in field command. He had nonetheless convinced the Minister of National Defense in July 1940 that he should and would, on relinquishment of the appointment of CGS, be permitted to replace the "somewhat too old and inflexible" Major-General Odlum as GOC 2nd Division. Crerar's subsequent promotion to the corps-level rank of lieutenant-general in the fall of 1941 did not dissuade him from this ambition. He instead proclaimed his willingness to accept a reduction in rank in exchange for divisional command. When it appeared that McNaughton would not be able to return to duty for an extended period, however, Crerar abandoned this altruistic stance and turned over CGS duties to Major-General Ken Stuart. Arriving in England on 23 December ostensibly to take over the 2nd Division, he in fact assumed unbroken command of the Canadian Corps from that date. According to Crerar, a "few weeks in Acting Command of the Corps convinced . . . [him] that a good many shifts in Unit and Brigade commanders were necessary if the command element was to be brought up to an adequately high standard." On discussing this matter with Montgomery, Crerar furthermore readily accepted the latter's offer to "visit each of the Canadian formations and give . . . his personal views.[8]

Montgomery, not surprisingly, had a better understanding of Canadian field capabilities and deficiencies than Crerar. He had witnessed Canadian performance on "Bumper" and had felt obligated to criticize the 2nd Division for being too slow in seizing upon an opportunity presented to attack an opposing formation in the flank. He further noted that Canadians, as well as the British, placed too much faith in the brigade group as a tactical formation.[9] Montgomery also prompted the Canadian Corps Study Week

19–23 January 1942, which was attended by all senior formation commanders and staff officers, as well as unit commanders. By means of a large cloth model the three Canadian infantry divisions, army tank brigade, and corps headquarters made separate presentations on the division in the approach march and contact battle, infantry-artillery cooperation, infantry-tank cooperation, all-arms cooperation in defense, and movement, organization, and new equipment. After discussion following the end of each session, Montgomery summed up, emphasizing among other things the vital importance of concentrated artillery fire in defense and the absolute necessity of adequate service support.[10]

During February and March the dynamic Scots-Irishman visited all nine Canadian infantry brigades and 27 infantry battalions, doubtlessly employing the highly effective approach he had devised, and evidently took pains to explain to Crerar in his "Some General Notes on What to Look for When Visiting a Unit" (see Appendix A). Based on these visits and previous and subsequent observations of Canadian participation on exercises, Montgomery rendered a host of constructive and critical comments that, taken as a whole, present a reasonably good picture of the state of Canadian military progress up to this point. What Montgomery principally identified was a fundamental weakness at the top. A number of brigadiers, in his estimation, were not fit for brigade command. Indeed, he felt that a certain Brigadier Archambault, already removed, had done the 8th Infantry Brigade "a very great deal of harm." It is nonetheless significant that out of eight brigadiers observed, Montgomery considered four as more than satisfactory.[11] As shall be seen, however, the modicum of professional competence exhibited at this level was not necessarily matched either above or below.

Montgomery's comments on battalion commanding officers ranged from "Commanded a battalion for 4 years in peace, and is now doing it again" to, in the case of a French-Canadian, "A very good little chap who commands his B[attalio]n in his own queer way." That Montgomery's judgments were generally free from all but professional bias there can be little doubt, for he differentiated primarily between those who were "completely useless" and those who were "teachable." He appears furthermore to have overlooked the factor of age whenever competence was evident as in the case of the CO who at "age 48 . . . [gave] the impression of being over 50 . . . [but who was] a strong character . . . [who ran] a very good show." For one "decent chap" he felt nothing but pity, since he was "completely out of his depth as a battalion commander, and . . . [knew] practically nothing about how to command and train a battalion." Of another battalion commander he wrote: "This is the worst and most ignorant C.O. I have met in my service in the Army." This case seems the more interesting because the CO in question, who trained neither his officers nor NCOs, many of whom were "very intelligent," was so bad at organizing training that his men became "bored with it." Yet, there were more COs who were keen and able, some even potential brigadiers, though Montgomery clearly recognized that it did not "necessarily follow that because he is a good B[attalio]n Com[man]d[er], he will make a good B[riga]de Com-[man]d[er]." Of 25 COs observed, Montgomery considered seven to be unacceptable.[12]

In respect of battalion seconds-in-command, Montgomery somewhat more severely named nine out of 16 unsatisfactory. He assessed many company commanders, nonetheless, as adequate through excellent. While he considered all but three of 17 adjutants encountered to be in the same category, Montgomery was struck by the excessive amount of paper in circulation within Canadian units and formations. Brigades literally foundered under paper, which by making "everyone office bound" had the effect of "cramping initiative, stifling training" and generally impairing "military efficiency." He found adjutants sitting "in their offices all day long trying to compete with it," when being responsible for unit discipline, they should have been out with their regimental sergeants-major (RSMs) every afternoon to "keep in touch with co[mpanies], keep their fingers on the N.C.O. pulse, and generally see that the machine . . . [was] ticking over properly." To overcome this problem, Montgomery advocated assembling a corps headquarters committee chaired by a brigadier to review means by which paperwork could be reduced and unnecessary returns eliminated. He estimated that it would be immediately possible to cancel at least 20 of the latter.[13] In response to this suggestion, Crerar, an unquestionably greater producer of ponderous paperwork than Montgomery, wrote: "The desirability of reducing the large amount of paperwork required of H.Q. was raised by me shortly after I took over command and an analysis has been under way for the last week."[14] Such a typically modern Canadian response seems to indicate, however, that the problem was never really solved.

Montgomery also had a lot to say about NCOs. He recommended the removal of eight RSMs for reasons of age or incompetence, the worst being described as "age 50, fat and idle." Definitely concerned that the majority of COs did "not seem to realize the immense importance of having a really first class cadre of N.C.O.'s," he was quick to note that some did "not even see . . . N.C.O.'s on promotion and talk to them." This was an especially telling comment and certainly points out the need for further investigation into the entire area of Canadian NCO training and employment. One particularly intriguing aspect was that in all but regular battalions, there also prevailed the "old peace-time system" of promoting NCOs within companies, which Crerar admitted "to be inherent in Canadian units . . . because in . . . many cases the battery or company was locally mobilized from a militia unit."

Montgomery further discovered that within several units, NCO training was "hardly carried out at all." He particularly noted that there was "no system for teaching privates how to be N.C.O.'s *before* they . . . [were]

promoted." Of all ranks commented upon, Montgomery seems to have been least impressed by Canadian company sergeants-major.[15] That this potential weakness concerned Crerar well into 1943 is evident from his warning that "a unit with an ignorant or undependable cadre of Non-Commissioned Officers is unfit to overcome the problems of the battlefield or withstand any severe strain on its discipline or morale." He accordingly urged COs to give priority to the development of "reliable, knowledgeable, self-respecting and loyal" NCOs. As one battle school report stated, however, the criteria for NCO promotion often placed parade smartness, administrative ability, and general peacetime efficiency above other soldierly virtues.[16] One suspects, as well, that the best were made into officers to the detriment of building up a strong NCO corps.

An even more serious shortcoming noted by Montgomery was the apparent inability of most Canadian commanders to conduct proper troop training. While a "great deal of time . . . [was] spent in teaching people how to make war and how to fight . . . little time . . . [was] spent in teaching officers *how to train troops*." The "real trouble," according to Montgomery, was "that officers generally ha[d] never been taught 'training' as distinct from fighting in battle" and they did "not really understand it." Company commanders who had "never been taught how to train companies" thus employed "old fashioned training methods that were in use 30 years ago," with the result that "much time [was] wasted and many men bored." Commanders, it appeared to Montgomery, were quite content just to know that training was happening; there was little supervision, let alone willingness "to investigate exactly how a CO . . . [might be] training his officers or N.C.Os." Suspecting that many Canadian officers did not even understand "skeleton force" exercises (telephone battles and signals exercises requiring minimal manning), he ventured that they would likely welcome "definite instruction about training principles and methods."

As it was, officer training tended to be conducted in "haphazard" fashion with little attention paid to shaking-out battalion and brigade headquarters, which "seldom seem[ed] to go out for a H.Q. exercise." Montgomery further noted that few battalions since November 1941 had actually exercised for any extended period as a unit, some having not operated as a battalion in the field, which he thought necessary once a month. When collective training did take place, moreover, it often suffered from improper organization; again, "much energy was wasted by wrong methods" and in many instances, unbelievably, there was "no testing of companies in turn by the C.O. and Brigadier." For the most part, company commanders were permitted to "direct" their own exercises, which usually saw seconds-in-command rather than company commanders in the "command" role. This was clearly anathema to Montgomery who chastised COs for not setting surprise exercises that would have forced company commanders to wield command themselves.[17]

Montgomery also expressed misgivings about the amount of time being devoted to training, an aspect that apparently disturbed several Canadian COs as well. Whereas the 1st Division allocated four days per week for construction of defenses (including antiboat and antitank scaffolding along beaches), a half-day for recreation, and one day off duty, only one and a half days were set aside for training. In Montgomery's view, this system merely served to dash any hope of serious accomplishment; it was far better, he suggested, to separate work from training and concentrate on each for longer periods of time so that more profitable results could be attained. He additionally prescribed what he termed "piece work," an incentive-oriented training approach that allowed individuals and groups to be dismissed from instruction the minute they fully grasped what had been taught.

As for field works, Montgomery disapproved of the 4th Brigade digging and wiring defensive positions in its "Stand to Area," pointing out in recognizably Fullerian tones that as divisional reserve its purpose was "to deal blows . . . not . . . receive them." He was similarly critical of the 3rd Division digging in its "Stand to Area" when it was unlikely to fight a defensive battle there. To start any battle "sitting in prepared trenches, behind barbed wire," Montgomery maintained, encouraged a "defensive mentality."[18] He could not "emphasize too strongly that the first requirement in the successful defeat of invasion . . . [was] NOT good defences," but rather "a good and well trained soldier."[19] In this respect it is clear that Montgomery reshaped Canadian tactical thinking: whereas 2nd Division Operation Instruction No. 12 issued 27 November 1941 was entitled "Defence of Sussex," it had by 3 January 1942 been amended to read "Plan to Defeat Invasion."[20] The Montgomery "school" stressed both training and the offensive spirit.

What is important to highlight in all this, however, is that McNaughton had presumed his Canadian Corps to be "thoroughly prepared for battle" by the fall of 1941. In his estimation, "ceaseless training by day and night in all the intricacies of armoured warfare, through all the phases from teaching skill at arms to the individual to the combination of units, divisions and larger formations" had ensured as much.[21] Montgomery, on the other hand, disagreed—and from almost ever angle and level. "We live," he warned that same fall, "in a sort of peace-time atmosphere . . . [where] such things as courts-of-enquiry, traffic accidents, reports and returns, inspections, work on coast defences, and the paper and routine of peace conditions, all tend to leave little or no time for . . . study of the things that *really* matter in war." "And so it often happens," he continued, "that officers forget what *are* the things that really matter."[22] This fundamental difference in approach not only distinguished the professional from the amateur, but explained much of the Canadian training predicament.

To Montgomery, the collective training of the Canadian Corps revealed "1st class" troops, but a high command found seriously wanting. "The training of commanders, such as Brigadiers, C[ommanders]. R[oyal].

A[rtillery]., [and] unit commanders," he advised Crerar in May 1942, "has not made the same progress as that of the lower levels; it has been neglected and . . . not . . . tackled properly." In Montgomery's judgment, the "weak point in the Canadian Corps" was the lack of "knowledge of commanders in the stage-management of battle operations, and in the technique of battle fighting generally, on their own level.[23] He had remarked after observing Exercise "Flip," part of the "Flip, Flap, Flop" series conducted by 2nd Division in April 1942,[24] that none of the operations attempted would have "succeeded against a good enemy, because commanders did not know their stuff."[25] During Exercise "Conqueror" he was again "very disturbed at the lack of knowledge on the part of many B[riga]de and unit commanders in the Canadian Corps of how to lay on the battle.[26]" But he was clearly most concerned about generals: "If the[y] . . . could only learn how to put their Divisions into battle properly, and how to keep firm control over the ship in a rough sea," he wrote, "then the corps would be unbeatable."[27]

Montgomery remained convinced that against "an enemy as good as the German it . . . [was] difficult, almost impossible, for a formation or unit to recover if it . . . [was] put into battle badly in the first instance." Initial errors were "increasingly difficult to rectify . . . owing to the great fire power available, speed of movement, use of armoured fighting vehicles, [and] air power." The days were past when "good troops could save a battle that had been badly teed-up"; other things being equal, victory would "go to that side . . . put into battle properly and which . . . [could] retain control throughout the fight."[28] Nowhere was this more important than in the "advance to contact" or "encounter battle," which subject Montgomery had addressed with great perception in 1937. Stressing that mechanization increased the significance of ground, he argued that the initial encounter between opposing forces was "likely to develop into endeavours to secure such ground as . . . [would] enable the subsequent battle to be staged successfully." He concluded, therefore, that even when faced with a paucity of information about the enemy, a commander had to "decide *before* contact . . . how he . . . [would] fight" to impose his will and attain his object; the absence of any plan to do so would inevitably mean "drifting aimlessly into battle . . . piecemeal" and "conform[ing] gradually to the enemy's plan."

Recognizing that information on the enemy would become progressively urgent and from a certain stage obtainable only through fighting, Montgomery further recommended reinforcing reconnaissance units with forces of all arms, including artillery, from the start. Such forward bodies, besides being strong enough to deal with minor opposition, could additionally hold any ground secured. He saw the main body, in the meantime, "directed towards some area the possession of which . . . [would] give . . . [a commander], the advantage in . . . operations . . . follow[ing] the gaining of contact." In such circumstances commanders had also to "be trained to be in the right place at the right time"; initially, "well forward" so as to be able to influence the battle on the basis of first-hand information and give orders to subordinates in proximity to relevant ground, and, after gaining contact, not so far forward as to become "unduly influenced by local situations" to the detriment of effective planning ahead.[29]

It is revealing that when these concepts were incorporated in Montgomery's "14 points essential to success in battle," a policy directive promulgated in December 1941, the stage-management of battle headed the list. Planning the "contact battle," seizing the tactical initiative, and maintaining control through correct positioning of command elements constituted the fourth, fifth, and sixth points or "lessons learnt during the first two years of war." He also elaborated upon the necessity for the "cooperation of all arms," stressing in particular the advantage of using divisional artillery "as a 72-gun Bty [battery] under the CRA," the commander of the divisional artillery and gunner advisor to the divisional commander. Lesson eight, while pointing to the decisive influence of "armoured forces," suggested using them "to create opportunities for the employment of ordinary divisions." The stated object of "Anti-Panzer" defense was to strip enemy tanks of their infantry protection and seek "to destroy as many . . . as possible, and not merely . . . stop them."

The ninth and tenth lessons referred to the crucial importance of commanders and staffs thoroughly understanding the technique of "road movement" and holding the enemy in "the grip of . . . [their] observation and sniping from the beginning, and NOT vice versa." No enemy movement was to be allowed; any enemy seen was to be shot. Lessons eleven and twelve covered the requirement for "protection" against surprise enemy ground attack and hostile air action. The thirteenth lesson dealt with the means by which isolated subunits using "concealment" and "deception" were to continue to "fight the battle on a locality basis, taking under their command all small and isolated sub-units of other arms in the vicinity" until such time as reserves came into action. In this regard, the high standards of physical fitness, endurance, and "fighting spirit" demanded by the third lesson also applied. The last lesson accented the value of achieving tactical surprise and urged that it be included as "an essential part of every plan." Significantly, Montgomery placed "sub-unit efficiency" immediately after the stage-management of battle in his order of "lessons learnt." As he saw it, "once battle . . . [was] joined the issue passe[d] to the junior leader and his sub-unit . . . the infantry company and its platoons, the tank squadron and its troops, the artillery battery and its troops, the field company R[oyal] E[ngineers] and its sections." If these groups lacked the requisite skills, initiative, and leadership, the best higher plan was unlikely to succeed.[30]

Montgomery, ever the didactic commander, impressed his tactical approach upon the Canadian Army at every turn. During Exercise "Flip" he reminded formation commanders of the importance of directing subordinate headquarters to move on axes near their own headquarters in order to facilitate control. He also accorded special emphasis to the vital infantry company commander-artillery forward observation officer (FOO) relationship in formulating the details of simple artillery, mortar, and machine-gun fire plans. As Montgomery rightly put it, "in whatever way . . . used, the fire plan . . . restore[d] impetus . . . lost, and . . . [gave] a good 'kick-off'." He clearly did not like the Canadian practice of assigning a task to a battalion, stating it would be supported by a field regiment, and leaving the battalion CO, who possessed fewer artillery coordination means, to execute it alone. In all such cases he found no proper fire plan "laid on" and precious artillery resources wasted. To Montgomery, it was the duty of the higher headquarters to assist the lower.

Providing brigade staff organized the fire plan, a reserve battalion near to its "start line" with a supporting battery already deployed could mount a fresh attack supported by a field regiment in one and a half hours. In Montgomery's estimation, a brigade attack supported by three field regiments could be "teed-up" in three to four hours if participating units were in reasonable proximity along the line of march. To speed up the execution of fire plans, he insisted that all artillery reconnaissance parties include one "pistol" gun; in this way anticipated battery targets could be registered before the arrival of the bulk of the guns, which often occurred after dark. Again, Montgomery underscored the need for "thinking ahead" at all levels, warning that "hurrying units into battle without giving them time to make their preparations . . . merely add[ed] to . . . casualties." Again, the "theory of how to . . . [stage-manage the] tactical battle" was viewed as the best method of ensuring as much.[31]

On exercises "Conqueror," "Beaver III," and "Beaver IV," which ended 13 May 1942, Montgomery repeatedly noted the inability of Canadian divisional commanders to seize the initiative in battle. Citing the "offensive use of reserves" as the best means by which to achieve this, he did not reason that vague and imprecise information on the enemy precluded quick and aggressive reaction by a division in reserve. The main thing was to start reconnoitering, "and *at the same time* . . . set the division in motion to meet the threat" from a position favorable to launching offensive operations. Again, there remained a requirement for a simple but definite plan aimed largely at "securing such ground as . . . [would] assist . . . further operations." The enemy, if met, was to be hit and subjected to fresh blows "as a result of the first clash."[32] In advancing to contact, he recommended the employment of "forward bodies, or advanced guards, moving in rear of Rec[onaissan]ce Troops . . . prepared to act offensively as soon as the [latter were] . . . held up."

Montgomery's emphasis on "forward bodies," which resembled the current Soviet concept, was pronounced, innovative, and based on the assumption that there would always "come a time when further and more detailed information . . . [could] not be obtained without fighting." "It does not seem to be understood," he complained, that "complete information about the enemy [will never be gained] by the use of rec[onaissan]ce troops and air *alone*." To "attack the enemy and make him dance to your tune, you have first got to gain contact with him and obtain *by fighting* the further and more detailed information which will enable you to plan the offensive battle successfully." In "Beaver III" and "Beaver IV" such a system, which also called for divisional commanders to be forward, was not employed by Canadian formations in the advance; consequently, when reconnaissance elements were held up, divisional headquarters tended to wait for information, which was slow in coming, while brigades "consolidated" and "settled in."[33]

The 1st Canadian Infantry Division was in Montgomery's judgment especially "badly handled" on Exercise "Beaver III." Neither did its peacetime "stunt" of changing battalions between brigades particularly impress him; to hazard the loss of good formation teamwork on the possible chance of "misleading the enemy" was considered unsound practice in war. To Montgomery, it "was not the fault of . . . regimental officers and men that i [*sic*] Division failed badly. It was the fault of the Divisional commander." To fight bravely was not enough, "for the braver the men, the more . . . [would] be the casualties." If the "fine material" of 1st Division were to perform well in battle, Montgomery concluded, it had to have a commander other than Major-General Pearkes who seemed "unable to appreciate the essentials of a military problem and . . . formulate a sound plan." A "gallant soldier without . . . brains," Pearkes "would fight his Division bravely till the last man was killed" and, Montgomery added, "the last man would be killed all too soon." Stating that there was "good material to hand," he recommended relieving, in addition to the divisional commander, two of his brigade commanders, Brigadiers A. E. Potts and H. N. Ganong (the latter assessed earlier as a "good Brigadier, hard and tough . . . a grand fighter" but no great trainer).[34]

Montgomery formed a similar opinion of the 3rd Division during "Beaver IV," 10–13 May 1942, for which he held the divisional commander clearly responsible. The performance put on by Major-General Basil Price was simply "lamentable" and "completely ineffective." He did not, Montgomery continued, "possess that military ability and professional knowledge, that forceful determination, and that 'drive' to get things done, which are essential qualities in a commander in war." On the contrary, he failed to inspire, instilled no confidence, and generally forfeited his grip on the activities of the division in the field. Though "a very delightful person," Price was a "complete amateur, one totally unable to train his Division," which was behind the others in readiness for war. Montgomery, having first expressed doubts about Price in February, concluded that he "was unfit to command a Division in a field army."[35] Paradoxically, for he had appointed Price while CGS, Crerar agreed. Indeed, he had written to McNaughton on the occasion, referring also to the coincident appointment of Lieutenant-General Ernie Sansom to command the 5th Armoured Division, "I think these are good appointments and should result in credit to the Commands as well as to their Commanders."[36]

Put simply, Montgomery did not think it "possible to produce good Divisions unless you . . . [had] good Divisional Commanders." Without "a first class professional soldier" commanding it, the 3rd Division had little hope of becoming "the very fine division it could become." In respect of the stage-management of battle he considered it "quite impossible to make progress . . . unless Divisional Commanders . . . [were] themselves competent to train their subordinates, and . . . fully conversant with the handling of a Division in battle." Since men's lives were at stake, Montgomery insisted that "plain speaking" was necessary: "Those . . . commanders known to be bad . . . [had] to be told they . . . [were] bad," but they also had to be "*taught so that they . . . [would] become good.*" Significantly, he believed that most Canadian brigadiers and unit commanders were "excellent material, and only require[d] to be taught." He also expressed faith in the "very sound, but . . . not in any way brilliant" commander of the 2nd Division, Major-General J. H. "Ham" Roberts.[37]

Clearly, Montgomery's candid assertions cast new light on the interpretation that incompetent regimental officers were a major factor in impeding Canadian Army training progression in Britain and, subsequently, its operational performance in Normandy. This was certainly Stacey's opinion, which held that the army overseas "got rather less than it might have" from training because it possessed "a proportion of regimental officers whose attitude towards training was casual and haphazard rather than urgent and scientific." Presumably, as better ones rose in rank and responsibility, the situation worsened. Stacey's analysis of Normandy operations confirmed his impression, since the inadequacies of poor regimental officers "appeared in action," often with serious consequences.[38] After the war, Crerar reinforced this view by agreeing entirely with Stacey's assessment.[39] Yet, as the Montgomery correspondence has shown, many officers in this category were "teachable," willing, and of reasonable, if not always outstanding, caliber. To blame regimental officers, in short, clouds the issue that the Canadian high command did not know how to train them properly and, but for Montgomery's intervention, would have likely left them to learn the profession of arms though a process of osmosis.

Crerar himself attempted to imitate much of Montgomery's military approach. In echoing the latter's cry that the army was not "a mutual congratulation society," he stressed that good work should be praised and bad work stamped upon. His speaking notes on "Conqueror" were essentially a regurgitation of Montgomery's confidential memorandum to him on the same subject.[40] Crerar also recorded that Montgomery's personal views on Canadian commanders "very largely indeed, corroborated the conclusions... [he] had separately reached."[41] No doubt Montgomery's victory at El Alamein in November 1942 greatly reinforced the influence of his thinking upon the inexperienced Crerar. In October of the following year the Canadian corps commander recirculated "to be thoroughly absorbed" Montgomery's "Some Lessons Learnt during the First Two Years of War." For whatever reason, he chose to add "one qualification" in his covering memorandum: "that the title might better read 'Some Lessons Learnt during Two Thousand Years of War.'"[42]

In a previous report upon his visit to the Eighth Army in February 1943, Crerar had also insisted that "he saw nothing new in General Montgomery's tactics,"[43] which begs the question why then Canadian senior officers had such difficulty in mastering the art of higher field command. True, Montgomery had showered some praise upon Crerar for his handling of the Canadian Corps during Exercise "Tiger" in May, but it was unquestionably couched in terms that clearly (and cleverly) recognized the extreme importance of the "Ludendorff behind Hindenburg," the staff officer behind the commander. "You did splendidly," wrote Montgomery, "and you have a first class BGS in [Brigadier G. G.] Simonds... I thought he was very good and when I say you did well, I mean it."[44] There was, of course, a rather significant difference between Simonds on the one hand and Crerar and his nominee Price on the other; namely, that the junior had escaped through his very youth the ravages of unprofessional compromise that afflicted his seniors. It is truly doubtful that Crerar even with the full benefit of Montgomery schooling ever really knew as the master knew. There is little question, however, that McNaughton was but the "father of the Canadian Army" in a political sense. Montgomery was its military godfather.

NOTES

1. Record Group (RG) 24, Vol. 12,358, Translation of Extract from the German Army "Manual of the British Army," dated early April 1942.

2. Carlo D'Este, *Decision in Normandy: The Unwritten Story of Montgomery and The Allied Campaign* (London: Pan, 1984), p. 510.

3. Ronald Lewin, *Montgomery as Military Commander* (New York: Stein and Day, 1971), pp. 2–9, 266–270 and his "Field-Marshal Viscount Montgomery," *The War Lords: Military Commanders of the Twentieth Century*, ed. Field Marshal Sir Michael Carver (Boston: Little Brown, 1976), pp. 500–508; Richard Lamb, *Montgomery in Europe 1943–1945: Success or Failure?* (London: Buchan and Enright, 1984), pp. 20–21, 62–63, 405–406, 417; Gen. Omar N. Bradley, *A Soldier's Story* (New York: Henry Holt, 1951), pp. 208–209; D'Este, *Decision in Normandy*, pp. 46, 455, 510; and Russell F. Weigley, *Eisenhower's Lieutenants: The Campaign of France and Germany, 1944–1945* (Bloomington, Ind.: Indiana University Press, 1981), p. 37. Lamb writes: "Montgomery was brilliant at organization; all his working life was devoted to studying how to make army staff work more efficient. He understood every

branch of the army and its weapons; he was expert at moving great numbers of men and huge quantities of stores and vehicles at great speed across large distances; above all, his personality was always good for the morale of his troops. . . . And, provided he was in sole charge, he was good at commanding the troops of other nations" (Lamb, *Montgomery*, p. 20). The "reports on individual Canadian brigades which Montgomery sent to Crerar," writes Stacey, "give a fascinating glimpse of a great trainer of troops at work." Col. C. P. Stacey, *Arms, Men and Governments: The War Policies of Canada, 1939–1945* (Ottawa: Information Canada, 1974), p. 231.

4. Nigel Hamilton, *Monty: The Making of a General 1887–1942* (Sevenoaks: Hodder and Stoughton, 1984), Vol. I, pp. 117–118, 143–144, 156–165, 180–199, 227–245, 303–304, 470; Anthony John Trythall, *'Boney' Fuller: Soldier, Strategist, and Writer 1878–1966* (New Brunswick, N.J.: Rutgers University Press, 1977), pp. 93–96, 118–120; D'Este, *Decision in Normandy*, p. 482; Brig. B. L. Montgomery, "The Major Tactics of the Encounter Battle," *The Army Quarterly*, 2 (July 1938): 268–272; and his "The Problem of the Encounter Battle as Affected by Modern British War Establishment," *Canadian Defense Quarterly (CDQ)*, 1 (October 1937); 13–25 (first published in the *Royal Engineers Journal*).

5. Maj.-Gen. F. W. von Mellenthin, *Panzer Battles: A Study of the Employment of Armor in the Second World War*, trans. H. Betzler, ed. L. C. F. Turner (Norman, Okla.: University of Oklahoma Press, 1983) p. 241. Withdrawal under enemy pressure is probably the most difficult and perilous of all military operations. When Moltke the Elder was told by an admirer that his generalship would rank with the great captains, he supposedly replied, "No, for I have never conducted a retreat" (Ibid).

6. Gen. H. D. G. Crerar Papers (CP), Vol. 2, Notes re Enclosed Correspondence with C.-in-C., South-Eastern Command.

7 Reginald H. Roy, *For Most Conspicuous Bravery: A Biography of Major-General George R. Pearkes, V. C. Through Two World Wars* (Vancouver: University of British Columbia Press, 1977), pp. 136, 152, 166.

8. CP, Vol. 2, Notes re Enclosed Correspondence with C in C South-Eastern Command; and Vol. 1, letters Crerar to Montgomery, 6 January 1942, and Crerar to McNaughton, 11 January 1942. McNaughton left Britain 23 January 1942, returning on 28 March; the First Canadian Army was formed 6 April 1942. By Crerar's own admission, he had held no field command, whereas Pearkes had commanded a brigade, a division, and now a corps: "as a com[man]d[er] he had a reputation— as such I had none." On the basis of such obvious discrepancy, it is evident that field command ability, if thought about at all, was assumed to be something that automatically came with appointment. Not surprisingly, Crerar's relationship with Pearkes was stormy. Whereas "the headquarters of the other divisions and formations had invited me to dine with them," complained Crerar, "the 1st Division had done no such thing." On 9 May 1942, he told Pearkes that during "the last months his attitude had, perhaps unknowingly, made my position and our relationships extraordinarily difficult" (CP, Vol. 1, Crerar "Most Confidential" Note to File, 9 May 1942). In the end Montgomery solved Crerar's problem.

9. DHist CMHQ Historical Officer Report No. 49, Conference on Exercise "Bumper," dated 27 October 1941; and RG 24, Vol. 13,746, WD GStaff 2nd Canadian Infantry Division (hereafter CID), Exercise "Bumper" Exercise Instructions and Narratives.

10. DHist CMHQ Historical Officer Report No. 60, Canadian Corps Study Week 19–23 January 1942, Corps Training Programme, Winter, 1941–42, dated 29 January 1942.

11. CP, Vol. 2, Notes on Inf Bdes of Canadian Corps, Numbers 1–7, 3 February 1942 to 4 March 1942. Of the brigade commanders Montgomery commented upon, H. L. N. Salmon of the 7th Brigade rated first: "a far better and more knowledgeable soldier than any other Brigadier in the Corps," he was "fit to command a Division." K. G. Blackader of the 8th Brigade was "excellent," a future division commander, and the relief in the brigade "at seeing the last of Archambault [wa]s very evident." Montgomery also considered G. V. Whitehead of the 5th Brigade a "good Brigadier" as he had a "good brain" and was firm and decisive. Southam of the 6th Brigade was additionally "first class," while R. F. L. Keller of the 1st went unobserved. H. N. Ganong and Haldenby, respectively of the 3rd and 9th Brigades, were good though Montgomery later expressed reservations about the latter and eventually recommended the relief of the former. A. E. Potts of the 2nd Brigade and C. B. Topp of the 4th, while each a "nice person," were neither fitted for brigade command. Of Topp, Montgomery wrote: "He does not hear a great deal of what is said, and in consequence he does not know a great deal of what goes on in his Brigade." While Potts, who commanded a brigade for six years in peace, "may have done good work in the past," Montgomery added, "he is beyond it now. . . . He knows the officers in his Brigade, but beyond that he knows very little of what is going on" (Ibid). Montgomery also found Brig. R. A. Wyman of the 1st Canadian Army Tank Brigade a "vigorous commander," who could with advice be expected to perform well. He also noted that his Brigade Major, R. W. Moncel, was "very good" (CP, Vol. 2, 1 Canadian army tank brigade notes, 7 May 1942).

12. CP, Vol. 2, Notes on Inf Bdes of Canadian Corps, Numbers 1–7, 3 February 1942 to 4 March 1942. Montgomery rendered equally direct comments like "dead wood," "lacks guts," and "is idle and taken to drink" about officers of British formations [Imperial War Museum (hereafter IWM), Field Marshal Viscount Montgomery of Alamein Papers (hereafter MAP), BLM 25, Notes on 4th Division, Notes on 50th Division, and Notes on Portsmouth Area 25 July, 1940]. The first CO referred to was Lieutenant-Colonel J. R. Kingham of the Canadian Scottish Regiment, the second, Lieutenant-Colonel Chouinard of the Le Régiment de la Chaudière. The third CO mentioned was Lieutenant-Colonel G. H. Basher of the Royal Regiment of Canada. The fourth cited, Major D. G. MacLauchlan, had been in command for only two weeks, having spent the previous "three months at the Holding Unit." He eventually won the Distinguished Service Order at the battle of Clair Tizon in Normandy in August 1944. The last CO alluded to was Lieutenant-Colonel Hendrie of the 48th Highlanders. Among those COs who impressed Montgomery were: Sherwood Lett of the South Saskatchewan Regiment who replaced Topp; H. D. Graham of the Hastings and Prince Edward Regiment; Bernatchez of the Royal 22nd Regiment; T. E. D'O. Snow of the Royal Canadian Regiment; and T. J. Rutherford of the Stormont, Dundas, and Glengarry Highlanders. "We could do with some more C.O.'s like Rutherford" noted Montgomery (CP, Vol. 2, Montgomery to Crerar, 26 February 1942). The point of all this, of course, is that Canadian soldiers were being trained by these officers. There is thus a certain validity to Montgomery on observing one unshaven CO carrying a tired soldier's rifle that "this may be magnificent but it is not war." Actually, the CO, Lieutenant-Colonel

Calkin of the North Shore Regiment, should at the time have been ahead of his battalion reconnoitering a defensive position. Montgomery considered Calkin a "good man" with limited training ability who would do well with guidance.

13. CP, Vol. 2, Notes on Inf Bdes of Canadian Corps, Numbers 1–7.

14. CP, Vol. 2, letter Crerar to Montgomery, 3 February 1942.

15. CP, Vol. 2, Notes on Inf Bdes of Canadian Corps; and CP, Vol.2, letter Crerar to Montgomery, 2 March 1942.

16. RG 24, Vol. 13,685, letter Crerar to All Commanders and Commanding Officers, 1 Canadian Corps, 18 June 1943; and RG 24, Vol. 9764, Report on First Course at G.H.Q. Battle School.

17. Notes on Inf Bdes of Canadian Corps, Number 1–7, 3 February 1942 to 4 March 1942.

18 Ibid.; and CP, Vol. 1, memorandum Crerar to B.G.S., Cdn Corps, 11 January 1942.

19. RG 24, Vol. 13,684, [South Eastern] Army Commander's Personal Memorandum No. 2, dated 21 March 1942.

20. RG 24, Vol. 13,746, WD GS 2 CID, 2 DS(G)1–1–23 2 Cdn Div Operation Instruction No. 12 Defence of Sussex, 27 November 1941, and 2 DS(G)1–1–23 H.Q. 2 Cdn Div Plan to Defeat Invasion Amdmts to 2 Cdn Div Operation Instruction, 3 January 1942.

21. John Swettenham, *McNaughton* (Toronto: Ryerson, 1968), Vol. II, p. 172.

22. RG 24, Vol. 13,760, memorandum Army Commander's Address, 22 December 1941 under Trg 7–1–1 H.Q. Cdn Corps, Brigadier, General Staff to Distribution, 12 December 1941.

23. CP, Vol. 2, Notes on Beaver IV, 13 May 1942.

24. RG 24, Vol. 13,746, WD GS 2 CID 2 DS(G)1–5 HQ 2 Cdn Div, 9 April 1942, signed by GOC.

25. CP, Vol. 2, Notes on Exercise "Flip," 14 April 1942.

26. CP, Vol. 2, Exercise "Conqueror," 16 April 1942.

27. IWM, Lt. Col. Trumbull Warren Papers (hereafter TWP), letter Montgomery to Warren, 27 June 1942.

28. RG 24, Vol. 9804, Notes on Address by Army Commander, 22 December 1941, "Some Lessons Learnt During the First Two Years of War Sep 1939-Sep 1941"; and CP, Vol. 2, Exercise "Conqueror."

29. "The Problem of the Encounter Battle as Affected by Modern British War Establishment," pp. 13–21. For many years the composition of an advanced guard was based on an infantry unit or formation with emphasis on its covering or guarding mission. Fuller was always warning of the dangers of allowing an enemy's plan to interfere with the progress of one's own; being forced to change one's plan, in short, implied a loss of initiative.

30. Notes on Address by Army Commander, 22 December 1941.

31. CP, Vol. 2, Notes on Exercise "Flip,"; Notes on Beaver IV; and Some further notes on Beaver III, 25 April 1942. On "pistol" or "pocket" guns, see Brig. A. L. Pemberton, *The Second World War, 1939–1945, Army, The Development of Artillery Tactics and Equipment* (London: War Office, 1951), pp. 99, 149–150.

32. CP, Vol. 2, Exercise "Conqueror."

33. CP, Vol. 2, Some Notes on the Broader Aspects of Beaver III, 23 April 1942; and Notes on Beaver IV, 13 May 1942. One of the better Canadian brigadiers

(Sherwood Lett) did not finish giving orders for an attack to his COs at brigade headquarters until 1630 hours, when the attack was due to commence at 1715 hours.

34. CP, Vol. 2, Some Notes on the Broader Aspects of Beaver III; Beaver III Notes on Commanders, 25 April 1942; Notes on Beaver IV; and Notes on Inf Bdes of Canadian Corps, No. 6, 2 March 1942, 3 Inf Bde. Montgomery thought Potts and Ganong both made very poor showings on "Beaver III"; they were, in his opinion, too old and rigidly set in their ways. As for Pearkes, he wrote: "His mind works in a groove and he gets the bit between his teeth, puts on blinkers, and drives ahead blindly." Montgomery criticized the 1st Division for attacking its objective oblivious to a threat developing on its right flank. He felt that Pearkes should have protected his attack against this blow, which, when it did come, would have in Montgomery's estimation destroyed the 1st Division under real war conditions. The division also did not do well in the withdrawal. Still, Montgomery believed the 1st Division had "very fine material and should be a first class division."

35. CP, Vol. 2, Notes on Inf Bdes of Canadian Corps, No. 2, February 23, 7 Inf Bde 24 February 1942; and Notes on Beaver IV, 13 May 42, and Appendix "A" Notes on Commander 3 Div. On Montgomery's opinion of Pearkes, Price, Potts, and Ganong see also TWP, letters Montgomery to Warren, 25 April 1942, 1 June 1942, 27 June 1942, 27 July 1942, and 10 August 1942.

36. CP, Vol. 1, Crerar to McNaughton, 4 March 1941. Crerar later wrote to McNaughton: "I have come to the definite conclusion that as a Divisional Commander . . . [Price] is handicapped in two important respects. He does not possess what might be termed a "sense of tactics." He is unable quickly to appreciate a military situation and to dominate it with the requisite speed and decision" (CP, Vol. 1, Crerar to McNaughton, 10 Aug 1942).

37. Some Notes on the Broader Aspects of Beaver III; Beaver III Notes on Commanders, 25 April 1942; Notes on Commander 3 Div. Appendix "A" 13.5.42; Notes on Beaver IV; and Exercise "Conqueror." Montgomery thought the 2nd Division well-handled on "Beaver III"; he also considered Roberts "teachable." He did remark, however, upon the very positive influence on the division of the GSO 1, Lieutenant-Colonel C. C. Mann (from 28 January 1944 COS First Canadian Army) and suggested that Roberts not be left without a "really good officer" in that staff position. He thus implied that an average division commander "would always do well if he ha[d] a good G.S.O. 1" (CP, Vol. 2, Beaver III Notes on Commanders).

38. Col. C. P. Stacey, *Official History of the Canadian Army in the Second World War*, Vol. I: *Six Years of War: The Army in Canada, Britain and the Pacific* (Ottawa: Queen's Printer,1966), p. 253, and Col. C. P. Stacey, *Official History of the Canadian Army in the Second World War*, Vol. III: *The Victory Campaign: The Operations in North-West Europe* (Ottawa: Queen's Printer, 1966), p. 275.

39. CP, Vol. 21, Crerar to Stacey, 10 March 1959.

40. CP, Vol. 2, Notes on Conqueror, undated, following Exercise "Conqueror."

41. CP, Vol. 2, Notes re Enclosed correspondence with C in C South Eastern Command; and Memorandum on Conversation with Lt.-Gen. B. L. Montgomery, Commanding S.E. Army on 4 July 1942 Commencing 1800 hrs.

42. CP, Vol. 1, GOC/3–6 Comd 1 Cdn Corps to all Commanders and Commanding Officers, 1 Canadian Corps. 6 October 1943.

43. Personal copy CLFCSC Collection, Report on Visit to 8th Army Lt.-Gen. H. D. G. Crerar, C. B., D.S.O. Appendix "J": A few Personal Observations.

44. CP, Vol. 2, note Montgomery to Crerar, 30 May 1942. The Canadian Corps "is now beginning to become known as a good Corps," wrote Montgomery, "after 2 ½ years" (TWP, Montgomery to Warren 27 June 1942).

Epilogue

Final Tempering

Infantry battalions will be exercised in the attack, following close behind a moving barrage (which may be simulated by thunderflashes or other devices).

2nd Canadian Infantry Division
"Training Instruction No. 24," 22 April 1944[1]

If by the Montgomery measurement the Canadian Army overseas was found operationally wanting in 1942, the year 1943 witnessed a series of events that in their unfolding forced major organizational changes and exposed even more flaws. Indeed, the top blew off the Canadian high command. Unfortunately, the subsequent smoke screen generated by Canadian nationalism obscured the harsh realities behind this development and certain of its repercussions. The closely associated decisions in April and October to dispatch Canadian troops to the Mediterranean theatre, thereby effectively splitting the Canadian Army overseas into two rather distinct groups, coincidentally raised the question of the future of the First Canadian Army. In October, the CGS even went so far as to suggest that the best interests of Canada would be served by placing 2 Canadian Corps and ancillary Canadian troops remaining in Britain under a new army commanded by a battle-experienced British officer supported by experienced British staff officers.[2] It is in light of these important developments that Canadian training up to D-Day is discussed in the following pages.

There can be little doubt but the Dieppe debacle of August 1942 most severely impeded the progress of First Canadian Army training. The virtual destruction of the 2nd Division's 4th and 6th Infantry Brigades forced them to revert during the process of reconstitution to individual and platoon level training. The 4th Canadian Armoured Division, which had in the meantime arrived, anticipated reaching squadron (tank company) level in collective training by 15 February 1943. The 5th Canadian Armoured Division, having in 1942 extended squadron training to late December, was not much more advanced. Combined operations training, with its highly specialized amphibious overtones and inherent interservice complexity, had also since the autumn offered a change of training pace to the 1st and 3rd Divisions. The dangers that such specialized training posed to land operations proper seems to have been appreciated by Simonds, however, for as GOC 1st Division he warned: "In an assault landing troops tend to become obsessed with the idea of the 'battle for the beaches' and, unless actively combatted during training, inertia is likely to set in."[3] The more time spent on combined operations training, moreover, the less there was available to practice for open warfare.

During the famous GHQ Exercise "Spartan" 4–12 March 1943, the First Canadian Army, less the 1st and 4th Divisions, had ample opportunity to demonstrate its operational capacity for open warfare. The object of this largest troop maneuver since "Bumper" in the fall of 1941 was to practice breaking out of a secure bridgehead, the very role assigned to the First Canadian Army. As described by McNaughton, it was "a dress rehearsal for the full-scale invasion of the Continent." In brief, it called for the First Canadian Army (notionally, and ironically, the "British Second Army") supported by 19 air squadrons to attack and seize Huntingdon, the capital of a fictitious "Eastland" lying north of the River Thames. The task of the "German Sixth Army," represented by 8 and 11 British Corps also supported by air, was to defend Huntingdon. As finally organized, McNaughton's force included 1 Canadian Corps (2nd and 3rd Divisions), 2 Canadian Corps (5th Canadian and Guards Armoured Divisions, each of one armored and one infantry brigade), 12 British Corps (43rd and 53rd Divisions), and the 1st Canadian Army Tank Brigade. Oddly, while the 4th Canadian Armoured Division had been excused "Spartan" for lack of advanced training, Headquarters 2 Corps had since 19 January been included at McNaughton's insistence.

In the event, 2 Corps not only suffered deficiencies in signals capability, but was up to the last minute issued new equipment with which its operators were unfamiliar. Without the benefit of a preliminary command-post exercise,[4] the training value of this corps's participation was clearly questionable. Even more difficult to understand was the decision to assign both armored divisions to the most inexperienced corps commander. One of the key lessons of "Tiger," a year earlier in May 1942, had been that a corps of one armored and two infantry divisions was a well-balanced formation for all normal operations. It had been prescribed that any corps headquarters should be able "to handle efficiently up to three infantry divisions, or three armoured divisions, or *any combination* of the two types." Although armored divisions were obviously new and had to be handled differently, there was no requirement for special armored corps headquarters per se; the best results came from employing them in combination with infantry divisions and other arms.[5]

The enemy received a day's head start in deployment on commencement of "Spartan." McNaughton in the interim decided to forsake the better "going" round the western reach of the Thames for a direct, surprise attack on Huntingdon. This involved not only crossing a major water obstacle but also traversing difficult country following the establishment of a bridgehead. It meant additionally that he could not bring his considerable armored superiority to bear. The enemy reacted to this initiative by initially commencing bridge demolitions and, ultimately, contesting the successful advance of 1 and 12 Corps across the Thames. When it became clear that the enemy was in fact reinforcing his center from the western reaches, McNaughton decided to swing 2 Corps over to the better "going" in a westward pincer movement.

Unfortunately, McNaughton's newly formed 2 Corps advanced slowly due to traffic snarl-ups and problems of gasoline resupply, obvious indicators of a low standard of staff work. Signals shortcomings further ensured the loss of wireless contact between corps and army headquarters for 15 hours. Also in a highly dubious move, the commander of 2 Corps, Lieutenant-General E. Sansom, ordered his armored divisions divided, placing the infantry brigades designed to support tanks under the 5th Armoured Division and the two armored brigades under Guards Armoured. Although McNaughton quite correctly countermanded this order, his action came too late to prevent the regrouping from taking place. The Guards Armoured Brigade subsequently, for lack of infantry support, suffered umpire-simulated destruction by antitank action. Again, one of the lessons stressed since "Tiger" was not to split the armored division, which had been specifically structured to ensure all arms and especially tank-infantry cooperation.

McNaughton's handling of his command also reflected a lack of professional knowledge that could have been acquired through study. Evidently, he actually contemplated passing 2 Corps through 1 Corps on the night 7/8 March, a maneuver that would have bordered on the impossible. That McNaughton had no idea a corps required a minimum of 24 hours warning in order to execute a major task is borne out by the following timings: at 2335 hours on 6 March, he directed 2 Corps to advance east across the Thames through 1 Corps; at 1615 hours, the next day he gave counter orders to effect the western envelopment that night; at 2130 hours on 10 March, he issued orders for operations the following day; and at 2259 hours 11 March, he gave orders for operations on 12 March.[6] When faced with bridging difficulties on 7 March, his reaction was to go immediately to the local scene,[7] a rather extraordinary step for an army commander who should always be looking well beyond operations in current progress. In sum, McNaughton failed to demonstrate that critical capacity of a higher commander to plan sensibly and order not hours, but days ahead.

Sir James Grigg, British Secretary of State for War, observed the Canadian GOC-in-C's performance on "Spartan." He reported that he was "appalled at McNaughton's indecision" as "he stood in front of his situation map hesitating as to what to do and what orders to issue."[8] General Alan Brooke also called on McNaughton on 7 March, which visit Stacey implies may have been the catalyst that caused McNaughton to countermand his 6 March order to pass 2 Corps through 1 Corps at night. Whatever the case, Brooke recorded in his daily diary that the visit went a long way toward "proving my worse fear that... [McNaughton] is quite incompetent to command an army!" He added that: "He does not know how to begin the job and was tying up his force into the most awful muddle." It was "Quite clear," Brooke finally noted, "that Paget was incapable of realizing how bad Andy McNaughton is!"[9] Years later, even Crerar recalled "that it became patently obvious to all" during Exercise "Spartan" that McNaughton "was totally unsuitable for high operational command." According to him, both Grigg and Ralston witnessed McNaughton's "inability to sum up the situation and issue precise clear cut orders."[10]

In a post-exercise memorandum to McNaughton based on a review of all "Spartan" reports, Major-General Simonds, his former B.G.S., wrote: "the main conclusions [of the C-in-C Home Forces] indicating weaknesses in organization and training... [were] substantiated by events during the exercise." Most noticeable, he added, "forward brigades... acted with less energy than they did in exercise TIGER" in "getting to grips with the enemy." Road movement also remained a serious problem, particularly at bridgeheads and other defiles where special traffic control and routing arrangements had to be made to avoid congestion.[11] Revealingly, 2 Corps recommended that night movement of armored formations be kept to a minimum, and then be executed only with full lights! Simonds dismissed this on the grounds that the Eighth Army had conducted such moves highly successfully without lights. He likewise dismissed another 2 Corps suggestion, to collocate Advanced and Rear components of corps headquarters so that supply, transportation, and maintenance heads could be kept better informed, because it was "useless for Heads of Services [normally at Rear] to be in the tactical picture if they... [were] not in a position to control their units and give an up to date 'state' and forecast of requirements to the A/Q Staff." If there had to "be a gap somewhere," argued Simonds, "it should be between Advanced HQ and the Heads of Services rather than between the Heads of Services and their units."[12]

Crerar corroborated most of these points in his reports on "Spartan" and "Trojan," a formation headquarters signals exercise held on 31 May and 1

June to train replacement officers in their operational responsibilities. Apart from mentioning the perennial bogey of failure to pass on vital information, he commented upon the necessity "to appreciate the time required between the ordering of a Brigade or Divisional attack and the launching of its battalions supported by co-ordinated fire power." A commander once decided on a general plan of action had to look ahead, "to think out . . . the course he . . . [would] pursue *after* the immediate battle ha[d] been fought"; this could not be done were he "required to check on the detailed implementation by his staff, of the plan already decided upon." In this respect Crerar was especially hard on the 2nd Division, which had been censured by C-in-C Home Forces for inadequate coordination of infantry and artillery action and not digging-in after attack. Indeed, it was his failures during "Spartan," rather than at Dieppe, that cost the GOC, Major-General Roberts, his command.[13]

The most striking aspect of Crerar's commentary, however, was how much it actually parroted Montgomery. From stressing the need to fight for information in the establishment of contact and the advantageous use of ground, through the stage-management of battle and the correct location of the commander, he reflected the master's language and approach. At the same time, judging from its acceptable performance on "Spartan," 1 Corps was evidently the better for it. The same day that Brooke reported so adversely upon McNaughton he also visited Crerar and his headquarters where he saw "a real good show." The latter, in Brooke's words, had "improved that Corps out of all recognition."[14] Still, the extensive changes in command and staff appointments that followed "Spartan" left Crerar convinced that his corps had "lost some ground . . . in respect of functional efficiency." At the end of Exercise "Trojan," he asked commanders to concentrate on three things: training themselves and their staffs in their respective operational roles; developing a dependable NCO cadre; and training all ranks to the highest standard in weapon and equipment handling skill.[15]

Brief mention should, of course, be made of two aspects that continued to characterize Anglo-Canadian operations. One related to the two sides of road movement. First, restricting movement to roads to avoid damage to crops and civilian property inculcated in many troops a general reluctance to leave roads at all. Second, road movement congestion itself signaled an overabundance of vehicles, a problem identified on Exercise "Tiger" by Montgomery who sought at the time "to reduce the mass of transport that . . . accompanie[d] fighting units into battle."[16] The other aspect related to the "fetish" of commanders going forward from their headquarters and leaving "confusion" in their wake. After Exercise "Spartan," doctrine stressed that commanders "on the higher levels c[ould] fight their battles only from their HQ where they . . . [were] fully in the picture and ha[d] their full signals facilities."[17] Notably, in the German system of shared commander-COS responsibility, this was not so pronounced a problem, and commanders were constantly reminded that "the Knight's Cross is not won at Battle Headquarters, but forward with the victorious fighters."[18]

Barely a year now remained in which to finally prepare the First Canadian Army for operations on the soil of France. To provide a basis for forward planning, the army training program directive for April prescribed unit training for the period 1–31 May and formation training to brigade level during 1–30 June 1943. Significantly, however, it stipulated that where facilities were available, combined operations training would "take precedence over all other." While battle drills to produce "a habitual framework of action to typical situations" continued to be emphasized, special studies were also called for on how to cross wire, water, and minefield obstacles by day and by night. Headquarters training likewise stressed the special study of operations related to expanding and breaking out from a bridgehead formed by other troops and movement during pursuit. At the same time, the First Canadian Army directive demanded that close order drill periods be held once a week and ceremonial parades, to foster morale and *esprit de corps*, "from time to time as opportunities and facilities m[ight] permit." Again, this accorded with the direction after "Spartan" for a definite period of "smartening up."[19]

In April, largely due to pressure exerted by the Canadian government, the 1st Canadian Infantry Division and the 1st Army Tank Brigade replaced equivalent British formations in the order of battle for the assault on Sicily. The intention was to have them return to disseminate formation-level battle experience among Canadian land forces for the invasion of northwest Europe, but this was clearly not the primary factor underlying their deployment. Given shipping availability, of course, this would have been a far better scheme for gaining much needed operational experience than the policy, begun in January 1943, of attaching for three months at a time individual Canadian officers and NCOs to the First British Army fighting in Tunisia. Ultimately, however, the latter did prove to be the main source of battle experience within the First Canadian Army, for in early October authorities decided to dispatch to Italy the 1 Canadian Corps and 5th Canadian Armoured Division, which had exercised as a division for the first time on "Spartan." Again, this was a direct consequence of Canadian governmental entreaty, spurred considerably by Mackenzie King's growing suspicion that casualties in Normandy could be heavy and might be avoided by sending troops to Italy.[20]

These decisions naturally put the whole future of the First Canadian Army in doubt, for it was left with but one national corps. Ralston had already warned McNaughton in July that sending a corps to the Mediterranean might conceivably jeopardize the "idea of a Canadian Army." Paget as commander of the 21st Army Group now designated for the invasion of Europe broached the matter of proposed changes in October; he informed

Figure E.1
1 Canadian Corps Ancillary Troops

1st Armoured Car Regiment (The Royal
Canadian Dragoons)

7th Anti–Tank Regiment

1st Survey Regiment

1st Light Anti–Aircraft Regiment
(Lanark and Renfrew Scottish Regiment)

Royal Canadian Engineers

   9th Field Park Company

   12th Field Company

   13th Field Company

   14th Field Company

1st Corps Signals

1st Corps Defence Company (The Lorne Scots)

Royal Canadian Army Service Corps

   1st Headquarters Corps Car Company

   1st Corps Transport Company

   No. 31 Corps Troops Company

   No. 32 Corps Troops Company

No. 1 Corps and Army Troops
Sub–Park (Royal Canadian Ordnance
Corps)

1st Corps Troops Workshop

1st Canadian Infantry Division	1st Canadian Army Tank Brigade (later Armoured Brigade)	5th Canadian Armoured Division

McNaughton that for the invasion the 21st Army Group would comprise
"an American Army, the Second British Army, and a combined Anglo-
Canadian Army" based on the First Canadian Army. Both Paget and Brooke
accepted the practicality of maintaining the existing staff structure and an-

Figure E.2
1 Canadian Corps

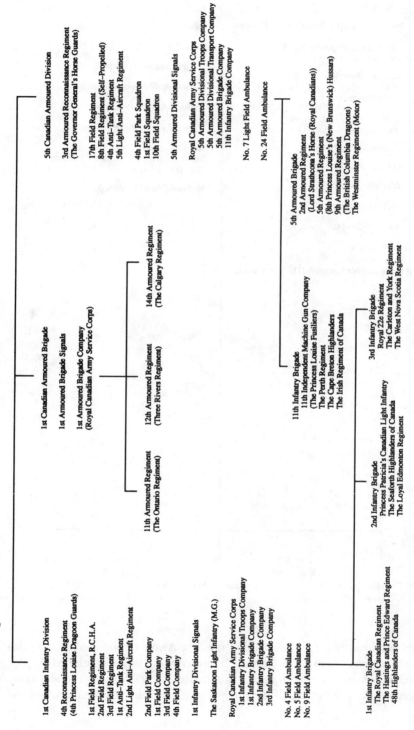

1st Canadian Infantry Division

4th Reconnaissance Regiment
(4th Princess Louise Dragoon Guards)

1st Field Regiment, R.C.H.A.
2nd Field Regiment
3rd Field Regiment
1st Anti-Tank Regiment
2nd Light Anti-Aircraft Regiment

2nd Field Park Company
1st Field Company
3rd Field Company
4th Field Company

1st Infantry Divisional Signals

The Saskatoon Light Infantry (M.G.)

Royal Canadian Army Service Corps
1st Infantry Divisional Troops Company
1st Infantry Brigade Company
2nd Infantry Brigade Company
3rd Infantry Brigade Company

No. 4 Field Ambulance
No. 5 Field Ambulance
No. 9 Field Ambulance

1st Infantry Brigade
The Royal Canadian Regiment
The Hastings and Prince Edward Regiment
48th Highlanders of Canada

2nd Infantry Brigade
Princess Patricia's Canadian Light Infantry
The Seaforth Highlanders of Canada
The Loyal Edmonton Regiment

3rd Infantry Brigade
Royal 22e Régiment
The Carleton and York Regiment
The West Nova Scotia Regiment

1st Canadian Armoured Brigade

1st Armoured Brigade Signals

1st Armoured Brigade Company
(Royal Canadian Army Service Corps)

11th Armoured Regiment
(The Ontario Regiment)

12th Armoured Regiment
(Three Rivers Regiment)

14th Armoured Regiment
(The Calgary Regiment)

11th Infantry Brigade
11th Independent Machine Gun Company
(The Princess Louise Fusiliers)
The Perth Regiment
The Cape Breton Highlanders
The Irish Regiment of Canada

5th Canadian Armoured Division

3rd Armoured Reconnaissance Regiment
(The Governor General's Horse Guards)

17th Field Regiment
8th Field Regiment (Self-Propelled)
4th Anti-Tank Regiment
5th Light Anti-Aircraft Regiment

4th Field Park Squadron
1st Field Squadron
10th Field Squadron

5th Armoured Divisional Signals

Royal Canadian Army Service Corps
5th Armoured Divisional Troops Company
5th Armoured Divisional Transport Company
5th Armoured Brigade Company
11th Infantry Brigade Company

No. 7 Light Field Ambulance

No. 24 Field Ambulance

5th Armoured Brigade
2nd Armoured Regiment
(Lord Strathcona's Horse (Royal Canadians))
5th Armoured Regiment
(8th Princess Louise's (New Brunswick) Hussars)
9th Armoured Regiment
(The British Columbia Dragoons)
The Westminster Regiment (Motor)

Note: Canadian Dental Corps, Royal Canadian Ordnance Corps, Royal Canadian Electrical and Mechanical Engineers, and Canadian Provost Corps not shown.

cillary troops, though the latter intimated that a change of army number might be required. The possibility of 12 British Corps being placed under First Canadian Army command brought forth the suggestion to add appropriate British staff officer representation. A War Office proposal that this proportion not exceed 50 percent was subsequently accepted by Canadian authorities. What was also clear, however, was that neither Brooke nor Paget was prepared to accept the generalship of McNaughton. Unfortunately, Montgomery's abrupt refusal to let McNaughton visit the 1st Canadian Division in Sicily in July 1943 raised a nationalist furor that over the years has clouded the central issue of his lack of command ability.[21]

In the meantime the 3rd Canadian Division and the 2nd Canadian Armoured Brigade, newly arrived from June, had also been selected in July for assault landing training with 1 British Corps; neither were to revert to Canadian command until 11 July 1944. This left the First Canadian Army with the 2nd Infantry and 4th Armoured Divisions preparing for Normandy exploitation operations up to and across the River Seine. It was not until October 1943 during Exercise "Grizzly II," however, that the latter operated for the first time as a division with all arms and services functioning. Here again problems in traffic control and infantry-artillery coordination surfaced. Poorly briefed patrols that invariably got lost confirmed the low standard of training of its infantry brigade. A better showing reputedly occurred in the following month when the 4th Division opposed the 9th British Armoured Division in Exercise "Bridoon." Headquarters 2 Canadian Corps for its part directed "Grizzly II" and practiced controlling the 1st Polish Armoured and 61st British Infantry divisions in Exercise "Link" during September.[22]

From "Spartan" onward, Canadian formations and headquarters remaining in Britain continued to suffer from various training shortcomings. The unproductive habit of commanders appointing themselves exercise "directors" rather than actively practicing their own function seems to have persisted at the higher level. During both exercises "Elm" in February and "Pickaxe" in August, Brigadier G. V. Whitehead acted in the role of division commander, while the latter "directed."[23] At a lower level, the 4th Canadian Armoured Division having "gone through . . . many upheavals" did not reach squadron level training until August 1943. Only in mid-September did it embark upon regimental (battalion) level training. The 2nd Armoured Brigade, at about the same time, carried out training up to unit level between 15 September and 31 October. It is not surprising, therefore, that autumn formation-level training revealed imperfections in patrolling, traffic control, artillery movement, and fire coordination. Even the "drill of firing and then moving the pos[itio]n of the t[an]k . . . [did] NOT seem to be known" in one unit of the 4th Armoured Brigade.[24]

Thus it was that, only a few months before D-Day, Canadian units continued to emphasize the basics. Priority during the period 1 January–31

March 1944 was given to individual training as it was the "last opportunity to make the men of . . . units fighting fit, and fit to fight." Collective training received secondary priority, up to platoon and equivalent slated to be conducted in January, up to company in February, and up to battalion in March. Within the 2nd Division, collective unit training continued from 24 April, with infantry battalions being exercised to attack following close behind a moving barrage often simulated simply, and unrealistically, by pyrotechnics. At the same time, most training programs stressed the need for battle drill and initiative on the part of junior leaders.[25] While commanders were expected to have their units ready for action in all respects by the end of this training period, however, it should be noted that problems were still being experienced with battalion three-inch mortar platoons in February.[26] The intent here is not to compile a litany of training shortcomings, but to put to rest the myth that Canadian soldiers overtrained for four years in Britain. As can be seen, the standards attained varied between units and formations. But ready or not, by May all field firing ceased as they moved to their final D-Day deployment positions.

At this point it is worth recalling that when McNaughton relinquished his command in December 1943, an army that was but months before earmarked for major assault and exploitation operations on the Continent,[27] was now left almost entirely without effectual field leadership at the very top. On 21 December, the Chief of the General Staff, Lieutenant-General Stuart, assumed the newly created post of COS at Canadian Military Headquarters (CMHQ), and took over as Acting Commander of the First Canadian Army. Stuart was neither in the best of health,[28] nor inclined to get involved in field army matters. Citing security reasons, he advised the army COS (formerly BGS) that he did not wish to be made aware of details of tactical plans. His primary responsibility in Britain, as he saw it, was not to deal with training, but with "questions of policy" that had previously gravitated to McNaughton. Although intended as but a temporary measure pending the arrival of the more favored Crerar, Stuart's incumbency as acting army commander lasted until 20 March 1944, when the former took over on return from Italy. Ironically, Crerar arrived having not participated as a corps commander in any major operations.[29]

It was only at this critical juncture, little more than two months before the Normandy invasion, that command of the First Canadian Army became characterized by a singular dedication to the conduct of operations. CMHQ now assumed responsibility for policy and administrative matters that, previously, occupied the eclectic attention of McNaughton and skewed his focus away from army command. Always a too willing workhorse, he was also an insatiable dabbler, one who just had to have a finger in every pie. The effect, as has been seen, was disastrous. To Crerar, "McNaughton was primarily an administrator, organizer and technician; but . . . [one] apt to get immersed in detail . . . unable to stand back and view the whole picture as a senior operational commander must." Though "extremely competent at mobilizing, equipping, and preparing an army, he could not give it, or its senior commanders the higher training that was essential."[30] From his Royal Twenty Centres of prewar days to his Canadian Army in Britain, McNaughton's interests do not seem to have lain with the real profession of arms. He clearly did not regard the operational field as a discipline requiring equally intense study as, say, medicine or engineering, with which he displayed his pronounced affinity.

This, essentially a problem of high-command application and vocation, more than any "casual and haphazard" attitude on the part of regimental officers was the underlying reason that the Canadian Army got "rather less than it might have" from its training period in Britain.[31] Again, the perennial problem of too frequent changes in command and staff appointments, which in itself reflected the greater malaise, exacerbated the situation. As late as January and February 1944, the 2nd and 4th Divisions suffered changes in commanders; the first for reasons of operational expediency, the second due to the age of the incumbent.[32] In such circumstances proper training focus and effective command and staff cohesion could hardly be maintained. The grass roots projection of battle drill, on the other hand, was symptomatic of an overall dearth of higher training direction. The long winters of Canadian institutional neglect of the essential elements of the profession of arms could not be easily or quickly overcome.

NOTES

1. Record Group (RG) 24, Vol. 13,750, WD GS 2CID Trg Instr No 24, 22 April 1944.

2. Col. C. P. Stacey, *Official History of the Canadian Army in the Second World War,* Vol. I: *Six Years of War: The Army in Canada, Britain and the Pacific* (Ottawa: Queen's Printer, 1966), pp. 222–223 and Col. C. P. Stacey, *Official History of the Canadian Army in the Second World War,* Vol. III: *The Victory Campaign: The Operations in North-West Europe, 1944–1945* (Ottawa: Queen's Printer, 1966), pp. 30–32.

3. McNaughton Papers (MP), Vol. 157, GOC/1–0 memo to All Comds and CO's 1 Cdn Div from GOC 1 Cdn Div, 15 May 1943; and Stacey, *Six Years,* pp. 245–248, 387. The 4th Canadian Armoured Division arrived in Britain in a somewhat more advanced state than the 5th Armoured as it had trained on tanks in Canada. Both formations had to wait to be kitted out in the United Kingdom.

4. RG 24, Vol. 9792, Exercise "Spartan" Instructions; John Swettenham, *McNaughton* (Toronto: Ryerson, 1968), Vol. II, pp. 271–286; and Stacey, *Six Years,* pp. 249–251.

5. RG 24, Vol. 12,301, S. E. Army Exercise "Tiger" Final Conference, 4 June 1942. Remarks of Army Commander, 4 June 1942.

6. RG 24, Vol. 9793 and MP, Vol. 159, GHQ Exercise "Spartan" March 1943 Comments by Commander-in-Chief GHQ Home Forces March 1943. By the calculations of the GOC 2 Corps, the length of an armored division, less its "B echelon" maintenance element, was 74 miles at 30 vehicles to the mile and 56 miles at 40

vehicles to the mile. Given safety allowance road movement calculations, this meant it needed at the former density two routes to cut the columnar length to 50 miles and three routes to cut it to 34 miles. At the latter density, two routes shortened the length to 35 miles and three to 26 miles; heavier density, of course, made a division more vulnerable from the air (RG 24, Vol. 13,710, Appreciation by Lt.-Gen. E. W. Sansom, DSO, GOC 2 Cdn Corps, 18 February 1943). The impression is gained that McNaughton only dabbled superficially in the military art since his admittedly superior performance in the Great War, which, it must not be forgotten, was mainly in counter-battery work. When he went to Camberley after the war it was reported that "much of the work which he . . . [did] at the Staff College . . . [was] new to him." Swettenham, *McNaughton*, I, 193.

    7. Swettenham, *McNaughton*, II, 277, 286. There were not enough crossing sites for three corps so the army commander went down himself to urge the engineers on. Swettenham goes to extreme lengths to defend McNaughton's performance on "Spartan," failing to mention several significant military aspects covered in the GHQ Home Forces report. He himself does not seem to have appreciated the time-space problem in issuing orders and instructions to large army formations. General Omar N. Bradley, in ordering the redeployment of VII Corps from the Cherbourg area in 1944, gave Lieutenant-General J. Lawton Collins "five days for the turnaround of his corps: one for rest, two for the move, another for reconnaissance, and a fifth on which to issue the attack orders." Bradley described it as a "tall order even for 'Lightning Joe' Collins, a taller one for his troops." [Gen. Omar N. Bradley, *A Soldier's Story*, (New York: Henry Holt, 1951), p. 319].

    8. University of London, King's College, Liddell Hart Centre for Military Archives (hereafter LHC), Alanbrooke Papers (hereafter AP), 12/XII/5/5, Sir James Grigg interview by Mrs. M. C. Long, November 1954.

    9. LHC, Alanbrooke Diaries (hereafter AD), 5/6a 29 June 1942 to 4 May 1943. The Brooke entry cited is for 8 March 1943, which could be a mistake. He records he "left at 9 AM . . . to see 'Spartan'." Stacey states McNaughton's diary "establishes that General Brooke visited him on the morning of 7 March" [Col. C. P. Stacey, *Arms, Men and Governments: The War Policies of Canada, 1939–1945* (Ottawa: Information Canada, 1974), p. 235]. Swettenham's charge that Brooke bore a grudge against McNaughton since the Great War seems to have been concocted by the latter. An examination of Brooke's diary from that period reveals he hardly mentioned McNaughton at all and then only in the most innocuous way. From a Brooke fully prepared to record that Australian General Sir Thomas Blamey "looks entirely drink sodden and somewhat repulsive" (LHC, AD, 5/8, May 5, 1944), one might have expected more had he actually borne a grudge against McNaughton. Similar evidence has been produced by Gen. Sir David Fraser, *Alanbrooke* (New York: Atheneum, 1982), p. 188.

    10. LHC, AP, 12/XI/4/61, Crerar interview by Mrs. M. C. Long, November 1954.

    11. By using a DAQMG (Moves) and closely coordinating "G" and "AQ" at the divisional level, 1 Corps movement appears to have worked well on "Spartan" (GHQ Exercise "Spartan," March 1943 Comments by Commander-in-Chief GHQ Home Forces March 1943).

    12. MP, Vol. 161, Memorandum GOC, 2 Cdn Div to GOC-in-C First Canadian Army, 29 April 1943. Simonds took over 2nd Division on 13 April 1943. Mc-

Naughton produced his own comments on "Spartan," but Crerar recommended that Stacey not include a quotation from them in the official history (CP, Vol. 21, Crerar to Stacey, 7 June 1952).

13. MP, Vol. 157, Memorandum GOC, 1 Cdn Corps on Particular Training Requirements as Revealed by Exercise "Spartan," 18 April 1943, and Vol. 158, Address by GOC, 1 Cdn Corps on Exercise "Trojan" 31 May–1 June 1943; and C. P. Stacey, *A Date with History* (Ottawa: Deneau, 1983), p. 116. Just before Dieppe, Roberts had remarked that while "Montgomery was an admirable trainer of troops . . . he was getting a little old to lead them into battle" [Nigel Hamilton, *Monty*, Vol. I: *The Making of a General 1887–1942* (Sevenoaks, U.K.: Hodder and Stoughton, 1984), p. 527].

14. LHC, AD, 5/6a, 8 March 1943.

15. MP, Vol. 158, Address by GOC, 1 Cdn Corps on Exercise "Trojan," 31 May–1 June 1943, and Vol. 157, Memorandum GOC, 1 Cdn Corps on Particular Training Requirements as Revealed by Exercise "Spartan," 18 April 1943. It is noteworthy that while Crerar deprecated 3rd Division's too frequent practice of holding orders conferences when acting as enemy force on 12 British Corps's Exercise "Harold" in July 1942, he felt obliged to repeat this same message to all formations of the 1st Canadian Corps in February 1943 (CP, Vol. 1, GOC 1–0 memorandum to distribution from GOC 1 Cdn Corps, 25 February 1943; RG 24, Vol. 9792, Exercise "Harold" 25–31 July 1942 Instructions; and Stacey, *Six Years*, pp. 99, 245).

16. RG 24, Vol. 14,136, S.E. 5740/Trg circular Montgomery to Commander 12 Corps and Canadian Corps, 11 May 1942. The Canadian Army was well equipped with "B" (soft-skinned) vehicles. (RG 24, Vol. 12,214, Vehicle Provision—Canadian Army Overseas, 17 June 1944).

17. MP, Vol. 157, Memorandum GOC, 1 Cdn Corps on Particular Training Requirements as Revealed by Exercise "Spartan" 18 April 1943.

18. RG 24, Vol. 12,358, HG/INT/89/1 GS(I) GHQ Home Forces 17 September 1942 excerpt from a captured document, Notes for Commanders by C-in-C Sixth German Army, 3 June 1940.

19. MP, Vol. 157, First Cdn Army Trg Directive No 12 of 13 March 1943, and Trg Directive Number 14 Period 1 May–30 June 1943 of 17 April 1943.

20. Col. G. W. Nicholson, *Official History of the Canadian Army in the Second World War*, Vol. II: *The Canadians in Italy*, 1943–1945 (Ottawa: Queen's Printer, 1956), pp. 20–26, 340–344; and Stacey, *Six Years*, pp. 248–249, 416–417 and *Arms, Men and Governments*, pp. 229, 234–237. While American formations were already fighting in North Africa, some Canadian troops were about to spend their fourth Christmas in Britain. A total of 201 officers and 147 other ranks were sent to the First British Army; eight were killed and 17 made casualty. During final preparations for the Normandy assault, just about every major Canadian unit had men with North African service on its strength. Many practical fighting tips were brought back by these soldiers (RG 24, Vol. 13,788, Active Service Notes from Experiences of Lt. T. G. Bowie, 21 Cdn Armd Regt, as a Troop Leader Att to an Armd Regt in the Tunisian Campaign, 1943).

21. Stacey, *Arms, Men and Governments*, pp. 224–227, 234, 237–239, 245–247. Montgomery on asking Simonds whether he wished McNaughton to visit received the reply, "For God's sake keep him away." While Stacey is of the opinion that McNaughton had a perfect right to visit, he admits he probably showed poor

judgment in choosing such an inopportune time to do so. For the most thorough treatment of McNaughton's removal, see Ibid., pp. 231–245.

22. Stacey, *Six Years*, p. 252 and *The Victory Campaign*, pp. 30–40, 166; RG 24, Vol. 13,710, WD GS 2 Cdn Corps, Artillery Trg Instr No. 1 of 8 June 1943, WD GS 2 Cdn Corps Director's Comments [Grizzly II], and Comments on Director's Notes Exercise "Link," 26 October 1943; and RG 24, Vol. 9792, Exercise "Link" Report of Senior Umpire 2 Cdn Corps, 20 September 1943.

23. RG 24, Vol. 13,749, WD GS 2 CID 2 DS(G)/4–1–C–4 HQ 2 Cdn Div 9 February 1943 Exercise "Elm" Instructions and 2 DS(G) 4–1–0–4 GS 2 Cdn Div 1 August 1943 Exercise "Pickaxe" Instructions. "Elm" had as its object to exercise commanders in the approach march, deployment, and contact battle.

24. RG 24, Vol. 13,788, WD GS 4 CAD 4 Cdn Armd Div Trg Instr Number 16, dated 12 August 1943; and RG 24, Vol. 13,710 WD GS 2 Cdn Corps Director's Comments.

25. RG 24, Vol. 13,711, 2 Cdn Corps Weekly Progress Report to Canada, Week Ending 3 December 1943 of 4 December 1943; RG 24, Vol. 13,711, 2 Cdn Corps Trg Instr No 12 (Based on First Cdn Army Directive No 18) period 1 January 1944–31 March 1944 of 23 December 1943; RG 24, Vol. 13,750, 2 Cdn Inf Div Trg Instr No. 21 Period 1 January–31 March 1944 of 28 December 1943; RG 24, Vol. 13,788, WD GS 4 CAD 4 Cdn Armd Div Trg Instr Number 16, dated 12 August 1943 and 4 Cdn Armd Div Trg Instr Number 18 (Based on 2 Cdn Corps Trg Instr Number 12) period 1 January 1944–31 March 1944, dated 24 December 1943; RG 24, Vol. 13,750, WD GS 2CID Trg Instr No 24 of 22 April 1944; RG 24, Vol. 13,710 WD GS 2 Cdn Corps Director's Comments; and RG 24, Vol. 13,685, 1 Canadian Corps Training Instruction No. 31, Period 15 September–31 October 1943, dated 6 September 1943.

26. RG 24, Vol. 13,750, WD GS 2 CID 2 DS(G)/4–4–22 GS 2 Cdn Inf Div 14 February 1944 Report on 3 in Mortar Pls. Instances were brought to light where COs were still employing mortars in single detachments; in one instance training had even been undertaken where a detachment was sent out to train with a rifle company. All platoons were short of equipment and that of one battalion needed to be reorganized and trained for "one month free of duties."

27. MP, Vol. 161, Memorandum of Conversation General McNaughton—General Paget 1130 hrs, 17 June 1943.

28. Crerar had remarked of Stuart in 1941 that "he is not fit and if things get too strenuous he is liable to crack up"(CP, Vol. 1, Crerar to McNaughton, 4 March 1941).

29. Stacey, *Six Years*, pp. 221–229, *Victory Campaign*, pp. 29–31, *Date*, pp. 124–126, and *Arms, Men and Governments*, pp. 231–247, 426–427; and Nicholson, *Canadians in Italy*, pp. 340–344.

30. LHC, AP, 12/XI/4/61 Crerar interview by M. C. Long, November 1954.

31. Stacey, *Six Years*, p. 253.

32. Lt.-Gen. E. L. M. Burns, *General Mud: Memoirs of Two World Wars* (Toronto: Clarke, Irwin, 1970), pp. 118–119. Maj.-Gen. E. L. M. Burns departed the 2nd Division 10 January 1944 to take command of the 5th Armoured in Italy. Major-General F. F. Worthington left the 4th Division on 29 February 1944 and returned to Canada, where he served as GOC-in-C Pacific Command from 1 April 1945 to 22 January 1946 (Stacey, *Six Years*, pp. 417–419, 541–543).

Book Two

Half-Forgotten Summer

Three miles or so south of Caen the present-day tourist, driving down the arrow-straight road that leads to Falaise, sees immediately to his right a rounded hill crowned by farm buildings. If the traveler be Canadian, he would do well to stay the wheels at this point and cast his mind back to the events of 1944; for the apparently insignificant eminence is the Verrières Ridge. Well may the wheat and sugar-beet grow green and lush upon its gentle slopes, for in that now half-forgotten summer the best blood of Canada was freely poured out upon them.

C. P. Stacey, *The Victory Campaign*

Chapter 7

The Imprint of Doctrine

The creation of an effective military force depends upon more than the provision of adequate resources, the building of advanced weapons, or the availability of manpower. Military forces must be organized, equipped, and trained properly. Doctrine is the substance that binds them together and makes them effective.

Robert Allan Doughty, *The Seeds of Disaster*[1]

The First Canadian Army that fought in Normandy was also the last great British imperial army. It is impossible therefore to look upon Canadian operations during that half-forgotten summer in strictly national terms. The common image of prairie boys temporarily downing plows to take up arms against an odious enemy overseas, returning triumphantly home once the job was done, is inevitably incomplete. Though no formal alliance existed between Britain and Canada, the forces of both nations were more closely integrated than those of the NATO allies today. Canadian and British formations were completely interchangeable and their artillery and staff systems perfectly gloved. It follows, then, that a better understanding of Canadian army operations beyond the bridgehead can be gleaned by examining, however briefly, previous British Commonwealth experience in fighting the Germans. To put it more bluntly, Canadian army operations in Norman fields had an African genesis. In the course of this chapter the doctrinal implications of this facet will be examined and the related factors of enemy and equipment touched upon.

As the way an army fights is a function of its training, the importance of doctrine—that is, the body of corporate knowledge officially approved to be taught—cannot be overemphasized. Loosely defined as the "fundamental principles by which military forces guide their actions in support of objectives,"[2] doctrine has traditionally affected not only training, but army organization, equipment, and employment as well. Given the rather complex relationship of these elements plus the accident and chance of the battlefield, however, doctrine has of necessity always tended to be dynamic. Indeed, it was only through doctrinal change and refinement, thanks largely to the concerted efforts of Brooke, Montgomery, and Paget, that British arms were ultimately able to stand up to German forces in the field. From 1940 onward, the War Office published a series of pamphlets, *Notes from Theatres of War* and *Current Reports From Overseas*, that contained tactical accounts, practical hints, and lessons drawn from actual combat. The Canadian Army, as it naturally embraced British doctrine, published *Canadian Army Training Memoranda* that reproduced material from *Current Reports* and British *Army Training Memoranda*.[3]

Between Dunkirk and the summer of 1944, a particular Commonwealth style of war fighting emerged. Initially, with the eyes of the non–Germanic world riveted upon the tank after the Battle of France, the tendency was to neglect or downgrade the value of artillery and infantry. It is true, of course, that Allied artillery in 1940 had failed to carry out its role, the vast array of towed field guns having been rendered impotent by Stuka action and the fast-moving pace of German panzers. The rapid collapse of the French front, moreover, seems to have been precipitated by gunners passing despondent messages over their efficient communication links.[4] Events in France also convinced many that fighting by divisions was too unwieldy and slow. A committee headed by Gen. Sir William H. Bartholomew to investigate the lessons of operations in Flanders subsequently recommended basing the tactical handling of the division on a brigade group of all arms, "the lowest self-contained fighting formation."[5] The problem was that while this may have yielded a handier, more mobile grouping, it involved "penny packeting" tanks, engineers, and especially artillery within the division.[6]

The practice of permanently allotting artillery regiments to brigades unfortunately undermined the system for massing artillery fire. The divisional artillery adviser, the CRA, now came to be regarded as redundant. A movement also developed to abolish the CCRA (Commander Corps, Royal Artillery) whose similar function at corps level had also eroded. Whereas before Dunkirk the CCRA had under him a commander replete with headquarters, staff, and communications to effect tactical control of corps medium artillery, after 1940 he had to perform all these functions himself. This naturally posed a dilemma as the CCRA was first and foremost responsible to his corps commander for all artillery matters including air defense. By leaving the corps headquarters for the medium headquarters to command guns, however, he lost the necessary contact with the latter to enable him to fulfill his principal task. The result was that in most corps, the medium and reinforcing heavy artillery was parceled out to divisions whose CRAs, looked upon as staff officers, continued the process of decentralization down to brigade. As might be expected in such circumstances, when one brigade of a division was attacking or defending against attack, none of the guns of the others could be switched to its support. The unpardonable sin of letting guns sit idle much of the time was thus committed over and over again.[7]

In the Home Forces, all of this ceased in 1941 with Exercise "Bumper," which saw artillery command and control turn into a shambles. When regrouping of divisions between corps took place on one occasion, all the reserve artillery in one army inadvertently ended up within one corps, and, unfortunately, in the wrong place. As a result of "Bumper," the artillery situation was restored. Commanders of reserve artillery formations were reintroduced, and the positions of CCRAs and CRAs buttressed within the artillery chain of command, which remained inviolate. At the same time, infantry commanders were left in no doubt as to their ultimate responsibility for fire planning. Significantly, much of this was due to the influence of Montgomery who, convinced of the correctness of orthodox artillery doctrine, had once stated that "the business of Gunner C.O.s was first to train their regiments, and then to train infantry brigadiers to use them properly."[8] As previously mentioned, he also saw the infantry company commander-FOO relationship, so important in building up the detailed fire plan, as the key to quickly overcoming organized enemy resistance encountered during decentralized offensive mobile operations.[9]

Largely through the efforts of Brigadier H. J. Parham, the Royal Artillery was, after Dunkirk, technically able to perfect a highly efficient gunfire control system capable of producing, in a matter of minutes, a massive blow to deal with such emergencies. Unlike German dive bombers, it could also attack roughly the same targets by day or night in all kinds of weather. As Parham determined, improved radio communications and circumvention of the normal hierarchical chain of command permitted quicker responses to requests for gunfire. The pursuit of extreme accuracy was in these instances forsaken in favor of bringing overwhelming fire rapidly to bear. Under the Parham, or "Uncle" target system, designated artillery officers were empowered to order the fire of all guns within range. To a call prefaced by "Uncle target! Uncle target! Uncle target!," the entire divisional artillery would respond. Likewise, "Mike" called for a regimental shoot, "Victor" corps, "William" army, and "Yoke" AGRA.

When this system fully evolved by mid–1943, gunner commanders were integrated at every level and linked together by an intricate radio network. Along the front, junior troop commanders serving as FOOs occupied a series of OPs. Initially, special OPs manned by majors or lieutenant-colonels, "CRA's representatives," were superimposed upon this layout in critical areas and authorized to fire the full weight of divisional artillery. These gradually withered away, however, as troop and battery commanders (as "CO's representatives") proved equally capable of controlling massed gun fire. Eventually, artillery batteries, each of two four-gun troops, were intimately affiliated with armored regiments and infantry battalions. Artillery regiments in their turn were affiliated with brigades, the gunner CO acting as artillery adviser to the brigade commander from whom he was inseparable. At higher levels, the CRA and CCRA, ever wrestling with the thorny problem of forward displacement, commanded the movement and allotment of guns, for it was a tenet of the Parham system that every gun within range be laid, loaded and ready to respond to a request for fire.[10]

Behind the divisional and corps artilleries stood the AGRA. These were reinforcing army artillery brigades, the handling of which was practiced for the first time on "Spartan." Of no fixed composition, they usually consisted of three medium and one or two field and heavy regiments in proportions considered most suitable to the mission assigned. To gain maximum effect from the longer range and greater throw weight of medium and heavy guns, they were best employed as single-fire entities and not in "penny packets" along a front. In theory, AGRA were organized "for the purpose of giving an army commander a wide measure of flexibility in the rapid allotment of artillery resources to the right place at the right time"; in practice, they were almost invariably used as affiliated corps troops to reinforce divisional artilleries. With CCRAs each retaining a basic element that included an antitank regiment, a light antiaircraft regiment, and a survey regiment, a corps could expect to be strengthened by one or more AGRAs for bombardment or counter battery tasks. In anticipation that the requirement for reinforcing artillery would increase directly as the enemy attempted to stabilize the battle, an AGRA or one of its medium regiments might further be placed in support of a division during fluid operations. Always, however, the guiding principle was that "decentralization of resources . . . not preclude their concentration in the greatest possible strength when required."[11]

The allotment and movement of AGRA, so important in smashing unexpected resistance or repelling counterattacks, warranted careful consideration. As the overriding factor was that gunfire be concentrated at the right place at the right time, premature deployment had to be avoided. Filling up roads with a large number of guns for which an ample supply of ammunition might not be immediately forthcoming had also to be balanced against leaving forward formations room to maneuver. On the other hand, it was desirable to get guns well forward to minimize movement later during battle. Here the role of the BRA was important, for CCRAs had to be early advised of how many AGRA they would have at their disposal so that they, in turn, could warn CRAs of the number of AGRA regiments that would have to be accommodated within their respective divisional areas. Obviously, because of the potential for confusion, advance planning that incorporated simple and straightforward moves was vital. In situations of uncertainty, AGRA that were not decentralized were as a rule held well back; when conditions were better known, AGRA reconnaissance parties were thrown well forward, often with leading divisions. In the event that divisions were no longer able to make headway, the CCRA resumed responsibility for counterbattery and bombardment operations, the divisional battle merging into a more centralized corps effort.[12]

Turning now from a mainly artillery perspective, it is instructive to examine briefly the impact of the war in the Western Desert where an associated doctrinal saga involving all arms was played out. Here the jejune nature of the arena, plus the perception that German actions in France had validated the precepts of the radical all-tank school, tended to give armored forces center stage. This was most pronounced in the British case where a tactical division reflecting social stratification further characterized armored doctrine. The 1930s decision to mechanize the cavalry had, in fact, left the Royal Tank Regiment (RTR, formerly the Royal Tank Corps) exclusively responsible for infantry support. The more numerous cavalry regiments, on the other hand, continued in the traditional reconnaissance and independent mobile role. In general, most of the RTR units were grouped in army tank brigades of slower, heavily armored "I" tanks, while the cavalry, equipped with lighter, faster "cruisers," were assigned to armored divisions. Unfortunately, for reasons related to tank design, training, suspicion of misemployment, and even snobbery, armored brigades often viewed the infantry support role with a degree of distaste.[13]

The spectacular victory by Lieutenant-General Richard O'Connor over the Italians at Beda Fomm in early 1941 seemed nonetheless to confirm the soundness of the foregoing doctrine. The economy of force practice of employing "Jock" (after Lieutenant-Colonel J. C. Campbell, VC) columns of a battery of field artillery, occasionally some tanks, and a company of motorized infantry also appeared valid. With the advent of what became the *Deutsches Afrika Korps* under Lieutenant-General Erwin Rommel, however, reverses and doubts began to plague British arms. Confidence in equipment eroded, even though German tanks possessed no appreciable technological advantage over British variants at the time. In fact, Matilda and Valentine "I" tanks could withstand all enemy tank guns at but the shortest ranges. The two-pounder gun with which all British tanks were equipped and the 37 mm on the U.S. Stuart were both, moreover, slightly superior in penetrating power to the short-barrelled 50 mm on the Mark III panzer and the low-velocity 75 mm on the Mark IV. The Grant tank, which arrived in May 1942, could with its 75 mm sponson gun also penetrate the thickened front plate of the Mark III and IV at 650 yards, while its own frontal armor could stand up to the long-barreled 50 mm at 1,000 yards.[14]

The real secret of German success in armored warfare was the antitank gun. The easily concealed 50 mm *Panzerabwehrkanone* (Pak) 38 delivered a far greater wallop than the short 50 mm on the Mark III and proved to be one of the most effective weapons in the desert. It was backed up by the formidable dual-purpose 88 mm *Flugzeugabwehrkanone* (Flak), though initially not in large number, and later by the highly effective 75 mm Pak 40. The often overlooked fact was that the Germans actually *preferred* to destroy tanks not with relatively feeble tank armaments, but with antitank guns. Since British tanks fired no high explosive shells, this gave them a special edge, the more so because the short 50 mm on the Mark IIIH and the short 75 mm on the Mark IV were both capable of hurling high explosive to suppress targets other than armor. In the 75 mm of the Grant, of course, the British at last acquired the capability to fire a useful high-explosive shell at enemy antitank guns. Unfortunately, the requirement to engage targets with this lower sponson-mounted armament, as opposed to the turret-mounted 37 mm, meant unnecessarily exposing most of the tank to destructive enemy fire.[15]

Although the two-pounder antitank gun could penetrate enemy armor at normal battle ranges of about 800 yards, it was easily suppressed by the Mark IV short 75 mm, which could throw a 14-pound high explosive shell accurately over distances up to 3,000 yards. When mounted "portee" on an unarmored wheeled vehicle, the two-pounder proved too vulnerable. This naturally left Eighth Army infantry relatively powerless against enemy armor. Only after April 1942, when the six-pounder antitank gun arrived in sufficient quantities, was it able to meet German panzers on something approaching equal terms. In the meantime, two-pounder limitations in the antitank role resulted in artillery 25-pounders almost always being deployed primarily as tank killers, which meant that they were frequently unavailable to provide concentrated indirect artillery fire. The perceived inadequacy of the two-pounder main armament on Crusader cruiser and Matilda and Valentine "I" tanks at the same time led British armor to seek safety in dispersion. A vicious circle now developed as the vulnerable infantry, to compensate for the dissipation of artillery support, sought the protection of armor, which as a consequence often found itself forced to fight when it should have evaded. Such was the cycle that gave rise to the charge that the two-pounder was the weapon that almost cost the British the war.[16]

Given such circumstances, it is not surprising that British armor began to look upon the infantry as a tactical liability, while the latter became embittered at what they perceived to be the failure of armor to support them. According to one New Zealand brigadier, at a certain stage there developed "throughout the Eighth Army . . . a most intense distrust, almost hatred, of . . . [friendly] armour."[17] In large part this situation arose because of doctrinal differences, which were no doubt exacerbated by the distinction made between "I" tanks for infantry support and "cruiser" models intended to do what their descriptive naval term implied. At the same time, old-fashioned thinking prevailed. "The British, reckoning that their infantry should be able to take on anything with the bayonet," charged Major-General Francis Tuker of the 4th Indian Division, "kept on setting theirs out for Rommel's combine harvester."

British cruiser armor meanwhile, unlike the versatile and flexible German panzers that performed any task demanded of them, tended to believe it had but one role: that of a free-ranging exploitation force. Again in Tuker's view, "armoured commanders were still imbued with the idea of the concentrated cavalry charge, the *arme blanche*, the weapon of physical shock." During the battle of First Alamein in July 1942, which was won mainly by six-pounder antitank action and concentrated artillery fire, a New Zealand division request for tank support was met with the response that the 1st Armoured Division "had been trained to act independently and not in close cooperation with infantry." Despite such superciliousness, however, the weight of *Materialschlact* had already begun to countervail against the idea of runaway armored victory, which the earlier glittering successes of *Blitzkrieg* still tended to foster. More and more, battles between roughly equal and determined opponents assumed the form of hard pounding.[18]

The predilection of British armor for tank versus tank actions naturally played into enemy hands, for the basis of German tactics lay in the combined action of all arms, including most significantly the aggressive deployment of camouflaged antitank guns. Whenever German armor encountered strong resistance, it could retire under their protection, often luring to them in the process unsuspecting British tanks, which after taking casualties from antitank fire could be subjected to counterattack by tanks. Rommel, to be sure, was quite content to let British tanks run themselves to death against his gun line. Indeed, it took British tank crews a very long time to realize that their tanks were actually being knocked out not by the more obvious panzers, but by deadly, unseen 50-mm Pak 38s from afar. Their initial reaction was to credit the German tank guns with more firepower and greater range than they possessed. The all tank school and cavalry concept, in short, foundered miserably before the theory of all-arms cooperation so effectively practiced by the Germans.[19]

The overbalanced British armored division of two armored brigades, each of three tank regiments and a motorized infantry battalion, plus a "pivot" or support group that included another infantry battalion, antitank and antiaircraft elements, and a 32-gun field regiment, never managed to fight as a single formation. While the armored brigades tended to act independently, the support group was more often than not left holding static positions or strongpoints that by themselves were useless. Even after the armored division was restructured in 1942 to comprise divisional troops and an armored and lorried infantry brigade (which reflected a better infantry-tank ratio of 4:3 in units), the fragmented style that marked British tactics since the introduction of "Jock Columns" persisted. Here again the vulnerability of infantry played its part. The armor, meanwhile, instead of calling on supporting artillery and infantry to help clear the way when its own 75-mm Shermans and self-propelled 105-mm howitzers proved unable to subdue German antitank guns, continued to engage in fruitless and costly piecemeal attacks. Ultimately, the defeat of armor caused the entire system to collapse.[20]

While Montgomery on taking over the Eighth Army expressed reservations about its general state of training, he harbored particular doubts about the armor, which he likened unto "the cavalry . . . hunting . . . the fox." At Alam Halfa, over the protests of the GOC 7th Armoured Division, he refused to consider unloosing the armor against Rommel, who actually hoped that British armor would indeed attack. Stealing a page from his adversary, Montgomery instead ordered Lieutenant-General Brian Horrocks, 13 Corps, to dig in his tanks and antitank guns on Alam Halfa ridge and arrange to lure the Germans onto it in "a case of dog eat rabbit." Montgomery's growing realization that his armor was not up to the task being asked of it additionally prompted him to revise his plan of battle for Second Alamein but two and a half weeks before D-Day. One of the most striking features of that 12-day slogging match, which was closer run than commonly supposed, was the lackluster performance of his armor as compared with that of his infantry and artillery.

That Montgomery was able to identify this operational limitation among his troops stands to his credit as a commander, for it most probably made the difference between victory and defeat in both battles, notwithstanding the 2:1 numerical superiority of Commonwealth forces. Lack of an armored element suitably integrated within the army as a whole further explains why success was not exploited to the extent it perhaps could have been.[21] Armored shortcomings were almost certainly perpetuated in doctrine, since Desert War experience, whatever its validity in other theaters, continued to attract the attention of Home Forces. As late as April 1943 in Tunisia, the armored brigades of the home-trained 6th Armoured and desert-trained 1st Armoured divisions both launched attacks unsupported by artillery and infantry vainly against what was but a last-ditch German gun line defense. Not surprisingly, such repulses and their associated losses had long before begun to sap the dash and confidence of many British armored formations, some of which by Second Alamein were tending to display extreme caution rather than the romantic élan of a previous military age.[22]

Doctrinally, this change could be seen in the virtual disappearance of the originally emphasized first echelon in the tank-infantry assault. As explained in Chapter 5, the first echelon was an all-tank array that, with the support of artillery, was to precede the infantry onto an objective at best tank speed and momentarily dominate it until the arrival of the latter arm. The enemy, as one instruction put it, was to be demoralized by artillery, dominated by tanks, and killed by infantry. The defeating power of deep minefields and

Map 7.1
The Montgomery Touch

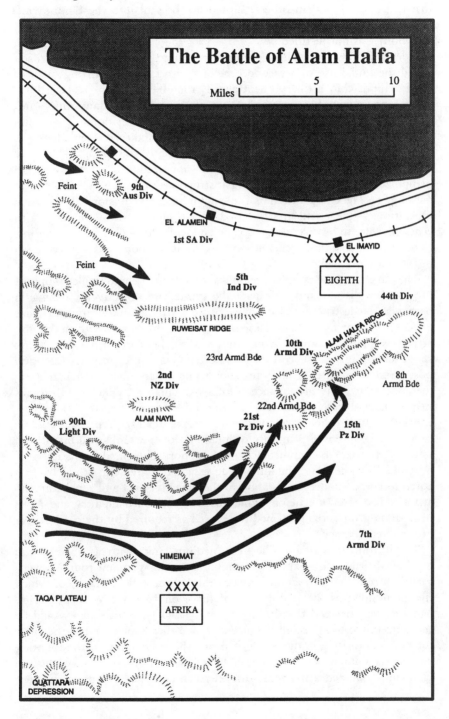

The Battle of Alam Halfa

Miles 0   5   10

Feint

9th
Aus Div

EL ALAMEIN

1st SA Div

EL IMAYID

XXXX
EIGHTH

Feint

5th
Ind Div

44th Div

RUWEISAT RIDGE

10th
Armd Div

ALAM HALFA RIDGE

23rd Armd Bde

8th
Armd Bde

2nd
NZ Div

22nd Armd Bde

ALAM NAYIL

21st
Pz Div

15th
Pz Div

90th
Light Div

7th
Armd Div

HIMEIMAT

TAQA PLATEAU

XXXX
AFRIKA

QUATTARA
DEPRESSION

other obstacles protected by antitank guns, however, led many to conclude that tanks "no less than others, should not be sent into the Unknown." Where information was "not positive or lacking," it was decreed, "a First Ech[elon] was not justified."[23]

Indeed, for assaults against prepared positions, the armored corps itself urged the initial use of a second echelon, with tanks supporting infantry from behind while artillery "neutralized" the objective. The rearward position for armor was recommended as tanks were "blind at any time" and, if leading, could not "see what the infantry . . . [were] doing"; tank fire from flanks and hull-down positions (all but gun and turret defiladed) was also thought to be "more effective than actual physical support."[24] Further direction on "the construction of echelons" appeared in a 21st Army Group pamphlet based on Army Training Instruction No. 2 of May 1943. According to "The Cooperation of Tanks with Infantry Divisions in Offensive Operations," the terms first, second, third, and fourth with respect to echelons were to be discontinued. The tank-infantry attack was henceforth to be conducted in three echelons only—assault, support, and reserve—each of two or more waves.[25]

The purpose of the assault echelon was to advance behind artillery support "to assault, disrupt and dominate the immediate objective," seeking in particular the destruction of any surviving enemy antitank weapons. Again, experience from fighting in Tunisia confirmed that, even with maximum artillery support, assault echelons composed solely of armor moving at tank speed seldom proved successful. More often than not, enemy machine-gun posts came to life after artillery fire supporting the assault echelon had lifted; these served to delay the advance of follow-on infantry, which left the tanks tied to their objectives and terribly vulnerable to counterattack. For these reasons, assault echelons in deliberate attacks against prepared positions came to be composed primarily of infantry alone or tanks and infantry in ratios appropriate to circumstances. The support echelon, also characterized by tanks "shepherding" infantry as an essential ingredient, stood by prepared to complete the subjugation of the objective area and repel counterattacks. The reserve echelon, which usually contained infantry and tanks in separate groupings, remained to be used as required by the commander of the overall attack.[26]

The introduction of the Sherman medium tank, with its 75-mm gun capable of firing high-explosive, smoke, or armor-piercing rounds, eventually blurred the distinction between the cruiser and "I" tank, of which the Churchill was the last. In a conference on 13 January 1944, in fact, Montgomery decreed that henceforth only two types of tanks would be recognized: the light reconnaissance tank and the "capital" tank, the latter category comprising both the Sherman and the heavier Churchill mounting either a six-pounder or 75-mm gun. There was to be no difference between Churchill-equipped army tank and Sherman-equipped armored brigades;

Figure 7.1
Three-Echelon Formation

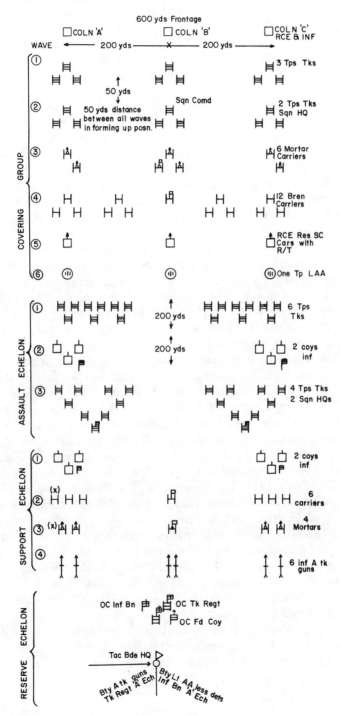

all were to be prepared to work with infantry and to be employed as main battle tanks in any role.[27] The armored division also had to be prepared to fight its way forward, even to the extent of making its own penetrations in breakthrough operations as infantry-created gaps, often incomplete, invited counterattack. The division's infantry brigade was to follow-up the armored brigade, "taking over and holding, as a series of pivots, ground won by the armoured brigade."[28]

The "pivot" as practiced within the 4th Canadian Armoured Division amounted to an all-round defensive position or stongpoint, usually assumed on ground vital to the enemy, around which armored elements could maneuver or, if need be, within which they could retire for protection. An infantry brigade pivot bristling with antitank guns backed up by artillery defensive fire could expect to occupy an equilateral triangular area roughly 1,800 to 2,400 yards.[29] Maintaining and restoring mobility to the tanks was also an infantry task. If armor was held up by antitank fire or difficult terrain and its maneuver restricted, infantry was to forge ahead, making up for lack of sustained fighting capability through speed of action. When advancing in open country where it was generally held that armor would lead by day and infantry by night, most attacks by the latter were foreseen as taking place in "half-light" (before last light) or at night. Obviously, the intent was to advance round the clock. The key areas that received emphasis in the training of infantry brigades in armored divisions were thus "first speed, and secondly night work."[30]

Canadian armor, though removed from the vagaries of British military social strictures, trained in accordance with the foregoing doctrinal developments. The 4th Canadian Armoured Division in the months most immediately preceding D-Day drew attention to "The Cooperation of Tanks with Infantry Divisions in Offensive Operations," describing it as "recent" and making it the subject of study. Army Training Instruction No. 2, "The Co-operation of Infantry and Tanks," had in the meantime also been published as a Special Supplement to *Canadian Army Training Memorandum* Number 28 of July 1943. The message implicit in all these post-Alamein documents, however, was that "against prepared defenses the tank cannot normally lead the attack and put the grateful infantryman on the ground. The mine and the obstacle dictate the order of events."[31] The 2 Canadian Corps Training Instruction No. 12 for the period ending 31 March 1944, while urging the study of "The Cooperation of Tanks with Infantry Divisions in Offensive Operations," further directed that "the clear distinction between ... SHERMAN equipped ... and ... CHURCHILL equipped ... [armoured brigades] be stressed."[32]

The significance of this direction was that, despite Montgomery's decree, Sherman and Churchill brigades trained differently in infantry-tank cooperation. Indeed, as stated in "The Cooperation of Tanks with Infantry

Divisions in Offensive Operations," the characteristics of the lighter armored Sherman, easy prey to the 50-mm Pak, "made it clear that... [it could] not carry out the infantry tank role in the deliberate attack." The doctrine writers recommended accordingly that Sherman brigades remain "backers-up to the assaulting troops and not, as infantry tanks, partners in the assault." Shermans could best support infantrymen on foot by sitting "back in hull or turret down positions" using "their very effective high explosive guns and, to a limited extent, their machine guns" to gnaw through a defensive position. While admitting that "gnawing [wa]s a slow methodical process," the authors insisted that this was, in "fact and not opinion," the best way of handling Shermans in the infantry support role. This meant, of course, that the hapless infantryman was once again left setting the pace in the face of organized resistance.[33]

Fortunately, the introduction of the six-pounder, a weapon superior to the 50-mm Pak 38, enabled the infantry division not only to stand its ground against panzers, but to defeat strong attacks inflicting heavy losses. At Medenine, Tunisia, on 6 March 1943 the tremendous power of a concealed antitank defense disposed in depth was demonstrated by three divisions of 30 Corps. Here the British held their fire until the last moment to entice the Germans into a "killing zone," and the latter uncharacteristically obliged by attacking frontally with 100 tanks supported by infantry, artillery, and aircraft. The carefully coordinated defensive fire of over 200 field and medium guns, including new and powerful 17-pounders, broke up numerous German assaults causing heavy infantry casualties. Of 52 German tanks lost, no less than 43 were destroyed by infantry six-pounders that were dug in but unprotected by minefields or wire. After the Battle of Medenine, the "Valmy of the antitank gunner," infantry morale was described as "being absolutely top of the line."[34]

Within a month the offensive capability of infantry was also spectacularly demonstrated by a remarkable feat of arms at Wadi Akarit. This battle Simonds had the opportunity to observe. During the moonless night of 5 April 1943, the 4th Indian Division under the superb tactical command of Major-General Tuker captured the Zouai-Fatnassa massif in a silent attack. Painstakingly rehearsed on sand models, with artillery support planned in detail but on a contingency basis only, the operation was a classic example of an infiltration battle, the successful outcome of which depended upon the training and skill of individual platoon and section commanders. The effect of this action, which cost the 4th Indian Division relatively modest casualties, was to turn an Axis force of some 38 battalions and 200 guns out of an exceedingly strong defensive position. Unfortunately, the Battle of Wadi Akarit that "had been won single-handed several hours before the formal attack began" was now compromised. The armored exploitation force for reasons related to command and control arrangements failed to arrive on time; when elements finally did appear they were decisively checked by no more than three 88-mm antitank guns for lack of artillery suppressive fire.[35]

That not all Commonwealth infantry were trained to such high standards is evident from a 21st Army Group letter dated July 1943, which charged that "the average soldier is not as skilled in the use of his personal weapons as the German or American soldier."[36] Tuker had himself observed on "the many examples [in late 1942] of the limitations of the battle training . . . given to infantry and armoured formations and even . . . individuals in the United Kingdom." He also noted "the predilection that some infantry commanders had for the barrage," which to his mind cast away "their most effective weapon—surprise." Although the barrage proved especially useful in gapping minefields and when enemy dispositions were not precisely known, it may have discouraged the detailed search and study of ground, while encouraging the selection of linear objectives. Another problem with the barrage was that it sometimes outran the infantry it was shielding, leaving them vulnerable to enemy pockets of resistance that inevitably survived. Accordingly, troops had to learn to "lean into" the barrage, which often assumed the nature of a "crutch" that militated against the ability of infantry to use its own weapons to fight its way forward.[37]

According to Field-Marshal Lord Carver, it was in the attack that the Germans inevitably proved more effective than the British. Tuker attributed their capacity to execute swift and concentrated actions directly to all-arms cooperation, "the outcome of constant training, of the perfecting of a battle drill which [wa]s not learnt on the square."[38] Ironically, during Infantry Training Conference No. 1 at the School of Infantry, Barnard Castle, in April 1944, most delegates expressed reservations about "Battle Drill generally." While accepting that "Parade Square Battle Drill [wa]s required in the initial stages of tr[ainin]g . . . [they were] afraid that the hard and fast rules concerning the sequence of orders m[ight] tend to make Pl[atoon] com[man]d[ers] forget to appreciate ground and think that every situation calls for only one of three responses, i.e. right flanking, left flanking or pincer movement." Drills previously taught for attacking strong points, woods clearing, tank hunting, attacks off the line of march, and reorganization were collectively denounced as "too rigid."[39]

Of associated significance was the conclusion that too much stress had been placed upon attack technique to the neglect of the defense. The speed and power of German counterattacks naturally served to reinforce this concern, especially as it pertained to retaining captured ground through rapid reorganization drills. Since such "firm basing" consumed proportionally more time in action than attacking, the consensus was that defense be taught before attack, rather than afterward as previously. Junior officers were also to be made aware that "surprisingly few Huns [were killed] . . . by attacking them. The big 'killings' [we]re made when they attack[ed] . . . unsuccessfully." Indeed, with well-organized and rehearsed fire plans and counter-attacks, a defender could even yearn for the Germans to attack. The advantages of reverse slope defense, the increased importance of snipers, and the desirability of devoting much more attention to the handling of unit mortars—each of which was supposedly first and best appreciated by the Germans—received additional emphasis. Curiously, the school's stated object with respect to "Battle Discipline" was to "acknowledge and over-come the amazing lethargy of the British soldier."[40]

The soldier within the fighting section, of course, constituted the guts of the infantry. In response to a query by First Canadian Army delegates concerning section fighting structure, the school's position was that the war establishment of two NCOs and eight men was sound. Spokesmen also suggested that, without being dogmatic, the division of this number into three fire and movement groups would yield tactical advantages. With section battle strength rarely expected to exceed one NCO and six men, however, school representatives advocated a normal deployment organi-zation of two groups: a "Bren [light machine gun] Group" of two men controlled by the section commander; and a "Rifle Group" of four men, including the second-in-command. For those not infrequent occasions when battle strength ran to but one NCO and four men, the recommendation was one group. As demonstrated in a mock battalion attack through a depth of 700 yards from front to rear, leading sections moved in either "two tight little g[rou]ps or blobs of three and four men each." The blob formation supposedly helped "overcome the feeling of loneliness . . . [of] the individual soldier," facilitated control, and enabled the blobs "to break out in open order speedily if they c[a]me under aimed fire." Not surprisingly, all agreed that the artillery fire plan had to be made to conform practically to infantry movement, especially with respect to controlling barrage fire.[41]

Obviously, there existed a conflict between the barrage and battle drill approach. More often than not, because enemy locations were rarely ever precisely known, attacking infantry followed a creeping barrage. A battalion in the assault usually deployed with two companies forward and two in depth. Its integral six three-inch mortars, 13 Bren gun carriers, and six six-pounder towed antitank guns provided support; if required, this was but-tressed by heavier machine guns and mortars from a machine-gun unit. Since handheld PIATs were only effective against armor at short range, it was imperative that six-pounders moved forward quickly during consoli-dation to ward off enemy counterattacks. In contrast, Canadians in North Africa had already witnessed with some fascination the German "pepper potting" method of infiltration attack. This involved light machine-gun groups of four to five men filtering forward, one supporting another, all aimed at sowing confusion and getting at least one gun in the rear of their objective. Liberal automatic weapon and mortar fire intended to attack morale enhanced the effect of these "confusion tactics."[42]

On a much higher plane, Crerar had, during his February 1943 visit to North Africa, already been advised by Montgomery that infantry divisions "should comprise *at least* one half the force of any Army." To overcome prepared enemy positions protected by minefields up to 4,000 yards deep, which process encompassed "break-in," "crumbling," "breakthrough," and pursuit stages, the "solid killing" had perforce to be done by infantry in strength. Once broken into, defensive systems could only be reduced by infantry, most efficiently operating in a series of thrusts along different axes. Ideally, armored divisions then passed through "gaps" to hold panzer divisions at bay, not attack them, while this process continued. "Throughout all attacks," emphasized Montgomery, "there has stood the need for Inf[antry]." In his view, the "new model" division of one armored and two infantry brigades, which was introduced in October 1942 for the purpose of making infantry division commanders familiar with armor, was not operationally satisfactory. In the decisive "fight to kill," there was no substitute for the "power of the well-trained Inf[antry] Div[ision]" of three infantry brigades. To Montgomery, as Crerar duly noted, "the foundation of attack" was the infantry and artillery program, with the latter the "secret of success."[43]

Given the time lag that invariably prevailed between battlefield action and the adoption of doctrine, it is clear that Canadian fighting style in Normandy largely reflected the experiences of the Desert and Tunisia. The lessons of Italy, though disseminated, do not appear to have been as deeply embedded or, for that matter, always relevant. If independent armored maneuver had become suspect before, it was hardly resuscitated in the struggle up the boot of Italy, which became a wearisome trial of "one more river, one more mountain." Described as a "dreadful . . . bloody affair, a war of attrition," the Italian campaign assumed an infantry-artillery character faintly reminiscent of the Western Front in the Great War. Unceasing rain during the winter months turned the countryside into a quagmire, making it tricky or impossible for tanks to maneuver off roads. Difficulty in spotting antitank guns over the next rise, moreover, often forced tank commanders to get out on foot and lead their armored charges safely onto new fire positions. As Canadians discovered, even unsolicited armored divisions like their 5th were not wanted, there "already . . . [being] as much armour in the Mediterranean as . . . [could] usefully [be] employ[ed] in Italy." Tactical demand for more infantry was so great, in fact, that British armored divisions, and later the 5th Canadian Armoured, were restructured on the basis of one armored and two infantry brigades.[44]

Of course the undiminished importance of infantry had been amply demonstrated in fighting in Russia and Asia as well as in North Africa and Italy.[45] Unfortunately, this was not to the advantage of either the British or Canadian armies, both of which shared an abiding fear of not being able to sustain sufficient foot soldiers in the field. The third attempt by the

British Army to rescue France was likely to be its last, a critical factor never lost sight of by Montgomery in his approach to the conduct of operations in Normandy. Indeed, as Russell Weigley so perceptively suggested, the very existence of the First Canadian Army with its mixed composition of Canadians, Britons, and Poles was a clear indication that the bottom of Britain's manpower barrel had been reached. After it, there would be no more British armies.[46]

NOTES

1. Robert Allan Doughty, *The Seeds of Disaster: The Development of French Army Doctrine 1919–1939* (Hamden: Archon, 1985), pp. x–xi.

2. Supplement 3, *Army Glossary*. See also Doughty's *The Evolution of US Army Tactical Doctrine, 1946–76* (Fort Leavenworth: Combat Studies Institute, 1979), pp. 1–2, 49. Doctrine has also been described as "the definition of the aim of military operations; the study of weapons and other resources and the lessons of history, leading to the deductions of the correct strategic and tactical principles on which to base both training and the conduct of war—*Sans doctrine les textes ne sont rien*" [Shelford Bidwell and Dominick Graham, *Fire-Power: British Army Weapons and Theories of War, 1904–1945* (London: Allen and Unwin, 1982), p. 2]. Another put it more simply: "Military doctrine is guidance for conduct of battle approved by the highest military authority" [Timothy T. Lupfer, *The Dynamics of Doctrine: The Changes in German Tactical Doctrine During the First World War* (Fort Leavenworth: Combat Studies Institute, 1981), p. vii].

3. For insight into the evolution of British doctrine, see Bidwell and Graham, *Fire-Power*, pp. 227–240. *Canadian Army Training Memoranda* (*CATM*) were widely read. DHist 113.3R4003 (D1) Research and Information Section, Vol. III, "Special Reports," Special Report Number 167, 9 January 1945, "*C.A.T.M.*" Whether doctrine should drive or merely reflects technological development remains a much debated point. As in the opinion of this writer the latter is probably the reality, Clausewitz's stress upon theory as study, because a positive doctrine is unattainable, makes great sense [Carl von Clausewitz, *On War*, ed./trans. Michael Howard and Peter Paret (Princeton, N.J.: Princeton University Press, 1976), pp. 140–141.].

4. Shelford Bidwell, *Gunners at War: A Tactical Study of the Royal Artillery in the Twentieth Century* (London: Arms and Armour, 1970), pp. 132–133; and John A. English, *On Infantry* (New York: Praeger, 1984), pp. 80, 124.

5. Tactical Doctrine Retrieval Cell, Staff College Camberly, "The Bartholomew Report," Bartholomew Committee Final Report (1940). The Bartholomew Committee included, besides the chairman, Major-Generals C. C. Malden and N. M. S. Irwin and Brigadiers D. G. Watson and W. C. Holden (three infantrymen and two gunners). It also recommended that divisions have their own armored reconnaissance units and battalions their own antitank platoons. It further called for all troops when outflanked or surrounded to continue to hold out from alternate positions.

6. Ronald Lewin, *Man of Armour: A Study of Lieut.-General Vyvyan Pope and the Development of Armoured Warfare* (London: Leo Cooper, 1976), pp. 127–128, 143–144; and Bidwell, *Gunners*, p. 133.

7. Bidwell, *Gunners*, pp. 132–136; Brig. A. L. Pemberton, *The Second World*

War, 1939–1945, Army, The Development of Artillery Tactics and Equipment (London: War Office, 1951), pp. 118–119; and (for details of artillery problems) Bidwell and Graham, *Fire-Power,* pp. 195–201.

8. Bidwell, *Gunners,* pp. 132–137

9. Nigel Hamilton, *Monty* Vol. I: *The Making of a General 1887–1942* (Sevenoaks, U.K.: Hodder and Stoughton, 1984), pp. 434–435.

10. Bidwell, *Gunners,* pp. 138–144; Pemberton, *Artillery Tactics,* pp. 161–162, 169; and Bidwell and Graham, *Fire-Power,* pp. 199–201. The U.S. Army never trusted its forward observers to such a degree; they recommended, but never commanded, fire. As Bidwell and Graham point out, in the Great War artillery became highly scientific, mastering the arts of counterbattery and the "break-in" battle. The "Uncle" target system superseded neither accurate survey (which was essential in preparing large, map-predicted fire plans) nor the normal engagement of targets of opportunity or the registration of local fire plans by battery observers. It was simply a means of rapidly landing a hammer blow to repel a counterattack or smash unexpected resistance (Bidwell and Graham, *Fire-Power,* pp. 195–201).

11. McNaughton Papers (MP), Vol. 156, The Employment of Army Groups Royal Artillery and Excerpts from COHQ Monthly Infm Summary No. 4 Appendix "E" Handling of Divisional and Corps Artillery (less Anti-Tank and Anti-Aircraft) in Attack, 2 November 1943; Record Group (RG) 24, Vol. 9793, GHQ Exercise "Spartan" Comments by Commander-in-Chief Home Forces March 1943; Col. G. W. L. Nicholson, *The Gunners of Canada: A History of the Royal Regiment of Canadian Artillery,* Vol. II: *1919–1967* (Toronto: McClelland and Stewart, 1972) p. 111; and Bidwell and Graham, *Fire-Power,* p. 258. The advantages of regiments serving under the same commanders (CAGRA) and affiliating AGRA with formations was stressed. AGRA were almost called Royal Artillery Groups, but the acronym "RAG" was not preferred.

12. MP, Vol. 156, The Employment of Army Groups Royal Artillery and Excerpts from COHQ Monthly Infm Summary No 4 Appendix "E" Handling of Divisional and Corps Artillery (less Anti-Tank and Anti-Aircraft) in Attack, 2 November 1943. The CCRA was responsible for coordinating bombardment as well as counterbattery. He had no staff for fire planning, details of which were worked out by CRAs and AGRA commanders (CAGRA). The BRA was responsible for directing the coordination of artillery throughout the army and for advising the army commander in all artillery matters.

13. Kenneth Macksey, *The Royal Armoured Corps and its Predecessors 1914 to 1975* (Beaminster: Newton, 1983), pp. 58–60; FM Michael Carver, *Dilemmas of the Desert War: A New Look at the Libyan Campaign 1940–1942* (London: Batsford, 1986), pp. 14–15, 142–143; and Lt. Gen. Sir Gifford le Q. Martel, *Our Armoured Forces* (London: Faber and Faber, 1945), pp. 19–20, 50–51, 91. The political impossibility of disbanding the cavalry, according to Bidwell and Graham, had led to that "most mentally inert, unprofessional and reactionary group in the British army" gaining proprietary right to the tank. Social rather than tactical or military considerations also originally accounted for the wholesale conversion of the exclusive 60th Rifles and Rifle Brigade to the tank support role as "motorized" infantry. In their words, the cavalry simply "did not mix with lesser beings" (Bidwell and Graham, *Fire-Power,* p. 227). Though Hore-Belisha merged the Royal Tank Corps and the cavalry into one Royal Armoured Corps in 1939, Sir John Dill noted as CIGS in 1940 that

it was the practice of some cavalry regiments "to choose officers according to their income" (Macksey, *The Royal Armoured Corps*, pp. 11, 66, 119).

14. Field Marshal Sir Michael Carver, *Dilemmas of the Desert War: A New Look at the Libyan Campaign 1940–1942* (London: Batsford, 1986) pp. 15–16, 51–52, 68–69; John Wheldon, *Machine Age Armies* (London: Abelard-Schuman, 1968), pp. 87–88, 112–117, 222–225; Macksey, *The Royal Armoured Corps*, pp. 100–101, 106–107; and Maj.-Gen. Sir Howard Kippenberger, *Infantry Brigadier* (London: Oxford University Press, 1951), p. 138. The Grant was a British-modified Lee with a high velocity 37-mm turret gun and a 75-mm close support weapon in its hull sponson. Up to 1942 no German tank save the Mark IIIJ (Special) with the L60 long 50-mm gun, of which there were but 19 in the summer of 1942, could penetrate any British tank frontally. Four Mark IVF2 (Special) panzers with the more powerful long, high-velocity 75 mm also arrived in May 1942.

15. Bidwell and Graham, *Fire-Power*, p. 234; Gen. Sir David Fraser, *And We Shall Shock Them: The British Army in the Second World War* (London: Hodder and Stoughton, 1988), pp. 158–159, 224; Maj. Gen. E. K. G. Sixsmith, *British Generalship in the Twentieth Century* (London: Arms and Armour, 1970), p. 179; Bidwell, *Gunners*, pp. 159–160; and Macksey, *The Royal Armoured Corps*, pp. 105, 121–123, 127 and *Panzer Division: The Mailed Fist* (New York: Ballantine, 1968), pp. 12–13, 61.

16. Macksey, *The Royal Armoured Corps*, p. 106; Wheldon, *Machine Age Armies*, p. 222; Lt.-Gen. Sir Francis Tuker, *Approach to Battle* (London: Cassell, 1963), pp. 12–15, 384; Bidwell and Graham, *Fire-Power*, pp. 227, 230–231; and Bidwell, *Gunners*, p. 131. See also *Current Reports from Overseas (CRFO)*, 1 (September 1942): 9–10; and Col. H. C. B. Rogers, *Tanks in Battle* (London: Sphere, 1965), p. 102. Senior artillery commanders in such circumstances were first reduced to advisor status, then dismissed like the CRA and his headquarters in the 50th Infantry Division before the Gazala battle [Shelford Bidwell, "Letters to the Editor," *Journal of the Royal United Services Institute (JRUSI)*, 1 (March 1982) and 3 (September 1982)].

17. Maj.-Gen. Sir Howard Kippenberger, *Infantry Brigadier* (London: Oxford University Press, 1951), p. 180. On the mistrust between arms see also Carver, *Desert Dilemmas*, pp. 51, 141.

18. Tuker, *Approach to Battle*, pp. 122, 151–155, 161, 173, 209, 232; Maj.-Gen. E. K. G. Sixsmith, "The British Army in May 1940—A Comparison with the BEF 1914," *JRUSI*, 3 (September 1982): 9; and John Strawson, *El Alamein: Desert Victory* (London: Dent, 1981), p. 169.

19. Macksey, *The Royal Armoured Corps*, p. 105; Carver, *Desert Dilemmas*, p. 52; Bidwell and Graham, *Fire-Power*, pp. 229–230, 234–237, 239–240; James Lucas, *War in the Desert: The Eighth Army at El Alamein* (New York: Beaufort, 1982), pp. 87–89, 99–100.

20. Bidwell and Graham, *Fire-Power*, pp. 224–225; Tuker, *Approach to Battle*, p. 185; Bidwell, *Gunners*, pp. 67, 161, 169; and John A. English, *On Infantry* (New York: Praeger, 1984), p. 126. The tank strength of a British armored division was thus reduced by half. The "column" was adopted as a useful expedient during a period when the British were numerically weak. They were, in fact, little more than mobile batteries escorted by an infantry company and often a tank troop; their original purpose was to lend artillery weight to forward screens and to harass the enemy. The invention of Brig. "Jock" Campbell, VC, a gunner, they were elevated possibly because of his reputation as a fighter from minor to major tactical status.

On the fragmentation of British tactics, see Bidwell, *Gunners*, pp. 164–177. The brilliant discussion carried on by Barnett, Bidwell, and Carver through letters to the editor in the *JRUSI*, 3 (September 1981), 1 (March 1982), and 3 (September 1982) over British doctrine is also most instructive.

21. Hamilton, *Monty*, I, 606–612, 641–644, 648, 655, 706–709, 735, 748, 761–763, 768–769, 773–774, and II, 11–23; R. W. Tooley, "Montgomery as Military Trainer: Preparation for Alamein" (unpublished M.A. thesis, University of New Brunswick, 1984), pp. 27–28, 32–33, 89, 98–100, 183–186; Bidwell and Graham, *Fire-Power*, pp. 242–243; Carver, *Desert Dilemmas*, pp. 138–139, 143; and Strawson, *El Alamein*, pp. 72–78, 88–174. On 25 October, the GOC 10th Armoured Division was ten miles behind his leading elements when he recommended withdrawal. Montgomery, ever hard-nosed, sorted him out (Strawson, *El Alamein*, 111–113). Lacking sufficient infantry to attack gun lines in front of Rahman track, the army commander also reluctantly decided to employ armor in precisely the way it should not have been used (Lucas, *War in the Desert*, pp. 203–204, 235, 239–244). Given the choice, Montgomery was not prepared to sacrifice rifle companies for tanks. See Ronald Lewin, *Montgomery as Military Commander* (New York: Stein and Day, 1971), pp. 110–111.

22. Bidwell and Graham, *Fire-Power*, pp. 239–240, 242–243; Hamilton, *Monty*, I, 773; Tuker, *Approach to Battle*, pp. 11–12; and MP, Vol. 156, GHQ Monthly Training Letter April 1943, Appendix C, Some Lessons of Alamein—Armour.

23. RG 24, Vol. 13,761, WD GS 3CID 3CD4-2-1-5 Headquarters 3 Canadian Infantry Division, 31 August 1943 circular, Cooperation of Churchills with Inf, Extracts from DRAC Monthly Liaison Letter No 3; and "Armour in the Battle of El Alamein," *CATM*, 28 (July 1943), p. 11.

24. Ibid.

25. MP, Vol. 156, The Cooperation of Tanks with Infantry Divisions in Offensive Operations, issued by Commander-in-Chief 21 Army Group, pp. 1–15, 20–25 and 21 Army Group Letter July 1943 Co-operation of Army Tanks and Infantry. Matching one regiment of five troops each of three tanks to a battalion was considered ideal. Squadrons were never to be split between echelons.

26. Ibid; and *CRFO*, 8 (24 July 1943): 5–9.

27. RG 24, Vol. 13,711, 53-SD G 2 Cdn Corps 14 January 1944 Minutes of a Conference held by General Montgomery HQ 21 Army Group 0930 hrs, 13 January 1944; Rogers, *Tanks in Battle*, p. 184; and Macksey, *The Royal Armoured Corps*, pp. 87, 140–143. The armored brigade of an armored division included a motorized infantry battalion, while the independent armored brigade intended to support an infantry division did not. The Churchill "I" tank had given a good account of itself in Tunisia.

28. "Notes on the Handling of Armour," *CRFO*, 7 (17 July 1943): 9–10.

29. RG 24, Vol. 13,788, WD GS 4CAD, 4 Cdn Armd Div, Trg Bulletin Number 49 "The Pivot," 12 October 1943; and 4 Cdn Armd Div Trg Instr Number 16 of 12 August 1943. The pivot was to be established in areas where armor could maneuver, which meant planning it in advance.

30. "Notes on the Handling of Armour," pp. 9–10.

31. RG 24, Vol. 13,788, WD GS 4CAD, 4 Cdn Armd Div Trg Instr Number 18 (based on 2 Cdn Corps Trg Instr Number 12) Period 1 January 1944–31 March

1944; and Supplement "Army Training Instruction No. 2 May 1943," *CATM*, 28 (July 1943).

32. RG 24, Vol. 13,711, 2 Cdn Corps Trg Instr No 12 (Based on First Canadian Army Trg Directive No 18) Period 1 January 1944–31 March 1944.

33. "The Cooperation of Tanks with Infantry Divisions in Offensive Operations," pp. 26–28. One tank in three in a Churchill brigade had a 75 mm capable of firing armor-piercing or high-explosive shells. There were two close support tanks per squadron armed with howitzers that could fire high explosive or smoke. The remaining tanks mounted six-pounders.

34. "The RA Story of the Battle of Medenine—6 Mar 43," *CRFO*, 3 (19 June 1943): 1–5; Bidwell, *Gunners*, pp. 186–187; MP, Vol. 156, 21 Army Group Letter July 1943; and "The German Ten Commandments for Employment of Tanks," *CRFO*, 4 (26 June 1943): 14–15. The point observed here was that the defensive position was built around the antitank defense, which had to be in depth and properly coordinated. The primary role of the antitank gun was the destruction of tanks and not the protection of friendly infantry, whose mission was to protect the gun from enemy infantry attack (see Tuker, *Approach to Battle*, pp. 283–284 and Bidwell and Graham, *Fire-Power*, pp. 245–246). The 17-pounder had a performance slightly superior to the dreaded 88 mm, being able to defeat almost four and one-half inches of armor at 1,000 yards as opposed to the latter's four.

35. Tuker, *Approach to Battle*, pp. 311–332; Bidwell, *Gunners*, pp. 191–199.; "The Battle of Wadi Akarit," *CRFO*, 6 (10 July 1943): 8–13, 16; "Some Notes on Night Operations by the Commanding Officer of a Gurkha Battalion," *CRFO*, 38 (20 May 1944): 1–4; and "The Value of Infiltration," 46 (January, 1945), p. 19.

36. MP, Vol. 156, 21 Army Group Letter, July 1943, p. 12.

37. Bidwell and Graham, *Fire-Power*, pp. 112–114; Tuker, *Approach to Battle*, pp. 185, 238–245. The "fire roller" or creeping barrage had been perfected in the Great War to provide a protective curtain of shrapnel for attacking infantrymen, particularly over the critical "last 300 yards" before they disappeared into the melee. Tuker was very much opposed to barrages, wrongly according to Bidwell, who nonetheless described him as a "gifted and unusual officer who took the trouble to concern himself in artillery matters, as opposed to merely demanding results" (Bidwell, *Gunners*, p. 192).

38. Carver, *Desert Dilemmas*, p. 142; and Tuker, *Approach to Battle*, p. 35.

39. RG 24, Vol. 9868, 2/Sch of Inf ⅓ (SD(A)) Memorandum to File Infantry Training Conference No 1 20–24 April 1944, dated 27 April 1944.

40. Ibid.

41. Ibid. Twenty-five Bren magazines were issued per section and the school insisted that picks and shovels be carried in lieu of the wretched entrenching tool.

42. Majors R. P. Bourne and N. A. Shackleton, "Analysis of Firepower in Normandy Operations in 1944," NDHQ Operational Research and Analysis Establishment; and Personal copy CLFCSC Collection "Report of Experiences and Lessons Learnt During My Three Month Attachment to 1st Army, North African Theatre" by Capt. R. H. Lane.

43. DHist Report on Visit to 8th Army Lt.-Gen. H. D. G. Crerar, C.B., D.S.O., Appendices "B,""D,""F," and "G"; and MP, Vol. 157, Notes on a Common Doctrine for the Emp of Inf and Tks under 61–2–1/Trg HQ First Cdn Army 23 June 1943. Three types of divisions were authorized in October 1942: infantry, of

three infantry brigades; armored, of one armored and one lorried brigade; and a "new model" infantry, of two infantry and one armored brigade (which was precisely the organization of the armored division in Italy). Paget claimed the mixed divisions served their purpose in acquainting infantry commanders with armor and upon their disbandment took the armored brigades into GHQ reserve [MP, Vol. 156, 20/Gen/6059 (S.D.1), 1 October 1942, signed by G. W. Lambert, and Vol. 161, Memorandum of Conversation Gen. McNaughton and Gen. Paget, 1120 hrs, 17 June 43].

44. English, *On Infantry*, pp. 136–138, and "Reflections on the Breaking of the Gothic Line," *Infantry Journal*, 12 (Autumn 1984): 45–51; and Dominick Graham and Shelford Bidwell, *Tug of War: The Battle for Italy, 1943–1945* (London: Hodder and Stoughton, 1986), pp. 19, 113–114, 431.

45. See my *On Infantry* and Paddy Griffith, *Forward into Battle* (Chichester: Antony Bird, 1981).

46. Russell F. Weigley, *Eisenhower's Lieutenants: The Campaign of France and Germany, 1944–1945* (Bloomington, Ind.: Indiana University Press, 1981), pp. 46, 51, 55.

1. Infantry training, 1941. Courtesy of National Archives of Canada/PA–177348.

2. Canadian soldiers on assault course, Bordon, Hampshire, 1941. Courtesy of National Archives of Canada/PA–177349.

3. Victors and vanquished at Carpiquet. Courtesy of National Archives of Canada/
PA–132860.

4. Mediums of 2 AGRA in action, Operation "Spring." Courtesy of National
Archives of Canada/PA–116516.

5. Canadian division commanders: Major-General Rod Keller of the 3rd Division (left), Major-General Charles Foulkes of the 2nd (right). Courtesy of National Archives of Canada/PA–116519.

6. Master and disciple: General Sir Bernard Montgomery and Lieutenant-General G. G. Simonds. Courtesy of National Archives of Canada/PA–129125.

7. The best tank country has the least antitank guns. Courtesy of National Archives of Canada/PA–131375.

8. Forming up for Operation "Totalize." Courtesy of National Archives of Canada/
   PA–132904.

9. Preparing for Operation "Tractable": an M10 tank destroyer is in the foreground.
   Courtesy of National Archives of Canada/PA–116525.

Chapter 8

Cast of Commanders

An unsuccessful or unlucky commander is not to be pitied: he need not have accepted his appointment. Of all those affected by his failure, he is least to be pitied.

Lieutenant-General Sir Francis Tuker,
Approach to Battle[1]

The distance between the English coast and the fields of Normandy in the summer of 1944 was better measured in terms of lifetimes rather than miles. The English Channel was more than just a geographical barrier: it was also a physical reminder of the gap that existed between practice and doctrine, which military training in Britain purportedly intended to bridge. The extent to which the Canadian Army bridged this gap, though difficult to gauge precisely, can best be seen in operations conducted beyond the assault phase of "Overlord." The First Canadian Army had, after all, been earmarked for exploitation operations, breaking out from a bridgehead, since late 1942. Indeed, in "Spartan" it had been exercised for this exact role. As has been shown, however, events after "Spartan" left the First Canadian Army somewhat less Canadian and suffering from a crisis in command that, ultimately, saw it forfeit its spearhead role. Developments from this point, particularly as they pertain to Canadian high command in Normandy, will be examined in the course of this chapter.

On 17 June 1943, Paget told McNaughton that the latest invasion plan envisaged the First Canadian Army commanding its own assault divisions and following them in to enlarge the bridgehead.[2] A new plan completed in July by Lieutenant-General F. E. Morgan, Chief of Staff to the Supreme

Allied Commander (COSSAC), projected a Canadian army of five divisions centrally deployed after the assault phase between American and British armies, respectively comprising seven and six divisions, right and left. As late as December 1943, the COSSAC plan called for a three-division sea-borne assault on a thirty mile front by the First U.S. Army, initially composed of 1 British and another American corps. Once two British corps were securely ashore, the First Canadian Army was to land and take them under command; both armies were then to come under the British commander of the 21st Army Group, the British Liberation Army.[3]

Montgomery discarded the COSSAC plan when he assumed command of the 21st Army Group in January 1944. He called instead for an initial assault by five divisions, protected on both flanks by airborne landings, on a frontage sufficient to accommodate two attacking armies, the First U.S. and the Second British, each of two corps. Behind these were to come two "follow-up" armies, the First Canadian and the Third U.S., also operating under the 21st Army Group. Montgomery made it abundantly clear as early as 21 January at the first Supreme Commander's Conference, Norfolk House, that the task of Anglo-Canadian forces would be to shield American forces operating against Cherbourg and the Brittany peninsula from the enemy main body approaching from the east. Ideally, he sought to entice the Germans to counterattack him on ground of his own choosing as he had at Alamein.[4] If Crerar is to be believed, however, Montgomery did not originally appreciate that the first shock of armor would fall on the British sector. In Crerar's words, the 21st Army Group "assumed that the east flank of the bridgehead, at Caen, would *not* be under pressure by German forces following the landing," and it was only after he disputed this assessment in April that Montgomery came to accept the former view.[5]

Whatever the derivation of the foregoing strategic scenario, except for the 3rd Division and the 2nd Armoured Brigade assigned to the assault landing, the operational and training focus of the First Canadian Army lay inland beyond the bridgehead. Unlike the Third U.S. Army, however, it was not to make its operational debut in spectacular fashion. From a leadership perspective, of course, the contrast between the First Canadian Army and its sister "follow-up" army was so striking as to invite comment. Whereas the former drifted essentially leaderless as a result of its commander being fired, the thrusting Lieutenant-General Patton, formerly fired as an army commander for slapping shell-shocked soldiers, assumed command of the Third Army from January 1944. Contrary to popular belief, Patton's accomplishments as Seventh Army commander in the Sicilian campaign had earned him the respect and admiration of Montgomery. Unknowingly perhaps, Montgomery even accepted Patton's appointment to command the Third Army against the wishes of the latter's erstwhile subordinate, Lieutenant-General Bradley, who privately nurtured an increasing dislike of his former superior.[6]

A 1915 graduate of West Point and classmate of General Dwight D. Eisenhower, Bradley received word in September 1943 that he would command the First U.S. Army. Having previously served as Infantry School commandant and divisional commander twice over, he had earlier that year been named Eisenhower's deputy in North Africa. Following the American defeat at Kasserine Pass in February, he became deputy to Patton, the new commander of II U.S. Corps. When Patton took over the Seventh Army, Bradley went on to command II Corps in the final days of the Tunisian campaign and the battle for Sicily. This made Bradley the most experienced U.S. corps commander, of whom 34 commanded in battle during the Second World War. Significantly, all but one were staff college graduates, while 29 of their number had passed through the war college. Twenty-six, ranging in ages from 52 to 62 were older than Bradley, who at 51 was eighth youngest.[7]

A calm, circumspect, infantry tactician, Bradley would in Normandy actually delay the activation of the Third Army for fear the impetuous Patton might compromise his efforts to escape the deadlock of the bocage. Similarly, Montgomery delayed the introduction of the First Canadian Army, possibly because he preferred instead to rely upon the commander of the Second British Army, Lieutenant-General Miles Dempsey, to handle several corps. Dempsey had commanded an infantry brigade at Dunkirk and, like Bradley, two divisions; at Montgomery's request he assumed command of 13 British Corps from December 1942. A former student of Montgomery's at Camberley 1930–31, the introverted Dempsey complemented his more extroverted master and, absolutely unflappable, possessed an uncanny ability to read a map. Dempsey was also well known and popular among Canadians for having served a year as McNaughton's BGS in 7th Corps. He was a very good friend of Simonds, whom he considered the best of his corps commanders in Normandy.[8]

Of the four army commanders slated to lead their formations in the invasion of Europe, Montgomery placed the least faith in the "prosy and stodgy" Crerar, who also struck Patton as "not impressive."[9] Though neither a student of war in the league of the older Patton or Montgomery, nor as experienced as the younger Bradley or Dempsey, the politically well-connected Crerar had nonetheless had more of a silver spoon career than any of them. He graduated from RMC in 1909, the same year Patton left West Point, and finished the Great War in McNaughton's footsteps as counter-battery staff officer in the Canadian Corps. Except for a brief third tour as a battery commander during the interwar years, Crerar spent all of his service on staff. He attended Camberley Staff College as a brevet lieutenant-colonel during 1923–24 on the same course as then Major Georges Vanier, future diplomat and Governor-General, and Captain A. E. Percival, who would later at Singapore surrender 80,000 troops. After a two-year exchange at the War Office and a posting to RMC as a tactics instructor,

Crerar attended the IDC in 1934. From 1935 he served as Director of Military Operations and Intelligence in Ottawa and from 1938, on promotion to brigadier, as commandant of RMC. In October 1939 he proceeded to Britain as the Senior Combatant Officer, returning to Ottawa in the summer of 1940 to take up the post of CGS.[10]

Since Crerar's preoccupations during the interwar years were similar to those of McNaughton, he inherited army command by anointment. He did not, however, immediately fill the void created by the latter's departure. Lieutenant-General Simonds on appointment to command 2 Canadian Corps temporarily assumed de facto leadership of the Canadian Army remaining in Britain. At this juncture he was Canada's most experienced general, both from the standpoint of staff employment and of commanding a large formation in action. Although only 40, fifteen years younger than Crerar, his very youth had saved him from professional debilitation as he progressed along the operational path to competent generalship. A 1925 graduate of RMC, Simonds attended Camberley Staff College during 1936–37. In 1938 he was promoted temporary major and posted as a tactics instructor to RMC where Crerar was commandant. The next year he trooped to Britain as GSO 2 (Operations) with the 1st Canadian Infantry Division. Following a brief sojourn as CO of the 1st Field Regiment, Royal Canadian Horse Artillery, Simonds in 1940 established the field staff officer training course at Ford Manor.

After conducting the first Canadian war staff course, Simonds was appointed GSO 1 of the 2nd Canadian Infantry Division and, subsequently, BGS of the Canadian Corps. Early in 1943 he relinquished command of the 1st Canadian Infantry Brigade and assumed the position of BGS, First Canadian Army.[11] Shortly after witnessing the Eighth Army victory at Wadi Akarit in early April 1943 as a staff observer, he took command of the 2nd Division. Only two weeks later, on the death of Major-General H. L. N. Salmon[12] in a plane crash, he was transferred to command the 1st Division, then slated to come under the operational direction of the Eighth Army for Operation "Husky," the invasion of Sicily. During the course of the campaign in Sicily and southern Italy, Simonds distinguished himself as a division commander, drawing particular praise from Montgomery. To gain further experience in handling an armored division, Simonds was at the latter's urging transferred to command the 5th Canadian Armoured Division. Unfortunately, the division received but a trickle of its tank establishment up to January,[13] which effectively precluded Simonds from acquiring experience in the command of such a formation.

In fact, the only action undertaken by 5th Division troops while Simonds was GOC was the so-called "Arielli Show." It is significant because it was directed by the commander of the 11th Canadian Infantry Brigade, Brigadier George Kitching, whom Simonds later chose to command the 4th Canadian Armoured Division in Normandy. Simonds, eager to see his infantry formation "get its first experience of contact with the enemy," had arranged for the 11th Brigade to relieve the 3rd Canadian Infantry Brigade on the 1st Division's front north of Ortona. At first light on 17 January 1944, it was launched against a series of enemy strongpoints southeast of the Arielli River. For some reason the plan called for successive barrage-covered assaults across the Riccio River, first by the Perth Regiment on the left, then by the Cape Breton Highlanders on the right. Opposed by the seasoned 1st Parachute Division deployed in well-prepared river line defenses, the piecemeal attack foundered disastrously in spite of overwhelming artillery support. It cost the brigade almost 200 casualties. Having advanced to within 200 yards of their objectives, many of the soldiers of the assaulting battalions not only "straggled back," but in several instances threw their Bren guns and rifles away.[14]

Simonds assumed command of 2 Canadian Corps on 30 January 1944, finally replacing Sansom who since his dismal performance on "Spartan" had been protected from removal by McNaughton, in spite of GHQ Home Force recommendations to the contrary. Immediately upon his arrival in London, Simonds met personally with Montgomery, newly appointed ground force commander for the Allied invasion of France, after which he swept into 2 Corps like a new broom. Reluctant to deal with unknown quantities and apparently unimpressed by the performance of certain 2 Corps staff officers and commanders, he, like Montgomery, brought in his own team from Italy. By the end of March he had replaced among the more important appointments the BGS, the CCRA, and the Chief Engineer; of seven senior staff officers at 2 Corps headquarters only two retained their jobs. Within the 4th Armoured Division veteran officers of the Italian campaign assumed command of the 4th Armoured and 10th Infantry Brigades. As previously intimated, Simonds's former GSO 1 in 1st Division and commander of the 11th Brigade, 33-year-old Major-General Kitching, took over the 4th Armoured Division on 1 March.[15]

While it was unquestionably prudent to bring Simonds back to command 2 Corps, which tacitly confirmed that all was not well in its ranks, he had precious little time in which to correct training faults. The new GOC 4th Division, who lacked armored experience in any case, never did manage to exercise his formation as a whole in a field exercise before its eventual commitment to battle. The 2nd Canadian Infantry Division, also newly commanded by Major-General Charles Foulkes since 11 January 1944, fared somewhat better; during Exercise "Step" conducted in early April it practiced breaking out of a bridgehead on a single thrust line, crossing a river, and assaulting an enemy position with live ammunition. April and May found the same division with corps and army elements engaged in Exercise "Kate," practicing the crossing of a tidal estuary on the River Trent in Yorkshire. Since it seemed distinctly possible that an assault crossing of the lower Seine in the face of enemy opposition would be required in any breakout from a bridgehead, 4th Armoured Divison infantry and engineers practiced similar operations on a lesser scale on the River Medway in Kent. Unfortunately, First Canadian Army operations did not actually follow this pattern in the event.

That Simonds found 2 Corps training deficient is evident from his corps commander's conference of 4 March 1944. Here he observed that not enough had been accomplished with respect to all-arms cooperation. Stressing that too much training was ill-organized and poorly prepared, he directed brigades to run unit tactical tests monthly using permanent umpire teams. He additionally insisted that training be carried out on the basis of not operating at war establishment. At a higher level, Exercise "Studiedum" conducted in mid-January aimed at effecting closer liaison between corps and division staffs. In February, Exercises "Jing" and "Jang" saw formation and artillery commanders and staffs of the 4th and 2nd Divisions, respectively, practicing the allotment of artillery fire during an advance and the preparation of divisional fire plans. In Exercise "Last" held mid–April, Simonds managed to practice all commanders and headquarters down to unit level in operations immediately following a breakout from a bridgehead.[16] Simonds had also, in the meantime, issued comprehensive personal instructions on 2 Corps operational policy and efficiency in command. Significantly, both documents were sent to Montgomery and Dempsey who gave them their unqualified blessing.[17]

That Simonds was a disciple of Montgomery is obvious, and they both owed their fortune to plane crashes. What is less evident is that Simonds's very competence may nearly have cost him his career. Indeed, it is highly unlikely that professional ability alone would have saved him from the malevolence of Crerar who increasingly envied the rising fortune of his once quite junior subordinate. The depth of his rancor was most balefully demonstrated in Italy, sparked by what can only be described as an exceedingly bizarre, picayune incident. During a visit to 5th Canadian Armoured division headquarters in Cassoria in late 1943, Crerar expressed a rather puerile interest in the construction of Simonds's caravan, a three-ton lorry office cum sleeping quarter, which Crerar referred to as a "home from home." Crerar was so impressed with its layout, in fact, that he subsequently dispatched a maintenance captain to obtain its exact measurements. When the officer eventually appeared unannounced at 5th Division headquarters, which had moved, he obtained the permission of a staff captain to enter the GOC's caravan. As might be expected, Simonds returned to what was essentially his private quarter only to find it apparently commandeered by a stranger bent on getting its measurements and taking notes. Understandably he put the run on the hapless captain who, much put out, reported the incident.

Crerar's reaction to this "personal discourtesy," which he admitted he could have chosen to ignore, was to remind Simonds "of a good many reasons, extending over a number of years, which should induce in you feelings, for me, of loyalty and appreciation." One suspects, however, that this pathetic expression of hurt feelings was merely symptomatic of a deeper underlying concern. More ominous was the veiled threat that because the episode indicated Simonds's "nerves . . . [were] over-stretched and that impulse, rather then considered judgement, [might] . . . begin to affect . . . [his] decisions," Crerar should be "extremely worried." Warning Simonds that he was "reaching a position in the Army when balance . . . [was] becoming even more important to . . . [his] future than brilliance," Crerar, incredibly, asked him "to undertake a self-examination, and . . . diagnosis of . . . [his] mental and physical condition."[18]

Not content to let the matter drop, the more so because of Simonds's arbitrary 11 December removal of Brigadier R. O. G. Morton, CRA of the 5th Division, Crerar went on to advise Montgomery that he had "serious cause to doubt . . . [the] suitability [of Simonds] for higher command." In Crerar's judgment, though Simonds possessed "all the military brilliance for higher command in the field with his tense mentality, under further strain through increased rank and responsibilities, he might go 'off the deep end' very disastrously indeed." To reinforce this point Crerar confided that Simonds had "always been high strung . . . with a tendency to be introspective, rather than objective, when faced with acute problems." Crerar's main concern, however, appears to have been Simonds's lack of deference to him. Despite the brave claim that, "till now, I have always been able to handle Simonds successfully," Crerar seems himself to have become highly unsettled by the perception that his erstwhile subordinate would "resent . . . any control or direction on . . . [his] part."[19]

Montgomery's response to Crerar was characteristically straightforward: he continued to entertain the "highest opinion of Simonds"; though he had "tried to go off the rails once or twice when he first went into action with his Div[ision], he had been "pulled . . . back . . . and taught . . . his stuff." Here, of course, Montgomery may have been referring to Simonds's poor handling in July of his 1st Brigade commander, Brigadier Howard Graham. Recognizing immediately that both were good commanders, Montgomery wisely intervened to save the junior and counsel the senior.[20] In like manner, he also bluntly pointed out to Crerar that Simonds would "be a very valuable off[ice]r in the Canadian Forces as you have no one else with his experience." The commander of the Eighth Army went on in markedly astute fashion to suggest that Simonds "must therefore be handled carefully and trained on." By way of comparison, he rated Simonds's replacement as GOC 1st Division, Major-General Chris Vokes, "not even in the same parish." "I am trying hard to teach him," lamented Montgomery, "but he will never be anything more than a 'good plain cook.' "[21]

Discounting Montgomery's "primary interest in field command," Crerar now impugned Simonds in the area of "Canadian policies and business," which "higher . . . responsibilities of . . . an independent C[ana]d[ia]n Com[man]d . . . he might conduct very disastrously indeed." In a letter to the COS, CMHQ, Crerar expressed his concern about Simonds's "egocentric state of mind," explaining that he had "under most confidential arrangements" consulted his medical authorities "to obtain . . . their technical advice on the fitness of Simonds continuing in command, or of assuming still higher responsibilities, in view of his mental condition." According to Crerar, the "medicals" on perusing the correspondence related to the caravan incident and the removal by Simonds of Morton, determined that "in spite of marked egocentricity, Simonds . . . could be relied upon to function effectively as a Senior Commander though preferably *not* as an independent C[ana]d[ia]n force Com[mande]r." His suspicions thus confirmed, Crerar committed the information to bureaucratic file as "background" for "some possible future time when the employment of . . . [the] brilliant, and comparatively young, [Simonds came] up for consideration." He nonetheless confirmed Simonds's selection as "the only present 'bet' " for corps command.[22]

Around the same time Crerar was reaching this conclusion about Simonds, Montgomery was coming to another about Crerar. From a Commonwealth military perspective it contrasted starkly with the assessment of the New Zealander, Lieutenant-General Sir Bernard Freyberg, whom Montgomery considered the best fighting division commander he had met. On 23 December 1943, the very day he learned of his appointment to command the 21st Army Group and Allied invasion ground forces, Montgomery wrote to Brooke: "The more I think of Harry Crerar the more I am convinced that he is quite unfit to command an army in the field at present. . . . He has already (from Sicily) started to have rows with Canadian generals under me; he wants a lot of teaching."[23] Crerar's earlier refusal during the administrative buildup of 1 Canadian Corps to take temporary command of the 1st Division to gain operational experience, as Montgomery strongly urged him to do, apparently contributed to this assessment.[24]

It is also most probable that the shrewd victor of Alamein heard about the troop dissatisfaction generated by the excessive paperwork emanating from 1 Corps headquarters and Crerar's insistence on Canadian soldiers following dress regulations to the letter. Crerar clearly disapproved of the Eighth Army's relaxed approach to dress and forbade the practice of drivers painting pictures and names of girlfriends on vehicles. When one of his division commanders protested, he in bloody-minded fashion amended his orders to permit the painting of a name one inch high on the dashboard where only the driver could see it. Montgomery, on the other hand, was anything but strict in such matters and claimed he only once issued an order on Eighth Army dress. Ironically, this was prompted by the occasion of a naked Canadian soldier leaning out of his truck and doffing a top hat in salute as the army commander drove by. After a good laugh, Montgomery decided there were limits and issued the one line order: "Top hats will not be worn in Eighth Army."[25]

It is, of course, true that Montgomery's proposal for Crerar to take over a division would have left him virtually following in the footsteps of Simonds, whose performance in the field had already netted him a recommendation for future corps command. As it was, Crerar had his first meeting with Montgomery at the end of October and the 1 Canadian Corps took over a static sector on the Adriatic front 1 February 1944; after a month in the line Crerar returned to Britain "without having participated in any major operations in Italy and without any formal report being made on his capacities as a commander in the field."[26] The battle-experienced Simonds, on the other hand, was considered by Montgomery at that time to be too young to command an army; he had, however, already recommended to Brooke on 23 December 1943 that Simonds "go to UK *now* to command the 2nd Canadian Corps."[27] In Kitching's view, "it was a great mistake on . . . [Crerar's] part [to not temporarily command the 1st Division] because it was his one opportunity to establish himself as a real commander. Instead . . . he remained just a kindly figurehead." While false pride may have been a factor here, simple jealously was obviously another. Indeed, Kitching suspected that the main intent behind Crerar's decision to equip his corps headquarters with vehicles before the 5th Armoured Division was "to make Simonds sit idle for some ten weeks and thus not be able to command the division in operations."[28]

In contrast to his attitude toward Simonds, Crerar seems to have maintained an almost unshakable faith in the GOC 3rd Division, Major-General Rod Keller, whom he considered a "first class commander." Keller had been a year ahead of Simonds at Camberley and on the same course as then Captain F. W. "Freddy" de Guingand who later became Montgomery's famous COS. In June 1942, Crerar had placed Keller first in line within 1 Canadian Corps for appointment to command a division. For whatever reason, he did not rate Brigadier Salmon, regarded by many as outstanding and the best qualified officer available to command a division in the field, quite as high as Keller for promotion.[29] Even when in March 1943 he felt compelled to counsel Keller on alleged "misbehaviour in the matter of over-indulgence," as reported by British and Canadian general officers, Crerar maintained that "he had no doubt as to his abilities as a Commander."[30] As late as 16 May 1944 Crerar wrote: "I believe that Keller would make a two-fisted and competent Corps Com[man]d[er] in the field."[31] Apparently, Keller's assault landing training of 3rd Division within 1 British Corps gave Crerar a certain sense of personal satisfaction. "The technique . . . employed by Second Brit[ish] Army [of which 1 British Corps was part]," he immodestly wrote, was "almost in its entirety, that developed by me when 3 Cdn Inf Div was under my com[man]d in 1 Cdn Corps."[32]

Crerar's confidence in Keller's "two-fisted leadership" would be abruptly shattered within a few weeks after the invasion of Normandy. On 5 July 1944 the GOC 1 British Corps, Lieutenant-General John Crocker, advised Dempsey that Keller was "not really fit temperamentally and perhaps phys-ically (he is a man who has the appearance of having lived pretty well) for such a responsible command." According to Crocker, the 3rd Canadian Division had "lapsed into a very nervy state" after "the excitement of the initial [assault] phase had passed". Except for the 7th Brigade, which "stood considerable enemy pressure with great fortitude," the division "became jumpy and . . . far too quick on the trigger," submitting "exaggerated re-ports of enemy activity and . . . [its] own difficulties." Again, to paraphrase Crocker, the "steadying hand" required to combat this "general attitude of despondency" was not forthcoming; "indeed the state of the Div[ision] was a reflection of the state of its Commander" who "was obviously not standing up to the strain and showed signs of fatigue and nervousness (one might almost say fright) which were patent for all to see."[33] Crocker's assessment was corroborated by Dempsey who also observed the division's "highly strung state in . . . the first three or four days ashore" and its loss of offensive spirit thereafter. Blaming Keller for failure to properly control and inspire his formation, Dempsey remarked that had it been a British division he would have recommended his removal at once.[34] Montgomery in a letter to Crerar concurred, giving his opinion that Keller "was not good enough to command a Canadian division."[35]

As heir apparent to McNaughton, of course, Crerar had long been able to play a kingmaker role in the appointment of Canadian officers to senior command. In October 1939 he even indicated that he felt "very strongly that R.M.C. [graduates] should have first claim on all P.F. (C.A.S.F.) commissions."[36] He was instrumental, moreover, in selecting Lieutenant-Colonels C. Foulkes and C. C. Mann, respectively GSOs 1 of 3rd and 2nd Divisions, for promotion to brigadier and possible assignment to either command or staff posts. The latter was subsequently appointed BGS, 1 Canadian Corps on 13 July 1942 and the former replaced Simonds as BGS, First Canadian Army. By the time Crerar belatedly took over the First Canadian Army on 20 March 1944, Foulkes had been GOC 2nd Division since 11 January and Mann BGS/COS, First Canadian Army from 28 Jan-uary. The even later return from Italy of newly promoted Brigadier E. R. Suttie in February to command 2 Canadian AGRA and Brigadier R. A. Wyman in April to command 2nd Armoured Brigade rounded out the slate of key Canadian staff officers and commanders for the Normandy invasion.[37]

Ironically, Simonds and Foulkes, who both attended Camberley in 1937 as senior and junior division candidates respectively, were also destined to have a serious falling out. The source of this antagonism may even have been the Staff College, where Simonds reportedly graduated at or very near the top of his class. The more pedestrian Foulkes, a regular force infantry officer, appears to have been exceedingly ambitious and as unpopular with his fellows as he was humorless. He was a cold fish. Simonds, on the other hand, was intolerant, hot tempered, and headstrong, which admitted short-comings he attempted to hold in check, occasionally vainly, by maintaining a glacial-like composure. Though totally unable to inspire their soldiers like Montgomery, Simonds and Foulkes both evinced a similar ruthlessness of character. Together with Crerar, who possessed a nasty streak of his own[38] and was obviously prepared to cajole and intimidate through "old age and treachery," they constituted the pithy kernel of the Canadian high command in Normandy. The more personable Kitching and Keller were in another category. Behind them all, of course, stood a largely unsung array of gunners[39] and a weight of artillery doctrine.

Significantly, when the First Canadian Army became operational on 23 July 1944, Crerar almost immediately got into a quarrel with his sole corps commander. With Simonds's 2 Corps astride the Caen-Falaise road remaining under command of Dempsey, the First Canadian Army initially assumed responsibility only for the eastern sector of the front held by Crocker's 1 British Corps. Crerar's assigned task was "to advance [First Canadian Army's] left flank eastwards so that OUISTREHAM w[ould] cease to be under direct enemy observation and fire . . . [in order that] use c[ould] then be made of the port of Caen." To achieve this, Montgomery suggested, it would be "necessary to push the enemy back to the east side of the R. DIVES, and to occupy such positions as will ensure that all territory to the west of the river is dominated by our troops."[40] On 22 July Crerar dispatched a written instruction to Crocker repeating this general direction and ordering him to draw up the necessary plan, which Crerar indicated he wished to discuss on the morning of 24 July. In the same instruction Crerar stipulated that the "immediate task" would be "to gain possession of the general line of the road which runs from BREVILLE 135745 through LE MARAIS 161777 to the road junction LE PETIT HOMME 170792."[41] At the 24 July meeting, however, Crocker voiced strong objections to such detailed tactical direction, and, at Crerar's request, put them in writing the same day.

In Crocker's judgment, the operation ordered by Crerar would have involved "an attack on a narrow front through close and difficult country where the enemy [wa]s well posted in some strength and would, in its later stages, [have] involve[d] clearing an extensive build-up [sic] area." Instead of achieving the "object . . . enabl[ing] the OUISTREHAM–CAEN Canal to be brought into use," Crocker argued, "the proposed advance to "BRE-VILLE–LE PT. HOMME r[oa]d, would . . . merely result . . . to purposeless losses, and an extended front which could only be held with dispropor-tionate daily casualties from the enemy artillery EAST of R DIVES and the undisturbed mortars and short range weapons in the GONNEVILLE 1676–VARAVILLE–BAVENT area." He accordingly requested Crerar to "reconsider his specific direction, adding that as GOC he was "not prepared, personally, to be responsible for carrying it out." As an alternative to attacking on a narrow front, Crocker proposed earmarking 3rd Division to capture Troarn and Bures as a first priority task, which he estimated would require a brigade with full air and ground support. On success of this phase, he saw a division again supported by air advancing on a broad front "to the line BAVENT–GONNEVILLE–MERVILLE, with exploitation to VARAVILLE and towards CABOURG."[42]

Crerar's same-day reaction was to defensively annotate and forward Crocker's written objections to Montgomery and "call upon [the latter] for aid." Whether for personal reasons or "because of the fact that I am a Canadian," Crerar whined, "Crocker gave . . . the immediate impression . . . that he resented being placed under my command and receiving any directions from me"; he exhibited "no tact, nor desire to understand my views." The stern Crocker's longer experience in command of a corps in action may have been the catalyst that pushed Crerar to react this way. Crocker's recent attempt to fire the favored Keller may also have sowed resentment. In any event, Crerar admitted to being "quite convinced that Crocker . . . [was] temperamentally unsuited to be one of . . . [his] Corps Com[man]d[er]s" and asked that he be exchanged for either of the commanders of 12 or 30 Corps, both of whom Crerar had served with and claimed to know well. They "will work with me," he wrote. "Crocker never will."[43] Tellingly, Lieutenant-General G. C. Bucknall, who had been Crerar's GSO 2 when the latter was Commandant at RMC, was destined to be relieved as commander of 30 Corps, his tenure there being later described as a "non-event."[44]

On 25 July Montgomery once more interviewed Crerar on the matter of an apparently recalcitrant subordinate. While allowing that the GOC 1 Corps could be "somewhat difficult," he reproached Crerar for not using persuasion rather than formal orders to harness Crocker's energy and proven ability, especially since he had just come under command. Montgomery also refused to transfer Crocker to another corps on the rather sensible grounds that such reassignment, besides requiring staff changes during a difficult period in operations, would only restrict future flexibility as it might still be necessary under certain conditions to place Crocker's corps under the First Canadian Army. Crerar in acknowledging that he had "not given full weight to this prospective situation" agreed to "go more than half way" toward salvaging the situation. He nonetheless requested Montgomery to speak with Crocker to "straighten out . . . the . . . relationship" and confirm that "what was urgently wanted was the clearance of OUISTREHAM and the CAEN Canal from close enemy observation and mortar fire at an early date, along the lines of [Crerar's] instructions." Montgomery promised to see Crocker the following morning, advising Crerar to meet his corps commander later that day to "go over . . . the tactical problem" once more "with the air cleared and good prospects of mutual understanding."[45]

The next day Montgomery advised Crerar by letter that he had instructed Crocker to quit bickering and be "a loyal subordinate," one prepared "to lead the way . . . in saying what an honour it [wa]s to serve in the Canadian Army." Montgomery similarly counseled Crerar that an "Army Commander should give his Corps Commanders a task, and leave it to them as to how they do it." While keeping in touch, he "must stand back from the detailed tactical battle . . . the province of his Corps Commanders," intervening "only if he thinks it is not going to be a success." To reinforce this point Montgomery repeated in a postscript that, in an army of but one corps, the higher commander "will, if he is not careful, find that he is trying to command that Corps himself in detail"; with "not enough to do . . . he is inclined to become involved in details which are the province of his subordinates." In Montgomery's unequivocal view, "John Crocker [wa]s a very experienced fighting commander," who because he knew "his stuff" had to be led rather than "driven." Remarking that it "takes all sorts to make a good Army," Montgomery went on to stress to Crerar that "once you can get the confidence and trust of your subordinates, then you have a pearl of very great price." This was not likely to be attained, however, "without a very great deal of hard work, and very considerable subordination of self."[46]

In the same letter, Montgomery urged Crerar to "cut down paper in the field." He further suggested, no doubt in direct reference to Crerar's written instruction to Crocker, that "best results [were obtained] by dealing verbally with . . . Corps commanders," who could then give their views. That Crerar also chose to issue a tactical directive to all senior formation commanders on 22 July seems to have caused Montgomery some additional irritation, for he insisted "it would be a good thing to tell Crocker that you sent him several copies . . . only in case he wanted to send them on to his subordinates, and that there is no need to send them on unless he so wishes." As Montgomery explained to Crerar, "*in the field* it[wa]s wrong to send tactical directives to anyone except your immediate subordinates—as *they* are responsible to you, and *their* subordinates are responsible to *them*." Having "expressed this opinion many times," Montgomery found Crerar's action in this regard "definitely contrary to . . . [his] wishes."[47]

Crocker's reaction to the directive can only be surmised. It is unlikely, however, that he was greatly impressed by its content. The first three pages consisted largely of extracts taken from a translation of a report by *Panzer Lehr* Division (which he may already have read) covering its experiences during the period 6–22 June. It was useful perhaps for highlighting how the Germans had taken the measure of certain British tactical methods, one of which was the attack on a very narrow front. But Crerar's assessment was gallingly superficial in its thrust: to "aim at maximum *surprise*, as well as maximum fire power." The last three pages were also extracts, taken directly from an address given by Crerar on 14 May 1944, itself a patchwork effort taken almost verbatim from paragraphs in previous letters and memoranda. All told they remain more revealing of a commander who never had an original idea of his own than they were stimulating. Indeed, the narrow emphasis placed upon the employment of barrage fire and the necessity for infantry—"deploy[ed] in width, rather than in depth"—to keep close to it during the "Break-in" battle even suggested a trench warfare mentality. The use of armor was by comparison hardly mentioned, except in the most general sense.[48] On the whole, Crerar's directive, especially in its non-artillery facets, suffered from vagueness and superficiality.

In a larger sense the foregoing incident seems to confirm a persistent lack of judgment, if not tactical naiveté, on the part of Crerar. Montgomery, by now practiced in settling disputes among senior Canadian commanders, expressed his exasperation in a letter to Brooke on 26 July:

> Harry Crerar has started off his career as an Army Comd by thoroughly upsetting everyone; he had a row with Crocker the first day, and asked me to remove Crocker. I have spent two days trying to restore peace; investigating the quarrel, and so on. As always, there are faults on both sides. But the basic cause was Harry; I fear he thinks he is a great soldier, and he was determined to show it the very moment he took over command at 1200 hrs 23 July. He made his first mistake at 1205 hrs; and his second after lunch. I have had each of them to see me—separately of course. I have told Harry in quite clear terms that in my opinion the basic fault lies with him, in this quarrel. I have seen Crocker, and told him he must play 100%.... I now hope I can get on with fighting the Germans—instead of stopping the Generals fighting amongst themselves.[49]

According to the late Brigadier Richard Simpkin, a key element in the effective central direction of a field army is "an unbroken chain of trust and mutual respect running from the controlling operational commander to the tank or section commander."[50] As can be seen, however, this was hardly the case in the First Canadian Army as Crerar assumed command. Part of the problem was doubtless of his own making, a result of his inability to recognize operational talent when it stared him in the face. At the same time, the half-generation gap that existed within the Canadian high command further signified a relative lack of depth. By way of comparison, the youngest U.S. corps commander, Major-General J. Lawton Collins, was seven years older than Simonds; in the German army, moreover, less than two percent of corps commanders were under 45![51] When all evidence is weighed, nonetheless, it is difficult to dispute Montgomery's assessment of Crerar, which in respect of First Canadian Army deployment was a consequential factor. Indeed, the once leaderless army had gained little in the way of stature with its new head. While noting on 24 June that Bradley and Dempsey were both "first class . . . Army [Commanders] and . . . very willing to learn," Montgomery wrote: "I have grave fears that Harry Crerar will not be too good; however, I am keeping him out of the party as long as I can."[52]

NOTES

1. Lt.-Gen. Sir Francis Tuker, *Approach to Battle* (London: Cassell, 1963), p. 144.

2. McNaughton Papers (MP), Vol. 161, Memorandum of Conversation Gen. McNaughton—Gen. Paget, 1130 hrs, 17 June 1943. Operation "Overlord" was the code name for the liberation of western Europe. Operation "Neptune," the assault phase, aimed at securing a lodgement on the Continent from which further operations could be developed to attain this end.

3. Col. C. P. Stacey, *Official History of the Canadian Army in the Second World War*, Vol. III: *The Victory Campaign: The Operations in North-West Europe, 1944–1945* (Ottawa: Queen's Printer, 1966) pp. 18–21, 28–30; Nigel Hamilton, *Monty*, Vol. II: *Master of the Battlefield 1942–1944.*, (Sevenoaks: Hodder and Stoughton, 1987), pp. 475–488; Omar N. Bradley, *A Soldier's Story* (New York: Henry Holt, 1951), pp. 201–204, 213–217, 221, 226–227; and Carlo D'Este, *Decision in Normandy: The Unwritten Story of Montgomery and the Allied Campaign* (London: Pan, 1984), pp. 34–39, 55–68.

4. Hamilton, *Monty*, II, 501–502, 549–552; Stacey, *Victory Campaign*, p. 30; D'Este, *Decision in Normandy*, pp. 62–65; and Omar N. Bradley and Clay Blair, *A General's Life* (New York: Simon and Schuster, 1983), pp. 232–234. Hamilton points out that the minutes of this meeting were denied to historians for almost 40 years. According to D'Este the "Montgomery master plan is as much of an enigma now as it was in 1944" (D'Este, *Decision in Normandy*, p. 476).

5. Crerar Papers (CP), Vol. 21, Crerar to Stacey 7 June 1952. It does appear, however, that the Allies were reasonably certain of the effectiveness of Operation "Fortitude South," the elaborate deception effort that painted the Normandy invasion as a feint and kept the 18 divisions of the Fifteenth German Army tied up in the area of the Pas de Calais in anticipation of a main landing there [Ronald Lewin, *Ultra Goes to War: The Secret Story* (London: Hutchinson, 1978), pp. 313–318; and Barry D. Hunt, "Operation Fortitude: D-Day and Stategic Deception," *Canadian Defense Quarterly* (CDQ) 1 (Summer 1984): 44–47].

6. Richard Lamb, *Montgomery in Europe 1943–1945: Success or Failure?* (London: Buchan and Enright, 1984), pp. 75–76; Carlo D'Este, *Bitter Victory: The Battle for Sicily July–August 1943* (London: Collins, 1988), pp. 129, 558–560; Bradley, *Soldier's Story*, pp. 229–230; and Hamilton, *Monty*, II, 330–333, 511, 589–591. Patton's initial impression of Montgomery as a military professional was highly favorable: "small, very alert, wonderfully conceited, and the best soldier—or so it seems—I have met in the war" (D'Este, *Bitter Victory*, p. 68). On the eve of the Normandy invasion, Patton wrote in his diary "I have a better impression of Montgomery than I had" (Hamilton, *Monty*, II, 590). It has been argued that Montgomery and Patton, "the outstanding Allied field commanders on the European side of World War II," were in many ways alike [Martin Blumenson and James L. Stokesbury, *Masters of the Art*

of Command (Boston: Houghton Mifflin, 1975), pp. 230–239]. According to Ladislas Farago, Patton readily conceded that Montgomery was "a good and ingenious commander, somewhat like himself" and "the only general in the Allied camp with whom he would have to compete and who was worth competing with" [Ladislas Farago, *Patton: Ordeal and Triumph* (New York: Dell, 1975), p. 492]. Patton was the only American officer to attend Montgomery's Tripoli Study Week 15–17 February 1943. At that time Montgomery described him as "an old man of about 60," which was roughly correct (Hamilton, *Monty*, II, 143).

7. Russell F. Weigley, *Eisenhower's Lieutenants: The Campaign of France and Germany, 1944–1945* (Bloomington, Ind.: Indiana University Press, 1981), pp. 80–85, 170–171; Bradley, *Soldier's Story*, pp. 69–70, 211; and Robert H. Berlin, "United States Army World War II Corps Commanders: A Composite Biography," *The Journal of Military History*, 2 (April, 1989): 149, 152, 157–158.

8. Hamilton, *Monty*, II, 146; D'Este, *Decision in Normandy*, pp. 59–60; John Swettenham, *McNaughton* (Toronto: Ryerson, 1968), Vol. II pp. 121–122, 179, 269; Lt.-Gen. Sir Brian Horrocks, *Corps Commander*, (London: Sidgwick and Jackson, 1977) pp. 21–24; and Ronald Lewin, *Montgomery as Military Commander* (New York: Stein and Day, 1971), p. 227.

9. Montgomery of Alamein Papers (MAP), BLM 126, M508 Montgomery to Brooke, 7 July 1944; and Hamilton, *Monty*, II, 146.

10. *Canadian Army Training Memorandum (CATM)*, 48 (March 1945), pp. 15–18; Robert Speaight, *Vanier: Soldier, Diplomat and Governor General* (Toronto: Collins, 1970), p. 99; and *Owl Pie* (Camberley: Staff College, 1923 and 1924). Crerar graduated thirteenth out of 30 at RMC. Son of a prominent Hamilton family, he had attended Upper Canada College, the closest thing to Eton in the Dominion. See also Lester B. Pearson, *Mike: The Memoirs of the Right Honourable Lester B. Pearson*, Vol. I: *1897–1948* (Toronto: Signet, 1973), pp. 136, 199; and J. L. Granatstein, *The Ottawa Men: The Civil Service Mandarins, 1935–1957* (Toronto: Oxford University Press, 1975), pp. 86–87, 123.

11. *CATM*, 50 (May 1945), pp. 18–19. See also J. S. McMahon's touching paean, *Professional Soldier: A Memoir of General Guy Simonds* (Winnipeg: McMahon, 1985).

12. Salmon was a regular officer of the Royal Canadian Regiment who had been wounded twice and awarded the Military Cross in the Great War. A stickler for detail and a hard taskmaster, he was generally recognized as a good trainer. For other impressions of Salmon, see Tony Foster, *Meeting of Generals* (Toronto: Methuen, 1986), p. 253; Lt. Gen. Howard Graham, *Citizen and Soldier* (Toronto: McClelland and Stewart, 1987), pp. 112–114, 126, 134, 137; and Maj.-Gen. George Kitching, *Mud and Green Fields* (Langley: Battleline, 1986), pp. 140–141, 146–147. The first is anti, the second pro, and the last probably the most balanced.

13. Col. G. W. L. Nicholson, *Official History of the Canadian Army in the Second World War*, Vol. II: *Canadians in Italy, 1943–1945* (Ottawa: Queens Printer, 1956), pp. 264, 346, 354; and Lt.-Gen. E. L. M. Burns, *General Mud: Memoirs of Two World Wars* (Toronto: Clarke Irwin, 1970) pp. 123–124.

14. Lt.-Col. J. A. English, "Reflections on the Breaking of the Gothic Line," *Infantry Journal*, 12 (Autumn 1984): 44; Nicholson, *Canadians in Italy*, pp. 364–371 and *The Gunners of Canada: A History of the Royal Regiment of Canadian Artillery*, Vol. II: *1919–1967* (Toronto: McClelland and Stewart, 1972), 184–185; and Burns,

General Mud, pp. 124–126. For the brigade commander's rendition of the Arielli action, see Kitching, *Mud and Green Fields*, pp. 186–189.

15. W. E. J. Hutchinson, "Test of a Corps Commander: Lieutenant-General Guy Granville Simonds, Normandy 1944" (unpublished M.A. thesis, University of Victoria, 1982), pp. 149–151; Col. C. P. Stacey, *Official History of the Canadian Army in the Second World War*, Vol. III: *The Victory Campaign, The Operations in North-West Europe, 1944–1945* (Ottawa: Queen's Printer, 1966), pp. 33–34, Vol I: *Six Years of War: The Army in Canada, Britain and the Pacific* (Ottawa: Queen's Printer, 1966), p. 417, and *Arms, Men and Governments: The War Policies of Canada, 1939–1945* (Ottawa: Information Canada, 1974) p. 233. The British recommended firing Sansom after "Spartan." For a while there was talk of Simonds taking 1 Corps (Stacey, *Six Years*, p. 223). Lieutenant-Colonels E. L. Booth of the 12th Armoured Regiment (Three Rivers Regiment) and J. C. Jefferson of the Loyal Edmonton Regiment skipped a rank in accordance with Commonwealth practice to command as brigadiers, respectively, the 4th Armoured and 10th Infantry Brigades. Simonds also brought with him his 1st Division artillery commander, Brig. A. B. Matthews, who took over as CCRA; his engineer commander, Lt.-Col. Geoffrey Walsh, on promotion to brigadier assumed the post of Chief Engineer. Brig. H. V. D. Laing remained DA & QMG of 2 Corps and Brig. S. F. Clarke the Chief Signals Officer. Brig. R. A. Wyman left the 1st Armoured in Italy to command the 2nd Armoured Brigade in the Normandy invasion.

16. Record Group (RG) 24, Vol. 13, 750, WD GS 2CID Summary of Events entries 1 April–23 April 1944; RG 24, Vol. 13, 711, WD GS 2 Corps papers on Exercises "Last," "Kate," and "Studiedum"; RG 24, Vol. 10, 800, 2nd Canadian Corps Commander's Conference 4 March 1944; Nicholson, *Gunners*, II, 270–271; James Alan Roberts, *The Canadian Summer*, (Toronto: University Press, 1981), p. 46; Hutchinson, "Corps Commander." pp. 151–154; and Stacey, *Victory Campaign*, pp. 38–41 and *Six Years*, pp. 252–253.

17. Crerar Papers (CP), Vol. 7, 1–8/Ops Operational Policy—2 Cdn Corps 17 February 1944; and 58–1SD Efficiency of Command, 19 February 1944, Montgomery to Simonds 23 February 1944, and Dempsey to Simonds 27 February 1944 from personal copy of Canadian Land Forces Command and Staff College collection.

18. CP, Vol. 7, Crerar to Simonds 10 December 1943. Simonds's caravan had apparently broken down the day previously, and he had requested his batman/driver to get it set up before he returned. When he arrived he found this had not been done due to the presence of an officer and other rank who claimed they were working for Crerar. On learning that they needed another four hours to complete their task, Simonds exploded with "the caravan had been built from a sketch . . . [he] had made in ten minutes" (Simonds to Crerar 15 December 1943). In the same letter, Simonds charged that Crerar had "strongly opposed. . . [his] appointment as B.G.S., that . . . [Crerar] disapproved of . . . [his] being there and that [he] . . . expect[ed] to be removed very shortly after [Crerar] took over." This was denied by Crerar.

19. CP, Vol. 7, Crerar to Montgomery 17 December 1943 and Crerar to Simonds 15 December 1943. Simonds's six-page explanatory rebuttal to Crerar was matched by the latter's five-page bureaucratic "memorandum to file" that addressed Simonds's letter paragraph by paragraph (CP, Vol. 7, Memorandum by GOC 1 Cdn Corps on contents of letter dated 15 December 1943 from Maj.-Gen. Simonds Comd 5 Cdn Armd Div, 21 December 1943). For an unsubstantiated pro-Crerar view of

this entire exchange, see Jeffrey Williams, *The Long Left Flank: The Hard Fought Way to The Reich, 1944–1945* (Toronto: Stoddart, 1988), pp. 24–25.

20. Lt.-Gen. Howard Graham, *Citizen and Soldier* (Toronto: McClelland and Stewart, 1987), pp. 158–164; Stacey, *Arms, Men and Governments*, p. 228; and Hamilton, *Monty*, Vol. II, p. 335. Simonds has been criticized for his handling of the battle for Agira in Sicily [Christopher H. N. Hull, "A Case Study of Professionalism in the Canadian Army in the 1930's and 1940's: Lieutenant-General G. G. Simonds" (unpublished M.A. thesis, Purdue University, 1989), pp. 50–57]. Here a timed program of artillery concentrations on suspected enemy locations, as opposed to a creeping barrage, supported a battalion attack. The enemy were not where they were expected, the infantry fell behind, and the attack failed. Two more separate attacks by 1st Brigade battalions were also unsuccessful. Agira was finally taken by the 2nd Brigade in two battalion actions [Graham, *Citizen Soldier*, pp. 173–177; Maj.-Gen. Chris Vokes with John P. MacLean, *My Story* (Ottawa: Gallery, 1985), pp. 113–117; and J. B. Conacher, "The Battle for Agira, July 24–8, 1943; An Episode in Canadian Military History," *Canadian Historical Review* 1 (*CHR*), (March 1949): pp. 1–21].

21. CP, Vol. 7, Montgomery to Crerar 21–12–43. Vokes attended Camberley 1935–36.

22. CP, Vol. 7, Crerar to Stuart, 13 January, 1944 and Crerar to Simonds, 8 January 1944. Crerar actually had the army's chief psychiatric advisor, Col. F. H. Van Nostrand, flown out to examine Simonds, who had just come out of the hospital to take over command of the 5th Division near Caserta. Van Nostrand was supposedly intercepted before reaching Simonds's headquarters, which was probably most fortunate. [Tony Foster, *Meeting of Generals* (Toronto: Methuen, 1986), p. 394].

23. Hamilton, *Monty*, II, 18, 453–454, 464–465.

24. Nicholson, *Canadians in Italy*, pp. 354–355. After his visit to Sicily in August 1943, McNaughton proposed to have Crerar take over "the 1st Division for a few months," but Simonds's incumbency rendered this impossible. A month later, on learning that Simonds had fallen ill, McNaughton signaled Montgomery that Crerar would be content to serve in a lesser rank if accepted as a division commander. The political nature of the dispatch of 1 Canadian Corps to the Mediterranean, however, found Crerar charged with the responsibility to bring all Canadian units and formations in Italy under his command. The Eighth Army, having never been asked, had at the same time little requirement for an armored division and still less for a corps headquarters foisted on it by Ottawa politicians. On the matter of Crerar's refusal to step down as GOC 1 Corps to command 1st Division, see also Col. Dick Malone, *Missing From the Record* (Toronto: Collins, 1946), pp. 65–68, 73–74.

25. Field-Marshal The Viscount Montgomery, *Memoirs* (London: Collins, 1958), p. 185; Vokes Papers (VP), "The Adriatic Front"; Vokes, *My Story*, pp. 152–153; Malone, *Record*, pp. 45–46, 77–79; and D'Este, *Bitter Victory*, p. 102. Vokes wrote that "Paper instructions dealing with training and administration descended on . . . [his] division in a continuous deluge," but he found it "most irritating when it verged on the stupid" (VP, "The Adriatic Front"). Canadians appear to have worn top hats on more than one occasion. Simonds was less impressed than Montgomery (Graham, *Citizen Soldier*, p. 173).

26. Stacey, *Arms, Men and Governments*, pp. 219, 245.

27. Malone, *Record*, p. 73; and Hamilton, *Monty*, II, 466.

28. Kitching, *Mud and Green Fields*, pp. 176, 178–179, 181. Crerar was not always kindly and in fact treated many lower ranking subordinates very poorly. According to Stacey, who witnessed him publicly tear a strip off his personal pilot much to the embarrassment of many within earshot, there "was some element of terror in his manner of command" [C. P. Stacey, "Canadian Leaders of the Second World War," *CHR*, 1 (March 1985): 68; and Foster, *Meeting of Generals*, p. 394]. Montgomery recommended that Dempsey be given command of the First Canadian Army and Lt.-Gen. Sir Oliver Leese the Second British. His rationale was that "the Canadians would gladly accept a British general whom they know and trust rather than have the troops mishandled by an inexperienced general of their own. Dempsey has served with them and they all know and like him. As soon as they can produce their own general, then he takes over at once; until that time, give the Canadian army to Dempsey" (Hamilton, *Monty*, I, 465).

29. CP, Vol. 5, Crerar to McNaughton, 6 June 1942, and Vol. 2, SO CMHQ to Crerar, 17 April 1942. In any event, Keller and Salmon each took command of their respective divisions, the 3rd and 1st, on 8 September 1942, several months ahead of Simonds who, after brief service as a brigade commander under the latter, became GOC 2nd Division on 13 April 1943.

30. CP, Vol. 1, Crerar memorandum to file, 3 May 1943.

31. CP, Vol. 8, Crerar to Stuart, 16 May 1944.

32. CP, Vol. 2, Crerar memorandum to COS, CMHQ 24 April 1944.

33. CP, Vol. 3, Crocker to Dempsey, 5 July 1944. "I am very sorry to have to write in this vein," reported Crocker, "because I have appreciated very much the great privilege it has been to have a Canadian Div. under my command." Crocker has been described as "stern and humourless," but one whose "long experience with armoured forces made him an excellent choice as the corps commander whose units would spearhead the invasion of . . . Normandy" (D'Este, *Decision in Normandy*, pp. 60–61). Crocker had won a DSO and MC as a Second Lieutenant in the Machine Gun Corps. He attended Staff College while still a subaltern, and was Hobart's BM in the 1930s. His command experience ran from the 3rd Armoured Brigade in France to the 6th Armoured Division, 9 and 11 Corps in North Africa. According to Field Marshal Lord Carver, "to serve him was an education in itself." The Editor, *British Army Review*, described him as follows: "A man of legendary personal courage and absolute integrity, he had the unusual gift of being as fine a staff officer as he was a commander in battle" ["Thoughts on Command in Battle," *British Army Review*, 1 (July 1978): 5].

34. CP, Vol. 3, Dempsey to Montgomery, 6 July 1944.

35. CP, Vol. 3, Montgomery to Crerar, 8 July 1944. He added that "the Canadian soldier is such a magnificent chap that he deserves, and should be given, really good generals."

36. CP, Vol. 14, Crerar to Maj.-Gen. H. H. Matthews, 3 October 1939.

37. CP, Vol. 2, SO CMHQ to Crerar, 17 Apr 42; Nicholson, *Gunners*, II, 190, 271; and Stacey, *Six Years*, pp. 331, 343. Brigadier H. O. N. Brownfield had gone to Italy in the last two months of 1943 to be CCRA of 1 Corps. He returned to resume the appointment of Brigadier Royal Artillery (BRA), First Canadian Army in December 1943.

38. Hutchinson, "Corps Commander," pp. 74–75, 78–79; CP, Vol. 7, Simonds

to Crerar, 15 December 1943; and Stacey, "Canadian Leaders of the Second World War," pp. 68–69. DS at Camberley during this period included Lieutenant-Colonels W. J. Slim and E. E. Dorman-Smith, later COS Eighth Army (Hutchinson, "Corps Commander," p. 74). On Foulkes, see Foster, *Meeting of Generals*, pp. 84–85, 340, 424–425 and Kitching, *Mud and Green Fields*, pp. 206, 226–227. On Simonds, see W. Denis and Shelagh Whitaker, *Tug of War; The Canadian Victory that Opened Antwerp* (Toronto: Stoddart, 1984), pp. 77–79.

39. The CCRA of 2 Corps was Brig. A. B. Matthews, the CRA 2nd Division Brig. R. H. Keefler, the CRA 3rd Division Brig. P. A. S. Todd, the CRA 4th Division Brig. J. N. Lane, and the Commander 2 AGRA Brig. E. R. Suttie.

40. CP, Vol. 2, 21 Army Group M512 of 21–7–44; and Memorandum on Conference with C-in-C 21 Army Group held at Tac HQ, 21 Army Group at 2100 hrs, 20 July 1944.

41. CP, Vol. 2, Crerar to Crocker, 22 July 1944.

42. CP, Vol. 8, Crocker to Crerar, 24 July 1944.

43. Cp, Vol. 8, Crerar to Montgomery (whom he calls "Monty"), 24 July 1944; and Comments by GOC-in-C First Canadian Army on Memorandum Dated 24 July 1944, Submitted by GOC 1 Brit Corps.

44. D'Este, *Decision in Normandy*, p. 194.

45. CP, Vol. 8, Memorandum of a Meeting with C-in-C 21 Army Group at Tac HQ 21 Army Group commencing 1500 hrs, 25 July 1944. Eventually two operations, much like Crocker suggested, were planned: Operation "Rawlinson" to be conducted by the 3rd British Division south of the Bois de Bavent; and Operation "Byng" to be carried out by the 49th Division north of the wood. The detachment of the 3rd Division for Operation "Bluecoat" on 1 August precluded these operations from ever being executed (Stacey, *Victory Campaign*, pp. 198–201). In 21 Army Group M515 of 27–7–44, Montgomery stated he "realized" that limited resources "may prevent the full implementation" of M512 direction concerning the advancement of the First Canadian Army left flank. Given that the German 12-cm mortar could hurl a 35-pound bomb 6,500 yards and the feared 15-cm six-barrelled *Nebelwerfer* several 75-pound bombs more than 7,000 yards, easily reaching past the objective line selected by Crerar, it would appear that Crocker might well have been the more tactically astute.

46. CP, Vol. 8, Montgomery to Crerar, 26 July 1944. That Crerar absorbed this lesson is obvious from his later remarks: "The C-in-C would not give a direct order to a particular Div. He would tell me what action he wanted carried out. Indeed, under normal conditions, I, as Army Comd, would not instruct Gen Simonds, a Corps Comd, which tps should be employed by him to carry out my requirements, though I might suggest that, say, the P.A.D. [Polish Armoured Division] seemed to be well placed to do the job." (CP, Vol. 21, Crerar to Stacey, 23 July 1947).

47. CP, Vol. 8, Montgomery to Crerar, 26 July 1944; and see Stacey, *Arms, Men and Governments*, pp. 223–224.

48. CP, Vol. 3, Tactical Directive by Comd, First Cdn Army, 22 July 1944, under GOC-in-C 3–4 Crerar to Comd 1 Brit Corps, A/Comd 2 Cdn Corps, and A/GOC 4 Cdn Armd Div. Regarding the 14 May speech, see CP, Vol. 1, GOC 3–6 Crerar to Comds 1 Cdn Inf Div, 5 Cdn Armd Div, 1 Cdn Armd Bde, 26 February 1944.

49. Alanbrooke Papers (AP), 14/1 Montgomery to Brooke, 26–7–44.

50. Richard Simpkin, *Race to the Swift: Thoughts on Twenty-First Century Warfare* (London: Brassey's, 1985), p. 230.

51. Berlin, "United States Army World War II Corps Commanders," p. 152; and Maj. French L. MacLean, "The Unknown Generals—German Corps Commanders in World War II" (unpublished M.A. thesis, US Army Command and General Staff College, 1988), pp. 40, 116.

52. Hamilton, *Monty*, II, 675; and VP, "The Adriatic Front." When Montgomery expressed these same sentiments to the CIGS on 7 July 1944, the latter wrote back: "It is evident that the Canadians are very short of senior Commanders, but it is equally clear that we shall have to make the best use of the material we have. . . . I want you to make the best possible use of Crerar. . . . You can keep him busy small and give him the less important roles." MAP, BLM 126, M508 Montgomery to Brooke 7 July 1944 and BLM 1/101 Brooke to Montgomery 11 July 1944.

Chapter 9

Throes Beyond the Beach

Ask GOC when he comes to lunch today to bring for Corps Comd an explanation of why his Div has lost in 2 days 158 brens, 65 Piats, 46 2″ mortars.

Operations Log 2nd Canadian Infantry Division, 24 July 1944[1]

With the First Canadian Army relegated to a follow-up role, Dominion participation in the D-Day amphibious assault was provided by the 3rd Canadian Infantry Division and 2nd Canadian Armoured Brigade, both part of 1 British Corps, in the Second British Army. That they and all other Allied formations failed to attain their objectives on 6 June set the tone for later operations beyond the bridgehead. The 2nd Armoured Brigade, for example, came nowhere near capturing Evrecy southwest of Carpiquet and east of the Odon River from where it was to patrol forward to the Orne. Most unfortunately, the unexpected presence and piecemeal commitment of the 21st Panzer Division prevented the 3rd British Division from securing Caen, an inland port and communications center of 54,000 located at the confluence of both rivers. Naturally, since the city and rivers together constituted serious barriers to movement, the Germans viewed this area as a gateway to Paris and key to the defense of Normandy.

On the afternoon of D-Day, 1st SS Panzer Corps under *SS-Obergruppenfuehrer* Joeseph "Sepp" Dietrich assumed responsibility for defense of the Caen sector with orders to hurl the invaders back to the sea.[2] From this point onward the struggle in Normandy devolved into a series of bitterly contested local actions. Here the Canadian Army incurred its heaviest casualty days of the war. Indeed, it has been demonstrated that in northwest Europe 1944–45, the Canadian combat infantryman stood a greater chance of being killed or injured than his father had in an equivalent period on the Western Front in the Great War. The restricted battlefield of Normandy, which reflected a German troop-to-space density two and a half times that of the Russian front, established this pattern. As Carlo D'Este put it, "Despite the vast array of sophisticated and deadly weapons of war available to both sides, success or failure in Normandy ultimately became the ability of the foot soldier to take or hold *ground*."[3] Lightning war had come to be conducted at a more earthly pace.

In the Canadian sector north and south of Caen, a gently rolling plain of meadowland and wheatfields, termed corn in British accounts, characterized the Norman countryside. Running roughly along the line Bayeux-Caen-Falaise, it abounded in small woods, orchards, and innumerable hamlets of solidly constructed stone houses and farm buildings. The occasional large forest marked its southern reaches, while the heights to the east of the River Dives presented another barrier. To the west of Falaise lay the true bocage, a patchwork of small fields bounded by ditches and earthen embankments crowned with virtually impenetrable thickets whose roots had been undisturbed for years. Behind these embankments, which were as high as a man, troops could move concealed from fire and view, even from the air. Interconnected by numerous narrow roads and tiny hamlets, the bocage was anything but ideal for armor; it not only restricted main gun range, but in climbing banks and crossing roads, tanks invariably heaved up, exposing their soft undersides to the deadly short-range infantry *Panzerfaust*. On the Caen plain, on the other hand, armored attackers faced longer range tank killers like the 88-and 75-mm Pak 40 deployed within a defensive grid based on woods and hamlets, backed up by a system of violent panzer counterattack.[4]

The 3rd Canadian Division and the 2nd Canadian Armoured Brigade, trained principally as assault forces, were among the first to encounter such defenses. They also learned the hard lesson that the best tank country was implicitly that with the fewest antitank weapons. But it was in the bocage on the early morning of 13 June, after the firm establishment of the bridgehead, that the Second British Army lost a golden opportunity to envelop Caen. As a result of Dempsey's personal intervention within Bucknall's 30 Corps, the 7th Armoured Division managed in a bold stroke to penetrate as far as Villers Bocage. There seemed to be little appreciation within the division, however, that tanks could not go it alone in this type of terrain, which called for even more intimate tank-infantry cooperation than the desert. The reluctance of commanders in the absence of orders to disperse their squadrons or regiments off roads further increased the vulnerability of the division. Unfortunately, they also encountered the Tiger tank.

Map 9.1
The Bocage

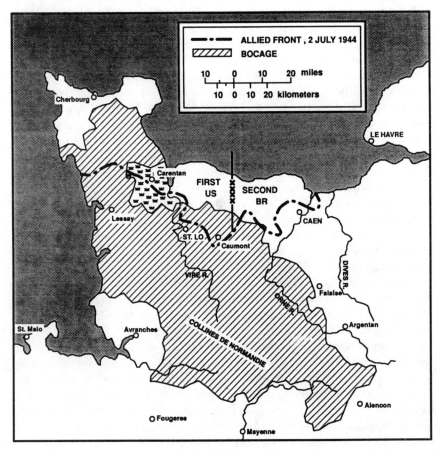

In a series of audacious attacks with four of these behemoths, plus several other tanks and infantry, *Obersturmfuehrer* Michael Wittmann, commanding No. 2 Company, 101st Heavy Tank Battalion, 1st SS Panzer Corps exacted a heavy price for such faulty local tactics. The quick action of this tank ace, credited with 119 kills on the Eastern Front, knocked out nearly 30 tanks and several other vehicles, completely shattering the leading columns of the 22nd Armoured Brigade and throwing the 7th Armoured Division onto the defensive. The intervening arrival of the 2nd Panzer Division made it clear that the British lacked sufficient infantry to enable them to hold out. Having chosen not to reinforce the success of the 7th Armoured initially, and choosing further not to consult Dempsey, Bucknall now made the fateful decision to order the division to withdraw.[5] More than a month's hard fighting would be required before the British returned.

A New Zealander, Brigadier James Hargest, observed the 7th Armoured during this period and noted that on 11 June outside Tilly-sur-Seulles, north of Villers Bocage, the infantry of the 131st Brigade were three miles behind the tanks, whose junior officers complained to him about lack of infantry. On mentioning this to the division commander, Hargest apparently received the reply that the "pace was too hot for infantry" and that the latter "preferred to go on alone [with tanks]." Hargest concluded that "our tanks are badly led and fought. Only our superior numbers and our magnificent artillery support keeps them in the field at all." He attributed "a great deal of their failure . . . to the retention of the absurd Regimental system. Because there is no work for cavalry, the Cavalry Regts were given tanks. The officers are trained in armour not because they like armour, but because they are cavalry men. They are in armour because they like horses in other units." He went on to state that the Royal Tank Regiment was "sound and every unit in armour should belong to . . . [it]. At the moment we suffer because of the incompatibility and lack of the "will to fight" in the Armoured Corps."[6]

The fight back to Villers Bocage took until 4 August. In the meantime the perimeter of the narrow but contiguous Normandy bridgehead that had been established on 10 June looked, even to the less faint-hearted, precariously near becoming permanent. The arrival of the 2nd Panzer in the Villers Bocage area, which ominously represented the commitment of German reserves, caused Montgomery on 14 June to suspend all offensive operations for 48 hours in order to regain his balance. Within the Second British Army, 1 Corps received orders to adopt an aggressive defensive posture in the Caen sector, while 30 Corps was warned for offensive action against the Villers Bocage-Caumont area to arrest the movement westward of the 2nd Panzer. Lieutenant-General Bradley, charged with the reduction of Cherbourg and breaking-out, successfully argued at the same time he would have to postpone the latter task as the First U.S. Army could not do both. While Montgomery momentarily revived the idea of a double envelopment of Caen, he eventually dropped it for lack of deployment space within the Orne bridgehead.

Montgomery instead finally directed the Second Army to launch 8 Corps of upward of three divisions in a major thrust between Carpiquet and Rauray striking southeast to the Orne. Operation "Epsom" as this 25–29 June attack was called, intentionally resembled Montgomery's blitz attack at El Hamma, which had seen 10 Corps supported by the Desert Air Force successfully flank the Mareth Line in late March 1943. Indeed, El Hamma, which witnessed the first recorded use of forward air controllers (FACs) in battle, confirmed that the problem of air support for the army had been satisfactorily worked out. There is reason to believe, however, that Montgomery himself did not fully appreciate the difficulties of fighting through the bocage. In the course of establishing a bridgehead over the Odon, 8 Corps precipitated a battle of attrition that approached Great War dimensions. Casualties in the infantry ran well in excess of 50 percent, losses that could ill be afforded, but which nonetheless attested to the nature of the fighting.[7]

While "Epsom" did not attain its territorial objectives, the Germans had been forced to use all available reserves to stem its onslaught. The 2nd SS Panzer Corps of the 9th SS (*Hohenstauffen*) and 10th SS (*Frundsberg*) Panzer Divisions, which had been ordered back to France on 12 June after having blunted the Red Army spring offensive at Tarnopol, was prematurely committed in a costly countermove that succeeded in pushing back, but not eliminating, the Odon bridgehead. Indeed, from "Epsom" up to the breakout on 25 July, between 560 and 725 panzers continuously deployed against the British sector, whereas during this same period the Americans rarely faced more than 190. Four of the seven divisions opposing the British and Canadians were also SS, which each fielded two more infantry battalions than normal army panzer divisions.[8] In the Panther battalion of their panzer regiments, of course, the Germans evinced an overall qualitative superiority in armament that issued from the Eastern Front. The Sherman 75 mm could not pierce the frontal armor of a Panther and could only deal with a Tiger from the rear or point-blank from enfilade. Ironically, Anglo-American field armies were also being made to suffer for the technologically advanced military state of their Russian allies.

Significantly, Montgomery from 25 June ordered the suppression of reports that commented adversely upon the inadequacies of Allied tanks and equipment as compared with the German. While concern for morale prompted him to take such action, he also seems to have been convinced that when Allied weapons and equipment were intelligently used the German could be handled. Heavy 45-ton Panthers and clumsy 56-ton Tigers with their respective 75-mm and 88-mm high-velocity guns had, after all, been encountered in Tunisia and were found to be vulnerable to six- pounder fire on their sides and rear. Then, too, they could be stopped as were the 9th and 10th SS on the Odon by massive artillery fire from medium and heavy guns. The 17-pounder was also more than a match for the 100-mm frontal armor of the Tiger, as it could penetrate 111 mm at 2,000 yards. In mounting this gun into some of their Shermans, the British ensured that the Allies had at least one tank, renamed the Firefly, which could take on German models.[9] Unfortunately, the Firefly, which initially lacked a good high-explosive round, was only issued on a limited scale and naturally became a prime enemy target. As a result of experience gained, the 2nd Canadian Armoured Brigade organized its squadrons on a four troop basis, with one Firefly per troop. While the position of the troop leader was left for units to decide, it was thought prudent to have him lead in a less conspicuous Sherman, leaving the troop sergeant back in the Firefly to cover troop movement.[10]

Yet, despite serious technological disadvantages in tanks, it was additional infantry not armor that Montgomery really needed. On 24 June he informed Crerar that Guards Armoured and the 4th Canadian Armoured Divisions were being "phased back . . . [to] come in at the end of the 'build-up' ". The congested state of the bridgehead, which figured prominently in this decision, seems also to have presented Montgomery with an opportune excuse for keeping Crerar "out of the party" as long as possible. Until the Second British Army had gained sufficient "elbow room" to the northeast, east, and southeast of Caen, he asserted, there was neither sufficient frontage nor depth to employ or deploy another army. The battle area could handle another corps, but not all the ancillary army troops that would perforce accompany the First Canadian Army headquarters. There also remains the distinct possibility, of course, that Montgomery at this critical juncture was simply unwilling to take a chance on Crerar.

Montgomery proposed instead to build up 12 British Corps with the 53rd and 59th Infantry Divisions, and then introduce the 2nd Canadian Infantry Division and Headquarters 2 Canadian Corps with its corps troops. Dempsey had in the meantime been requested to place the 3rd Canadian Infantry Division under Simonds as soon as he could assume operational responsibility. Following the arrival of 2 Canadian Corps, Crerar's Head-quarters First Canadian Army with army troops would be brought in, prepared to take over the eastern sector of the 21st Army Group with initially 1 British and later 2 Canadian Corps under command. But until Caen and the line of the River Dives were secured, Montgomery preferred to have Dempsey in charge, even it meant his having to command five corps.[11] This also ensured that Simonds commanded "all Canadians in France," for he was "far and away the[ir] best general . . . the equal of any British Corps Commander, and . . . far better than Crerar."[12]

As outlined earlier in March 1944, the task set for the First Canadian Army had been envisioned as that of taking over the eastern sector and advancing to capture Le Havre and Rouen in an operation code-named "Axehead." On 7 May, however, 21st Army Group had cautioned that as the "type of country immediately South of the initial bridgehead d[id] not favour a rapid advance . . . and a period may supervene round about D + 14, when there will be a grave risk of operations stabilising on a line which gives the Germans advantages in defence." It had also warned that once through the bocage when greater scope for armored maneuver would exist, the "aim . . . [w]ould be to contain the maximum enemy forces facing the Eastern flank of the bridgehead."[13] On 18 May Crerar produced Operation "Pintail," an appreciation of the "problem of the defence of the Eastern sector of the Allied bridgehead against heavy and determined German at-tacks" by two to three panzer plus seven to eight infantry divisions.

The appreciation assumed that the First Canadian Army would take over the eastern sector on or after D + 25 (1 July) and that it would extend as far south as the Argentan-Evreux road. In concluding that he should base his coastal flank on the River Touques and broaden his frontage to include the Argentan-Falaise road, Crerar identified a requirement for three corps. From detailed topographical and intelligence studies, the Argentan-Falaise axis was selected for its "minimum of transverse obstacles" to be the most likely enemy thrust line. Should the enemy "penetrate to the high ground between ARGENTAN and FALAISE," recorded Crerar, he would dominate the valley of the River Dives south of Mezidon and "gravely imperil the maintenance of any of our forces East of R DIVES and NORTH of the road LISIEUX-CAEN."[14]

As actual operations developed, Crerar's army did not become operational until 23 July, seven weeks after D-Day and 12 days after 2 Canadian Corps took over a sector of the Second British Army front. By this time the 3rd Canadian Infantry Division supported by the 2nd Canadian Armoured Brigade had been in action for 48 days. On Juno beach on D-Day, the 3rd Division had taken heavier casualties than its sister British formations, but it had also advanced farther inland than any other Allied division. In striving the following day to attain its D-Day objective, the general line of Putot-en-Bessin and Carpiquet, it had run into what its commander feared most: panzer counterattack. During the afternoon of 7 June, in what may have been an ambush, 25 Panzergrenadier Regiment of the 12th SS (*Hitlerjugend*) Division launched three infantry battalions supported by artillery and a battalion of Mark IVs against the left flank of the leading tank and infantry elements of the 3rd Division. This reverse, which saw the Canadians thrown out of Buron and Authie, may have been avoided had the 3rd Division's SP guns been within range as they should have been.[15] The next morning, Dempsey visited Keller and "impressed on him the importance of getting his artillery and armour properly under control."[16]

On the morning of 8 June the 2nd Battalion, 26 Panzergrenadier Regiment also counterattacked the Royal Winnipeg Rifles occupying Putot-en-Bessin. Believing themselves surrounded by panzers and superior enemy forces, three companies of the Winnipegs attempted to withdraw under cover of smoke, losing heavily in the process. In reality, no German tanks participated in the attack, though it does appear that British tanks of the 24th Lancers did counterattack from the northwest. The Germans attacked with but three panzergrenadier companies of the 2nd Battalion/26 Panzergrenadier Regiment infiltrating between the Winnipeg companies. Significantly, each SS company possessed on average two to three MG 42 general-purpose machine guns per section as compared to one Bren in each Canadian equivalent. That evening, however, the Canadian Scottish Regiment supported by a squadron of tanks and two field artillery regiments counterattacked behind a creeping barrage to retrieve the situation, which ultimately cost the Canadians nearly 400 casualties.[17]

The 12th SS Panzer Division and its Siegfriedesque commander, *Stan-*

Map 9.2
Panzer Counterattack, 7 June 1944

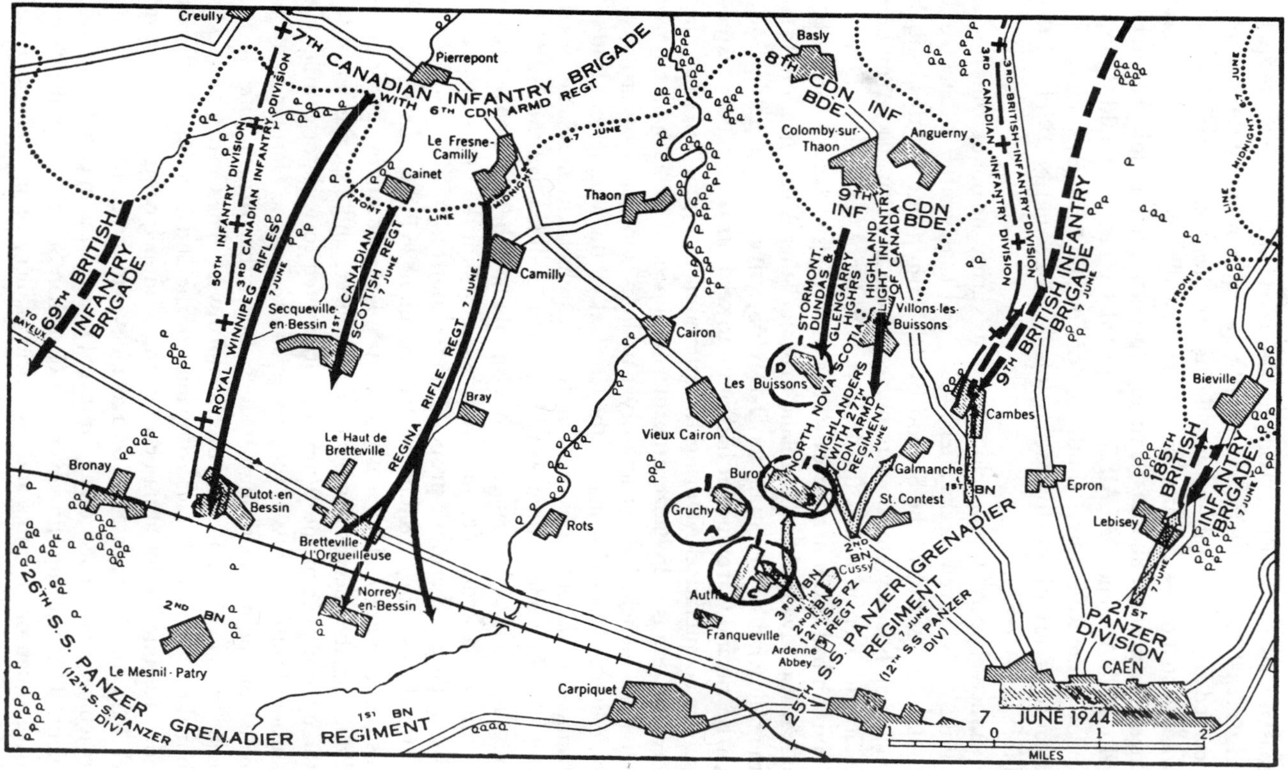

Map 9.3
Infantry Counterattacks, 8 June 1944

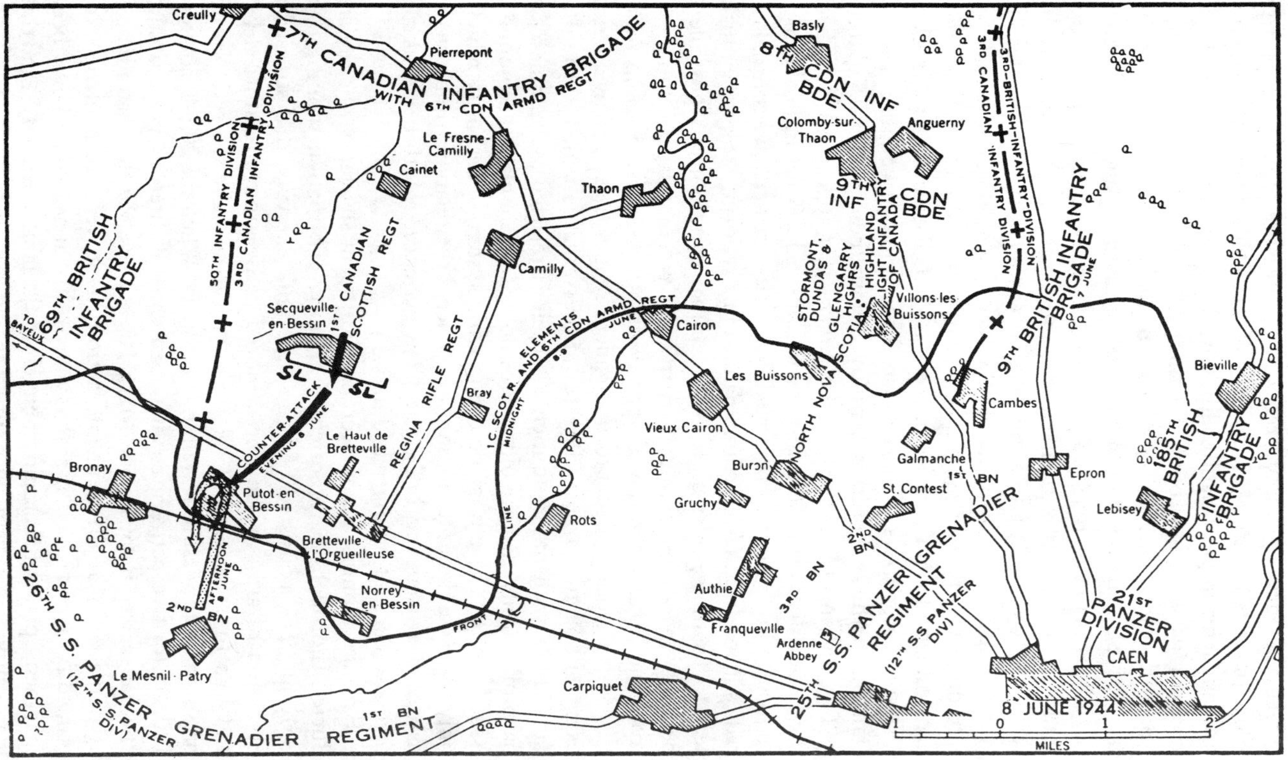

dartenfuehrer Kurt Meyer, were to remain the scourge of Canadian arms throughout the Normandy campaign. They also became the standard by which Canadians proudly preferred to measure their battlefield prowess. Now practically part of Canadian folklore, Meyer and his men continue to hold an arresting fascination. Like the 3rd Canadian Infantry Division, the *Hitlerjugend* went into battle for the first time in Normandy. Dubbed the "baby division with the milk bottle badge" by a disparaging Allied press, the 12th SS Panzer Division had been formed in June 1943 almost entirely of youths between 16½ and 17 years of age. This was a consequence of a Hitler Youth Organization scheme, introduced after Stalingrad, to induct selected young men into a volunteer division, which on passing the test of war would serve as a model for the incorporation of additional volunteers into other German divisions. While command cadres of officers and NCOs came mostly from the experienced 1st SS (*Leibstandarte Adolf Hitler*) Panzer Division, organizers quickly grasped that innovative rather than standard training methods should be employed with these youthful volunteers.[18]

The training philosophy of the *Hitlerjugend* appears to have been more boy scout than orthodox military in approach. Great importance attached to inculcating a sense of responsibility, self-sacrifice, and comradeship. Parade square drill, hardly countenanced in any form, took very much a back seat to training under as realistic combat conditions as possible for impending operations. Fieldcraft, particularly camouflage techniques learned from the Russians, received special attention. Marksmanship training focused on shooting not on formal gallery ranges, but exclusively in the field using silhouette targets. Physical fitness was attained through sports, "marching with full equipment . . . [being] rejected as . . . unnecessary and harmful." Only 18-year-olds were allowed cigarettes, those younger being issued candy. There was "no dominating system of authority which knows only orders and unquestioning obedience," the relationship between battle-hardened officers and NCOs and inexperienced youth being likened unto that of older and younger brothers.

For nine months, despite certain equipment shortages, the division conducted thorough, battle-oriented training. Formation training, begun in early in 1944, consisted of large-scale tank exercises that stressed the co-operation of arms within the armored battle group (reinforced battalion) and live fire. By April 1944 the division had already suffered 15 dead, presumably the result of training accidents. When the 20,540 soldiers of the 12th SS (of two panzergrenadier regiments of three infantry battalions and one panzer regiment of one Mark IV and one Panther battalion, 141 operational tanks in all) went into action, they were considered "excellently trained, as well trained as scarcely any other division ha[d] ever been . . . so that their operational employment c[ould] be fully justified." And this, more than simple fanaticism, was surely their great forte.[19]

The last major Canadian operation undertaken against the 12th SS during

Map 9.4
Le Mesnil–Patry Action, 11 June 1944

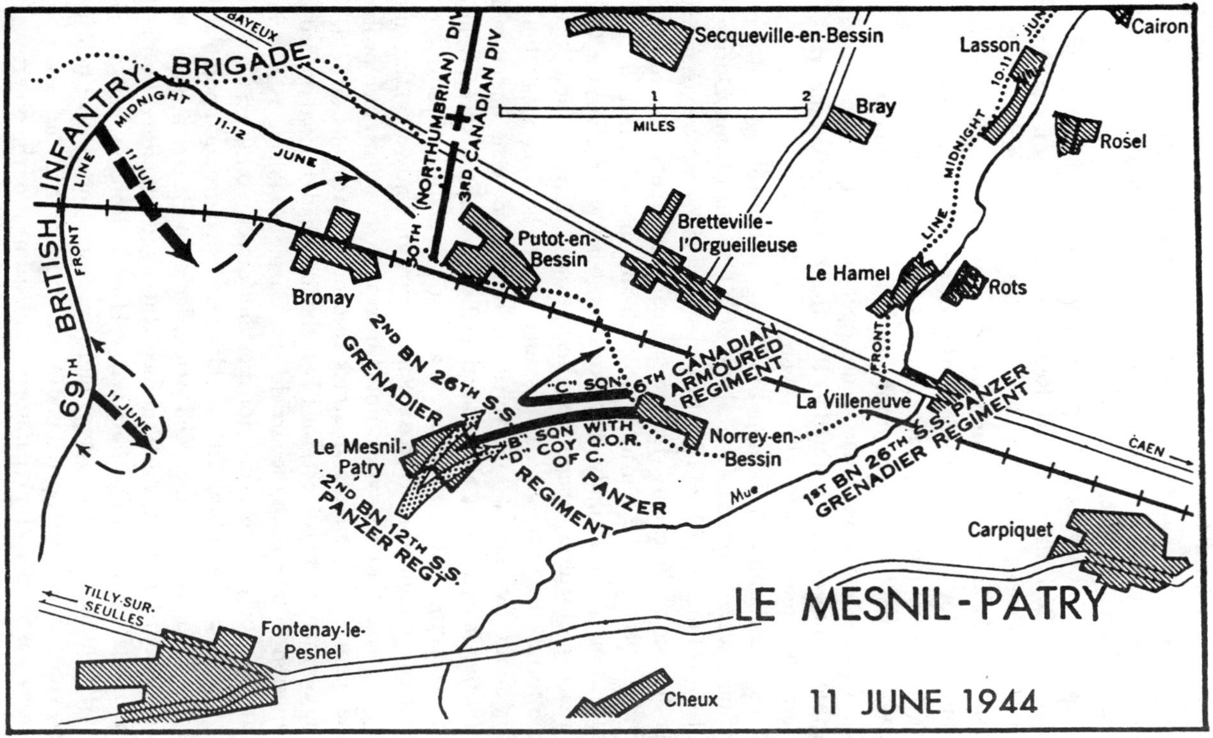

LE MESNIL - PATRY

11 JUNE 1944

the month of June was "a complete and costly failure." At 1430 hours 11 June, Wyman's 2nd Canadian Armoured Brigade, having been warned at 0800 hours, launched the 6th Armoured Regiment (1st Hussars) and the Queen's Own Rifles toward Le Mesnil-Patry in an effort to secure the high ground south of Cheux. Incredibly, a squadron of tanks with a company of infantry riding on them led the advance. Forced to dismount by mortar and machine-gun fire, some of these infantrymen managed to accompany the tanks into Le Mesnil-Patry, which was defended by elements of the 2nd Battalion, 26 Panzergrenadier Regiment. Unhappily for the attackers, the 2nd (Mark IV) Battalion, 12th Panzer Regiment, had just deployed to the south of the town. An immediate counterattack by elements of a panzer company, for the loss of three Mark IVs, resulted in the virtual annihilation of the leading Hussar squadron. In this disgraceful affair, the infantry company suffered 96 casualties, more than half of them missing. The action at Le Mesnil-Patry was the last major operation in June. Total Canadian casualties to this point amounted to 196 officers and 2,635 other ranks, slightly more than one-third of whom were dead.[20]

Despite continuous shelling, mortaring, and patrolling, the last two weeks of June were comparatively calm on the Canadian front. During the night of 16/17 June, the 7th and 8th Brigades even managed to exchange positions in the face of the enemy. Due to language differences, however, the interchange between the Canadian Scottish and the Regiment de la Chaudière turned out to be a highly dangerous and harrowing affair; the Chaudières, in fact, prematurely abandoned their position, leaving but a dozen men of the former regiment's reconnaissance parties holding a battalion frontage for about five hours.[21] Fortunately, this lapse went undetected by the *Hitlerjugend* who were also adjusting their dispositions largely in response to increasing 30 Corps pressure that, with Operation "Epsom," eventually exacted a terrible toll. Two days after "Epsom," however, the "impression arose at . . . [12th SS, which noted increased reconnaissance probing,] that the enemy was planning an attack to capture Carpiquet airfield."[22] In this the Germans were correct, for 1 British Corps had ordered the 3rd Canadian Division to take both the airfield and Carpiquet village as a prelude to its participation in a three-divisional assault directly on Caen.

Operation "Windsor," the attack across open ground upon Carpiquet on 4 July involved Brigadier Ken Blackader's 8th Canadian Infantry Brigade, augmented by the Royal Winnipeg Rifles and supported by the 10th Armoured Regiment (The Fort Garry Horse). Roughly 760 divisional and AGRA guns from one heavy, eight medium, and twelve field regiments provided artillery support. The 16-inch guns of HMS *Rodney* and a monitor, *Roberts*, assisted with preparatory bombardment of the objective area. Additional maneuver support provided included the heavy (4.2-inch) mortars and Vickers medium machine guns of the Cameron Highlanders of Ottawa (M.G.) and three squadrons of "special armor" (flail tanks for beating paths

Map 9.5
Operation "Windsor"

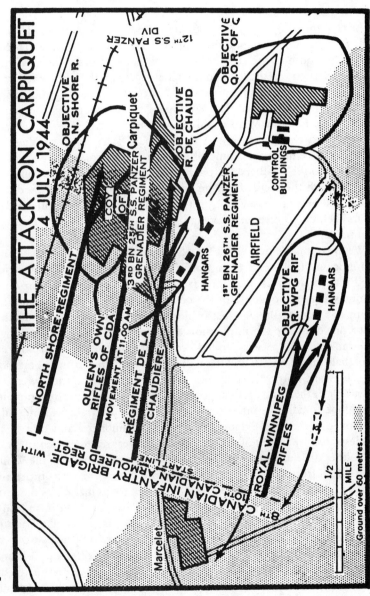

THE ATTACK ON CARPIQUET
4 JULY 1944

NORTH SHORE REGIMENT

OBJECTIVE N. SHORE R.

12TH S.S PANZER DIV

Carpiquet

3RD BN 25TH S.S. PANZER GRENADIER REGIMENT

OBJECTIVE R. DE CHAUD

OBJECTIVE Q.O.R. OF C

QUEEN'S OWN RIFLES OF CDA

MOVEMENT AT 11:00 AM

COY OF

RÉGIMENT DE LA CHAUDIÈRE

HANGARS

1ST BN 26TH S.S. PANZER GRENADIER REGIMENT

AIRFIELD

CONTROL BUILDINGS

8TH CANADIAN INFANTRY BRIGADE WITH 10TH CANADIAN ARMOURED REGT.

STARTLINE

ROYAL WINNIPEG RIFLES

OBJECTIVE R. WPG RIF

HANGARS

Marcelet

1/2

MILE

Ground over 60 metres....

through minefields, flame-throwing Crocodiles, and Assault Vehicles, Royal Engineers (AVRE) designed to hurl petards against strong points and provide armored cover for soldiers engaged on demolition tasks). Two squadrons of tank-busting Typhoon fighter-bombers were also on call to the brigade.

As elaborated in a 17-page operation order, the first phase of "Windsor" called for the concomitant capture of the village of Carpiquet and the hangars north and south of the airfield. This was to be accomplished by the North Shore Regiment on the left and the Chaudières on the right, each supported by a squadron of tanks reinforced by "specials," attacking the village from south of Villeneuve, while the Winnipegs simultaneously struck out for the south hangars from Marcelet. The Winnipeg attack was to be supported by the third tank squadron. A diversionary sally north to Vieux Cairon was also to be mounted from Villeneuve 15 minutes later by a squadron of the Sherbrooke Fusiliers. In phase two the Queen's Own Rifles were to pass through the secured village and seize the control tower and buildings at the east end of the airfield. In the event, the attack commenced at 0500 hours behind a creeping barrage fired by six field and two medium regiments.[23]

We now know that the 12th SS divined 8th Brigade intentions from monitoring "tank voice radio traffic" and proceeded to heavily mortar and shell Canadian attack positions from their time of occupation on 3 July. Minutes after the opening of the covering barrage on 4 July, the Germans dropped a counterbarrage just behind it, which not only caused substantial casualties but gave the impression that Canadian shells were falling short. The tanks and "specials" rolled on relentlessly toward Carpiquet village nonetheless, the AVRE and flamethrowers reducing strong points and German forward outposts. Armored mobility and effectiveness were reduced by rubble in the built-up area, however, and a fierce house-to-house infantry struggle ensued. The intense artillery support program had obviously not destroyed the essential fabric of a well-camouflaged and dug in defense orchestrated by barely 50 men from 25 Panzergrenadier Regiment.

Neither did the barrage effectively cover the movement of the Winnipegs, whose axis from Marcelet took them somewhat south of its protective fire. The battalion, mortared incessantly, also had to go it alone as the third tank squadron, earmarked for phase two, stayed back in reserve and only supported by fire. Although faced by the remnants of the 1st Battalion, 26 Panzergrenadier Regiment, which had been practically wiped out in "Epsom," the Winnipegs appear to have drawn the stiffer opposition; there were an estimated 17 tanks and SP guns dug in to the east of the airfield. Yet, in response to a personal appeal by the CO, the battalion was allocated only a reinforced troop of tanks for intimate support. When the two leading Winnipeg companies did finally reach the hangars at 0900 hours, the intensity of enemy fire was so great that it was impossible to hold on. Ordered to withdraw around 1300 hours, they were compelled by the nature of the open ground to retire half-way to their start line.[24]

Phase two was in the meantime set in train and the Queen's Own Rifles committed to battle. Unfortunately, Carpiquet had not been entirely cleared of enemy, and it took the battalion some time to reach the far end of the village. With the withdrawal of the Winnipegs from the south hangars, however, any Queen's Own Rifles thrust toward the control buildings risked exposing them to devastating flanking fire from that quarter. They were accordingly ordered to wait, while the Winnipegs, their first attack shattered, were sent in again. At 1600 hours the second attempt got underway with an armored squadron in support attempting a sweeping maneuver through low ground around the enemy left flank. Once again the infantry reached the hangars, but the tanks, having lost contact, were stalled by antitank fire and threatened by panzer counterattack. At 2100 hours brigade ordered the battalion to return to its start line. During the next two days the 8th Brigade fought off three German counterattacks to hold what was gained. The cost had been high: 377 casualties, of whom 117 were dead. Tank casualties in comparison were relatively light, except for the squadron supporting the Winnipegs which lost 6 out of 15.[25]

Obviously, the decision to launch the Winnipegs over two kilometers of open ground without any intimate direct fire support was highly questionable. The decision to hurl them in again with the minimum tank support they should have had in the first place could also be categorized as too little, too late. Whether or not disproportionate confidence in the capacity of massive artillery bombardment to overcome enemy resistance contributed to neglect of sensible maneuver arrangements, it is hard to fault the corps commander, Crocker, for attributing the "limited success of... [the Carpiquet] operation ... to a lack of control and leadership from the top." More divisional guidance should have been given and additional resources committed when "things started to go not quite right." The army commander agreed that "the operation was not well handled" and considered that it "proved ... quite conclusively that ... [Keller was] not fitted to command a Division." "At a time when the situation demanded a clear-cut decision and firm control," Dempsey charged, the divisional commander "failed to take a grip."[26] In a letter to Brooke, Montgomery wrote: "Keller has not proved himself to be quite fit to com[man]d a Div[ision]; he is unable to get the best out of his soldiers—who are grand chaps."[27]

The day after the attack on Carpiquet, the order for Operation "Charnwood," the capture of Caen, was issued by 1 British Corps to its participating three infantry divisions and supporting armored brigades. Planned for 8 July, the operation called for a concentric advance in five phases: first, an assault by the 3rd and 59th British Divisions from the north in a sustained drive on Caen; second, an attack by the 3rd Canadian Division from the northwest to secure the area as far south as Authie; third, a general push

Map 9.6
Operation "Charnwood"

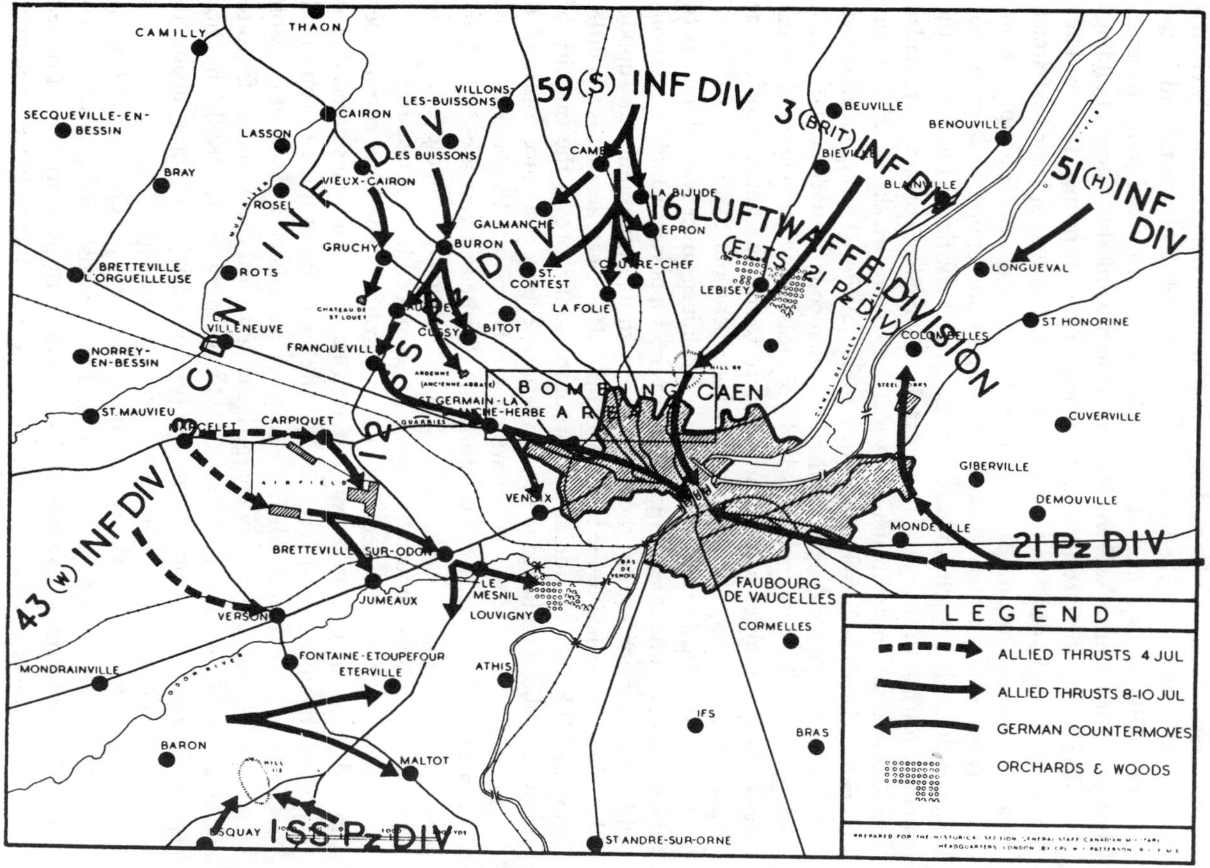

into Caen and toward the line Franqueville-Ardenne; fourth, the final reduction of Carpiquet and mopping-up to the River Orne; and fifth, consolidation and British divisional thrusts to obtain bridgeheads over the River
Orne. Support laid on for the attack included "special armour" from the
79th Division, the firepower of 3 and 4 AGRA, and naval gunfire from
several warships of the Royal Navy.

"Charnwood" also saw heavy bombers of Bomber Command employed
for the first time in a close support role on the battlefield. Apart from their
reputed salutary effect upon morale, however, these strategic engines of
destruction seem to have yielded little in the way of tactical advantage.
Indeed, because a 6,000 yard troop safety distance was required, the rec-
tangular target area finally chosen (4,000 yards long by 1,500 wide) lay well
behind the German forward ring of fortified villages and contained pitifully
few enemy defensive positions at all. The fact that 467 bombers dropped
2,562 tons of bombs between 2150 and 2230 hours on 7 July and the ground
attack did not commence until 0420 hours the following morning further
degraded their impact and served to alert the enemy of the imminence of
the latter.[28]

Notwithstanding this unusually heavy application of technology, the battle for Caen, by this point a symbol as much as an operational hinge,
degenerated into a brutal and primitive individual test of arms. Adolf Hitler
had decreed that the city be defended unto death. Montgomery, hounded
by detractors, was no less determined to carry it. In practical terms this
meant that the 3rd Canadian Division, along with elements of the 59th
British, had once more to close with the formidable 12th SS, albeit now
reduced to "four punch-drunk battalions" that "held no illusions about the
outcome." Just how much they had suffered on "Epsom" was recorded by
a young lieutenant:

> I was lying next to my Divisional Commander when, a few hundred metres
> in front of us, the remnants of the reconnaissance company of his former
> Panzer Grenadier regiment were run over by British tanks and mowed down
> by accompanying infantry. We couldn't even help with artillery fire, since all
> our ammunition had been used up. The Divisional Commander knew every
> one of these 17–18 year old soldiers, who were now fighting their last battle
> in front of us. When I looked toward the General, I saw tears in his eyes.[29]

Basically, there were three phases to Keller's 3rd Division plan of attack.
Phase one was to be executed by Brigadier Ben Cunningham's 9th Brigade
supported by the tanks of the Sherbrooke Fusiliers, with the Stormont,
Dundas and Glengarry Highlanders (SDG) taking Gruchy and the Highland
Light Infantry of Canada (HLI) capturing Buron. In phase two the SDG
were to secure the Chateau de St. Louet while the North Nova Scotia

Map 9.7
3rd Division Attack, 8 July 1944

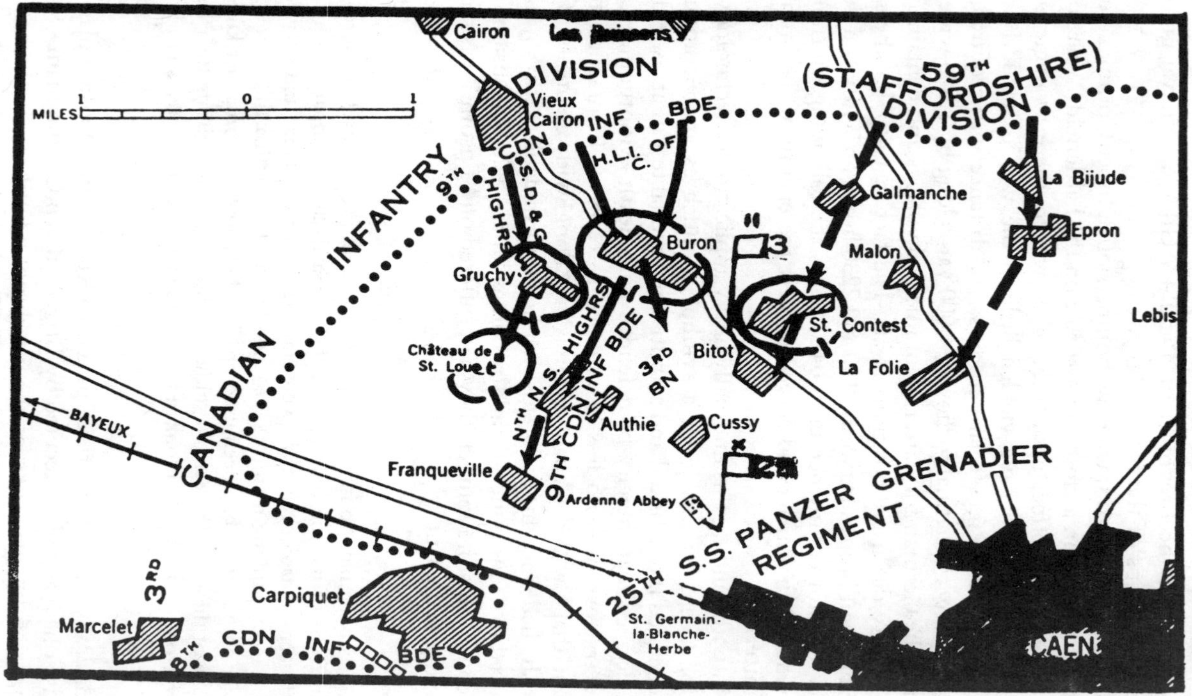

Highlanders took Authie-Franqueville. During phase three Brigadier Harry Foster's 7th Infantry Brigade supported by the 1st Hussars was to pass through the 9th to seize Cussy and the Abbaye Ardenne. Following this, Blackader's 8th Brigade supported by the Fort Garry Horse (FGH) was to capture the control buildings and southern hangars of Carpiquet airfield in Operation "Trousers."[30]

Keller's operations commenced at 0730 hours 8 July, at which time the 59th Division moved against St. Contest. The Canadian attack, supported by divisional artillery and guns from 3 and 4 AGRA, produced what was later reported as an "unbelievable" volume of fire. Still the *Hitlerjugend* fought on, responding with fixed line machine-gun fire and, as the artillery lifted, more intense observed indirect and direct shoots. Eventually, a charge by roughly 15 Bren gun carriers of the 7th Reconnaissance Regiment (17th Duke of York's Royal Canadian Hussars) assisted the SDG in taking Gruchy. Close support by their Sherbrooke armored squadron had not been forthcoming initially due to communications problems, although by day's end about a third of its tanks were knocked out. By 0945 hours "B" company, which had disappeared into the smoke around 0750, reported Gruchy secured. The company of 25 Panzergrenadier Regiment that had defended it was completely annihilated. It was not until 1430 hours, however, that the SDG pushed on to the Chateau de St. Louet. The following day the battalion had the honor of being the first to enter Caen; by 1330 it had two companies in the center of the city. After this ordeal, which cost Cunningham's 9th Brigade 616 casualties in two days of fighting, the SDG war diary recorded: "We are all very tired, having been in f[or]w[ar]d pos[itio]ns, attacking and fighting and patrolling from D-Day."[31]

The battle for Buron by the HLI, which represented its first major action, had delayed the advance of the SDG from Gruchy. The morale of the HLI could not have been higher as its four companies, deployed two up and two back, attacked the village in set-piece fashion, the troops following an artillery barrage "just like walking out in the rain." Outside of Buron, however, they encountered an antitank ditch 12 feet wide and 15 feet deep covered by machine gun, mortar, and artillery defensive fire tasks. Supporting tanks, out of communication, had in the meantime run into minefields and incurred casualties. Eventually the HLI fought their way into Buron and, with the help of two troops of Royal Artillery 17-pounders, were able to defeat enemy armored counterattacks. With 262 casualties, the HLI suffered the greatest loss of any unit on 8 July; the supporting tank squadron mustered but four out of 15 Shermans.

Following the reduction of Buron, the North Novas went on to secure Authie and Franqueville in a series of hotly contested actions. At 1730 hours the 7th Brigade commenced phase three of "Charnwood" and by 2300 hours, after much more hard fighting, Cussy was firmly in the hands of the Canadian Scottish. The enemy withdrew from the Abbaye Ardenne that night. The following day the 8th Brigade occupied Carpiquet airfield. On 10 July a ceremonial parade was held in Caen. "Charnwood" had cost 1,194 casualties, 330 fatal, which was heavier than the loss on D-Day. Obviously, many lessons had by this point also been learned, not least among them the discovery that "street fighting" training had been taught as too much of a drill. The limited effectiveness of prolonged artillery bombardment was additionally noted, as was the doctrinal tendency of armor to hang too far back.[32] More serious were the tensions that seem to have arisen among the Canadian field command.

On 11 July at 1500 hours Simonds's 2 Canadian Corps assumed responsibility within the Second British Army for roughly 8,000 yards of frontage along the River Orne through Caen. It had under command Foulkes's 2nd Canadian Infantry Division and Suttie's 2 AGRA, both recently arrived, as well as Keller's 3rd Division, and Wyman's 2nd Canadian Armoured Brigade, which formations were ordered to rotate regiments for rest and refit. The immediate task given to 2 Corps was "to hold the sector and by active patrolling to study the problem of gaining a br[idge]head over the R[iver] ORNE, SOUTH of CAEN." The last was the planning basis for Operation "Atlantic," the Canadian portion of Operation "Goodwood," a major attack to be executed 18 July by 8 Corps, of three armored divisions, striking east and south of Caen with the object of "writing down" German armored strength.

"Atlantic" called for the 3rd Canadian Division to clear the east bank of the Orne, thereby protecting the 8 Corps right flank, from Ste. Honorine into Fauberge de Vaucelles. Specifically, Blackader's 8th Brigade was to lead the advance east of the river, capturing Colombelles, Giberville, and Mondeville. Cunningham's 9th was then to pass through and clear Vaucelles, while Foster's 7th, in reserve west of the Orne in Caen, remained ready to cross over. Foulkes's 2nd Division was to advance southwards from Caen to seize, in succession, the high ground north of St. André-sur-Orne and the village of Verrières, which commanded the road to Falaise. To effect this, Brigadier Sherwood Lett's 4th Brigade was to capture Louvigny on the Orne and, if practicable, cross over to seize the high ground north of St. André. Brigadier Bill Megill's 5th Brigade was to cross at Caen and take the latter feature if it had not been secured by the 4th Brigade. Subsequent advance southward was to be undertaken by Lett's 4th or Brigadier Hugh Young's 6th Brigade as circumstances dictated.[33]

The main attack, Operation "Goodwood," was the largest yet mounted against the Germans in Normandy. As D'Este has demonstrated, it was the "brainchild" of Dempsey who managed to sell the idea of an all-armored stroke to a skeptical Montgomery. The latter, aware of the serious limitations of British armor since North Africa, had actually stated in January that he would never employ an armored corps. In Dempsey's concept, some 1,600 heavy bombers and 400 lighter aircraft striking from first light

Figure 9.1
2 Canadian Corps Ancillary Troops

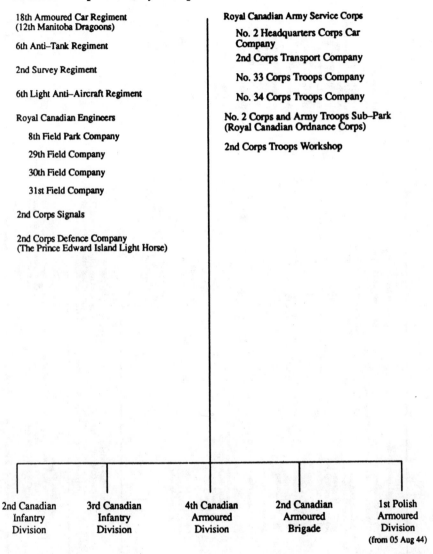

18th Armoured Car Regiment
(12th Manitoba Dragoons)

6th Anti–Tank Regiment

2nd Survey Regiment

6th Light Anti–Aircraft Regiment

Royal Canadian Engineers

    8th Field Park Company

    29th Field Company

    30th Field Company

    31st Field Company

2nd Corps Signals

2nd Corps Defence Company
(The Prince Edward Island Light Horse)

Royal Canadian Army Service Corps

    No. 2 Headquarters Corps Car
    Company

    2nd Corps Transport Company

    No. 33 Corps Troops Company

    No. 34 Corps Troops Company

No. 2 Corps and Army Troops Sub–Park
(Royal Canadian Ordnance Corps)

2nd Corps Troops Workshop

2nd Canadian Infantry Division	3rd Canadian Infantry Division	4th Canadian Armoured Division	2nd Canadian Armoured Brigade	1st Polish Armoured Division (from 05 Aug 44)

on 18 July were expected to cut a craterless swathe over which the armored assault could expeditiously pass. Excellent enemy observation over the congested "airborne" bridgehead east of the Orne, which compelled the armored divisions to cross one after another instead of simultaneously, made it an extremely difficult ground operation to launch, however. As it unfolded, "Goodwood" was to a large degree an armored-air experiment that succeeded on a grander plane,[34] but failed on a lower one for lack of infantry,

Figure 9.2
2 Canadian Corps

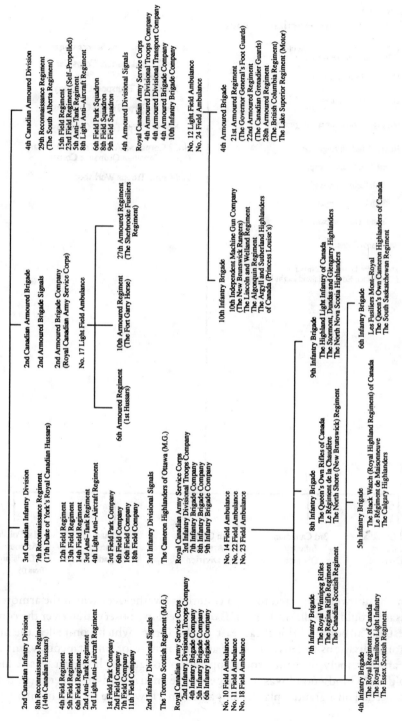

2nd Canadian Infantry Division

8th Reconnaissance Regiment
(14th Canadian Hussars)

4th Field Regiment
5th Field Regiment
6th Field Regiment
2nd Anti–Tank Regiment
3rd Light Anti–Aircraft Regiment

1st Field Park Company
2nd Field Company
7th Field Company
11th Field Company

2nd Infantry Divisional Signals

The Toronto Scottish Regiment (M.G.)

Royal Canadian Army Service Corps
2nd Infantry Divisional Troops Company
4th Infantry Brigade Company
5th Infantry Brigade Company
6th Infantry Brigade Company

No. 10 Field Ambulance
No. 11 Field Ambulance
No. 18 Field Ambulance

7th Infantry Brigade
The Royal Winnipeg Rifles
The Regina Rifle Regiment
The Canadian Scottish Regiment

3rd Canadian Infantry Division

7th Reconnaissance Regiment
(17th Duke of York's Royal Canadian Hussars)

12th Field Regiment
13th Field Regiment
14th Field Regiment
3rd Anti–Tank Regiment
4th Light Anti–Aircraft Regiment

3rd Field Park Company
6th Field Company
16th Field Company
18th Field Company

3rd Infantry Divisional Signals

The Cameron Highlanders of Ottawa (M.G.)

Royal Canadian Army Service Corps
3rd Infantry Divisional Troops Company
7th Infantry Brigade Company
8th Infantry Brigade Company
9th Infantry Brigade Company

No. 14 Field Ambulance
No. 22 Field Ambulance
No. 23 Field Ambulance

8th Infantry Brigade
The Queen's Own Rifles of Canada
Le Régiment de la Chaudière
The North Shore (New Brunswick) Regiment

5th Infantry Brigade
The Black Watch (Royal Highland Regiment) of Canada
Le Régiment de Maisonneuve
The Calgary Highlanders

4th Infantry Brigade
The Royal Regiment of Canada
The Royal Hamilton Light Infantry
The Essex Scottish Regiment

9th Infantry Brigade
The Highland Light Infantry of Canada
The Stormont, Dundas and Glengarry Highlanders
The North Nova Scotia Highlanders

6th Infantry Brigade
Les Fusiliers Mont–Royal
The Queen's Own Cameron Highlanders of Canada
The South Saskatchewan Regiment

2nd Canadian Armoured Brigade

2nd Armoured Brigade Signals

2nd Armoured Brigade Company
(Royal Canadian Army Service Corps)

No. 17 Light Field Ambulance

6th Armoured Regiment   10th Armoured Regiment   27th Armoured Regiment
(1st Hussars)   (The Fort Garry Horse)   (The Sherbrooke Fusiliers
                                                        Regiment)

10th Infantry Brigade
10th Independent Machine Gun Company
(The New Brunswick Rangers)
The Lincoln and Welland Regiment
The Algonquin Regiment
The Argyll and Sutherland Highlanders
of Canada (Princess Louise's)

4th Canadian Armoured Division

29th Reconnaissance Regiment
(The South Alberta Regiment)

15th Field Regiment
23rd Field Regiment (Self–Propelled)
5th Anti–Tank Regiment
8th Light Anti–Aircraft Regiment

6th Field Park Squadron
8th Field Squadron
9th Field Squadron

4th Armoured Divisional Signals

Royal Canadian Army Service Corps
4th Armoured Divisional Troops Company
4th Armoured Divisional Transport Company
4th Armoured Brigade Company
10th Infantry Brigade Company

No. 12 Light Field Ambulance
No. 24 Field Ambulance

4th Armoured Brigade
21st Armoured Regiment
(The Governor General's Foot Guards)
22nd Armoured Regiment
(The Canadian Grenadier Guards)
28th Armoured Regiment
(The British Columbia Regiment)
The Lake Superior Regiment (Motor)

Note: Canadian Dental Corps, Royal Canadian Ordnance Corps, Royal Canadian Electrical and Mechanical Engineers, and Canadian Provost Corps not shown

Map 9.8
Operation "Goodwood/Atlantic"

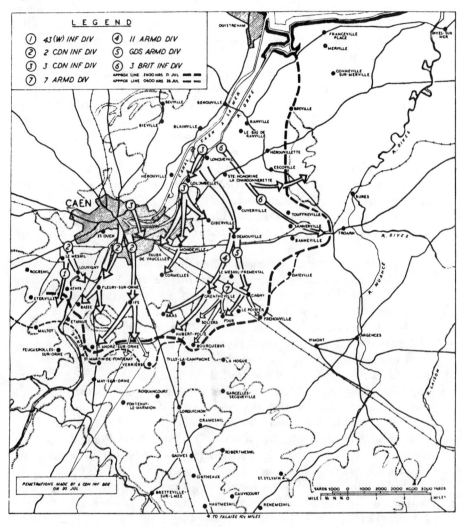

the general shortage of which partly accounted for its being undertaken in the first place.

"Atlantic," the secondary attack, was the much less glamorous affair. At 0745 hours the leading elements of Blackader's 8th Brigade crossed the start line on a two-battalion front "behind the most terrific barrages planned in the European sector of op[eration]s." The Queen's Own Rifles advancing on Giberville, however, watched helplessly as their barrage rolled away when they were forced to ground by German machine-gun fire from Colombelles; they now had to fight their way to their objective, which took from noon until 2210 hours to completely secure. The Chaudière advance on the right had in the interim slowed from 1040 hours as heavy resistance was encountered from the area of a chateau north of the Colombelle steel works. Lack of maneuver room, exacerbated by bombing craters on roads, resulted in a telescoping of forces at this point.[35]

A "scene of indescribable congestion" now developed in the order of march as the reserve battalion, the North Shore Regiment, and units of Cunningham's 9th Brigade closed up on the same axis. The artillery barrage had "moved uselessly to the south." At 1330, Brigadier Blackader called on *Typhoons* to destroy the chateau. When this failed, an "Uncle" target was brought down upon the place, some shells unfortunately landing among the SDG, which exacerbated an already confusing situation. Eventually the Chaudières assisted by the SDG began to make inroads, and the North Shores were directed to clear the steel works. At 1635 General Keller issued new orders. Cunningham's 9th Brigade now bypassed Blackader's with the North Novas moving on Vaucelles and the SDG against Mondeville, formerly an objective of 8th Brigade.

When it first became apparent that Cunningham's 9th Brigade would be delayed in getting into Vaucelles, Simonds had directed Foster's 7th Brigade to see if it could cross over into the suburb. Evening consequently found the Regina Rifle Regiment from the 7th Brigade established there before the North Novas and HLI from the 9th. By noon 19 July the 9th Brigade had cleared Vaucelles of enemy. Foster's 7th Brigade in the meantime had been ordered to capture Cormelles, an industrial suburb east of the main road to Falaise, which now constituted the boundary between the 3rd and 2nd Divisions. Reports that Cormelles was lightly held, but that it might not remain so, saw the preemptory dispatch of the HLI to that location, which led to additional confusion between brigades and further complaints of troops being shelled by friendly artillery. As it turned out, the HLI got two companies into Cormelles by late afternoon; they were relieved by the Canadian Scottish and Winnipegs that evening.[36]

All the while these actions were being fought, the command situation within the 3rd Canadian Division reflected certain strained relationships. On the afternoon of 10 July, Keller had called on his patron, Crerar, who was unavailable at the time, to discuss the removal of Cunningham from command of the 9th Brigade. Choosing to leave a message with the DA&QMG to be conveyed to Crerar, Keller explained that he was convinced such a change was necessary and had so informed Cunningham. His stated reasons were the latter's "failure to 'get-on' and hesitancy to use reserves promptly and aggressively, which had resulted in failure to exploit opportunities and in increased casualties." Keller went on to cite four instances that allegedly confirmed Cunningham's "lack of drive": the 9th Brigade's failure to take its D-Day objectives; the "delayed use of reserves" at Authie on 8 July; "hesitancy and lack of drive" at Caen the next day; and a failure to get patrols swiftly forward to the river line on the night 9/ 10 July. On receipt of this message Crerar had advised Keller to prepare a submission to Simonds, under whose command the 3rd Division was to shortly fall. Ironically, Crerar had the same day passed to Simonds the adverse letters that had been raised on Keller himself by Crocker, Dempsey, and Montgomery.[37]

While suggesting that it was "quite possible that Crocker's handling of Keller ha[d] not brought out the best in the latter," Crerar counseled Simonds "that until Keller's good judgement is established in *your* mind, you cannot give weight to his views concerning his own immediate subordinate." Oddly, Crerar's reservations about Crocker appear to have been based on "indications ... [of] his tendency ... to talk direct to the Brigadiers, tending to by-pass the Divisional Commander [in whom Crocker had obviously lost confidence]." Crerar, though he did not tell Simonds, also seems to have been of the opinion that "Cunningham was the 'white-haired boy' with Crocker and Dempsey before the assault."[38]

As if he did not have enough to worry about before "Atlantic," Simonds on 13 July reported to Crerar that "in his opinion, while Cunningham had failed on some occasions to show the speed and determination which might have been expected, generally, he appeared to have carried out his instructions intelligently, and well." Simonds expressed concern, however, "that Cunningham had not always received that direction and guidance from above which he was entitled to expect." The GOC 2 Corps further reported that he had shown Keller the comments made on his performance by Crocker, Dempsey, and Montgomery. Though Keller "was distinctly upset on reading ... [these] reports," Simonds was more surprised by his subsequent response "that ... he did not feel that his health was good enough to stand the heavy strain and asked that he be medically boarded as he felt that he would be found to be unfit."[39] In the event, both Keller and Cunningham commanded in "Atlantic."

As Keller's 3rd Division increasingly displayed signs of operational deterioration, Foulkes's 2nd Division in "Atlantic" engaged in its first major action since Dieppe. At 1800 hours 18 July, Lett's 4th Brigade sent a reinforced battalion, the Royal Regiment of Canada (RRC), supported by a squadron of FGH tanks to capture Louvigny under cover of a barrage, this being accomplished at a cost of 111 casualties by the following morning. In the meantime the Black Watch (Royal Highland Regiment of Canada) from Megill's 5th Brigade, like the Reginas from Foster's 7th, had crossed the Orne into Vaucelles. At 1402 hours 19 July, the Régiment de Maisonneuve, spearheading the three-phase 5th Brigade attack south from Vaucelles, reported that C and D companies had gone through A and B following up the barrage; the last mentioned had by mistake gone several hundred yards beyond their start line and were caught in the opening line of barrage fire. Fleury-sur-Orne, the Maisonneuve objective, was none-theless attained by 1425 hours.

Later that afternoon the Calgary Highlanders penetrated to Point 67 over-looking St. André-sur-Orne from the north. The Black Watch in turn seized the village of Ifs by dusk and successfully held it against counterattack. Developments to this point now persuaded both Foulkes and Simonds that the overall favorable situation was ripe for further exploitation. As an anticipatory measure the Queen's Own Rifles and Sherbrooke Fusiliers were even warned for a possible night attack. Hasty plans were also laid during the evening 19 July to send Young's hitherto uncommitted 6th Brigade, reinforced by the Essex Scottish Regiment from the 4th Brigade and supported by the Sherbrooke tanks, to attack Verrières ridge at 1200 hours the next day.[40] The effect of "Goodwood," however, had been to draw substantially greater German strength into the area of Bourgebus ridge. The Canadians faced more than the German 272nd Division, which had yet to see action.

Indeed, on the afternoon of 19 July, Dempsey ordered 2 Corps to take over Bras and Hubert-Folie from 8 Corps which, having lost around 270 tanks, had been severely mauled and was preparing to withdraw. The 3rd Division, in fact, relieved the nearly destroyed 11th Armoured. The 7th Armoured Division, ordered to complete the capture of Bourguébus, did so at first light the next day when both it and Guards Armoured Division came under Simonds's command. As might be expected, some 7th Armoured tanks advancing from the east had traversed as far as Beauvoir Farm along the ridge that the 6th Brigade was preparing to attack. While they momentarily considered taking Verrières, choosing not to for reasons of relative strength, their presence may have reinforced the presumption by Simonds that "opposition . . . was not great and that quick offensive action should break through readily the enemy screen."[41] In any case, the tanks were eventually withdrawn and Young's 6th Brigade attack on a 4,000-meter front went in at 1500 hours 20 July supported by artillery fire and rocket-firing Typhoon strikes.

On the right the Queen's Own Cameron Highlanders of Canada, with a Sherbrooke tank squadron available for counterattack in support, advanced in "T" formation (two companies up) through a field of wheat behind a barrage to secure St. André-sur-Orne. On the left, intimately accompanied by five tanks, Les Fusiliers Mont-Royal (FMR) attacked behind a barrage toward Beauvoir and Troteval farms on their way to their objective, Verrières village. Having moved continuously through the night and morning, the troops had not had a meal since 1700 hours the day before (the Camerons had not had lunch). Ominously, in the vicinity of Beauvoir and Troteval farms, where British tanks had previously roamed freely, enemy resistance began to grow; in attempting to press on after certain obvious locations had been cleared, leading FMR elements were attacked from the rear by

German infantry issuing from farm cellars. At the same time, enemy antitank guns and Panthers came into action. With its artillery FOO dead, its forward company cut off, and its antitank support not yet having come up, the battalion hung on grimly throughout the night, unable to move either ahead or back.[42]

A greater disaster by far occurred in the center where the South Saskatchewan Regiment (SSR), protected by a troop of tanks on each flank, assaulted through three kilometers of tall grain fields to the crest of Verrières Ridge. Tragically, the battalion on reaching its objective area after 1700 hours consolidated on an open slope dominated by a higher feature held by Germans. The exposed Canadians, under direct observation and subjected to murderous indirect artillery and mortar fire that could be accurately corrected, were now attacked by panzers from the left rear flank. Initially believing that the two flanking tank troops were sufficient to deal with the half-dozen roving panzers, the Sherbrookes were slow to dispatch their reserve squadron forward.

Enemy tanks working back and forth along defiladed approaches meanwhile wreaked havoc upon the demoralized and, from 1700 hours when a thunderstorm burst, rain-soaked troops of the SSR. Easily picking off a troop of supporting 17-pounders as they raced to rescue the besieged Canadian infantry, the powerful panzers also managed to hold Canadian tanks at bay. Around 1800 hours the 6th Brigade lost communication with the SSR. When information was received, it was to the effect that the acting commanding officer had been killed and, later, that the battalion was withdrawing. On learning this at about 2100 hours, Young instructed the SSR to reorganize immediately behind the Essex, which sleep-deprived battalion had been ordered forward at 1730 hours to establish a firm base between Beauvoir Farm and St. André.

On reaching this position, which was also exposed to enemy observation, the Essex encountered the retreating soldiery of the SSR streaming back and, in their wake, the devastating fire of counterattacking German panzers and infantry supported by mortars and artillery. Unable to consolidate, taking casualties, and out of touch with battalion, the two forward Essex company commanders after joint consultation decided to withdraw their subunits, at least one of which got out of control. Around midnight, by which time they had been "rounded up," Young personally addressed these companies and arranged with division the resupply of rifles, Brens, PIATs, and associated stores, which arrived at 0400. While the Essex were dispatched back to their lines, the SSR remained scattered to the wind.[43]

Instead of meeting light opposition, the Canadians had run into elements of the 2nd Panzer Division and the progenitor of the *Hitlerjugend*, the 1st SS Panzer Regiment of the 1st SS (*Leibstandarte Adolf Hitler*), which mustered in the neighborhood of 100 tanks. On 21 July they counterattacked. By this time Wyman's 2nd Canadian Armoured Brigade, which evidently much preferred to serve with the 3rd Division, had been placed under command of Foulkes's 2nd Division. Young's 6th Brigade, already given the Black Watch, now also received under command the 1st Hussars, which with the Sherbrookes were placed in close support of infantry to repel counterattack. Pressure on the front of the depleted Essex began to tell around 0900 hours, however, when the 1st Hussars reported that troops were moving to the rear. When this was shortly confirmed by a liaison officer, orders were given and patrols established to prevent any further rearward movement by the Essex Scottish.

This, of course, did not prevent increasing enemy infantry and tank infiltration of the Essex position. The Black Watch were accordingly warned to be prepared to counterattack at 1600 hours to restore the situation. In order for the artillery to complete the necessary arrangements, the attack was delayed until 1800 hours, at which time it was successfully carried out under cover of a creeping barrage. The line thus stabilized along the road St. André-Hubert Folie. Beauvoir and Troteval farms were at the same time lost, as were most men of the forward FMR companies. All together Foulkes's 2nd Division lost 1,149 casualties in Operation "Atlantic," a much higher figure than the 386 sustained by the 3rd; yet more than half were suffered by regiments committed on the second day in pursuit of a perceived opportunity. Total 2 Canadian Corps casualties were close to 90 percent or more of those suffered by 8 Corps in its "death ride of... armoured divisions."[44]

Simonds's 2 Canadian Corps was now blooded, but it had paid a high price. The attack on 20 July was by any measure a disaster. Canadian troops had fled in the face of the enemy, but the SSR could hardly be blamed for having been placed in such a tactically untenable position as they were. Unquestionably, they should have been intimately supported by tanks that far better than infantry chests could lean into a barrage and take a hit. Doctrine played a part here, as well as an armored corps perception that other arms failed to understand the limitations of armor, that tanks should not be expected to lead attacks against prepared enemy antitank positions.[45] Yet, as established casualty rates of 76 percent for infantry against seven percent for armor indicate,[46] most crews from shot-up tanks got away to fight another day. Here, of course, the buck must be passed back to higher command for not insisting, as Montgomery did, on making armor conform even against its will. However one looks at it, Canadian troops regardless of their experience level did all, and more, that could possibly have been expected of them in the attack on Verrières Ridge.

NOTES

1. Record Group (RG) 24, Vol. 13,750, Operations Log 2nd Canadian Infantry Division (2CID) entry 0955 hrs, 24 July 1944, from 2 Canadian Corps.

2. Carlo D'Este, *Decision in Normandy: The Unwritten Story of Montgomery and the Allied Campaign* (London: Pan, 1984), pp. 107–160; and CLFCSC Collection, Special Interrogation Report Genlt Edgar Feuchtinger, Comd 21 Pz Div (6 June 1944–25 August 1944) 25 August, 1945, and Special Interrogation Report Oberstgruppenfuhrer [*sic*] (Col.-Gen.) Joeseph "Sepp" Dietrich, Commander 1st SS Pz Corps and 6 SS Pz Army. The 16,000-man strong 21st Panzer Division of three panzer (Mark IV 75mm) and two panzergrenadier regiments had been deployed by Rommel specifically to defend Caen, which it did with some bumbling success. Unfortunately for the Germans, their high command structure was unnecessarily fragmented. Field Marshal Gerd von Rundtstedt at *Oberbefehlshaber West* (*OB West*) had under him Rommel's Army Group B of the Seventh and Fifteenth Armies and Army Group G south of the Loire. He had also formed in November 1943 Panzer Group West, which under Lieutenant-General Geyr von Schweppenburg was to cooperate with both. Rommel, who wished to fight the battle forward near the beaches, was only given two additional panzer divisions, the 2nd and 116th, but these remained in the Fifteenth Army sector. In March 1944 the 2nd SS Panzer Corps of the 9th and 10th SS Panzer Divisions left to stem the Russian winter offensive. Three remaining panzer divisions, the 1st SS, 12th SS, and *Panzer Lehr*, could be moved only with Hitler's express approval. The problem was that Hitler had been talked into believing, like Rommel and others fooled by "Fortitude," that the main Allied invasion would occur in the Pas de Calais area, the Fifteenth Army sector. See also Eversley Belfield and H. Essame, *The Battle for Normandy*, (London: Pan, 1983), pp. 31–37; and Charles Messenger, *Hitler's Gladiator: The Life and Times of Oberstgruppenfuhrer and Panzergeneral-Oberst der Waffen-SS Sepp Dietrich* (London: Brassey's, 1988), p. 117–125.

3. D'Este, *Decision in Normandy*, p. 153. The five heaviest casualty days were 6 June, 8 and 25 July, 8 and 14 August [Terry Copp and Robert Vogel, *Maple Leaf Route: Victory* (Alma: Maple Leaf Route, 1988) p. 106]. For Great War and Second World War casualty comparisons, see Jeffrey Williams, *The Long Left Flank: The Hard Fought Way to the Reich, 1944–1945* (Toronto: Stoddart, 1988), pp. 318–320. Brooke claimed the density in Normandy was 2.5 times that of the Eastern Front. [LHC, Alanbrooke Papers (AP), 14/1, Brooke to Montgomery, 28 July, 1944].

4. Crerar Papers (CP), Vol. 9, Appendices "A" and "B" to Ops/1–6–4, dated 18 May 1944 (Appreciation—Operation "Pintail"); Belfield and Essame, *Battle for Normandy*, pp. 23–26; D'Este, *Decision in Normandy*, p. 154; and John A. English, *On Infantry* (New York: Praeger, 1984), p. 141. The Caen-Falaise plain is today much more open than in 1944, presumably due to farm amalgamation.

5. D'Este, *Decision in Normandy*, pp. 174–198. It seems clear from reading his papers, especially his correspondence with Chester Wilmot, that Bucknall mishandled this situation. IWM, Lt.-Gen. G. G. Bucknall Papers. Wittmann had his Tiger shot out from under him by a six-pounder in Villers Bocage, where he lost two more Tigers plus a Mark IV Special.

6. Public Record Office (hereafter PRO), Kew, CAB 106/1060 Personal Copy of Notes by Brigadier James Hargest, Normandy Landing, June 1944.

7. Col. C. P. Stacey, *Official History of the Canadian Army in the Second World War*, Vol. III: *Victory Campaign: The Operations in North-West Europe, 1944–1945* (Ottawa: Queen's Printer, 1966), pp. 1421–151; Nigel Hamilton, *Monty*, Vol. II (Sevenoaks: Hodder and Stoughton, 1984), 194–207, 644–657, 665–667, 673–683; and

D'Este, *Decision in Normandy*, pp. 232–251. Montgomery knew from ULTRA intercepts that the 1st SS Panzer Division and 2nd SS Panzer Corps were moving toward Caen. He had also been advised by the War Office before D-Day that it could guarantee replacements only for the first month; after that, he would have to break up divisions or ancillary troops. The "British Army was a wasting asset" (D'Este, *Decision in Normandy*, p. 237, 250). On the development of tactical air support, see Shelford Bidwell and Dominick Graham, *Fire-Power: British Army Weapons and Theories of War 1904–1945* (London: Allen and Unwin, 1982. pp. 260–273.

8. Stacey, *Victory Campaign*, pp. 147–151; Ronald Lewin, *Montgomery as Military Commander* (New York: Stein and Day, 1971), pp. 206–207; Hamilton, *Monty*, II, 680–682, 699–700; John Keegan, *Waffen SS: the Asphalt Soldiers* (New York: Ballantine, 1971), pp 111–116; and Henry Maule, *Caen: The Brutal Battle and the Breakout from Normandy* (Vancouver: David and Charles, 1976), pp. 50–58. General F. Dollmann, commander of the German Seventh Army, ordered the immediate attack by 2nd SS Panzer Corps, which was soundly rebuffed. Hours later Dollmann poisoned himself (D'Este, *Decision in Normandy*, pp. 241–242).

9. Belfield and Essame, *Battle for Normandy*, pp. 51–56; Russell F. Weigley, *Eisenhower's Lieutenants,: The Campaign of France and Germany 1944–1945* (Bloomington, Ind: Indiana University Press, 1981) pp. 20–22; and Majors R. P. Bourne and N. A. Shackleton. "Analysis of Firepower in Normandy Operations in 1944," NDHQ Operational Research and Analysis Establishment. The Germans also had a technological edge in their machine guns, submachine guns, mortars (especially *Nebelwerfers*), hand-held antitank weapons, and small arms ammunition. See also Max Hastings, *Overlord: D-Day and the Battle for Normandy, 1944* (London: Pan, 1984), pp. 220–231. Panthers and Tigers were less mechanically reliable that Shermans, which nonetheless caught fire so easily they were christened "Tommy Cookers." Montgomery who believed in building a gun and putting a tank around it personally pressed for the conversion of Shermans to Fireflies. Montgomery of Alamein Papers (MAP), BLM 117, Montgomery to "Archie", 26 August 1943 and M506 21 Army Group Memorandum on British Armour 6 July 1944; and PRO, WO205/5D, D.O. Correspondence C.-in-C., DCIGS to Montgomery 5 August 1944.

10. Personal Copy CLFCSC Collection, 3 Cdn Div Questionnaire with Answers Submitted by 2 Cdn Armd Bde, 2 Cdn Armd Bde, Brit Western Expeditionary Forces, 26 June 1944. A Canadian tank regiment was organized into a headquarters (four tanks) and three squadrons, each having a headquarters (three tanks) and three troops of four tanks each. Formerly there were five troops of three tanks each (RG 24, Vol. 10,800, 2nd Canadian Corps, Corps Commander's Conference, 4 March 1944). Some British units organized Firefly troops and squadrons (see D'Este, *Decision in Normandy*, p. 140).

11. CP, Vol. 2, Notes on Conference C-in-C–GOC-in-C First Canadian Army, 24 June 1944; and Stacey, *Victory Campaign*, pp. 146–147.

12. MAP, BLM 126, M511 Montgomery to Brooke, 14 July 1944.

13. RG 24, Vol. 10,799, WD GS 2 Cdn Corps, Operation "Axehead" Appreciation and Outline Plan by H.D.G. Crerar, CB, DSO, GOC-in-C First Canadian Army 8 May 1944; and Stacey, *Victory Campaign*, pp. 39, 83.

14. CP, Vol. 9, Ops/1–6–4 Operation "Pintail" Appreciation by Lt.-Gen. H.D.G. Crerar CB DSO 18 May 44. Crerar proposed undertaking the "Pintail" study on 12 April. It was approved by the COS, 21st Army Group on 24 April.

15. Craig W.H. Luther, *Blood and Honor: The History of the 12th SS Panzer Division "Hitler Youth," 1943–1945* (San Jose, Calif.: Bender, 1987), pp. 127–142. According to former *Hauptsturmfuehrer* Hans Siegel, 12th SS, he was ordered by his regimental commander, *Standartenfuehrer* Kurt Meyer to leave his tank and take a motorcycle to reconnoiter forward for British tanks. Seigel, on locating the Canadian advance, reported back to Meyer, who ran the battle from an observation post in the Abbaye Ardenne (Conversation with Hans Siegel, CLFCSC Normandy Battlefield Study, May 1989).

16. PRO, WO 285/9, Dempsey Diary (hereafter DD), 8 June 1944.

17. Stacey, *Victory Campaign*, pp. 126–133, 135–136; Luther, *Blood and Honor*, pp. 157, 160; Col. G.W.L. Nicholson, *The Gunners of Canada: A History of the Royal Regiment of Canadian Artillery*, Vol. II: *1919–1967* (Toronto: McClelland and Stewart, 1972), p. 281; RG 24, Vol. 13,789, Tactics (Source: 2 Cdn Corps Int Summary); and Reginald H. Roy, *Ready for the Fray: The History of the Canadian Scottish, 1920–1955* (Vancouver, B.C.: Published by the Regiment, 1958), pp. 232–240. In this infiltration attack, it does appear that three German companies put three defending Canadian companies to flight [Interview with Lt.-Col. (Waffen SS, retired) Hubert Meyer, 6 March 1986]. Stacey also indicated as much. The Bren only fired 500 rounds per minute against the MG 42's 1,200.

18. Hubert Meyer, *MS # P-164, 12th SS Panzer Division "Hitlerjugend" June to September 1944*, Historical Division, Headquarters United States Army, Europe, 23 June 1954, pp. 7–9; and his *Kriegsgeschichte der 12.SS-Panzerdivision "Hitlerjugend"* (Osnabruck: Munin Verlag, 1987), Vol. II, pp. 619 (in English). See also Luther, *Blood and Honor*, pp. 24–40. 12th SS was originally raised as a panzergrenadier division. For a contrast in the formation of an SS division, see Charles W. Snydor, Jr., *Soldiers of Destruction: The SS Death's Head Division, 1933–1945* (Princeton, N.J.: Princeton University Press, 1977).

19. Meyer, *12th SS*, pp. 10–18; and Luther, *Blood and Honor*, pp. 57–79. The murder of 134 Canadian soldiers tarnishes the otherwise sterling battlefield performance of the 12th SS. For a detailed treatment of this blot, see Luther, *Blood and Honor*, pp. 181–194.

20. Stacey, *Victory Campaign*, pp. 139–140; Luther, *Blood and Honor*, pp. 199–202; and Nicholson, *Gunners*, II, 283. Siegel commanded the attacking panzer company. Although the Canadians thought their artillery preparations inadequate, Meyer described the weight of fire as strong (Meyer, *12th SS*, pp. 50–51). Copp and Vogel are on solid ground when they charge that Brig. Wyman, commander of the 2nd Armoured Brigade and a veteran of Italy, "was breaking every rule of... battle doctrine" [Terry Copp and Robert Vogel, *Maple Leaf Route: Caen* (Alma: Maple Leaf Route, 1983), p. 84]. Wyman had come close to being court-martialed by Crerar and replaced by Brig. Leslie Booth in May 1944 for a drinking bout following a mess party; in the interests of operational continuity the abstinent Montgomery advised dressing him down instead. MAP, BLM 119, Crerar to Montgomery, 14 May 1944 and Montgomery to Crerar, 15 May 1944.

21. Roy, *Ready for the Fray*, pp. 248–250; and Stacey, *Victory Campaign*, p. 140.

22. Meyer, *12th SS*, pp. 56–73.

23. Stacey, *Victory Campaign*, pp. 153–155; Personal Copy CLFCSC Collection, HQ 8 Cdn Inf Bde Op "Windsor" 8 Cdn Inf Bde 00 No 14 of 3 July 1944; R. H., Roy, *1944: The Canadians in Normandy,* Canadian War Museum Historical Publi-

cation No. 19 (Ottawa: Macmillan, 1984), pp. 45–50; RG 24, Vol. 13,766, WD GS 3CID Summary of Events and Information (hereafter SEI), 2–3 July 1944, and 3CID Intelligence Summary No 17, 4 July 1944; RG 24, Vol. 14,140, WD HQ 8th Canadian Infantry Brigade (hereafter CIB) SEI 3–5 July 1944; RG 24, Vol. 14,129, WD HQ 7 CIB SEI, 2–5 July 1944; and R.E.A. Morton, *Vanguard: The Fort Garry Horse in the Second World War* (Published by the Regiment, circa 1945), pp. 30–35.

24. Ibid.; Meyer, *12th SS*, pp. 74–77; and DHist, CMHQ Historical Report No. 162 (8 November 1946), pp. 10–15.

25. Stacey, *Victory Campaign*, pp. 153–155; Roy, *Canadians in Normandy*, pp. 45–50; RG 24, Vol. 14,140, WD HQ CIB SEI, 3–5 July 1944; DHist, CMHQ Historical Report No. 162 (8 November 1946), pp. 10–15. The 43rd (Wessex) Division occupied Verson with the 5th Battalion, Duke of Cornwall's Light Infantry during the attack on Carpiquet. On failure of the attack, the position became untenable and was evacuated [Maj.-Gen. H. Essame, *The 43rd Wessex Division at War 1944–1945* (London: William Clowes, 1952), pp. 33–34].

26. CP, Vol. 3, Crocker to Dempsey, 5 July 1944, and Dempsey to Montgomery, 6 July 1944; DD, 4–5 July 1944; and Hamilton, *Monty*, II, pp 699.

27. MAP, BLM 126, M508 Montgomery to Brooke 7 July 1944. Montgomery added that "Harry Crerar once suggested to me that Keller would be next for a Corps. The idea is quite absurd. A B[riga]de Com[man]d is his ceiling" (Ibid).

28. RG 24, Vol. 13,711, WD GS 2 Cdn Corps SEI, 7 July 1944; Stacey, *Victory Campaign*, pp. 157–160; Roy, *Canadians in Normandy*, pp. 51–52; D'Este, *Decision in Normandy*, pp. 315–318; and CMHQ Historical Report No. 162, pp. 15–19.

29. Meyer, *12th SS*, pp. 66–67, 81.

30. RG 24, Vol. 13,766, WD GS 3CID SEI, 5–10 July 1944; RG 24, Vol. 14,140, WD HQ 8CIB SEI, 8–10 July 1944; and RG 24, Vol. 14,129, WD HQ 7CIB SEI, 8–11 July 1944.

31. RG 24, Vol. 15,271, WD SDG, 4–10 July 1944; Meyer, *12th SS*, p. 85; Stacey, *Victory Campaign*, pp. 160–163; Roy, *Canadians in Normandy*, pp. 52–63; and CMHQ Historical Report No. 169, pp. 20–22. In the first 24 hours, the Canadian divisional artillery handled 27,000 pounds of shell per gun (Nicholson, *Gunners*, II, 289–290).

32. RG 24, Vol. 15,076, WD HLI, 7–8 July 1944; RG 24, Vol. 14,129, WD HQ 7CIB SEI, 8–10 July 1944; Cap. J. Allan Snowie, *Bloody Buron: The Battle of Buron, Normandy—08 July 1944* (Erin: Boston Mills, 1984), pp. 64–65; Copp and Vogel, *Caen*, pp. 106–108; Stacey, *Victory Campaign*, pp. 160–161; Roy, *Canadians in Normandy*, pp. 55–57. When the North Novas received six officer and 61 other rank replacements on 9 July, they did not even have time to meet platoon or company commanders, but were hurriedly detailed off by numbers (RG 24, Vol. 15,122, WD North Nova Scotia Highlanders, 9 July 1944).

33. RG 24, Vol. 13,711, WD GS 2 Cdn Corps SEI, 11 July 1944; CP, Vol. 2, TAC. H.Q. 21 Army Group M510 10 July 1944; and Stacey, *Victory Campaign*, pp. 168–171.

34. Montgomery originally planned "Goodwood" for 17 July to coincide with "Cobra," a major attack by Bradley's First U.S. Army, slated for 19 July. He finally opted for 18 July, but "Cobra" was delayed to 24 July; aborted on that day due to bad flying weather, it finally took place successfully on 25 July [Martin Blumenson, *Breakout and Pursuit, United States Army in World War II, The European Theatre of*

Operations (Washington: Department of the Army, 1961), p. 189]. On Dempsey and "Goodwood," see D'Este, *Decision in Normandy*, pp. 354–355, 396.

35. Stacey, *Victory Campaign*, pp. 169–173; RG 24, Vol. 14,140, WD HQ 8CIB, 17–19 July 1944; RG 24, Vol. 10,797, WD GS 2 Cdn Corps Operations Notes, 18–23 July 1944; Belfield and Essame, *Battle for Normandy*, pp. 148–151; Roy, *Canadians in Normandy*, pp. 68–74; Terry Copp and Robert Vogel, *Maple Leaf Route: Falaise* (Alma: Maple Leaf Route, 1983), pp. 38–42, 48–51. The barrage advanced slowly, lifting 100 yards each four minutes; it was fired by the four field regiments of the 3rd Division and the 3rd and 4th Medium Regiments (Nicholson, *Gunners*, II, 295).

36. Ibid.; and RG 24, Vol. 14,140, WD HQ 7CIB SEI, 18 July 1944. At 1435 hours, 18 July, the SDG were told that an "Uncle" target was to be fired; they had five minutes to take cover. Claiming a medium troop was firing short, they recorded "again we come under our own arty fire." One officer and two other ranks were killed; two officers and 10 other ranks were wounded (RG 24, Vol. 15,271 WD SDG, 18 July 1944). Registering targets was a major problem for artillery, and it was considered fortunate if one or two guns from an entire divisional artillery could range on specific targets or barrage starting lines (Nicholson, *Gunners*, II, 296).

37. Personal Copy CLFCSC Collection, Personal and confidential handwritten memo to Army Commander from D.A. & Q.M.G. First Canadian Army, Brig. A. E. Watford, 10 July 1944.

38. Personal Copy CLFCSC Collection, Crerar to Simonds, 10 July 1944, and Crerar to COS, CMHQ, 10 July 1944.

39. CP, Vol. 3, Crerar memorandum to file, 14 July 1944.

40. RG 24, Vol. 14,109, WD HQ 5CIB 5 Cdn Inf Bde OO No 1, dated 18 July 1944, and message log, 19 July 1944; RG 24, Vol. 14,116, WD HQ 6CIB SEI, 19–20 July 1944; Roy, *Canadians in Normandy*, pp. 74–79; Stacey, *Victory Campaign*, pp. 172–176; and Copp and Vogel, *Falaise*, p. 54. Between 1200 and 2030 hours 18 July, there were four battalion "O" Groups (meetings at which subunit commanders were given orders) held in the Black Watch; the battalion was mortared during three of them (RG 24, Vol. 15,009, WD Black Watch, 18 July 1944).

41. RG 24, Vol. 14,116, WD HQ 6CIB SEI, 17–20 July 1944. The brigade was on two hours notice to move from 1200 hours 18 July. On the history of formations like the 272nd German Division, see W. Victor Madej (ed.), *German Army Order of Battle: Field Army and Officer Corps, 1939–1945* (Allentown, Pa.: Game, 1985).

42. RG 24, Vol. 13,711, WD GS 2 Cdn Corps SEI, 20 July 1944; Roy, *Canadians in Normandy*, pp. 80–84, 90–92; Copp and Vogel, *Falaise*, pp. 56–61; and Stacey, *Victory Campaign*, p. 174. H-hour was set at 1500 hours because it was "the earliest at which the air force could coop." The fire plan was quite correctly worked out by the brigade commander and the CRA (RG 24, Vol. 14,116, WD HQ 6CIB SEI, 17–20 July 1944).

43. RG 24, Vol. 14,116, WD HQ 6CIB SEI, 20 July 1944; Roy, *Canadians in Normandy*, pp. 84–89, 92–96; RG 24, Vol. 15,262, WD SSR, 20 July 1944; Personal Copies CLFCSC Collection, Accounts of the Attack by S Sask R on the High Ground 0459 in the Afternoon of 20 July 1944 Given by Maj. J. S. Edmondson, "B" Coy, Maj. L. L. Dickin, "D" Coy, Capt. Murray Stewart, Adjt, Capt Lane, Mortar Offr, and Lt. R. Matthews, "A" Coy, at La Villeneuve, 23 July 1944, Proceedings of a Court of Inquiry in the Field, 2 August 1944 (on losses of personal and unit equipment . . . sustained by The Essex Scottish Regt. and S. Sask. R. during

actions... on 20–21 July 1944), memo Lt.-Col. B.J.S. Macdonald to Maj.-Gen. Chas Foulkes 30 July 1944, and letter Lt.-Col. B.J.S. Macdonald to Lt.-Gen. G. G. Simonds 12 August 1944; and Stacey, *Victory Campaign*, pp. 175–176. The SSR were ordered to occupy the reverse slope, but the grid reference given them was forward. The ground in this area is very flat and open and almost all reverse slope, however, and dangerously exposed to the crest at Fontenay-le-Marmion, held by the Germans.

44. RG 24, Vol. 14,116, WD HQ 6CIB SEI, 21 July 1944, and Int Log 20–21 July 1944; RG 24, Vol. 13,766, 3CID Intelligence Summary No. 23, 19 July 1944; Roy, *Canadians in Normandy*, pp. 93–96; Copp and Vogel, *Falaise*, pp. 56–61; and Stacey, *Victory Campaign*, pp. 175–176. The 2nd Canadian Armoured brigade, which had trained with the 3rd Division from July 1943, supposedly found 2nd Division troops "jumpy, nervous, and green" (Copp and Vogel, *Falaise*, pp. 44–45). According to the War Diary of 21st Army Group, total casualties for 8 Corps were 1,818, for 2 Canadian, 1,614 (D'Este, *Decision in Normandy*, p. 385). Stacey gives the "total casualties of all Canadian units in the theatre of operations, for the four-day's fighting" as 1,965 in all categories.

45. RG 24, Vol. 12,304, 2 Cdn Armd Bde, Op Overlord, Part III, Lessons Arising from the Op.

46. CP, Vol. 29, Report on Survey of Reinforcement Situation—Canadian Army Overseas by Lt.-Gen. E. W. Sansom, Inspector General, 29 March 1945.

Chapter 10

Cold Eye on Death

It has been a source of deep regret to me that a fine battalion like the Black Watch suffered so heavily in . . . [Operation "Spring"]. I would prefer to make no statement on the subject for I dislike even suggesting criticism of those who lost their lives, but if a statement is required from me as a matter of record, I consider that the losses were unnecessarily heavy and the results achieved disappointing. Such heavy losses were not inherent in the plan nor in its intended execution. The action of the Black Watch was most gallant but was tactically unsound in its detailed execution.

Lieutenant-General G. G. Simonds, 1946[1]

What happened on Verrières Ridge had not occurred for lack of professional military thought on the part of Simonds. In "Atlantic" he had gambled, erroneously as it turned out, that the "Goodwood" onslaught had left the Germans on their last legs. As he later stated, however, "nobody had been optimistic enough to believe the Germans would fight south of the Seine." The expectation was that once all hope of liquidating the bridgehead faded they would pull back to that riverline; hence the requirement for Operation "Axehead" discussed in Chapter 9.[2] That Simonds anticipated the development of a more fluid stage in the fighting at this juncture is further evident from the operational policy he made explicit soon after taking over 2 Canadian Corps. As this policy, which received the personal blessings of both Dempsey and Montgomery, also provides substantial insight into the prescribed method by which Canadian operations were to be conducted, it is worth examining in some depth.

Unlike anything produced by Crerar, the 2 Canadian Corps operational policy enunciated by Simonds reflected originality, clarity, and completeness. Pointing out that corps were always of variable composition and could comprise several types of divisions, independent brigades, and AGRA depending upon assigned tasks and allotted frontages, he considered it "impracticable to lay down a clear-cut doctrine for . . . [its] employment." Simply put, a corps essentially operated "in a 'territorial corridor,' covering the communications along which it move[d] and [wa]s maintained." As Simonds saw it, once a firm beachhead had been established in Normandy, the probable role of 2 Corps would be to pass through and either follow up retiring enemy forces or mount attacks against organized defensive positions. In the follow-up role, the aim would be to overcome delaying detachments through "*Determined* infiltration, with quick artillery support controlled by forward observing officers [FOOs]." To deal with enemy rearguard positions established to prevent such attempts at infiltration, well-prepared and coordinated brigade attacks by leading divisions would be required.[3]

Depending upon whether the ground was open or close, either armored or infantry divisions could lead in follow-up operations, the latter division being given in such case an armored regiment under command. They were to "advance on a single thrust line, disposed in depth on a one-brigade front, opening a two-way maintenance route as they advance[d]." The one-brigade front was deemed necessary because the divisional artillery, even when reinforced by a proportion of corps medium and field guns, was considered "only sufficient to support attack by one brigade." If the enemy employed demolitions extensively, the divisional engineers were "only sufficient to open and maintain one all-weather two-way route." The leading brigades were to be preceded across the divisional front by strong combat and engineer reconnaissance. Within infantry divisions, brigades could be passed through one another, the leading brigade always being directed onto the ground of tactical importance where a firm base could be established to facilitate the passage through of the next. In this manner a division would be "disposed in depth with successive brigades established on firm bases covering centres of communication."[4]

In the armored division, a similar deployment procedure applied, though, again, whichever brigade led depended upon the suitability of the country for the employment of infantry or armor. In either instance, the second brigade was to provide a firm base for the forward movement of the first, which meant that in case of sudden German counterattack there always existed a basis for recovery. Leading brigades operating from such firm bases, which served as anchors and protected against deep flanking attack, were consequently expected to "act with great boldness." This system also ensured that whenever the enemy identified and concentrated strength against a thrust line, it could be advantageously countered by simply moving "a reserve brigade wide to a flank to force the enemy to dissipate his strength on a wider frontage." Simonds cautioned, however, that while it might be possible under such circumstances to site the divisional artillery to support either brigade, "the weight of artillery support must *NOT* be divided."[5]

Should the German ever choose to stand and fight a deliberate or properly prepared defensive battle, emphasized Simonds, "*attack without adequate re-connaissance and preparation will not succeed.*" The attack had to be "carefully organized" and its "frontage . . . limited to that on which really heavy [artillery] support may be given." Since the essence of the German system of defense was counterattack, forward localities tended to be held mainly in terms of fewer men with more automatic weapons, backed up by mortars capable of delivering a heavy weight of fire from positions 3,000 to 4,000 yards in the rear. The "well planned infantry attack, with ample fire support," warned Simonds, may "penetrate such a position with comparative ease, but the first penetration will stir up a hornet's nest." So long as German reserves were available, they could be expected to counterattack continuously, employing tanks and SP guns in support of infantry frighteningly close to objectives with considerable death-dealing and demoralizing effect.[6]

To Simonds it was quite clear that the "*success of the offensive battle hinge[d] on the defeat of the German counter-attacks*" and having "*sufficient . . . reserves in hand to launch a new phase as soon as the enemy strength has spent itself.*" It was also obvious to him that the "*defeat of . . . counter-attacks . . . [had to] form part of the original plan of attack.*" This meant deciding beforehand the forward movement of antitank guns, tanks, and medium artillery to "stand off" counterattacking German armor. Initial objectives had also to be selected to a depth of not less than 4,000 yards to ensure that German mortars were silenced; otherwise, they would be used to support counterattacks and impede consolidation. The alternative, to deal with them by prearranged counterbattery fire, had not generally proven effective due to the German practice of siting mortars behind very steep cover, then shooting and scooting. Since the "forward displacement of the bulk of the artillery," additionally meant that there was "bound to be a pause" when forward-attacking troops would be without full artillery support, Simonds recommended the employment of all available air resources at this point.[7]

In planning an attack on a prepared position, Simonds stressed the importance of correctly allocating troops to tasks and simplifying command arrangements. To best ensure the former he recommended that every commander "think two below his own command"—that is, a divisional commander keeping unit tasks in mind and a brigade commander possible company or squadron undertakings. By grouping these so that each "group of tasks" came "within the power of achievement of each of his immediately subordinate formations or units, each commander . . . [could] arrive at a correct allocation of troops without breaking up existing organization . . . always a bad practice in battle where team work counts for so much." Not surprisingly, Simonds urged commanders to explain their thought processes when allotting tasks and giving orders to subordinates. He further suggested that command arrangements could be simplified if "each distinct phase of an operation . . . [could] be carried through to completion without changes of responsibility in respect to command and changes of commanders of supporting arms working with the infantry or armoured commanders concerned."[8]

Every new phase, defined by Simonds as "the transfer of responsibility between units and formations and their commanders for continuance of operations," unfortunately involved a pause that gave respite to the enemy. As the pause became longer "the higher the level at which transfer takes place," he considered it "advantageous to operate formations and units in depth on narrow frontages . . . [which gave] them 'staying power,' rather than on wide frontages necessitating early relief by passing through new formations and units." Against prepared defenses protected by thick mine-fields or antitank obstacles, only the "sledge-hammer" infantry division possessed the necessary "staying power to carry an attack through in depth." The armored division, though capable of taking on a rearguard position, did not possess sufficient infantry to break through an organized defense; it was primarily a "weapon of opportunity" designed for more fluid operations.[9]

On 1 July Simonds issued further guidance on the conduct of the attack. He stressed in particular that while the effect of air and artillery bombardment was "90% moral," and actual casualties inflicted on defenders "always . . . very small," sudden and intense pounding served to paralyze an enemy for a short period. Since good troops recovered quickly, however, he considered it vital that attacking infantry lean into the barrage, which, though hazardous, yielded fewer casualties. He also stipulated that they "not stop . . . [or] open fire until the objective [wa]s reached," for if troops adopted fire positions it was "extremely difficult to get them on the move again." At the same time, all the ammunition they carried would be needed to repel the inevitable counterattack. The objective, once taken, had first to be "mopped up" [all defenders killed or captured], which called for the "detailed search of the position itself," and then prepared for defense. This included pushing out reconnaissance patrols, Simonds insisted, for nothing was "more dangerous than to sit down in front of the Boche and not know what he [wa]s up to."[10]

Unfortunately for Simonds, 2 Canadian Corps was not afforded the chance to conduct follow-up operations. After the debacle on the slopes of Verrières Ridge, planning continued for a fresh, more deliberate, attack to be mounted against the prepared German defense. As Montgomery explained in a detailed letter to Eisenhower on 24 July, 2 Canadian Corps was to spearhead a sustained offensive by the Second British Army down the Falaise road commencing the next day. The object of the 2 Corps attack was to capture the Fontenay-le-Marmion—Point 122 feature, also known as the "Cramesnil spur." This was to be followed by a 12 Corps attack west of the Orne on 28 July and a subsequent push by 8 Corps east of the Orne toward Falaise on 30 July. All three operations, if successful, were to be preliminary to another "Goodwood" style offensive, the results of which could not be foretold. If on the other hand they did not go well, it would still be possible to retire on the 2 Corps firm base and try again in early August. Though Operation "Cobra," the first full-scale U.S. attack, had to be aborted and postponed on 24 July because of poor weather, Montgomery informed Eisenhower that Dempsey had been instructed to carry on regardless. In the event, "Cobra" and the 2 Canadian Corps attack, Operation "Spring," were both launched on 25 July 1944.[11]

Planning for Operation "Spring" had been in progress since before 21 July when Simonds issued his preliminary orders. In his view, the high ground north of Cintheaux constituted the "key to the German main defence system south of Caen" and thus the "ultimate objective" and "necessary stepping stone" to continued advance. He further reasoned that the built-up areas of St. André-sur-Orne and May-sur-Orne to the west offered the best cover for an attack in which even a partial success might gain the "very important VERRIERES ridge." It was clear to him, however, that deployment for such an attack would have to be conducted in darkness and the crest of Verrières ridge captured before daylight. According to Simonds, his plan finally "legislated both for success and the lack of it," this aspect being well-understood by Dempsey who had also been advised it was probably too much to hope for a breakthrough.[12] Bearing in mind that Simonds was roughly aware of the opposition he faced, this would appear to make sense. Whereas the dreaded 1st SS Panzer held the front from Verrières eastward, the 272nd German Infantry Division occupied the area between there and the Orne. The degree to which the 272nd had been reinforced by elements of 2nd, 9th SS, and 10th SS panzer divisions does not appear to have been appreciated, however.[13]

On 23 July Simonds briefed all commanders down to brigadier on "Spring." The next day he held a final conference with Foulkes, Keller, and the GOCs of the 7th and Guards Armoured Divisions. In outline, the operation called for four phases, the first of which entailed simultaneous night attacks by the 2nd and 3rd Canadian Infantry Divisions astride the Falaise road to capture by first light, respectively, the objectives of May-sur-Orne—Verrières and Tilly-la-Campagne. In phase two the 2nd Division was to take Fontenay-le-Marmion and Roquancourt, while the 7th Armoured seized the high ground at Cramesnil-la-Bruyere, prepared to exploit forward to the area of Cintheaux. On the 7th Armoured reaching its objective, the 3rd Division, less one brigade, was to secure Garcelles-Secqueville. During the last phases, which were tentative only, the Guards Armoured was to pass through 7th Armoured and with the remaining brigade of 3rd Division capture La Hogue woods; the 7th Armoured was then to push on to Cintheaux. While considerable air support was allocated to "Spring," the operation was not deemed dependent upon it.[14]

For artillery support, the CCRA had 2 Canadian and 8 AGRA in addition to the divisional artilleries. A total of nine field, nine medium, and two heavy regiments actually fired in support of "Spring." With the exception of an initial harassing fire program laid on by corps, however, artillery support for the operation was planned and controlled mainly at the division level (presumably in support of divisional maneuver plans). Significantly, the divisional fire plans supporting the initial assault consisted of a series of timed and "on call" concentrations instead of the standard creeping barrages employed in Operations "Windsor," "Charnwood," and "Atlantic." The latter, it was now felt, not only wasted ammunition and served to warn the enemy of impending attacks, but also, by indicating start lines, led them to easily identify and bring fire to bear on forming-up places. On the other hand, creeping barrages had long proven themselves to be a most effective form of support when enemy dispositions were not precisely known.[15] Notwithstanding this consideration, it seems reasonably clear from the artillery support arrangements for "Spring" that divisional commanders had some latitude in the planning and execution of this operation.

The attack went in at 0330 hours 25 July under various diffusions of artificial moonlight provided by searchlight batteries attempting to shine their beams on low cloud cover. On Keller's 3rd Division front, Cunningham's strongly supported 9th Brigade acted as spearhead, launching the North Novas against Tilly-la-Campagne while holding the HLI ready to pass through to secure Garcelles-Secqueville. The North Novas advanced across a kilometer of open fields from Bourguébus with three companies up, initially in darkness because the searchlights failed to come on. When they did eventually light up, the reported effect was that the troops were silhouetted "so that they were good targets to the enemy." On reaching the environs of Tilly, the North Novas discovered that the artillery had not subdued the soldiers of the 1st SS who "shot and shouted and threw grenades like wild men." In the fighting and darkness the situation became terribly confused.

The CO of the North Novas, Lieutenant-Colonel Charles Petch, now mistakenly reported that two companies were on their objectives and the attack was progressing satisfactorily. At the break of dawn, by which time he had committed all companies and could see they were being bloodily repulsed, he requested the assistance of the FGH tank squadron waiting to support the HLI in the next phase. When that squadron moved up, however, it was engaged by counterattacking Panthers and concealed antitank guns; it consequently withdrew to the west of the village and attempted to shoot the infantry into it. In the process of doing so it lost 11 tanks and was given permission that afternoon to retire on Bourguébus. The infantry in the meantime had been ordered to dig in and hold where they were. That

Map 10.1
Attack on Tilly, 25 July 1944

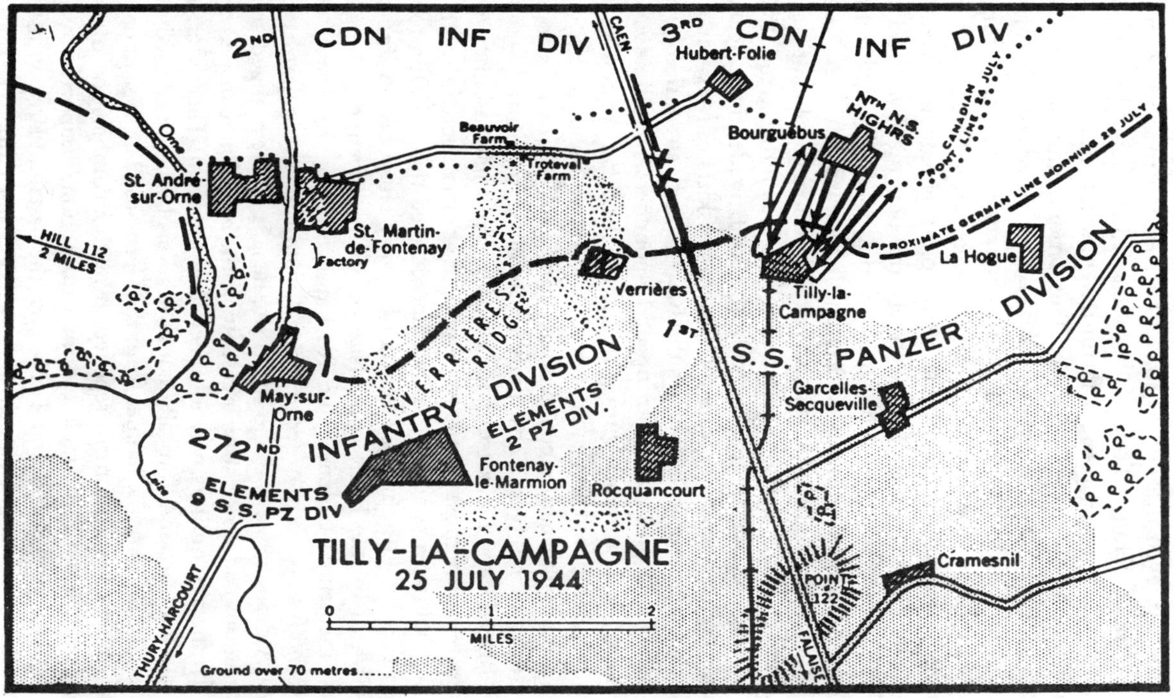

TILLY-LA-CAMPAGNE
25 JULY 1944

afternoon they were also given permission to make their way back under cover of darkness. With the failure of this battalion to take Tilly, Keller's 3rd Division attack foundered.[16]

The attack on Foulkes's 2nd Division front was a more complicated and, ultimately, even more disastrous affair. As the road between St. André-sur-Orne and Hubert-Folie had been selected as the start line, the 6th Brigade was ordered to secure St. Martin-de-Fontenay and the area of Troteval Farm in a preliminary operation. This action commenced on the evening of 24 July when the Camerons took on the wretched task of clearing through St. André toward St. Martin and a composite company from the FMR successfully attacked Troteval Farm. Tanks of the Sherbrooke Fuliliers assisted both units. The divisional plan from this juncture called for the 4th and 5th Brigades to pass respectively through the FMR and Camerons, taking each under command, thus creating a gap through which 7th Armoured Division elements could exploit forward.

Within the 4th Brigade, the Royal Hamilton Light Infantry (RHLI) was ordered to attack Verrières, after which the Royal Regiment of Canada was to advance to take Roquancourt. In the 5th Brigade, the Calgary Highlanders were directed to capture the eastern outskirts of May-sur-Orne, from which secure area at 0530 hours the Black Watch, supported by a squadron of 1st Hussar tanks and a troop of 17-pounders, would advance to seize Fontenay-le-Marmion. During this phase the 22nd Armoured Brigade of the 7th Armoured Division was also to move up from Ifs, prepared to counter possible panzer counterattacks and exploit forward as opportunities presented themselves. Those units not involved in the attack—the SSR from 6th Brigade, the Essex from 4th Brigade, and the Maisonneuves from 5th Brigade—were most curiously grouped as a reserve under the 6th Brigade.[17]

Difficulties in securing the start line delayed the 2nd Division attack on Verrières by 40 minutes. Reports of enemy tanks east of Troteval Farm, itself held by the FMR composite company, prompted the gutsy RHLI CO, Lieutenant-Colonel John Rockingham fresh from Staff College, to suspend his assault in order to mount a company attack to resecure his start line. Although this cost the RHLI the benefit of prearranged artillery concentrations and hence heavier casualties, the battalion managed under cover of darkness to fight its way into Verrières by dawn. Thereafter, assisted by 17-pounder fire and "on call" concentrations by field and medium guns, it wrested control of the hamlet from the Germans. The violent counterattack that followed was, in turn, repelled through a combination of six- and 17-pounder fire and PIAT tank hunting team action. Supported by a squadron of the 1st Royal Tanks and Typhoons, the battalion later withstood a similarly fierce onslaught launched against Verrières after 1700 hours. Sadly, this action was to be the only Canadian success that day. It remains notable in that it was attained by so-called inexperienced, but well led and handled, Canadian troops.[18]

Map 10.2
Action on Verrières Ridge, 25 July 1944

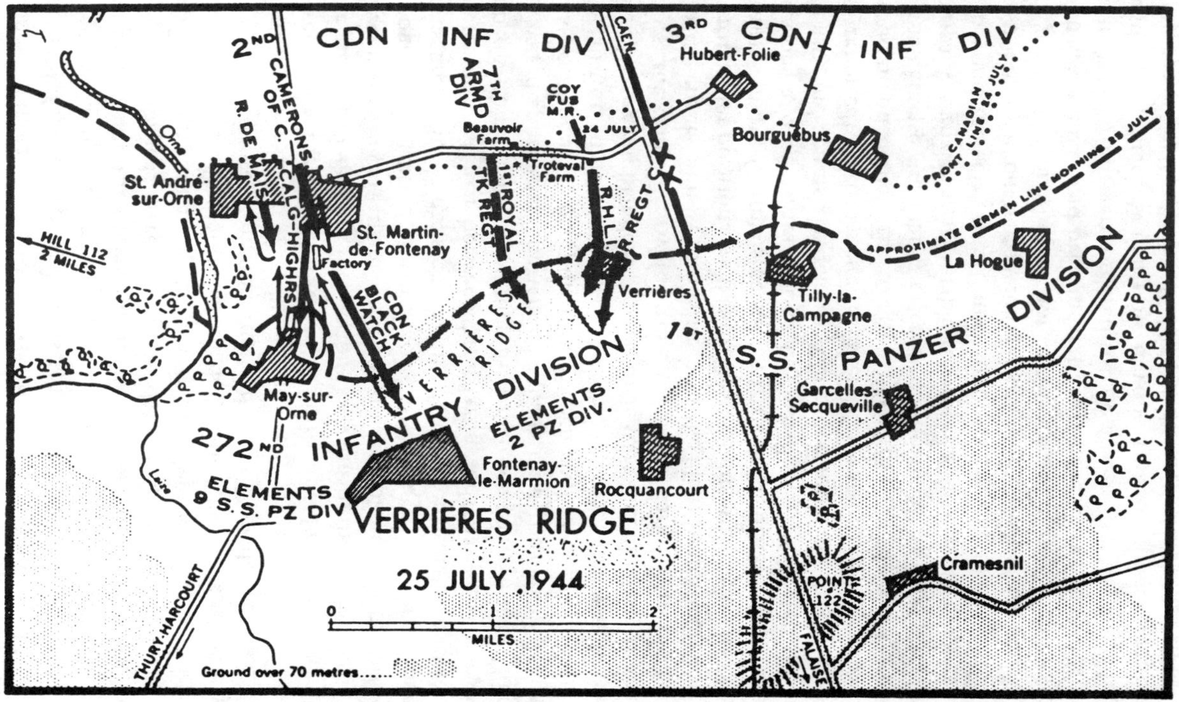

Once the RHLI reported they were firmly in Verrières, orders were issued to the Royal Regiment to commence phase two. The battalion moved out toward Roquancourt at 0600 hours, supported by a squadron of the 1st Hussars and paralleled by the British 1st Royal Tank Regiment to the west. With fighting still in progress in Verrières, the Royal Regiment CO, Lieutenant-Colonel J. C. H. Anderson, chose to skirt the village and push on, unfortunately without waiting to arrange artillery support. Once over the ridge, both units found themselves in the killing zone of an elaborate, and ingeniously camouflaged, German reverse slope defense that produced an avalanche of fire from antitank guns, panzers, machine guns, tank destroyers, mortars, artillery, and infantry. Enfiladed from Tilly-la-Campagne and similarly exposed to fire from the right, the 4th Brigade advance was abruptly and savagely halted. [19]

To the west where the Germans straddled both sides of the river, Megill's 5th Brigade attack had also run into serious snags from the beginning. The task of clearing the enemy from the built-up area of St. Martin proved simply beyond the capacity of the depleted Camerons, who had been under constant pressure in St. André since 20 July. The unconfirmed fact that the one kilometer open stretch between St. Martin and May-sur-Orne was honeycombed with mineshafts and tunnels, which would have afforded the Germans covered approaches, portended equally disastrous entanglements and assaults from the rear. A report by a French civilian on 23 July of the existence of an iron mine complex in the area went essentially unheeded. Even as the Calgary Highlanders crossed their start line, the last company at 0347 hours, the Camerons were struggling in the darkness to secure it.

A grim battle ensued almost immediately as the Highlanders were forced to clear position after position. Each time they assumed the enemy had been "blasted away," more Germans seemed to trickle in behind them. Poor communications and casualties among key personnel aggravated this increasingly nasty and confused situation. When one company shortly before 0600 hours reportedly did manage to enter May-sur-Orne, it was forced by heavy mortar and artillery fire to retire 200 yards to the north. A second company was likewise summarily ejected midmorning. At 0630 hours the reserve company signaled that, unable to progress, it was digging in but 300 yards beyond the start line. Fifteen minutes later Foulkes personally signaled it "not to dig in but to go wide and keep going." The Maisonneuves were shortly placed at one hour's notice to move and at 0715 hours the Black Watch, whose CO had been mortally wounded earlier that morning in fighting in St. Martin, were ordered to "go ahead."[20]

Command of the Black Watch now devolved upon a junior company commander, Major F. P. Griffin. Taking over just before the originally slated 0530 H-hour, and realizing that this timing could no longer be met, he proceeded to recoordinate artillery and tank support essentially along the lines of the previously planned attack. The report by an officer patrol

Map 10.3
Operation "Spring"

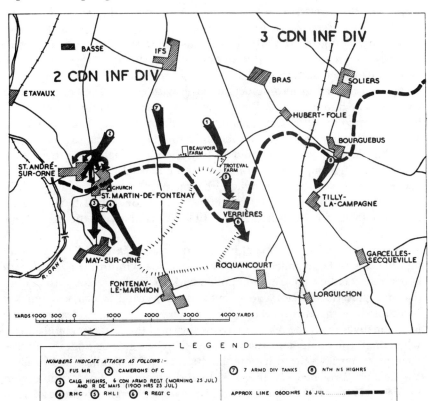

LEGEND

NUMBERS INDICATE ATTACKS AS FOLLOWS :-

① FUS M R   ② CAMERONS OF C   ⑦ 7 ARMD DIV TANKS   ⑧ NTH NS HIGHRS

③ CALG HIGHRS, 6 CDN ARMD REGT (MORNING 25 JUL)
   AND R DE MAIS (1900 HRS 25 JUL)

④ RHC   ⑤ RHLI   ⑥ R REGT C   APPROX LINE 0600 HRS 26 JUL

dispatched to reconnoiter May-sur-Orne that it appeared lightly held seems to have convinced Griffin to adhere to this plan, even though contact had not been made with forward elements of the Calgary Highlanders. A more skeptical Brigadier Megill, who actually considered it wiser to go into May-sur-Orne, before attacking Fontenay-le-Marmion, reluctantly acquiesced in this decision largely because of Griffin's enthusiasm and the promise it held for success. Griffin also apparently believed that a Black Watch drive directly on Fontenay-le-Marmion would assist the Calgary Highlanders in gaining May-sur-Orne (although their objective had been to secure a start line for Griffin's unit). What unfolded from this point was a tragedy of Great War dimensions.

At 0910 hours the Black Watch, with two companies up and two back, bravely advanced up the open slope toward Fontenay-le-Marmion from the factory area south of St. Martin. Due to lack of information as to the whereabouts of the Calgary Highlanders near May-sur-Orne, the battalion, now dangerously exposed on the right flank, may have gone without full artillery support. Only one of three allocated FOOs accompanied the advance, and his wireless set was soon put out of action. The squadron of the 1st Hussars *specifically assigned* to support the Black Watch somehow also ended up assisting the Highlanders around May-sur-Orne. On failing to properly "marry up" with the infantry it was supposed to support, the entire squadron sought to provide covering fire from that vicinity, but here its tanks were drawn into desperate battle with enemy antitank guns and panzers. The doomed Black Watch, under intense mortaring and raked by machine-gun cross fire, thus pressed on alone in the very face of counter-attacking Panthers coming into action, struggling as Simonds had urged them but days before to "uphold...[their] good name by...[their] conduct and...fighting." An estimated 60 all ranks led by Major Griffin reached the top of the ridge where the enemy was dug in and posted in even greater strength. Of 300 officers and men committed to this action not more than 15 made it back, the acting CO falling with the mass of his soldiers.[21]

During the Black Watch trial by fire, the enemy increased the pressure on the Calgary Highlanders from May-sur-Orne. Unfortunately, through a misunderstanding the battalion pulled back to St. André-sur-Orne rather than the prescribed factory area south of St. Martin, which was quickly reoccupied by the enemy. The Germans were thus able to deal with the Maisonneuves from the rear, exactly as they had the Calgary Highlanders, when the former battalion attacked May-sur-Orne at 1900 hours in a futile attempt to retrieve the situation. In the meantime, Foulkes had ordered Young's 6th Brigade to be prepared to attack Fontenay-le-Marmion from the general area of May-sur-Orne the following morning. In the course of planning this operation, however, Young became convinced that until the Germans were cleared from Hill 112 to the west of the Orne, further operations immediately east of the river were unlikely to achieve success. At 2000 hours he expressed these reservations to Foulkes, stating that he considered it "his duty to the men under his command" to do so. Foulkes, on his part, agreed and set out to make similar representations to Simonds.[22]

Simonds, as it turned out, had already seen Dempsey and received permission to suspend Operation "Spring," which, except for Dieppe, was the bloodiest day of the war for Canadian arms. When he precisely determined that events were not unfolding as they should have is not entirely clear. The erroneous report from the North Novas and confused communications emanating from the 5th Brigade, likely prompted by German counter movements, apparently led him to believe that Tilly and May-sur-Orne were in Canadian hands. Indeed, the perception that Tilly was being held against counterattack persisted within 2 Corps headquarters as late as 1625 hours. In any case, after having personally monitored the attack of the Black Watch and visited Dempsey, Simonds at 1500 hours ordered

Foulkes's 2nd Division to capture Rocquancourt with the corps artillery in support at 1830 hours, attack May-sur-Orne again at 2100 hours, and take Fontenay-le-Marmion the next morning. He also expected Cunningham's 9th Brigade to consolidate Tilly during the night. The strong German counterattack against Verrières around 1800 hours, however, appears to have finally convinced him otherwise.[23]

By any measurement "Spring" was an unmitigated tactical debacle and Simonds was obviously deeply upset about it. In postwar correspondence he maintained that despite the overall strength of German dispositions, "the objectives of MAY-SUR-ORNE, VERRIERES, and TILLY-LA-CAM-PAGNE could and should have been taken and held without heavy casualties." That they were not he attributed to faulty minor tactics, especially those points he elaborated upon at the beginning of July: neglecting to secure start lines properly; failing to keep close to supporting artillery fire; overlooking the need to search ground thoroughly when mopping up; and not consolidating quickly enough to meet counterattack. In his view, disregard of these basic tactical measures and "errors of judgement in minor tactics" largely accounted for the "failure to secure initial objectives" and the excessive and unnecessary casualties in operation "Spring."[24]

In light of the rather complicated and disconnected tactical plan of the 2nd Division, which must be attributed to Foulkes, these observations surely have some validity. The Camerons clearly pursued a task beyond their capacity, and without the entire 6th Brigade behind them to help out it remained difficult to attain within the required timeframe. Indeed, the clearance of St. André and St. Martin might better have been left to the 6th Brigade complete. A proper attack by the 5th Brigade supported by armor would likely have secured May-sur-Orne and, in turn, Fontenay-le-Marmion. One would have expected, as well, that Major Griffin, having just assumed command of the Black Watch, should have been *directed*, as Rockingham of the RHLI more wisely insisted, to alter his plan to fit obviously changed circumstances. Since there was a CRA's representative at 5th Brigade headquarters, one would also have thought that better artillery fire control and bombardment arrangements could have been made for the Watch attack. In short, it is difficult to escape the conclusion that both Foulkes and Megill could have done more to ensure that the fighting battalions of the 2nd Division were correctly launched into battle.[25]

The lot of 2nd Division units might have been made easier, of course, had 2 Corps taken greater pains in coordinating with 12 British Corps the masking or suppression of German daylight activity across the Orne to the west. Still, major responsibility for the disaster appears to lie at the divisional level of planning and execution. That Simonds was highly dissatisfied with the performance of the 2nd Division, with whom he passed most of the morning from 0800 hours, is evident from the disclosure that one of the "things ... uppermost in ... [his] mind on that day ... [was to] get rid of

General Charles Foulkes." For reasons possibly dating back to "Atlantic" or even before, Simonds had reached the conclusion that his old staff college classmate "did not have the right qualities to command . . . 2nd Division." On "at least three occasions," recalled Major-General Kitching, "Simonds confided in me that he was going to get rid of . . . Foulkes."[26] But Simonds never would get rid of Foulkes. Protected by Crerar, he went on in November to command 1 Canadian Corps in Italy, succeeding the dismissed Lieutenant-General E. L. M. Burns whom Keller was once slated to replace. Indeed, through the continued patronage of Crerar, Foulkes was eventually chosen to head the Canadian Army before Simonds.[27]

In later years Foulkes disputed Simonds's portrayal of "Spring" as a "holding action," maintaining that it was represented to him solely "as a break-through operation with prospects of success." He also expressed resentment at the proclivity of Simonds "to blame the inefficiency of our troops for our misfortunes."[28] But here, to refer back to the introduction, one can argue that Foulkes was even more prone to explain the failure of Canadian troops in terms of their relative inexperience (which also left him off the hook). Indeed, he was to be accused of doing exactly this after the bloody repulse of the 1st Division at the Lamone River in Italy on 4 December 1944. Yet, the failure of this formation to carry out its assigned task during Operation "Chuckle," as this "sacrificial holocaust" mounted by 1 Corps was "grotesquely" code-named, appears to have been less the fault of the fighting troops than an indirect result of Foulkes's unrealistic higher level planning. One brigadier, a battalion CO, and a second-in-command being practiced as a CO were nonetheless relieved.[29]

An equivalent number of heads similarly rolled as a consequence of "Spring," though in the long-suffering 3rd rather than the 2nd Division. It is doubly difficult, of course, to fathom why but one battalion should have spearheaded Keller's 3rd Division attack. Notwithstanding Simonds's expressed preference for operating "formations and units in depth on narrow frontages" to enhance "staying power," one of the major lessons learned by the 3rd Division after a month of offensive action was to launch attacks on a broad front. By attacking in this fashion the enemy was forced to disperse or split his defensive fire effort, which also precluded him from applying its weight in depth. If, on the other hand, a division "kick[ed] off with one or two b[attalio]ns, the enemy Div Arty and Mortars, and, if necessary, t[an]k res[erves] c[ould] be concentrated quickly against the attack." Nearby enemy company localities not under attack were also free to support defenders with enfilade fire.[30]

This is what appears to have happened in the attack upon Tilly-la-Campagne, which action subsequently became tactically contentious. When the North Novas continued to experience severe difficulty in attempting to secure their objective, the SDG were placed at notice to move to their assistance from 1125 hours. Since the latter unit had the day before been advised that because it had "had no rest" it would not be taking part in "Spring," this warning came as "a mental blow . . . felt by all ranks." That they were ordered to stand down at 1600 hours, seems mainly to have come about as a result of a heated confrontation in which Cunningham, Petch, and Lieutenant-Colonel G. H. Christiansen of the SDGs persuaded Keller of the futility of continuing the attack.[31] The following evening Keller discussed the matter with Simonds, who subsequently convened a board of inquiry into the failure of the North Novas to take Tilly.

This board, completed on 29 July, saw Cunningham and Petch both removed from command, the former to Kingston as commandant of the staff course.[32] Christiansen, in a 3 August letter to Keller professed a loss of confidence "in . . . leadership and command that kept every unit . . . in action continuously in spite of severe casualties, and culminated in the launching of several worn-out and disorganized men . . . into the attack on Tilly La Campagne on 25 Jul 44." Noting that he "was warned to be ready to go to their assistance" when "it was apparent that they could be written off," he added that "under the above circumstances, or similar ones, I would have, and will, refuse to put the S.D. & G. Highrs in." On receipt of this letter Keller raised an adverse report on Christiansen recommending "no further employment" and repatriation to Canada. Simonds, lamenting Christiansen's "impression that battles can be fought on a 'limited liability' basis," agreed that he was "unfitted to lead Canadian Troops with determination." Paradoxically, on 23 December Major-General H. W. Foster, GOC 1st Division and former commander of 7th Brigade during "Spring," specifically requested Christiansen to command the West Nova Scotia Regiment. He was supported in this request by Foulkes who, perhaps in a backhanded criticism of either Simonds or Keller, claimed to be "fully aware of [the] circumstances concerning Christiansen['s] removal."[33]

It would appear, however, that Simonds was even more aware of the command situation and critical state of morale that existed within the 3rd Division. In a 27 July letter to Dempsey reporting on Keller's fitness to command he pointed out that since D-Day the division had "never been out of contact" and had incurred some 5,500 casualties, most of them within rifle companies. This "wastage" plus "the fact that the division had been unable to get out of the line and re-organize properly ha[d] resulted in a deterioration of its fighting efficiency quite out of proportion to . . . actual losses." As casualties among junior leaders had been heavy, Simonds continued, within many sections and platoons "the men hardly kn[e]w one another or junior leaders their men and men their leaders." In short, "sub-units lack[ed] the cohesion in battle characteristic of a trained battle team." Simonds found as a consequence that "unit commanders and brigadiers [we]re apprehensive about operations not through fear of becoming casualties themselves or of having casualties, but because they fe[lt] their units [we]re unfitted in their present state of training to put up a good show."

He also sensed within the division "a feeling of some resentment" that due credit had not been given for hard fighting.

The impression was additionally widespread that the 3rd Division should have been "withdrawn into reserve to be re-organized" after the initial assault. While Simonds remarked that he had taken steps to quash such "erroneous ideas," he recommended against the removal of Keller on the grounds it "would have a most adverse effect on . . . morale . . . [and] be regarded as censure on the efforts of the division." In order to develop "the full fighting efficiency" of the 3rd Division, argued Simonds, it had to "be given a period out of the line to re-organize and train and absorb reinforcement personnel." Only after a "successful operation," however, did he "consider that a change in command could be made without affecting the feeling of the division itself." As for the "individual qualities" of Keller, Simonds thought them "unimportant . . . in comparison with the bigger problem of maintaining the morale of 3 Canadian Division." He had nonetheless "formed the impression that . . . Keller ha[d] not appreciated the vital importance of the moral aspects of higher command and the absolute necessity for the commander being a stabilizing influence in the give and take of active operations." Despite this, Simonds "believe[d] . . . Keller ha[d] failed to do his best, mainly through a feeling that it ha[d] been 'all censure and no encouragement.' "[34]

On 27 July, 2 Canadian Corps regrouped, the 7th and Guards Armoured Divisions reverting from command and the 4th Canadian Armoured Division and the 4th British Armoured Brigade coming under command. The general plan announced for the near future was to hold the corps front with the 2nd Division right and the newly arrived 4th Division left. The 2nd Canadian Armoured Brigade and the 3rd Division were scheduled at last to remove to rear areas for reorganization, refitting, training, and assimilation of reinforcements.[35] This accorded with the intentions of Montgomery who the very same day, anxious to further the successful breakout by American forces to the west, directed the Second British Army to deliver a strong right wing offensive, Operation "Bluecoat," in the Caumont area with not less than six divisions. To keep the enemy from transferring forces across to the western flank, he deemed it essential that the First Canadian and Second British Armies continue to attack the enemy vigorously in the east. As he so colorfully put it: "He must be worried, and shot up, and attacked, and raided, whenever and wherever possible." Subsidiary objects of these activities were to gain ground of tactical advantage and "write off" German manpower and equipment. Within 2 Canadian Corps this translated into a number of costly and largely unsuccessful battalion attacks on limited objectives, with Tilly-la-Campagne occupying center stage.[36]

As if to illustrate that there was nothing basically wrong with Canadian troops, a reinforced company of the Essex supported by artillery and the direct fire of a tank troop captured an enemy-held orchard midway between

Verrières and Tilly in a vicious, costly action on the night of 29 July. The next day the Calgary Highlanders were warned to be prepared to attack Tilly from this position in the early hours of 1 August; a company of the Lincoln and Welland Regiment from the 4th Division was at the same time earmarked to launch a diversionary feint from Bourguébus. Despite this assistance and the support of both divisional artilleries plus 2 Canadian AGRA, the Calgary attack was stalled west of the village by intense German machine-gun and counterbarrage fire, the last being perceived once more as Canadian shelling falling short. A second, daylight assault supported by a troop of the Royal Scots Greys enabled some Canadians to get into Tilly, but, unable to consolidate, they retired to the area of their original start line. A company of the Royal Regiment, pushed forward to assist in piece-meal fashion, met the Calgary Highlanders coming back. At this juncture Brigadier Megill ordered the shattered battalion to attack again at 1430 hours supported by a squadron of the Fort Garry Horse. This effort, with its attendant aura of the reinforcement of failure, was similarly repulsed short of Tilly by a like concentration of enemy fire.[37]

Apparently as a result of Montgomery's personal appeal to Crerar on the morning of 1 August to keep up the pressure on the 2 Corps front, the entire Lincoln battalion was now ordered to execute a silent attack that night against Tilly. As planned, two companies were to strike south from Bour-guébus and occupy blocking positions between Tilly and La Hogue to forestall an anticipated panzer counterattack from the latter quarter. The two other companies were then to advance directly on Tilly, the first seizing an intermediate position through which the second would assault the village. This actually amounted to a one company attack, albeit supported from first light by the fire of a reinforced squadron of the 29th Armoured Re-connaissance Regiment (The South Alberta Regiment), a troop of 17-poun-der antitank guns, and the divisional and corps artillery. As events unfolded, the intermediate position was secured, but the blocking companies were forced back to Bourguébus in some confusion.

Despite this reverse, the commander of the 10th Brigade, Brigadier Jim Jefferson, ordered the last company to assault Tilly. The *Leibstandarte* de-fenders, not surprisingly, stopped it cold. Two days later Jefferson informed the Lincoln officers "that insufficient determination had been shown in attacking what should have been a two-company objective." Jefferson had of course made the presentation on "Clearing Towns and Villages" during the 2 Canadian Corps Study Period 13–18 March 1944. A further attempt to capture Tilly made by the Argyll and Sutherland Highlanders of Canada (Princess Louise's) backed by a South Alberta squadron on 5 August also failed. The same day Montgomery remarked to Simonds, "Congratula-tions, you've been kicked out of Tilly again!" The strongly fortified village finally fell to the 51st Highland Division on 8 August, but only after having been cut off and following a protracted struggle by two Seaforth battalions

Map 10.4
Attack on Tilly, 1 August 1944

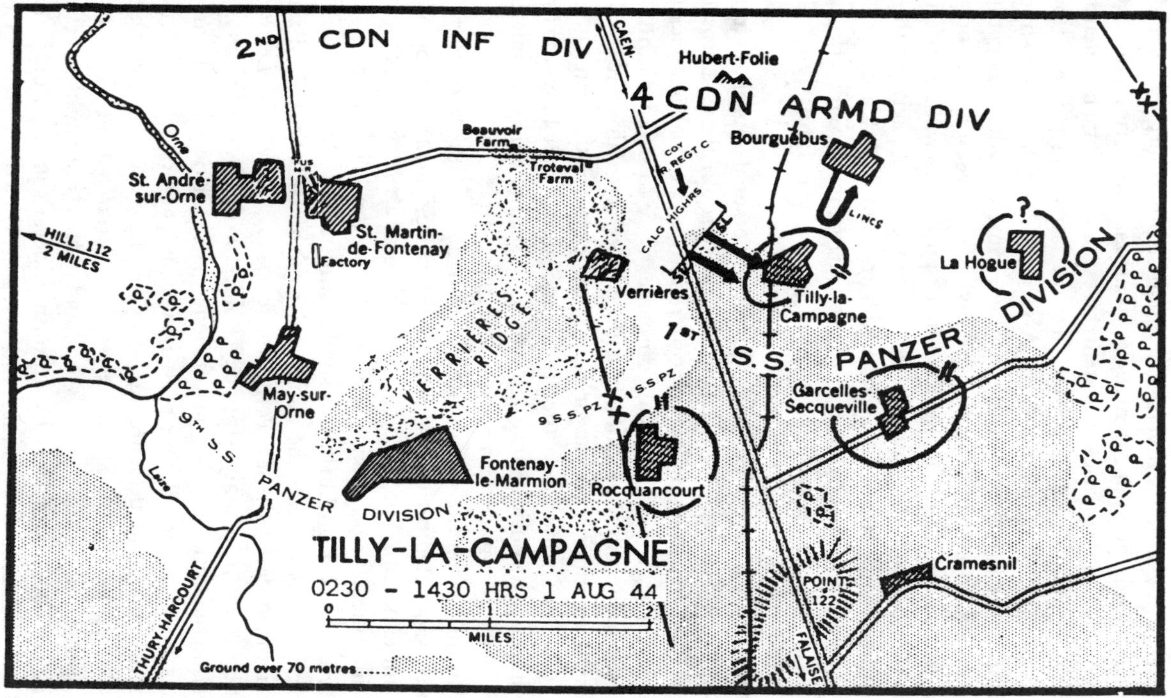

TILLY-LA-CAMPAGNE

0230 – 1430 HRS 1 AUG 44

0 MILES 1

Ground over 70 metres

2ND CDN INF DIV

4 CDN ARMD DIV

1ST S.S. PANZER DIVISION

9TH S.S. PANZER DIVISION

DIVISION

CAEN-

Orne

St. André-sur-Orne

St. Martin-de-Fontenay
(Factory)

May-sur-Orne

HILL 112
2 MILES

THURY-HARCOURT

Orne

Laize

Beauvoir Farm

Troteval Farm

Hubert-Folie

Bourguébus

L INCS

Verrières

CALG HIGHRS

LINCS

CGY REGT C

Tilly-la-Campagne

Garcelles
Secqueville

Fontenay-le-Marmion

Roquancourt

POIN
122

FALAISE

Cramesnil

La Hogue

CERRIERE
RIDGE

Map 10.5
Attack on Tilly, 5 August 1944

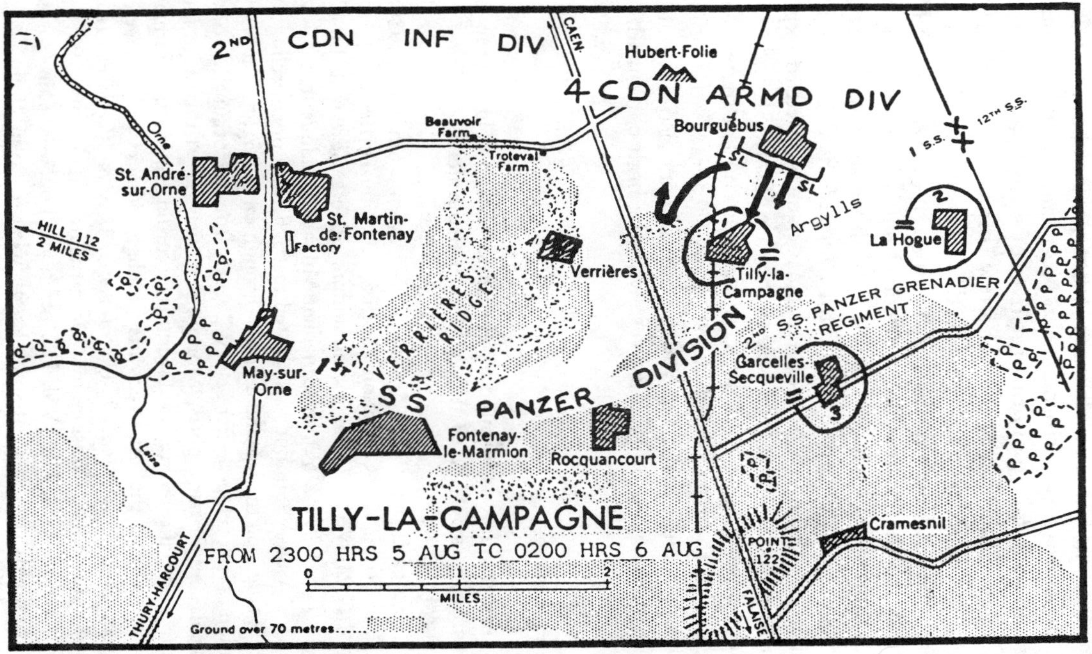

of the 152nd Brigade supported by armor.[38] The question thus remains whether Tilly was ever really a two-company objective.

It is easy to be wise after the fact, especially in the warmth and comfort of a writer's chair, but to conduct a military study without some degree of Clausewitzian critical analysis would be to defeat its very purpose. The old adage that one learns best from mistakes is not without foundation. Looking at Canadian Army performance in Normandy up to the end of July 1944, it would seem fair to say that the lives of many soldiers were unnecessarily cast away. While some, and not a few commanders, have argued that lack of combat experience related directly to loss of life, this contention cannot entirely be sustained. As has been shown in the case of the RHLI, and the 12th SS for that matter, inexperienced units did prevail in the face of the enemy, provided their commanders exhibited the requisite tactical skill and leadership. Judging from the performance of the 272nd Infantry Division, neither can the myth of German fanaticism be used to explain excessive Canadian losses. What then can? In the case of the SSR and the Black Watch the conclusion is inescapable: surely those who left them exposed in open wheatfields to be harvested like so many sheaves. As for other units introduced piecemeal to battle, and whose soldiers also gave all that mortals could, the responsibility must rest with the high command.

NOTES

The chapter title was inspired by the lines: "Cast a cold eye/On life, on death./Horseman, pass by!" W. B. Yeats, "Under Ben Bulben," *Collected Poems* (London: Pan, 1990), p. 401.

1. Record Group (RG) 24, Vol. 12,745, Memo Simonds to COS CMHQ on Attack by R. H. C.—Operation "Spring," 31 January 1946.

2. RG 24, Vol. 12,745, Memorandum of Interview with Lt.-Gen. G. G. Simonds, CB, CBE, DSO, at Canadian Military Headquarters, 19 March 1946 by Col. C. P. Stacey. Simonds also stated that "the idea of encircling the enemy by a holding attack on the left and a break-through on the right . . . was a product of the situation as it developed after D-day." Apart from the occupation of the Cherbourg peninsula and Brittany ports, Montgomery was not at this stage interested in the capture of specific geographical features; according to Martin Blumenson, his main aim was to retain the intiative while avoiding setbacks and reverses. [Martin Blumenson, *Breakout and Pursuit, United States Army in World War II, The European Theatre of Operations* (Washington: Department of the Army, 1961), p. 14].

3. Crerar Papers (CP), Vol. 7, Operational Policy—2 Cdn Corps, 17 February 1944. Simonds elaborated at some length what to do in "following up a German retirement." He cautioned, however, that the Germans, instead of stepping back "to a position some distance in the rear," might "alternatively . . . stabilize the initial beach-head operations in front of a position on which they are prepared to fight." He nonetheless intended in every instance to direct divisions on "centres of front-to-rear and lateral communication as their objectives," the capture of which would

increase friendly force momentum while restricting enemy power of maneuver (Ibid.).

4. Ibid.

5. Ibid. Simonds insisted that "one medium regiment w[ould] always be either in support or under command of a forward [leading] division." (Ibid.).

6. Ibid. On 13 July 1944, the Command-in-Chief Panzergruppe West observed that "the HKL [*Hauptkampflinie* or forward edge of the battle area] is still too closely manned. In it should be only about one-third of each company, the other two-thirds should be in two lines 600 and 1200 meters behind the HKL. Reinforce the HKL at night if necessary. Whoever puts most of his men into the HKL will have high casualties without being able to prevent a break-in of the enemy." A week earlier Panzergruppe West had directed that "counter thrusts with tanks against the British will yield inexpensive success only if they are made at once. Otherwise the enemy will have put out mines, and heavy casualties will be inflicted by artillery and low flying aircraft before reaching the starting point of an attack." The same document stated that only antitank "positions in depth make sense . . . [and they] should be in open ground." (RG 24, Vol. 13,712, Enemy Methods, "extracts from an order of 85 Inf Div and three orders of Panzergruppe West . . . captured 16 August 1944").

7. CP, Vol. 7, Operational Policy—2 Cdn Corps, 17 February 1944. Simonds in an earlier directive stressed that as the "Germans move forward heavy tanks firing shell at close range to support immediate counter-attacks by their infantry . . . all infantrymen must be thoroughly trained in manhandling the 6-pdr over all types of ground and obstacles." Getting these guns forward was the more important because it was sometimes "impossible to move our tanks close behind our assaulting infantry owing to delays imposed by minefields and anti-tank obstacles." Mc-Naughton Papers (MP), Vol. 157, COG/1–0 Operational Training, 15 May 1943. The Canadian artillery never really solved the tactical problem of countermortar.

8. CP. Vol. 7, Operational Policy—2 Cdn Corps, 17 February 1944.

9. Ibid.

10. RG 24, Vol. 10,799, Simonds's Draft of Lessons, 1 July 1944. Simonds saw the primary role of artillery as one of "neutralization" as opposed to old-fashioned "destruction" (the capability required against Japanese bunkers, for example, and still sought by Russian artillery today). See Brig. A. L. Pemberton, *The Second World War, 1939–1945, Army, The Development of Artillery Tactics and Equipment* (London: War Office, 1951) p. 330. Simonds also had views on patrols. Reconnaissance patrols, he stated, "should be as small as possible (two or at most, three men)," selected from among "those who like to play a lone hand or work with one or two tried companions." He further recommended grouping these men into a special platoon within units for this kind of work. Simonds additionally thought it "quite wrong to send out a fighting patrol on an undefined mission towards the enemy to take prisoners." Only after reconnaissance patrols produced a clear picture, he insisted, should fighting patrols, minor attacks, be contemplated. Badly organized fighting patrols, he reminded, usually ended in "getting ambushed and giving useful information to the enemy" (Ibid.).

11. Nigel Hamilton, *Monty*, Vol. II: *Master of the Battlefield 1942–1944* (Sevenoaks: Hodder and Stoughton, 1984), pp. 737–738; Crerar Papers (CP), Vol. 2, 21 Army Group M512 of 21-7-44; Col. C. P. Stacey, *Official History of the Canadian Army*

in the Second World War, Vol. III: *The Victory Campaign: The Operations in North-West Europe, 1944–1945* (Ottawa: Queen's Printer, 1966), p. 183; and Terry Copp and Robert Vogel, *Maple Leaf Route: Falaise* (Alma: Maple Leaf Route, 1983) pp. 62, 76–78. On the eve of "Spring" and "Cobra," seven panzer divisions (2nd, 21st, 116th, and 1st, 9th, 10th, and 12th SS) with a total of 645 tanks faced the Second British Army; of these, all but the 10th SS and elements of the 2nd and 9th SS Panzer were east of the Orne. On the U.S. front, there were two panzer divisions of about 190 tanks. About 60 infantry battalions opposed the First U.S. Army on 16 July, whereas roughly 70 battalions were opposite the Second British [Stacey, *Victory Campaign*, pp. 183–185; and Ronald Lewin, *Montgomery as Military Commander* (New York: Stein and Day, 1971), p. 207].

12. RG 24, Vol. 12,745, Memo Simonds to COS CMHQ on Attack by R. H. C.—Operation "Spring," 31 January 1946, Letter Stacey to Simonds, 16 March 1946, and Memorandum of Interview with Lt.-Gen. G. G. Simonds, CB, CBE, DSO, at Canadian Military Headquarters, 19 March 1946 by Col. C. P. Stacey.

13. Stacey, *Victory Campaign*, p. 185. According to Stacey, the 272nd Division was reinforced with a panzer battalion from the 2nd Panzer, a panzer grenadier battalion from the 9th SS, and a reconnaissance battalion from the 10th SS. The 9th SS and 2nd Panzer remained in close reserve and within striking distance respectively. The movement of the 2nd Panzer east from Caumont had gone undetected (Ibid.).

14. RG 24, Vol. 10,808, Gds Armd Div 00 No 2 Operation "Spring," 24 July 1944; and RG 24, Vol. 14,116, WD HQ 6 CIB SEI, 24–25 July 1944.

15. Col. G. W. L. Nicholson, *The Gunners of Canada: A History of the Royal Regiment of Canadian Artillery*, Vol. II: *1919–1967* (Toronto: McClelland and Stewart, 1972), pp. 301–302; and Pemberton, *Artillery Tactics*, pp. 235–237. The 2nd New Zealand Division employed the barrage as their normal method of artillery support. With a preferred density of one gun per 20 yards and a usual depth of about 4,000 yards, it took about 12 hours to prepare after receipt of the division commander's orders. In the opinion of one brigade commander, "provided the troops understood a barrage and kept right up to it, an attack under a barrage seldom failed." (Pemberton, *Artillery Tactics*, p. 279). Canadians began to feel that only 25 percent of artillery resources should be employed on the barrage, leaving the other 65 percent available to deal with outside but relevant enemy positions (Personal Copy CLFCSC Collection, 8th Cdn Inf Bde Barrage in the Attack).

16. Stacey, *Victory Campaign*, pp. 186–187, 189–190; Reginald H. Roy, *1944: The Canadians in Normandy*, Canadian War Museum Historical Publication No. 19 (Ottawa: Macmillan, 1977), pp. 103–109; RG 24, Vol. 15,122, WD North Novas 25 July 1944; RG 24, Vol. 10,800, Report by Lt. Col. McLellan GSO 1 (Liaison) 3 Cdn Inf Div on "Spring," 25 July 1944; and Copp and Vogel, *Falaise*, p. 70.

17. Stacey, *Victory Campaign*, pp. 187–188; Roy, *Canadians in Normandy*, pp. 102–103; and RG 24, Vol. 14,409, WD HQ 5CIB O. O. No. 1, 24 July 1944.

18. Personal copy CLFCSC Collection, Brig. J. M. Rockingham to Col. C. P. Stacey, 27 October 1948 and Account of the Actions of the Scout Pl RHLI in the Attack and Holding of Verrieres, 25 July 1944, as Given by Lt. Hinton, Scout Pl, to Capt. Engler at Louvigny, 5 August 1944; Stacey, *Victory Campaign*, pp. 190–191; and Kingsley Brown, Sr., Kingsley Brown, Jr., and Brereton Greenhous, *Semper Paratus* (Hamilton: RHLI Historical Association, 1977), pp. 243–250.

19. Stacey, *Victory Campaign*, pp. 188, 190–191; Nicholson, *Gunners*, II, 302–303; RG 24, Vol. 14,116, WD HQ 6 CIB SEI, 23–25 July 1944; and Roy, *Canadians in Normandy*, pp. 102, 109–117. Roy's description of the entire battle is as thorough an account as any published. Every survivor of "Spring" who could be found in England plus several in Canada were interviewed by army historians [C. P. Stacey, *A Date with History* (Ottawa: Deneau, 1983), p. 177].

20. Roy, *Canadians in Normandy*, pp. 102–103, 117–123; Stacey, *Victory Campaign*, pp. 188, 191; Maj. Roy Farran, *The History of the Calgary Highlanders, 1921–54* (Calgary, Alberta: Bryant, 1954), pp. 151–153; Copp and Vogel, *Falaise*, pp. 66, 74; and RG 24, Vol. 14,109, WD HQ 5 CIB Message Log, 24–25 July 1944, and SEI, 24–25 July 1944. The log entry for 1030 hours 25 July records that "A" company "walked into own barrage."

21. Roy, *Canadians in Normandy*, pp. 122–129 and his "Black Day for the Black Watch," *CDQ* 3 (Winter 1982/83): 34–42; Stacey, *Victory Campaign*, pp. 191–192; RG 24, Vol. 14,109, WD 5 CIB O. O. No. 1, 24 July 1944; RG 24, Vol. 15,009, WD Black Watch, 8–25 July 1944; and DHist Historical Section Report No. 150 of 12 February 1946. The Black Watch entries show "No more news of the missing boys" on 27 July and "No more news of the missing" 28 July. With 15 out of 300 returning, the Black Watch attack suffered 95 percent casualties; the Newfoundland Regiment on the first day of the Somme, 1 July 1916, attacking with 776 saw 68 return, a casualty percentage of 91.2. Brigadier Megill later claimed the "fire plan was fired on time exactly as arranged . . . however . . . due to enemy fire, the adv of the bn was too slow to take full advantage of it." He doubted the accuracy of reports that the battalion was fired on from behind as it crossed the start line, stating that it was probably due "to some plunging fire" being mistaken for fire coming from the rear, "a very common battle error" (RG 24, Vol. 12,745, Confidential Memo Megill to G 3 Cdn Inf Div CAOF, 29 January 1946).

22. Roy, *Canadians in Normandy*, pp. 113–114, 129–131; Stacey, *Victory Campaign*, pp. 192–193; Copp and Vogel, *Falaise*, p. 72; RG 24, Vol. 14,109, WD HQ 5 CIB SEI, 25 July 1944; RG 24, Vol. 14,093, WD HQ 4 CIB SEI, 25 July 1944; RG 24, Vol. 13,750, WD GS 2 CID Ops Log and SEI, 25–26 July 1944; RG 24, Vol. 14,116, WD HQ 6 CIB SEI, 25 July 1944. At 2240 the RHLI reported, "We are suffering cas[ualties] from our own guns." Foulkes, it appears, did not see Simonds about canceling "Spring" (Stacey, *Date with History*, p. 178).

23. Stacey, *Victory Campaign*, pp. 186, 192–193; W. E. J. Hutchinson, "Test of a Corps Commander: Lieutenant-General Guy Granville Simonds, Normandy 1944," (unpublished M. A. thesis, University of Victoria, 1982), pp. 174–179, 182; Dempsey Diary (DD), 25 July 1944; RG 24, Vol. 13,711, WD GS 2 Cdn Corps SEI, 25 July 1944. According to McLellan, "It was decided that Tilly must be held and re-inforced at night" since 2nd Division was in possession of May-sur-Orne (RG 24, Vol. 10,800, Report by Lt. Col. McLellan).

24. RG 24, Vol. 12,745, Memo Simonds to COS CMHQ on Attack by R.H.C.— Operations "Spring," 31 January 1946; and Hutchinson, "Corps Commander," p. 181. Hutchinson had access to Simonds's private papers, but all of the major source material he quoted is duplicated in the NAC.

25. Hutchinson, "Corps Commander," pp. 180–182; Roy, *Canadians in Normandy*, pp. 117–118, 123–125; Copp and Vogel, *Falaise*, p. 66; Brown and Greenhous, *Semper Paratus*, pp. 243–246; Stacey, *Victory Campaign*, p. 188; and RG 24,

Vol. 14,109, 5 Cdn Inf Bde O. O. No. 1, 24 July 1944. Megill's background was signals, not infantry.

26. Maj.-Gen. George Kitching, *Mud and Green Fields* (Langley: Battleline, 1986), p. 206; and Hutchinson, "Corps Commander," pp. 175–176, 178, 182. Plans had been made for 2nd Division to smoke off its right flank, with 3rd Division artillery on call if required.

27. Montgomery of Alamein Papers (MAP), BLM 1/101 Brooke to Montgomery, 14 July 1944; Col. G. W. L. Nicholson, *Official History of the Canadian Army in the Second World War*, Vol. II: *The Canadians in Italy: 1943–1945* (Ottawa: Queen's Printer, 1956), pp. 451, 606; and Lt.-Gen. E.L.M. Burns, *General Mud: Memoirs of Two World Wars* (Toronto: Clarke, Irwin, 1970), pp. 218–221. In considering future commanders on 16 May 1944, Crerar wrote: "Simonds and I are agreed that, as regards mentality, Foulkes possesses the necessary qualifications. On the other hand, he has not been tried out in the field and though he certainly possesses the brains and the outlook, he may not show himself equipped with the necessary mental and moral stamina." Crerar also compared Simonds and Burns: "In my opinion both Simonds and Burns are capable of successfully filling the appointment of Army Comd. Of the two, Simonds would probably be the more brilliant and show more drive in f[iel]d op[eration]s. Burns is the better balanced and looks further ahead" (CP, Vol. 8, Crerar to Stuart, 16 May 1944). Burns's Canadian divisional commanders would not probably have agreed that his "shy, introverted, and hummourless" manner marked him as a good field commander. According to Maj.-Gen. Chris Vokes, "No nicknames were ever more negative in their meaning than those given to General Burns, as he was known throughout 1 Canadian Corps as 'Laughing Boy' or "Smiling Sunray" [Vokes Papers (VP), Adriatic Front—Winter 1944].

28. Stacey, *Date with History*, pp. 174–178. Too much has always been made of whether or not "Spring" was a holding attack. As Tuker so simply put it: "A holding attack which actually engages, instead of a feint which does not engage, can seldom be effective if its attack fails, because the enemy is no longer under threat in that sector. He has won and can turn elsewhere" [Lt.-Gen. Sir Francis Tuker, *Approach to Battle* (London: Cassell, 1963), p. 255].

29. Farley Mowat, *The Regiment*, (Toronto: McClelland and Stewart, 1955), 252–269; Strome Galloway, *The General Who Never Was* (Belleville: Mika, 1981), pp. 236–241; Nicholson, *Canadians in Italy*, pp. 612–623 and *Gunners*, II, 249–251. Here Canadian troops were badly shelled by their own artillery, but it was not so much the fault of the artillery as high-level planners. Again, inadequate reconnaissance seems to have been the problem. The magnitude of the Lamone obstacle, 25-foot high flood banks on the land side and a 40-foot drop to the river, was grossly underestimated. In 12 hours, 164 casualties were incurred. There is also evidence that Foulkes mishandled his division in the Foret de la Londe outside Rouen, 27–29 August 1944 [Paul Douglas Dickson, "Command Relations in the Northwest Europe Campaign, 1944–45: Montgomery and the Canadians" (unpublished M. A. thesis, Acadia University, 1985), p. 62].

30. RG 24, Vol. 13,766, Headquarters 3 Canadian Infantry Division Lessons of War Number 1, 12 July 1944.

31. RG 24, Vol. 15,271, WD SDG, 25 July 1944. "We need rest and refit, having

been in the line since D Day," the diarist recorded. See also Tony Foster, *Meeting of Generals* (Toronto: Methuen, 1986), p. 354.

32. Hutchinson, "Corps Commander," p. 183.

33. CP, Vol. 1, Memorandum in the Case of Lt. Col. G. H. Christiansen. Petch had already been given command of the 4th Princess Louise Dragoon Guards on 18 December 1944 [Lt.-Col. H. M. Jackson, *The Princess Louise Dragoon Guards* (Published by the Regiment, 1951), p. 244].

34. CP, Vol. 3, Simonds to Dempsey, 27 July 1944. "Simonds handled both Keller and Cunningham very sensibly," Crerar wrote approvingly, "and both are carrying on in their respective appointments for the time being and until Simonds has reached more or less independent conclusions as to their abilities." He also noted that "in light of other information," he was "not sure at all of Keller being able to last the course." Keller had been considered a replacement for Burns as commander of 1 Corps (CP, Vol. 3, Crerar to Stuart, 15 July 1944; and Notes on Meeting with CIGS at Tac HQ C-in-C 21 Army Gp 1630-1730 hrs, 19 July 1944). There were also reports of looting and vandalism on the 3rd Division front at Colomby-sur-Thaon, Putot-en-Bessin, Les Buissons, and Villons les Buissons. Similar incidents were reported on the U.S. front (CP, Vol. 4, Maj. J. P. Manion, SO 2 Infm to SCAO, 26 June 1944; CP, Vol. 4, Crerar to Keller, 29 June 1944; and CP, Vol. 4, Brig. W. D. Wedd, SCAO First Cdn Army to DA&QMG, 11 July 1944).

35. RG 24, Vol. 13,711, WD GS 2 Cdn Corps SEI, 27 July 1944. "It is now D plus 55, and our first day out of the line," wrote the 3rd Division diarist (RG 24, Vol. 13,766, WD GS 3 CID SEI, 31 July 1944).

36. CP, Vol. 2, Tac. H. Q. 21 Army Group M515, 27 July 1944; RG 24, Vol. 13,751, WD GS 2 CID SEI, 1 August 1944; and Copp and Vogel, *Falaise*, p. 82. Operation "Bluecoat," which involved six divisions and two armored brigades, spelled the end of Operations "Rawlinson" and "Byng." It was at this time that Montgomery announced that the Belgian and Dutch contingents of about brigade size would be going to the First Canadian Army (actually 1 British Corps).

37. Copp and Vogel, *Falaise*, p. 84; Roy, *Canadians in Normandy*, 138, 141–142; Farran, *Calgary Highlanders*, pp. 154–156; and Stacey, *Victory Campaign*, p. 205. The CO of the Calgary Highlanders ordered artillery fire stopped to show the effects of the German counterbarrage. A message log entry for 0325 hours, 1 August, also recorded "Essex mortars shelling us. Stop fire" (RG 24, Vol. 14, 109, WD HQ 5 CIB Message Log 010325).

38. Stacey, *Victory Campaign*, pp. 206–207; MAP, BLM 20, 2 Cdn Corps Study Period 13–18 March, dated 16 February 1944; Hutchinson, "Corps Commander," p. 188; Roy, *Canadians in Normandy*, 144–146; and Maj. R. A. Paterson, *A Short History of the 10th Canadian Infantry Brigade* (Hilversum, Holland: De Jong, 1945), pp. 18–21. Tilly was a hamlet of about eight stone farm houses, each possessing an orchard surrounded by high stone walls. The Germans in fortifying Tilly strengthened the basements and "rubbled" the houses to withstand artillery. In 1942 Montgomery assessed Jefferson as "too slow, not a leader" (Kitching, *Mud and Green Fields*, pp. 203–204, 208). A company of the Lake Superior Regiment supported by two troops of tanks from the Canadian Grenadier Guards also assaulted La Hogue on 5 August. The company commander was given an hour and a half to prepare his attack, which, because of brigade staff underestimation of enemy strength and

failure to provide a secure start line, failed miserably [G. F. G. Stanley, *In the Face of Danger: The History of the Lake Superior Regiment* (Port Arthur: Lake Superior Scottish Regiment, 1960), pp. 147–150; and RG 24, Vol. 15,098, WD Lake Superiors, 5 August 1944].

Chapter 11

The Amiens Alchemy

While I would not wish to take any credit away from General Simonds, the basic plan for Operation "Totalize" was laid down by me, the fundamental tactics I required was that the forward movement should commence with the initiation of the fire support and not be delayed until long after the bombardment had started.

General H. D. G Crerar, 1952[1]

One suspects that if Operation "Spring" taught Simonds anything, it was that he could not trust the tactical acumen of either of his infantry division commanders too far. While they may have been better than the Sansoms and Prices that the Canadian military system first threw up, they had hardly been prepared by the McNaughton approach to training for higher operational command. Being relatively junior at the beginning of the war, they had fortunately been less exposed to the enervating influence of nonprofessional concerns, but it is doubtful that they in their military thought had kept pace with Simonds. Predictably, he was to retain a much tighter rein over the planning and execution of forthcoming operations ordered by Crerar. On 30 July, the day before 2 Corps reverted to being under the command of the First Canadian Army, the latter had advised Simonds to commence planning a thrust down the Caen-Falaise road "in about ten days time" to coincide with the success of the First U.S. and Second British Army operations. Deeply embarrassed and exasperated by the appalling performance of his subordinate formations in "Atlantic" and "Spring," he looked upon this as an opportunity to redeem a tarnished reputation.[2]

On 1 August, Simonds produced a remarkable written appreciation and outline plan for mounting an operation, code-named "Totalize," to break

Map 11.1
Operation "Totalize"

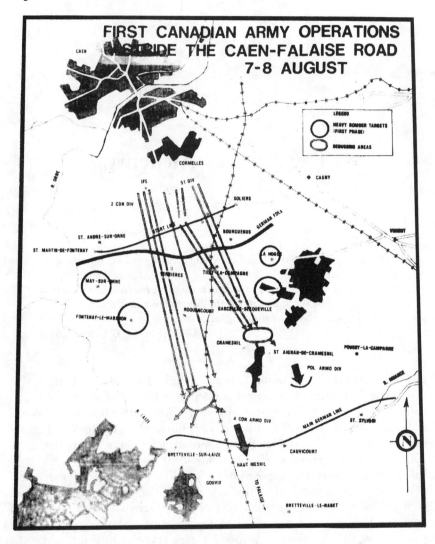

through the German defense. Noting that the enemy position was manned by the 1st SS right and the 9th SS left, each disposed with one infantry regiment back and one forward with all tanks and SP guns in support, he expected very heavy fighting. The presence of the 12th SS in close reserve also meant that a counterattack was likely on the eastern flank. Simonds thus envisioned one "break in" operation to penetrate the foremost prepared defensive zone along May-sur-Orne–Tilly-la-Campagne–La Hogue and a second to pierce the rearward partially prepared position along Hautmesnil–St. Sylvain. Given the open nature of the ground, which ideally suited the characteristics of German weaponry, he deduced that the defense would "be most handicapped in bad visibility—smoke, fog or darkness, when the advantage of long range[wa]s minimized."[3]

While Simonds recognized the impossibility of achieving tactical surprise "in respect to objectives or direction of attack," he believed it could still be attained "in respect to time and method." The essential problem was "how to get the armour through the enemy gun screen to sufficient depth to disrupt the German anti-tank gun and mortar defence, in country highly suited to tactics of the latter combination." Like Montgomery, Simonds seized upon the employment of heavy bombers as part of the solution. Yet, he reasoned, if all available air support were used for the first "break in," there would be little left for the second, which would also suffer from diminished gun support unless a "pause" were incorporated to move artillery and ammunition forward. On the other hand, if the initial "break in" could be accomplished by "infiltrating through the screen in bad visibility" with limited air support, say heavy night bombers, then heavy and medium day bombers would be available to deal with the next zone at the very moment artillery support was expected to slacken. Through this "novelty of method," which involved transporting infantry in armored carriers closely behind leading tanks, Simonds hoped to avoid a slackening pause and "maintain a high tempo to . . . operations."[4]

What Simonds proposed was a properly coordinated corps attack by three infantry and two armored divisions, two armored brigades, two complete AGRA plus the support of two additional ones, a searchlight battery for movement lighting in event of low cloud cover, four squadrons of special armor with flamethrowing *Crocodiles*, and the "whole of the available air effort." As originally conceived, the operation comprised three phases, the first of which involved a night attack on the Fontenay-le-Marmion–La Hogue position with two infantry divisions, each with an armored brigade under command. The task of the right division operating west of the Caen-Falaise road was to secure the line Caillouet-Gaumesnil and "mop up" its sector; east of the road, the left division was to capture the areas of Lourguichon, St. Aignan de Cramesnil, Cramesnil, Garcelles-Secqueville, and Secqueville-la-Campagne. There was to be no preliminary bombardment during the first phase, though commencing at H-hour RAF *Lancaster* bombers were to "obliterate" the areas of May-sur-Orne, Fontenay-le-Marmion, and La Hogue–Secqueville. At the same time, tanks and carrier-borne infantry of leading brigades were to assault under cover of a quick medium artillery barrage, advancing 100 yards in each minute, straight for their first objectives.[5]

In the second phase, one armored division and a fresh infantry division were to break into the Hautmesnil–St. Sylvain position. The task of the armored division was to capture Hautmesnil itself and the high ground northwest of Bretteville-le-Rabet; thereafter it was to be prepared to exploit forward west of the Caen-Falaise road. The infantry division following up was to protect the right flank by forming a firm base in the area of Bretteville-sur-Laize. It was subsequently to form a firm base for the third phase by relieving the armored division at Hautmesnil and Bretteville-le-Rabet. During the third phase it was to be prepared to exploit to St. Sylvain. The second phase, expected to commence at noon the following day, was to be heavily supported by fighter, medium, and United States Army Air Forces (USAAF) *Fortress* heavy day bombers. In the third phase, the already committed armored division was to exploit beyond Fontaine-le-Pin. The second armored division was to advance through Quesnay to a position just short of Falaise. Each armored division was to have one medium artillery regiment under command and the support of medium and fighter bombers, on call, to deal with possible threats from the 12th SS Panzer division. Two AGRA were also to be made available after a pause.[6]

Of key concern to the "Totalize" plan was how to move the infantry forward with the tanks at tank speed during the first phase. If the major threat to the tank was the long-range, hard-hitting 75-mm or 88-mm gun, the main danger to infantry came from concentrated artillery, mortar, small arms, and machine-gun fire. Fortunately, about this time the BRA of First Canadian Army, Brig. H.O.N. Brownfield, had decided to reconvert the 3rd Division artillery, which since D-Day had been equipped with U.S. 105-mm *Priest* SP guns, to towed 25-pounders. In a flash of inspiration, Simonds hit upon the idea that if they were stripped of their guns and reconfigured, they would be sufficiently roomy to afford protection to a 10-man infantry section against bullets and fragments. He accordingly requested and received permission to modify the *Priest* for this purpose. He also asked that troops be given a period of training on them so they would not feel "like a lot of sardines in a tin." In the event, many units only received two days training and the last of 70-odd *Kangaroos*, as the "unfrocked *Priests*" or "Holy Rollers" were subsequently named, arrived at troop locations but 24 hours before the attack.[7] Simonds later laid formal claim to having invented the armored personnel carrier (APC), though no patent was ever for good reason officially granted.[8]

As for the general concept of "Totalize," it can hardly be imagined that Simonds during his observation of the Wadi Akarit battle in April 1943 would not have heard tell of the "Blitz" of the El Hamma, which, having just happened on 26 March, would have been on everyone's lips. Here for the first time the Desert Air Force employed a new technique for ground-air coordination termed "taxi-cab rank" to support an Eighth Army attack. Strikes by 16 "*Kittybomber*" squadrons with five *Spitfire* squadrons flying "top cover" preceded and accompanied the forward movement of ground forces. An airborne aircraft and RAF officers with high-frequency wireless sets on the ground controlled the operation. A thin creeping barrage, which served as a moving bomb line, also preceded the 2nd New Zealand Division as it successfully attacked out of a setting sun. Most significantly, the tanks of the leading 8th Armoured Brigade advanced through the dust and smoke and into the moonlight without losing direction.[9]

As reported in *Current Reports From Overseas* in July 1943, the heavy sand storm that blew up to blind enemy antitank gunners during this action additionally served to remind that sufficient "consideration ha[d] not always been given by armoured formations . . . to the advantages of smoke." "Consider the factors," the article urged, "Defences are planned most carefully to cover avenues of approach"; with antitank guns sited to cover the fronts of neighboring positions at various ranges, depending upon penetration power, the "whole lay-out depends on visibility":

> Put down a fog upon it and it is helpless. Introduce into that fog, not a long straggling line of tanks, striving to see each other and painfully keeping direction, but a mass, a 'phalanx,' of tanks on a narrow front. What hope have the defenders got? Those in the path of the charge are overwhelmed from right, left, and centre. Those on the flanks hear the noise, but cannot see to interfere. The tanks, followed by (or carrying) their infantry, go through to their objective, consolidate it during darkness, and wait for pick up in the morning.[10]

El Hamma, Montgomery's suggested model for "Epsom," may also have been the precursor of "Totalize."

On 4 August Montgomery formally directed the First Canadian Army to "launch a heavy attack from the Caen sector in the direction of Falaise" no later than 8 August and, if at all possible, the day before. The main object of this operation was to "cut off the enemy forces . . . facing Second Army." [11] The magnitude of the moment and historic nature of the date doubtless increased Crerar's personal enthusiasm for Operation "Totalizer [*sic*],"[12] now clearly envisioned as a chance to repeat an attack like that delivered in 1918 at Amiens, which, spearheaded by the Canadian Corps, yielded such a decisive victory. Later, he would claim having "laid down . . . the basic plan" himself, "that the tactics, adopted for 'Totalize,' [we]re considerably based on" his tactical directive of 22 July 1944 discussed earlier in Chapter 8. The "two innovations brought in by Simonds in his detailed plan," Crerar concluded, were the "employment of Bomber Command on targets close to . . . own troops on each flank of the attacking front" and the use of APCs.[13]

On 5 August in an address to senior officers he submitted that "the potentially decisive period" of the war had been reached. He further expressed the "firm" conviction, if somewhat bumptiously, that "a highly successful, large scale operation, now carried out by one of the Armies of the Allied Expeditionary Force, *favourably placed for that purpose* [author's emphasis], will result in the crushing conviction to Germans, even of the S.S. variety, that general defeat of the German Armies on all fronts has become an inescapable fact." Expecting that a quick termination of the war would follow, Crerar obviously hoped that the results of "Totalize" would be decisive and historical. He purported to have "no doubt" about the First Canadian Army making 8 August 1944, the anniversary of the decisive Battle of Amiens, "an even blacker day for the German Armies than . . . [what was] recorded against that same date twenty-six years ago."[14]

If 8 August 1944 was to be made another historic date, however, Crerar felt that "certain basic things" had to "be firmly grasped by all ranks." Among these he accented the need to maintain the momentum, which in his understanding meant the early provision by commanders "of the direction and orders required to keep the movement, and fire support, alive and nourished." While underscoring the importance of initiative and condemning the general tendency among all ranks "to consider objectives on the ground as an end—rather than as a means to an end," (i.e., killing enemy), he nonetheless cautioned that on "reaching a 'pause' objective, prepare at top speed for the almost invariable quick, but determined, enemy infantry-cum-tank, small scale, counter-attack." Warning that "to surrender to German SS Troops is to invite death," he exhorted the infantry to "be seized with intention to drive on . . . by the use of their own weapons . . . in the absence of 'laid on' support." Clearly, in Crerar's view, the "idea . . . [was] far too prevalent that, without a colossal scale of artillery, or air support, continued advance of the infantry [wa]s impossible."[15]

Yet, as Montgomery was to report, the "desperately anxious" Crerar, worried about "fighting his first battle" at the head of the first Canadian field army, had himself "seemed to have gained the idea that all you want is a good initial fire plan, and then the Germans all run away!" He still had not realized, Montgomery continued, that "battles seldom go completely as planned."[16] Again, despite his occasional utterances to the contrary, it would appear that Crerar essentially harbored a trench warfare mentality. His performance as a corps commander in Italy at least convinced Major-General Vokes that his "whole outlook on tactics was influenced by his experience as a junior officer of artillery in the 1914–18 war." At one point Crerar even suggested bringing "tactical methods of attack . . . in line with those used in France and Flanders in World War I." When, according to Vokes, he expounded his views to general officers of the Eighth Army at a study period, he was "heard in stony silence by that battle-experienced galaxy."[17]

As might be expected, difficulties in coordinating air support for "Totalize" ensued from the start. The Commander-in-Chief of Bomber Command, Air Chief Marshal Sir Arthur Harris, was, due to genuine concern about troop safety, relatively lukewarm to the idea of close support heavy bombing by night. He agreed, however, that if it were "proved to the satisfaction of the 'Master Bombers' concerned that 'RED' or 'GREEN' coloured concentrations, fired by 25-p[ounde]rs could be clearly identified at night, then Bomber Command w[as] prepared to carry out the task." Otherwise it would commence twilight heavy bombing in accordance with the program at 2130 hours for 40 minutes, an alternative reluctantly accepted by Simonds at the time. Following a trial whereby one-minute bursts of red and green 25-pounder shells were put down on two selected points opposite the 1 British Corps front on the night of 6 August, the "master bombers" concluded that targets indicated by marker shells could be satisfactorily identified by night.[18]

The H-hour for the commencement of the first phase of "Totalize" thus continued to be 2300 hours 7 August, from which time both flanks of 2 Corps armored-infantry thrusts would be protected by heavy bombing. Air support for the second phase estimated to start at 1400 hours 8 August was more comprehensive and largely the responsibility of the USAAF Eighth Air Force. Significantly, in the course of discussion, the effect of "dust, smoke, and corruption" was recognized as a problem in the accurate bombing of successive targets. Forward troops and vehicles were accordingly warned to carry yellow smoke and yellow Celanese triangle strips for identification to friendly aircraft. Most important of all, however, all land force action was now locked into heavy bomber strike timings, which could not be altered without 24 hours warning. The only link with Bomber Command, moreover, was through First Canadian Army headquarters.[19]

New intelligence on changes in German dispositions prompted Simonds on the morning of 6 August to make a major modification to his original plan, for which orders had been issued the previous day. The 89th Infantry Division, believed to have left Norway on 12 June, had relieved the 1st SS Panzer in the line on the night of 5 August. As the 9th SS Panzer had already left for the Caumont area on 1 August to counter the threat from the Second British Army, the 89th in fact took over the entire forward defensive frontage between the Orne and La Hogue previously held by both SS panzer divisions. With an established structure of two regiments of three battalions each, the division fielded roughly 3,000 front line troops, many of whom were of non-German extraction. It nonetheless fielded 78 mortars and was backed up by two heavy artillery battalions, numerous *Nebelwerfer* multi-barrelled mortars, two SP antitank units, and about sixty 88-mm guns. The 89th had never been in action before and was not thought to be capable of offering great resistance in the face of heavy bombardment or deep penetration by an enemy. The 272nd Infantry Division had in the meantime sidestepped east and south of Cagny where on the night of 4 August it relieved the still formidable 12th SS Panzer, which took up a reserve position on the River Laison.[20]

The 12th SS was estimated to have about 2,500 front line troops (actually

1,500), 45 Mark IV panzers, and 35 *Panthers* (actually 37 and 9). The 101st
Heavy Tank Battalion, 1st SS Panzer Corps, with roughly 25 *Tigers* was
also assumed to be in the area, which it indeed was, attached to the 12th
SS. Simonds was also concerned that the 1st SS had retired to the area of
Bretteville-sur-Laize–St. Sylvain to strengthen the second position [it was
instead headed to participate with the 2nd and 116th Panzer and 2nd SS
(*Das Reich*) Panzer divisions in the abortive Mortain offensive against
Avranches ordered by Hitler on the night of 2 August]. Reckoning that the
"second 'break-through' might meet stronger resistance than originally anticipated," Simonds consequently decided to combine the second and third
phases by taking "advantage of the . . . air effort and maintain the momentum by launching 4 Cdn Armd and 1 Polish Armd Divs . . . simultaneously
and parallel . . . directly through to their final objectives in Phase II." As
counterattacks by the 89th and 272nd Divisions would "at best be half-
hearted efforts," the two infantry divisions attacking in the first phase were
expected to "be handled more boldly than . . . originally planned."[21]

The effect of this decision was so important that it deserves closer examination. With no change in the first phase, the 2nd Canadian Infantry
Division remained committed on the right of the Caen-Falaise road, with
the 2nd Canadian Armoured Brigade under command, to capture Caillouet
and Gaumesnil. It was also charged with mopping up St. André, May-sur-
Orne, Fontenay-le-Marmion, and Rocquancourt. On the left, the 51st
(Highland) Division with the 33rd British Armoured Brigade under command was charged with capturing Lourguichon Wood, St. Aignan de
Cramesnil, Cramesnil, Garcelles-Secqueville, and Sequeville-la-Campagne;
in phase two it was to exploit two kilometers to the south. The second
phase portion calling for the 3rd Division to follow the 4th Armoured on
its advance to capture Hautmesnil and the high ground northwest of Bretteville-le-Rabet was, however, cancelled. The task of the former in this case
would have been to secure both flanks by forming firm bases in Bretteville-
sur-Laize and the woods north of Cavicourt east of the main road, from
where it was to be prepared to exploit to St. Sylvain. Upon being relieved
in phase three by the 2nd Division in Bretteville-sur-Laize and the 51st
Division in St. Sylvain, the 3rd Division would have repositioned its brigades in the areas of Hautmesnil, Bretteville-le-Rabet, and Point 140 east
of Quesnay Wood. The 1st Polish and 4th Armoured Divisions would have
then advanced, left and right of the Caen-Falaise road, southward to their
most distant objectives, Points 159 and 206, respectively.

As amended, however, the plan called for the 2nd and 51st Divisions to
push on more boldly and themselves secure the right and left flanks in the
second phase. The 1 Polish Armoured and 4th Canadian Armoured were
during the same phase to dash to their final objectives. The 3rd Division
following the move forward of 1 Polish Armoured was to remain in reserve
north of Caen, prepared to move on Simonds's order to take over the areas

of Hautmesnil, Bretteville-le-Rabet, and Point 140.[22] In other words, two armored divisions, of but one armored and one infantry brigade each, were now expected to breach by daylight a defensive position in depth that was ostensibly more heavily defended than the foremost zone. Again, heavy bombing of the "Goodwood" variety was considered to be the technological key to success. Only this time, no matter how quickly the more powerful infantry divisions, each of one armored and three infantry brigades, broke through the first position, the armored divisions would have to await the air strike. Unless, that is, it could be cancelled in timely fashion.

The GOCs of the 4th Canadian and 1st Polish Armoured Divisions expressed serious reservations about being forced to attack on what they considered excessively narrow fronts. In a meeting with Simonds on the morning of 7 August, both Kitching and Major-General Stefan Maczek pointed out that this would detrimentally limit their ability to maneuver. The divisional frontage allotted Kitching was only 1,000 yards and at one point, between Gaumesnil and a quarry to the west, it narrowed to but 800 yards; that allocated to the 1st Polish Armoured Division was roughly the same, though heavily wooded areas lay to its front and flanks.[23] It is true, of course, that neither Kitching nor Maczek were experienced armored commanders, which may well be the reason Simonds refused to accept their remonstrations. At the same time, *Army Training Instruction No. 2* did state that the maximum frontage for a squadron of tanks attacking in two waves would "seldom exceed 300 yards." A deliberate attack by a "division... with two infantry... and two tank battalions up," according to this doctrinal yardstick, would therefore "normally operate on a frontage not exceeding 1,200 yards."[24]

Yet, as we have seen, Simonds could hardly have claimed to have been an experienced armored division commander either. His preference for fighting on narrow frontages, so clearly set forth in his instruction on operational policy, appears on the surface to have furthermore typified the proclivity of an artillerist. Like Crerar, Simonds was a member of the powerful gunner faction within the Canadian Army. In later life he would argue that "the artillery arm provide [d] the best schooling for high command of any of the arms." Being "technical enough to demand serious intellectual effort in the spheres of mathematics, mechanics and electronics," it also "as a principal supporting arm... require[d] a thorough knowledge of the tactics of infantry, armour and other troops... dependent on a sound 'fire plan.' " Whereas other arms veered toward a "more marked specialization," declared Simonds, the artillery developed a "balance between technical and tactical aspects of the military profession."[25] Despite his evident affection for his corps, however, it would be wrong to conclude that Simonds did not realize all arms working in concert produced an effect far greater than the sum of their parts.

In Italy Simonds had made clear his tactical approach during a 5th Canadian Armoured Division TEWT in which the armored brigade was depicted as having reached its objective and was now contemplating further action in the face of a disorganized enemy. When the commander of the 5th Armoured Brigade, Brigadier "Brad" Bradbrook, queried the need to wait "for another 24 guns" as he had "over 150 of them on . . . tanks," Simonds insisted that the correct course was to pause, reorganize, and wait for the artillery to catch up. The brigadier, possibly unaware of the African experience, was subsequently fired.[26] Significantly, a 1941 CJWSC exercise alluded to in Chapter 5 had placed similar emphasis upon the importance of artillery. Its scenario postulated a brigade attack supported by three regiments of artillery and the question was whether to delay it for an hour, despite the urgent need to take an objective, in order to obtain the support of a fourth regiment. The "suggested solution," which to some degree illustrated the depth of the tactical dilemma facing those who would command all arms, was to "wait for it, as the slight additional delay so caused will be more than made up for by the doubling [sic] of . . . gun support."[27]

Obviously, it is not possible to be categorical about the relative merits of fire power as opposed to maneuver, when, in theory, the former should complement the latter. So often in practical application, however, the artillery fire plan for sheer coordination problems related to gun and ammunition allotment, not to mention logistical considerations, may have dictated the limits of maneuver.[28] At the same time, infantry and armored ignorance of artillery planning methods and procedures often ensured the unpardonable loss of firepower advantage within whatever maneuver room existed. The key was knowing how to maneuver within the constraints of artillery requirements, trading one off against the other as the situation permitted. Sustained heavy emphasis upon artillery and air support may nonetheless have inculcated among some armored and infantry elements the mental attitude that they could do little on their own. In other words, the relationship fanned its own imbalance, bombing and especially indirect fire becoming a "crutch" that fostered an increasing maneuver arm dependence. The armored brigadier in Italy, though he may have been tactically naive, did display the requisite willingness, some might say recklessness, to fight his way forward using his own means.

As it was, doctrine as well as inferior weaponry determined the bounds of maneuver arm performance. Perhaps this naturally resulted from the artillery becoming, from the moment it is dealt the first shattering blows to enemy armor, the most battle-worthy and reliable corps in the Canadian and British armies. The essential dichotomy in tactical approach materialized in the argument over narrow frontages: simply put, attacking on a narrow front permitted the concentration of a greater weight of artillery offensive fire; on the other hand, it also allowed a mobile enemy to concentrate troops and defensive fire to defeat the thrust. Obviously, employing barrages or timed concentrations to put infantry on an objective, firing more concentrations on enemy locations that could possibly interfere, and using artillery on call thereafter, was best done on a narrow front. Against a skilled and almost invisible German defense in depth, however, the problem was not how to get the infantry there, but how to keep them there under intense mortaring and flanking counterattacks. One solution was to isolate the objective area by boxing it in with barrages, the other, to attack on a broad front.[29] Yet, as Simonds so correctly argued, to overcome a defense in depth one had to attack in depth, the conundrum of the broad front approach. Again, the secret was balance.

On "Totalize" in the oppressive heat and dust of 7 August, Simonds ensured that his maneuver elements formed up in concentrated formation. An armored and infantry brigade in both the 2nd and 51st Divisions constituted the main assaulting force. In each case they were organized in columns and given two "lines of advance" or axes. Within the 2nd Division, four columns were deployed with four vehicles abreast on a 16-yard frontage, which was roughly the width that could be cleared by four flail tanks. Every 10 feet along the length of a column there was another group of four vehicles. Each column was headed by two tank troops, followed by two mine-clearing flail troops and one lane-marking AVRE troop; marshaled behind these came an infantry battalion or, in one instance, a reconnaissance regiment mounted in Kangaroos or M3 White half-tracks. Further back in each column travelled the remainder of a tank squadron, two antitank troops, a machine-gun platoon, and an engineer section. The rear of all four columns was covered by a "fortress force" of one armored regiment less a squadron. Columnar deployment within the 51st Division, though similar, was limited to a left and right split, each based on an armored regiment and infantry battalion, roughly 200 vehicles strong, and including specially designated navigating tanks.

After dark all columns rolled closer to the start line, and punctually at 2300 hours 1,020 Lancaster and Halifax bombers commenced to drop a total of 3,462 tons of bombs on flank targets identified by artillery red and green marker shells. At 2330 hours both divisions crossed the start line in their respective formations, picking up a rolling barrage, fired by nine field and nine medium regiments, advancing 100 yards a minute in 200-yard lifts to a depth of 6,000 yards. In all, 720 guns with up to 650 rounds each were available to support the attack. To assist the phalanx in keeping direction, a Bofors tracer barrage, coordinated by the CCRA, was fired over divisional thrust lines. Artificial moonlight and wireless directional beams, two per divisional front, were also employed.[30]

On the 2nd Division front, the 2nd Canadian Armoured Brigade led off with the APC-borne 4th Brigade and 8th Reconnaissance Regiment (14th Canadian Hussars) under command. In addition to flails and AVRE, it was further bolstered by a company of medium machine guns, a platoon of heavy 4.2-inch mortars, a platoon of engineers, and two antitank batteries, one SP and the other 17-pounder Ram towed. The 5th Brigade with the FGH less one squadron, an SP antitank battery, a company of medium machine guns, and a platoon of heavy mortars followed behind prepared to restore momentum, if lost, by assaulting 2nd Armoured Brigade objectives. It was also to move on orders of the divisional commander to capture Bretteville-sur-Laize. The 6th Brigade with a squadron of Crocodiles, two antitank batteries, three heavy mortar platoons, and a company of medium machine guns was to commence "mopping up" operations at H-hour.[31] In spite of the slow rate of advance, a dense cloud of dust arose. Thickened by a ground mist and smoke, which the enemy quickly brought down, it proved impenetrable to searchlights.

After 15 minutes, because drivers could not see vehicles immediately ahead, taillights were turned on. In the ensuing confusion, heightened by German mortar and antitank fire, some tanks actually turned around to collide with oncoming APC's; others went missing for up to 36 hours. Not surprisingly, it became progressively difficult to keep direction; the Royal Regiment, for example, passed east rather than west of Rocquancourt, the RHLI ran straight through it, and the Essex went wildly astray. Nonetheless, by 0700 hours many columns of the 2nd and 51st Divisions were fighting in the vicinities of their first objectives and beginning to clear them. While more bitterly contested and casualty producing mopping-up operations were not completed until around 1700 hours, the first phase of "Totalize" was deemed to have been successfully completed by 0800 hours 8 August. The road to Falaise also lay open.[32]

From this juncture onward, however, "Totalize" assumed the character of a lesser "Goodwood," though without benefit of surprise, and the intrinsic risk associated with delay. At the same time that Kitching and Maczek had requested Simonds to broaden their attack frontages, they had mentioned the potential danger of "the long pause of about eight hours between Phase I and Phase II." Simonds, under the erroneous perception that the second zone was defended by the 1st SS, was nonetheless insistent that the armored divisions await the support of heavy bombers.[33] Given the renowned capacity of the Germans to react and the bitter experiences of "Atlantic" and "Spring," however, it is easy to appreciate Simonds's caution. That he should have been overruled is quite clear, but equally clearly it would have taken an army commander with the *Fingerspitzengefuehl* (fingertip feel) and stature of a Dempsey or Patton to do it. Crerar simply did not know as much as Simonds, which in effect left the 2 Corps commander without any of the usual counsel, help, and coercion that he might have received from an army headquarters. He could not have been more alone.

Unfortunately, the tactically clever *Oberfuehrer* Meyer reacted with more than customary German vigor. On the morning of 8 August he drove forward to assess the situation himself, personally rallying in the area of Cintheaux fleeing 89th Division soldiers. Standing in the middle of the road

Map 11.2
The Course of Operation "Totalize"

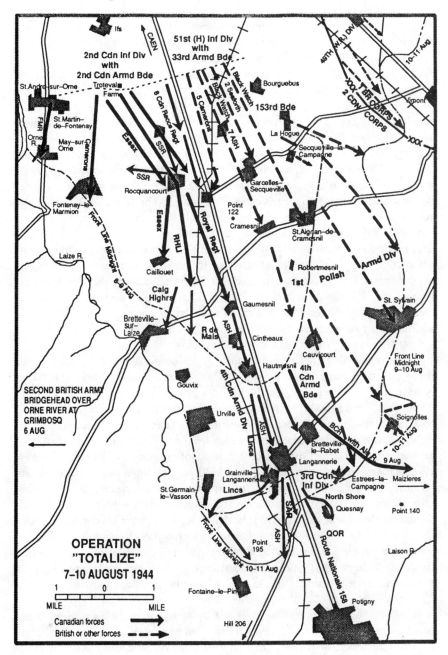

and calmly lighting a cigar, he had asked them in a loud voice if they were going to leave him alone to face the Allied attack. In the meantime, *Kampfgruppe Waldmuller* of two panzergrenadier battalions had been ordered to the area of Bretteville-le-Rabet and warned for further action. *Kampfgruppe Krause*, whose panzer and panzergrenadier battalions had been detached the very night "Totalize" commenced to assist in wiping out the Second British Army bridgehead north of Thury-Harcourt, was also directed to disengage and move 10 kilometers to occupy the heights west of Potigny, from which position it could defend the bottleneck between the "natural tank obstacles" of the Laison and Laize rivers. At 1130 hours *Kampfgruppe Waldmuller* reinforced by the 1st Panzer Battalion and roughly ten Tigers under Wittmann, a total of about 20 tanks, counterattacked the heights south of St. Aignan.[34]

The forward movement of *Kampfgruppe Waldmuller* and reports of counterattacks supported by panzers apparently convinced Simonds of the need to exercise caution and await the second air strike. To be sure, the intelligence picture was by no means clear at this point. The action of *Kampfgruppe Krause* in counterattacking the Orne bridgehead north of Thury-Harcourt seems to have especially confused the situation. The 2 Corps Intelligence Summary for the 24-hour period ending 2000 hours 8 August stated that: "With the complete absence of any clue to the identification of the armour on our front, an assessment of the enemy's immediate capabilities is almost impossible." While expecting the German "anti-tank line to be a source of some delay," it nonetheless ventured that "after moving 1 and 12 SS Divisions away to meet an immediate threat in the West" the enemy did not appear to have a "substantial reserve available."[35]

Notwithstanding the immense advantages conferred by "Ultra," better reconnaissance and patrolling, which was the main source of tactical information about the enemy, could have provided a more accurate picture. True, the German habit of moving only by night, aggressively closing up to Canadian-defended localities during darkness and pulling back in depth at dawn, often made this exceedingly difficult. It is also true, of course, that the 2nd Division as a "point of training" subsequently concluded patrol reports from 16 through 30 July to have been "most unsatisfactory." For lack of precise information and prisoners, a reasonably correct impression of enemy forward dispositions could not be gained. Significantly, it was only on 30 July that "steps . . . [were] taken to improve the standard of . . . patrols"; on 4 August a two-day divisional combat intelligence course was instituted for brigade intelligence officers.[36] It is difficult to believe that such shortcomings could not have been largely overcome during training in Britain, where the problem had already been observed.[37]

While Simonds was not well-served by army or corps intelligence, the movement forward of the 1st Polish Division produced additional problems of a purely practical nature. Into an area already brimming with matériel and dumping activity were now crowded an extra 650 armored and probably double the number lorried vehicles. The sheer volume of guns, equipment, and vehicles pouring into such an unusually restricted space created a traffic congestion that imposed a severe drag upon mobility. The grinding pace of mopping-up operations by preventing the forward and lateral dispersion of hundreds of infantry division vehicles ensured a further telescoping effect. By 0710 hours, with Fontenay-le-Marmion reported clear, Simonds ordered both armored divisions to "feed forward."[38] Here again difficulties were encountered as pockets of continuing German resistance threatened the security of predesignated forward gun deployment areas, many of which were subjected to machine-gun and mortar fire. Failure to capture Tilly before 0800 and Rocquancourt before 1215 hours seems also to have compromised the efficient forward deployment of armored division maneuver elements to their start positions.

In stark contrast, the attack by *Kampfgruppe Waldmuller* originally planned for 1230 hours was launched an hour earlier after a heavy bomber "flying command post" appeared as signaling the start of a major Allied air operation. Although the German counterattack proved unsuccessful and saw Wittmann die a warrior's death, it served to "spoil" the continued advance of the Polish Division for most of the day. Equally important, such "hugging" action left Meyer's tanks and soldiers well inside the "bomb line" behind which heavy bombers were not to strike for fear of destroying Canadian troop concentrations. Ironically, while forward German elements were spared, the Canadians and Poles were not so lucky. Indeed, two USAAF bomber groups accidentally unloaded upon them within these same safety limits.[39]

The start line for the second phase was the lateral road between Bretteville-sur-Laize and St. Aignan. The bomb line running north of Robertmesnil and Gaumesnil and south of the quarry east of Bretteville was forward of it. According to the air plan, Bretteville-sur-Laize on the right and St. Sylvain of the left were to be bombed preliminary to the advance of the 4th and 1st Divisions at 1400 hours 8 August. Once the dust settled, other noncratering strikes were to be carried out astride the Falaise road from Gouvix through Hautmesnil to Cauvicourt. Fighter bombers were to engage targets in the areas of Bretteville-le-Rabet, Quesnay Wood, and Estrées-la-Campagne. As it happened, weather forecasts on 7 August indicating visual bombing by *Fortresses* would have to take place earlier required the air attack to be advanced to 1226 hours, ending at 1355, which became the final H-hour for ground force movement.

Of the 492 USAAF Eighth Air Force bombers that attacked, unfortunately, one 12-plane group mistakenly engaged troops near Caen, while another erroneously dropped short in emulation of its badly hit leader. To their great shock, elements of the 1st Polish Division were struck in Cormelles. Within the 3rd Division the North Shore Regiment incurred about

100 casualties when attacked in Vaucelles. The main headquarters of the 2nd Canadian Armoured Brigade and the 3rd Division were also hit, as were 2 Canadian AGRA and 9 AGRA. Around 1330 hours 2 Corps requested the First Canadian Army to stop all bombing. In all, 65 soldiers were killed and another 250 wounded, one of whom was Keller, who had to be evacuated.[40] Though the attack inflicted far greater damage upon the enemy, it was not as effective as expected. At the same time, its incorporation within the second phase, more than any other factor, promoted a degree of inflexibility that by allowing the Germans to recover foreordained defeat.

As previously indicated, the 1st Polish Armoured Division was counter attacked in the area of its start line by *Kampfgruppe Waldmuller* just before H-hour. The advance of this now twice-stricken formation, whose traffic control capability had once been described as "quite efficient though there did not seem to be any definite system,"[41] was thus stopped almost before it started. On the right flank little better headway was made by the 4th Canadian Armoured Division. As intended, the 4th Armoured Brigade was to by-pass Cintheaux and Hautmesnil, capture Bretteville-le-Rabet, and push on to secure Points 195 and 206. The 10th Brigade was to take Cintheaux and Hautmesnil and relieve and mop up after the 4th Brigade in Bretteville-le-Rabet. A battle group comprising the 22nd Canadian Armoured Regiment (The Canadian Grenadier Guards), The Lake Superior Regiment (Motor), an antitank battery, and a squadron of engineers led the 4th Brigade advance.

Apparently in imitation of German practice it was called "Halpenny Force" after its commander, Lieutenant-Colonel Bill Halpenny. Apart from one distinguished troop action, however, "Halpenny Force" made no faster progress on crossing the start line than it had in closing up to it. Instead of having the Lake Superiors deal smartly with the small hamlet of Gaumesnil, which lay south of the bomb line and was originally to have been taken by the 2nd Division, it waited until the Royal Regiment secured it at 1530 hours. By 1800 hours "Halpenny Force" had only advanced beyond Cintheaux, but a kilometer away, at which time two companies of Argyll and Sutherland Highlanders from the 10th Brigade seized the village, while another two pushed south to take Hautmesnil. Shortly after this Halpenny decided in good doctrinal fashion to leaguer two of his tank squadrons in a "rear rally" near Gaumesnil to refuel and refit, an action that was completed around 2000 hours.[42]

Simonds maintained after the war that he had "stressed to the armoured divisional commanders that they . . . [were] not [to] get involved in probing out . . . position[s] before they called down fire or . . . fighter bombers." This presumably was why he had decentralized two AGRA, each of five medium regiments, one in support of each division.[43] To have made best use of such huge fire resources, however, called for more artillery staff planning expertise than units like the Grenadiers possessed. In short, the formation of battle groups like "Halpenny Force" saddled a single-arm commander with all-arms coordination problems that Canadian brigade staff organization was better equipped to handle. As Montgomery had warned, it was also an abrogation of tactical responsibility. The battle group idea appears nonetheless to have been embraced by the commander of the 4th Armoured Brigade, Brigadier Leslie Booth, who correctly reasoned that the tank had "little chance of success" against the German use of mixed groups of all arms. To combat such groups successfully, Booth asserted, one had to learn to "use 'battle groups' designed to beat the enemy" in numbers, equipment, offensive spirit, initiative, and close cooperation between arms.[44]

As so often with imitation though, certain important facets were overlooked: that the German *Kampfgruppe* system was rooted in a regimental structure that bore greater resemblance to the Canadian brigade than unit, and which included integral "infantry" guns of artillery caliber,[45] was one of these. According to Major-General "Pip" Roberts, moreover, when 11th Armoured Division finally did get its battle organization right it formed two mixed brigades, each of two armored regiments and two infantry battalions backed up by artillery as required. While all units were completely interchangeable with regimental-battalion groups organized and commanded according to assigned task, the most significant aspect of this structure was that the brigades themselves lost their separate armored and infantry character. Both brigadiers and their headquarters had to be equally competent at executing all-arms operations, which Montgomery held were best ensured at this level. Since artillery was still from a planning standpoint less closely integrated at the unit level than brigade, the suspicion thus lingers that "Halpenny Force" could have used some formation fire planning assistance. It is of course doubly significant that when Kitching, irritated over the delay of "Halpenny Force," was finally able to contact Booth "he was nearly two miles away from the battle and fast asleep in his tank."[46]

The opening of the second phase of "Totalize," while not a complete disaster, had clearly not gone well. A concerned Simonds now directed Kitching to press on through the night to secure Bretteville-le-Rabet and Point 195, the highest point before Falaise. Kitching, in turn, ordered the 4th Armoured Brigade to capture both objectives; the 10th Infantry Brigade was to follow up the armour and, after the seizure of Bretteville, occupy the villages of Langannerie and Grainville astride the Falaise road. The task of taking Bretteville still fell to "Halpenny Force," but was to be executed by two Grenadier tank squadrons and two infantry companies of the Lake Superiors at first light 9 August. The mission of capturing Point 195 was given to "Worthington Force," after the CO of the 28th Canadian Armoured Regiment (The British Columbia Regiment), which was accompanied by three infantry companies of the Algonquin Regiment. In many respects, the subsequent performance of this force in contrast with that of Halpenny's illustrated the depth of the tactical schizophrenia that gripped the armored corps of the British and Canadian armies.

During the early hours of 9 August, both forces set out for their objectives, momentarily passing each other in the dark around Bretteville-le-Rebat, which "Worthington Force" sought to avoid by skirting to the east. Once beyond the village its axis led south west across the Falaise road, north west of Quesnay wood, straight on to Point 195. "Halpenny Force," in the meantime, prepared to attack Bretteville, which fell to the Lake Superiors and Grenadier tanks in a hard-fought action against 89th Division elements sometime after 0600 hours. It was reported clear at 1400 hours, by which time 10th Brigade troops were fighting to secure Langannerie and Grainville. Unbelievably, the two Grenadier tank squadrons returned to leaguer in the "rear rally" near Gaumesnil after the action. They were only sent forward that evening to assume a mobile counterattack role.[47]

The fog of war now truly descended upon the battlefield. Just before 0700 hours "Worthington Force" reported that it was on its objective, and by 0800 hours 2 Corps was informed that the 4th Armoured Brigade was in possession of Bretteville-le-Rabet and Point 195. Within half an hour, however, the force requested artillery support as it was under severe panzer counterattack. When "Worthington Force" was queried around 0900 hours as to whether the support had been effective, it failed to reply. At 1030 hours the yet uncommitted 21st Canadian Armoured Regiment (The Governor General's Foot Guards) was ordered to proceed as quickly as possible to assist "Worthington Force" on Point 195. Supported by the last company and three-inch mortars of the Algonquins, a troop of antitank guns, flails, and a platoon of medium machine guns, this battle group did not get underway until after 1500 hours. For some reason artillery support was not immediately available, and the force was soon stopped by fire from the area of Quesnay Wood. Shortly before last light, having lost 14 tanks, it leaguered in Langannerie.

In the meantime suspicions were being confirmed that "Worthington Force" was not, as it had mistakenly reported, on Point 195. In fact, it had continued south east instead of south west in the rush to gain its objective before daybreak. Tragically lost, it had ended up on open ground east of Estrées-la-Campagne in the area of Point 140 to the Polish front. It was six kilometers away from its assigned objective. Soignolles, two kilometers to the north, still lay in German hands. Unfortunately for "Worthington Force," *Kampfgruppe Waldmuller* had also been ordered to the Point 140 feature. On discovering the presence of the Canadians, the Germans circled them from the west and east, counterattacking with Tigers and Panthers from *Panzerkampfgruppe Wunsche* and *Kampfgruppe Krause*. Subjected to a combination of withering tank, artillery, and mortar fire, "Worthington Force" was annihilated.[48]

Map 11.3
Destruction of "Worthington Force"

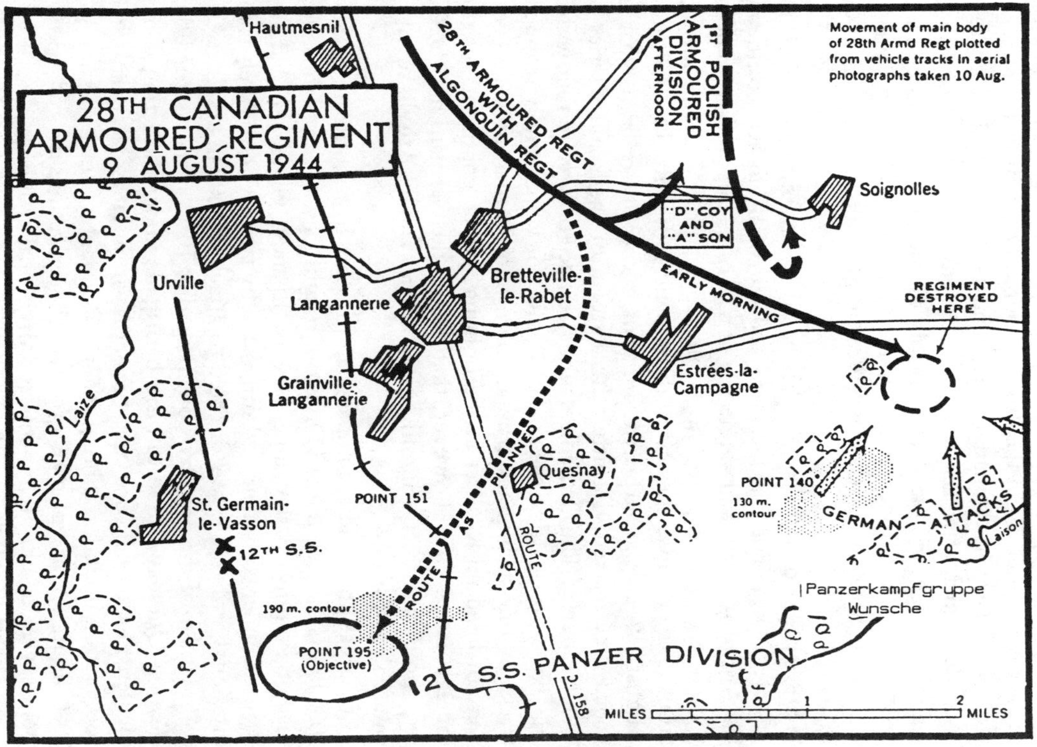

Movement of main body of 28th Armd Regt plotted from vehicle tracks in aerial photographs taken 10 Aug.

Soignolles

REGIMENT DESTROYED HERE

GERMAN ATTACKS

1 PanzerkampfGruppe Wunsche

POINT 140
130 m. contour

1ST POLISH ARMOURED DIVISION AFTERNOON

"D" COY AND "A" SON

EARLY MORNING

Estrées-la-Campagne

28TH ARMOURED REGT WITH ALGONQUIN REGT

Bretteville-le-Rabet

Quesnay

PLANNED ROUTE

158

S.S. PANZER DIVISION

HAUTMESNIL

28TH CANADIAN ARMOURED REGIMENT 9 AUGUST 1944

Langannerie

POINT 151

AS ROUTE

12

POINT 195 (Objective)

190 m. contour

Grainville-Langannerie

St. Germain-le-Vasson

12TH S.S.

Urville

Laize

MILES

MILES

2 MILES

The Canadians only gradually learned of the immensity of this disaster in the late afternoon of 9 August. The Poles whose tanks and artillery at one point fired upon "Worthington Force" until warned off by yellow recognition smoke were unable to effect its rescue. Stalled at Estrées-la-Campagne from about noon, they only managed to capture Soignolles the next day, which proved the final limit of their advance despite the exhortations of Simonds. On the 4th Armoured Division front, meanwhile, the connected hamlets of Langannerie and Grainville had fallen to the 10th Brigade, which after last light on 9 August had pushed on toward Point 195. That night in what was probably the single most impressive action of "Totalize," the Argyll and Sutherland Highlanders under Lieutenant-Colonel Dave Stewart seized the "Worthington Force" objective without a casualty.

Stewart, who later claimed that he always tried to protect his unit from "two enemies, The [*sic*] Germans and our own Higher Command,"[49] led his Argylls silently and single file in a daring, but well-reconnoitered approach march to capture the Point 195 feature. Without having unduly aroused the enemy, they were dug in and reorganized by first light on 10 August. When the surprised Germans eventually realized what had happened they reacted violently with a storm of shells and a series of strong counterattacks. The Grenadiers who had been ordered to follow the Argylls and exploit forward to the area of Point 206, were literally stopped in their tracks by one such attack around noon. Shortly thereafter the Foot Guards were ordered up to assist in the fighting, which continued for the rest of the day. It was clear, however, that neither the Germans nor the Canadians were going anywhere. Significantly, Stewart and his Argylls received hardly an accolade for this action.[50]

To break the resultant impasse and restore lost momentum, Simonds at 1000 hours ordered the 3rd Division to fight its way across the Laison River east of Potigny to the ridge west of Epaney. Given the 2nd Armoured Brigade under command and supported by two AGRA as well as the Polish divisional artillery, it was directed to attack at 1600 hours. The temporary commander of the 3rd Division, Brigadier Blackader, assigned the task of clearing Quesnay Wood to his 8th Brigade under the acting command of Lieutenant-Colonel Jock Spragge. For various reasons, delays in artillery coodination doubtless among them, this infantry attack did not go in until 2000 hours. A fire plan of grouped concentrations on call was provided from seven medium regiments and divisional artilleries.

The brigade attacked with two battalions up, the North Shores left and the Queen's Own Rifles right, in a south easterly direction that took the latter unit through Quesnay village. At first all went well and the lead Queen's Own company crossed a 150-yard cleared space on the edge of the wood with little opposition. When two following companies crossed it, however, the Germans opened fire with tanks, small arms, and mortars.

The North Shores, though greeted similarly, were driven out of the woods mainly by friendly shell fire. In reporting on this disastrous attack, the acting brigade commander complained that there had not been enough time for reconnaissance or to study artillery tasks. Information on the enemy was also considered "scanty" and not "sufficient upon which to make a sound detailed plan," which meant that artillery fire should have been more intense.[51] Indeed, the 8th Brigade attack appears to have been bloodily repulsed by the bulk of *Panzerkampfgruppe Wunsche* as well as *Kampfgruppe Krause*.[52] "Totalize" had fizzled out.

NOTES

1. Crerar Papers (CP) Vol. 21, Crerar to Stacey, 7 June 1952.

2. Record Group (RG), 24, Vol. 13,711, WD GS 2 Cdn Corps SEI, 30 July 1944; and RG 24, Vol. 10,797, 2 Cdn Corps GOC's Activities; and Hutchinson, "Corps Commander," pp. 186, 189.

3. RG 24, Vol. 10,808; and CP, Vol. 2, Operation "Totalize" Appreciation. Simonds briefed Crerar on it the day before.

4. Ibid. The range of the 25-pounder was 12,500 yards, the 5.5-inch medium, 18,200 (an 82-pound shell); located roughly one-third of this distance behind lines, their forward range was limited accordingly.

5. Ibid. Formations participating in "Totalize" were the 2nd and 3rd Canadian, the 51st (Highland), the 1st Polish and 4th Canadian Armoured, the 2nd and 33rd Armoured Brigades, and the 2nd Canadian and 9th AGRA.

6. Ibid.

7. Col. G.W.L. Nicholson, *The Gunners of Canada: A History of the Royal Regiment of Canadian Artillery*, Vol. II: *1919–1967* (Toronto: McClelland and Stewart, 1972), p. 310; and "Extracts taken from a lecture given by Lieutenant-General G.G. Simonds, CB, CBE, DSO . . . at Cabourg (Normandy) on 23 June 1947," DHist 693.013 (D2) Ops 2 Cdn Corps, *British Army of the Rhine Battlefield Tour Operation Totalize: 2 Canadian Corps Operations Astride the Road Caen-Falaise 7–8 August 1944*, Prepared under the direction of G (Training) HQ British Army of the Rhine (BAOR), pp. 31–33.

8. CP, Vol. 8, Simonds to Crerar 10 June, 1945; Col. C.P. Stacey, *Official History of the Canadian Army in the Second World War*, Vol. III: *The Victory Campaign: The Operations in North-West Europe, 1944–1945* (Ottawa: Queen's Printer, 1966), p. 210; and Reginald H. Roy, *1944: The Canadians in Normandy*, Canadian War Museum Historical Publication No.19 (Ottawa: Macmillan, 1984), pp. 150–152. It does appear, however, that the German three-quarter-tracked Sdkfz 251 issued before the war was, in fact, the first successful APC. See Richard E. Simpkin, *Mechanized Infantry* (Oxford: Brassey's, 1980), pp. 15, 22, 31. It is not the track that makes an APC, but the protection and cross-country mobility it offers to infantry; today, wheeled APCs are common. The U.S. White M3 half-track, also used by Canadian forces, had limited cross-country performance.

9. Brig. A.L. Pemberton, *The Second World War, 1939–1945, Army, The Development of Artillery Tactics and Equipment* (London: War Office, 1951), pp. 163–164; Nigel Hamilton, *Monty*, Vol. II: *Master of the Battlefield 1942–1944* (Sevenoaks,

U.K.: Hodder and Stoughton, 1984), pp. 194–201, 206–207, 587; and Shelford Bidwell and Dominick Graham, *Fire-Power: British Army Weapons and Theories of War 1904–1945* (London: Allen and Unwin, 1982), pp. 269–273.

10. *Current Reports From Overseas (CRFO)* 6 (10 July 1943), pp. 17–18.

11. CP, Vol. 2, 21 Army Group M516, 4 August 1944; and CP, Vol. 2, Crerar to Crocker and Simonds, 6 August 1944.

12. Personal copy CLFCSC Collection, Memorandum Operation Totalizer [*sic*] Re Planning Full Scale Air/Land Battle "Totalizer" Crerar to COS, 2 August 1944.

13. CP, Vol. 21, Crerar to Stacey, 7 June 1952 and 12 August 1957.

14. CP, Vol. 2, Remarks to Senior Officers, Cdn Army Operation "Totalize" by GOC-in-C First Cdn Army 051100, August 1944. The Battle of Amiens, which began at 0430 hours, 8 August 1918, was the greatest Allied triumph since the Marne. The Canadian and Australian Corps carried out the main attack under cover of a creeping barrage by 2,000 guns lifting 100 yards every three minutes. They captured three lines of objectives in a decisive action. Although the battle officially ended on 11 August, Ludendorff called 8 August the "black day of the German Army" in the history of the war [J.F.C. Fuller, *The Decisive Battles of the Western World 1792–1944*, ed. John Terraine (London: Paladin, 1981), pp. 373–384].

15. CP, Vol. 2, Remarks to Senior Officers by GOC-in-C First Cdn Army 051100 August.

16. Hamilton, *Monty*, II, p. 766.

17. Vokes Papers (VP), The Adriatic Front—Winter 1944.

18. CP, Vol. 2, Memo of Telephone Conversation Between C of S First Canadian Army, Speaking from HQ Bomber Command and Comd First Canadian Army, commencing at 1213 hours, 6 August 1944; and COS 1–1–0 Record of Tele Conversation, COS First Cdn Army and Col. GS First Cdn Army, from HQ AEAF to Main Army HQ at approx 052130B hrs, on the Decisions taken at a Joint Army/RAF Conference at HQ AEAF this afternoon, 5 August 1944; Personal copy CLFCSC Collection, Top Secret 17–1–2/Ops Main HQ First Cdn Army Operation "Totalize" Request for Air Support, 4 August 1944; and Stacey, *Victory Campaign*, pp. 211–213, 223.

19. CP, Vol. 2, C of S 1–1–0 Record of Tele Conversation COS First Cdn Army and Col. GS First Cdn Army, 5 August 1944; and *BAOR Battlefield Tour*, pp. 12–13, 83. All messages to Bomber Command had to go through the Senior Air Staff Officer at army headquarters, who put them into the RAF signals system. This was in stark contrast to the close communication that existed down to brigade level with aircraft of 84 Group of the 2nd Tactical Air Force, providing close air support to ground forces. [Reginald H. Roy, *1944: The Canadians in Normandy* (Ottawa: Macmillan, 1984) pp. 264–265].

20. *BAOR Battlefield Tour*, pp. 1–7 and Appendix "E," Addendum 6 August 1944 to 2 Cdn Corps Operation Instruction No. 4 issued 051200 B Aug; CP, Vol. 2, Simonds to Crerar, 6 August 1944; and Paper on Enemy's Reaction to Op Totalize by Lt. Col. P.E.R. Wright GSO 1 Int, 7 August 1944. The last document considered the 12th SS Division's role as counterattack to maintain the first or second defensive zones and assessed it as "insufficient . . . for either." See also Stacey, *Victory Campaign*, pp. 203–204, 214, 220–221, 232–233. The intelligence picture at this time was not clear. On 22 June, the 272nd Division supported by the 503rd Heavy Tank Battalion straddled the Orne between Maltot to the west and Verrières; from Ver-

rières east to La Hogue, the 1st SS Panzer held the line. As a result of "Spring," however, the 272nd and 503rd were moved to the area east and south of Cagny. The 9th SS Panzer Division west of Maltot now stretched east to cover the gap left by the 272nd. At the beginning of August, however, the 9th SS moved west with the 21st Panzer and the 503rd Heavy Tank Battalion to participate in the counter-attack at Mortain. The front was again reorganized with the 277th and 271st Divisions taking over west of the Orne and the 1st SS the sector between the Orne and La Hogue, from which the 272nd extended to Emieville. The 12th SS now withdrew into a reserve position on the River Laison. On the night of 4/5 and 5/6 August, the 1st SS also crept quietly away to Mortain, its place being taken by the 89th division, which deployed its 1055 and 1056 grenadier regiments left and right, respectively (*BAOR Battlefield Tour*, pp. 5–7, 10, 37).

21. CP, Vol. 2, Simonds to Crerar, 6 August 1944. Specific figures on German tank and SP gun strengths vary with every account. Stacey used German sources to state that when "Totalize" was launched, the 12th SS had 48 tanks, 37 of them Mark IVs with long 75-mm guns, nine Panthers, and two unidentified. They also had 19 Tigers from the 101st SS Heavy Tank Battalion and 88-mm guns in some number from the 3rd Flak Corps (Stacey, *Victory Campaign*, p. 221).

22. 2 Cdn Corps Operation Instruction No. 4 Operation "Totalize," 5 August 1944 and Addendum 6 August 1944; Appendices "D" and "E" to *BAOR Battlefield Tour*, pp. 75–80; and CP, Vol. 2, Simonds to Crerar, 6 August, 1944.

23. Maj.-Gen. George Kitching, *Mud and Green Fields*, (Langley: Battleline, 1986), p. 210; RG 24, Vol. 10,797, GOC's Activities; Roy, *Canadians in Normandy*, pp. 191–193, 349. Both divisional commanders considered the bombing unnecessary and too restrictive (Roy, *Canadians in Normandy*, p. 196).

24. CATM Special Supplement to *CATM* 28 (July 1943), p. 17. It also stated that in certain circumstances the tanks of a troop could be as close to each other as 20 yards, "but such density [wa]s exceptional." In open country it prescribed that tanks not normally be more than 100 yards from each other.

25. Hutchinson, "Corps Commander," p. 70.

26. Kitching, *Mud and Green Fields*, p. 183; and Col. G.W.L. Nicholson, *Official History of the Canadian Army in the Second World War*, Vol. II: *The Canadians in Italy, 1943–1945* (Ottawa: Queen's Printer, 1956), pp. 354, 692.

27. DHist 000.7 (D9) Syllabus for Cdn Jr War Staff Crse No 1 at RMC, August 1941, Exercise No. 8.

28. See, for example, William J. McAndrew, "Fire or Movement? Canadian Tactical Doctrine, Sicily—1943," *Military Affairs* 3 (July 1987): 140–145.

29. Personal Copy CLFCSC Collection, Combat Lessons—7th and 8th Cdn Inf Bdes. Elaborate box barrages had been used in the Great War. The suggestion was also made that attacks not be made at first light because infantry could not see the splash of shells.

30. RG 24, Vol. 10,800, 2nd Canadian Corps "Immediate Report" on Operation "Totalize," 7–9 August 1944, dated 18 August 1944; Stacey, *Victory Campaign*, pp. 216–218; Roy, *Canadians in Normandy*, pp. 163–165; Nicholson, *Gunners*, II, pp. 312–314; and *BAOR Battlefield Tour*, pp. 13–14, 17–21, 38–39.

31. 2 Cdn Inf Div 00 No. 2 Operation "Totalize," *BOAR Battlefield Tour*, pp. 81–83.

32. RG 24, Vol. 15,061, WD Essex SEI, 8 August 1944; RG 24, Vol. 14,117,

WD HQ 2 CAB SEI, 7 August 1944; RG 24, Vol. 14,093, WD HQ 4 CIB SEI, 7–8 August 1944; RG 24, Vol. 13,789, WD GS 4 CAD SEI, 7–8 August 1944; RG 24, Vol. 10,800, 2nd Canadian Corps "Immediate Report" on Operation "Totalize," 7–9 August 1944, dated 18 August 1944; Sawyer Papers (SP), Special Interrogation Report Brigadefuhrer Kurt Meyer, Comd 12 SS Pz Div "Hitler Jugend," 24 August 1945; BAOR Battlefield Tour, pp. 21–24; Stacey, *Victory Campaign*, pp. 218–220; Roy, *Canadians in Normandy*, pp. 165–183. Carrier-borne infantry casualties were seven killed and 56 wounded. The 6th Brigade had 54 killed and 155 wounded; the Queen's Own Camerons lost 30 killed. The Essex took Caillouet by 1100 hours.

33. Kitching, *Mud and Green Fields*, pp. 210–211.

34. Hubert Meyer, *MS# P–164, 12th SS Panzer Division "Hitler Jugend" June to September 1944* (HQ U.S. Army, Europe, 1954), pp. 98–101, 128–129; Roy, *Canadians in Normandy*, pp. 185–187, 196; Appendix "M" Account by Brigadefuhrer Kurt Meyer *BAOR Battlefield Tour*, p. 101; and SP, Special Interrogation Report Brigadefuhrer Kurt Meyer, Comd 12 SS Pz Div "Hitler Jugend," 24 August 1945. Meyer was promoted to *Brigadefuehrer* on 1 September. *Sturmbannfuehrer* (Major) Hans Waldmuller commanded the 1st Battalion, 25 Panzergrenadier Regiment, and Bernard Krause the 1st Battalion, 26 Panzergrenadier Regiment. *Obersturmbannfuehrer* (Lieutenant-Colonel) Max Wunsche commanded 12 Panzer Regiment [Craig W.H. Luther, *Blood and Honor: The History of the 12th SS Panzer Division "Hitler Youth," 1943–1945* (San Jose, Calif.: Bender, 1987), pp. 74–76, 141, 156, 232].

35. RG 24, Vol. 13,712, 2 Canadian Corps Intelligence Summary No. 28, ending 2000 hrs, 8 August 1944; and Roy, *Canadians in Normandy*, p. 191. The 1st SS were in action against the Americans on 7 August.

36. RG 24, Vol. 13,750, WD GS 2 CID SEI, 16 July and 30 July 1944; R.G. 24, Vol. 13,751, WD GS 2 CID SEI, 3 August 1944; and 2 CID Intelligence Summary No 6. The radio intercept "Y" service was often of more value than "Ultra," which gave little advantage in a "dog fight"' [Ronald Lewin, *Ultra Goes to War: The Secret Story* (London: Hutchinson, 1978), pp. 267, 284, 344].

37. RG 24, Vol. 13,750, WD GS 2 CID 2DS(G)4–1–0–6/GS 2 Cdn Inf Div Notes on Exercise Prodder, 1 November 43.

38. RG 24, Vol. 10,797, COS 2 Cdn Corps Handwritten Telephone Notes, 8 August 1944. Fontenay was not secured until 1700 hours.

39. Roy, *Canadians in Normandy*, pp. 189–197; Kitching, *Mud and Green Fields*, pp. 211–212; *BAOR Battlefield Tour*, p. 58; and Meyer, *12th SS*, pp. 101–102.

40. RG 24, Vol. 10,797, COS Notes 8 August and GOC's Activities; RG 24, Vol. 13,712, WD GS II Cdn Corps SEI, 8 August 1944; The Air Plan, *BAOR Battlefield Tour*; and Stacey, *Victory Campaign*, pp. 222–224; Roy, *Canadians in Normandy*, pp. 193–196; and Nicholson, *Gunners*, Vol. II, pp. 317–318.

41. RG 24, Vol. 9792, Exercise "Link" Report of Senior Umpire 2 Cdn Corps.

42. Stacey, *Victory Campaign*, pp. 222–224; Roy, *Canadians in Normandy*, pp. 197–202; George F.G. Stanley, *In The Face of Danger: The History of the Lake Superior Regiment* (Port Arthur, Ont: Lake Superior Scottish Regiment, 1960), pp. 158–161; and MP, Vol. 156, The Cooperation of Tanks with Infantry, pp. 3, 19.

43. Extracts from a lecture given by Simonds, 23 June 1947, *BAOR Battlefield Tour*, p. 33.

44. RG 24, Vol. 14,051, WD HQ 4 CAB Exercise "Iroquois," 1 July 1944. Booth directed this TEWT that dealt with battle groups (also in RG 24, Vol. 15,098).

45. RG 24, Vol. 12,358, German Assault Detachments, 14 August 1942, Notes on the Support of Armoured Attacks by Divisional Artillery (translation of a German document), and German Manual of Infantry Training No. 9. The Germans placed great reliance on 75-mm and 150-mm infantry guns also mounted as assault guns. [DHist 000.7 (D9) Syllabus for Cdn JWSC No 1 Aug 41 Intelligence Training Centre War Intelligence Course German Army (4) Tactics in General and the Attack].

46. Kitching, *Mud and Green Fields*, p. 213. On battle group organization, see Maj.-Gen. G.P.B. Roberts, *From the Desert to the Baltic* (London: William Kimber, 1987), pp. 159, 184–185; and Capt. Mike Cessford, "Mailed Fist: British Armour in Normandy 1944," *Armour Bulletin* (Summer 1989), pp. 31–39. In a 6 June 1944 report on artillery lessons learned, the CRA of the 5th Canadian Armoured Division in Italy criticized the functioning of FOOs and COs representatives at unit level. The former, he wrote, "failed in their duties," while the latter had to "show more initiative in controlling . . . FOOs" (Personal Copy CLFCSC Collection, HQ RCA 5 Cdn Armd Div Lessons from the Adolf Hitler Line to Frosinone by Brig. H.A. Sparling, CRA 5 Cdn Armd Div, 6 June 1944). The date of this document provides further evidence that many important lessons from the Italian theatre could not have been incorporated in training for Normandy.

47. Roy, *Canadians in Normandy*, pp. 203–207, 221–222; RG 24, Vol. 14,052, WD HQ 4 CAB SEI, 9 August 1944; RG 24, Vol. 13,789, WD GS 4 CAD SEI, 9 August 1944; RG 24, Vol. 10,797, Ops Log HQ 2 Cdn Corps, 9 August 1944 Serial 64; Stanley, *Face of Danger*, pp. 161–163; Maj. G.L. Cassidy, *Warpath: The Story of the Algonquin Regiment 1939–1945* (Toronto: Ryerson, 1948), pp. 76–78; and Kitching, *Mud and Green Fields*, pp. 213–214. The 4th Polish Armored Brigade reported "Worthington Force" as "badly shot up" with only seven tanks left.

48. RG 24, Vol. 10,800, 2nd Canadian Corps "Immediate Report" on Operation "Totalize" 7–9 August 1944, dated 18 August 1944; RG 24, Vol. 10,797, COS Notes 8–9 August 1944; Stacey, *Victory Campaign*, pp. 226–227; Roy, *Canadians in Normandy*, pp. 211–222; and Meyer, *12th SS*, pp. 103–107. The CRA even went aloft looking for "Worthington Force."

49. *"Albainn" Souvenir Edition*, The Argyll and Sutherland Highlanders of Canada Princess Louise's 1st Battalion Veteran's Association 5th Reunion, 12–13 May 1972, Hamilton, Ontario, p. 12. This information, part of a package on the capture of Point 195, was provided by Dr. Robert L. Fraser, who is currently working on a history of the Argylls.

50. RG 24, Vol. 10,800, 2nd Canadian Corps "Immediate Report" on Operation "Totalize," 7–9 August, 1944, dated 18 August 1944; RG 24, Vol. 10,797, Ops Log HQ 2 Cdn Corps 10 Aug Serial 8; RG 24, Vol. 14,052, WD HQ 4 CAB SEI, 10 August 1944; Roy, *Canadians in Normandy*, pp. 216–217, 221–225; Stacey, *Victory Campaign*, pp. 228–230; Kitching, *Mud and Green Fields*, p. 215; and Maj. R. A. Paterson, *A Short History of the 10th Canadian Infantry Brigade* (Hilversum, Holland: De Jong, 1945), pp. 22–24.

51. RG 24, Vol. 14,141, HQ 8 Cdn Inf Bde Report on Attack on Quesnay Wood (1047), 10 August 1944; RG 24, Vol. 13,767, WD GS 3 CID SEI, 10 August 1944; RG 24, Vol. 14,141, WD HQ 8 CIB SEI, 10 August 1944; RG 24, Vol. 10,797, Ops Log HQ 2 Cdn Corps, 11 August 1944 Serial 5; Stacey, *Victory Campaign*, pp. 230–231; Roy, *Canadians in Normandy*, pp. 226–228; Nicholson, *Gunners*, II,

p. 319; and W.T. Barnard, *The Queen's Own Rifles of Canada* (Don Mills; Ont.: Ontario Publishing, 1960), pp. 214–217.

52. SP, Special Interrogation Report Kurt Meyer; and Meyer, *12th SS*, pp. 104, 108.

Chapter 12

Case Hardening

We who have spent so many years in England think and speak constantly of England and our friends there... even to the point of appearing disloyal to Canada. The thought of returning there on leave sometime soon alone makes life supportable at times.

Canadian War Diary Entry, 31 August 1944[1]

The black day, *Der Schwarze Tag*, visited upon the German army on 8 August 1918 by the Canadian and Australian corps was not repeated in the half-forgotten summer of 1944. In the final analysis Operation "Totalize" was a failure. Despite overwhelming air and artillery superiority, five divisions and two armored brigades comprising upwards of 600 tanks could not handle two depleted German divisions, mustering no more than 60 panzers and tank destroyers. Contrary to popular belief, the bulk of roughly 80 88-mm antitank guns, mostly belonging to three *Luftwaffe* flak regiments, were deployed south of Potigny; only the divisional batteries were forward. It was thus mainly the 12th SS Division's resourceful handling of Tigers and Panthers that stemmed the Canadian attack. Yet, while these Eastern Front leviathans were more than a match for Shermans and Churchills, the Germans had nothing to compare with the Typhoon or "Jabo" (*Jagdbombern*) as their troops fearfully labeled it. Then, too, the 17-pounder in its Firefly, SP, and towed configurations possessed an ample margin of power over the Tiger as demonstrated since 1943.[2]

To Simonds, the problem was not weapons or machines, but rather a lack of proper handling of resources within armored divisions. Troops also displayed a tendency, traceable back to training in Britain, to stick to roads and thereby inevitably encounter the antitank guns sited to cover them.

Simonds had also expressly urged his armored commanders not to wait for infantry divisions to take out final objectives or "get involved in probing . . . before they called down fire or . . . fighter bombers." If he had given them narrow frontages, he had also allotted each division an AGRA of five medium regiments specifically to assist them in getting on quickly.[3] Kitching's reaction, however, was to attack with two brigades up, instead of in depth as per Simonds's operational policy, leaving them pretty much to their own devices. Booth, in turn, delegated tactical responsibility down to battle groups with the result that artillery was never effectively brought to bear against pockets of resistance like that initially, and critically, encountered at Gaumesnil.

That Canadian armor in "Totalize" exhibited both the dashing recklessness and excessive caution of their British brethren is, of course, striking. Such bifurcation no doubt reflected the doctrinal contradictions that grew out of Africa, and which battle experience in the static Italian campaign could hardly have been expected to resolve. Even the failure to employ available artillery resources approximated the British armored pattern, and one could well say that the operation foundered for not making better use of guns. At the same time, it might have been better had Simonds committed the 3rd Division supported by the 2nd Armoured Brigade to the "second break in" rather than the Poles. This would have at least alleviated communications difficulties due to language and seen two additional infantry brigades in action. It would appear, however, that the El Hamma model appealed more to Simonds than the lesson of Wadi Akarit, so convincingly demonstrated by the Argylls in taking Point 195.

Crerar simply blamed the Poles. The "bog-down" of the 2 Corps attack, as he saw it, was mainly due to the "dog fight" that developed between the 1st Polish Armoured Division and German elements in Quesnay Wood. Had the Poles smoked off and contained the enemy there and pushed on with the bulk of their strength, they would have widened the front and increased the depth for a tactically decisive advance. As it was, when dark came, they had advanced "not more than a few hundred yards."[4] It is worth noting, of course, the later criticism of Hubert Meyer, former first operations officer of the 12th SS, that it would have been wiser to have outflanked the *Hitlerjugend* to the east, an action that conceivably could have been initiated by Crerar himself much as Dempsey had in personally redirecting the 7th Armoured onto Villers Bocage on 12 June. Whether Simonds would have intervened in this manner had he been army commander is an intriguing matter of conjecture.[5]

The commander of the 12th SS, Kurt Meyer, considered "Totalize" an example of "inflexible, time wasting method," whereby staff planning and preparation "succeeded in burying the enemy under several thousand tons of explosives." Never once did speed, "the most powerful weapon of Armoured Warfare," appear to have been a paramount concern. In Meyer's view, the road to Falaise had been open and basically undefended from midnight 7 August to noon 8 August. *Kampfgruppe Krause*, for example, did not arrive from the west until shortly before midnight on 8 August. He attributed Canadian inaction after the initial breakthrough to be "the result of too much planning by the 2nd Corps" related to the employment of bombers. The development of the battle also convinced him that divisional commanders had not placed themselves "in the leading combat group, to see for . . . [themselves] to save precious time, and to make lightning decisions" to exploit "given opportunities."[6]

It seems clear that the failure of "Totalize" was less a product of troop inexperience, for Canadian soldiers had performed well when correctly employed, than the result of a flawed concept. Waiting for the second bomber strike guaranteed a loss of momentum. Had the strike been waived and high-command attention turned to the staff problem of getting troops and artillery forward, the tempo could have been sustained. But the strike could only have been cancelled through the First Canadian Army, which had expended so much effort in arranging strategic bomber support that it had become almost bureaucratically entrenched. Notwithstanding the requirement for 24 hours notification, it is highly unlikely that Crerar would have even felt disposed to request a cancellation of "Bomber" Harris, with whom he appears to have struck up a rather ingratiating relationship.[7] Besides, it was the one area in "Totalize" planning that because of its strategic overtones would have remained the sole prerogative of the First Canadian Army headquarters. Crerar no less than Simonds was also attracted to the technological expedient, which the Allied bomber barons at the strategic level had so mistakenly yet skillfully proselytized.

That another more tactical approach was feasible is evident from Meyer's postwar postulation of a "Red Totalize." After three years of combat experience in Russia, he was convinced the Soviets would not have permitted a "battle of phases" with a "first objective only three miles behind the enemy Front Line." The tasks of the 2nd and 51st Divisions would have been to advance behind a concentrated artillery attack "to smash the enemy defence on both sides . . . and open the road to Falaise." The armored brigades and carrier-borne infantry which accomplished this would have then "automatically take[n] over the task of advance force for the two attacking divisions," one brigade pushing toward St. Sylvain while the other seized Bretteville-sur-Laize. At the "first sign" that the road was open, the advance force of the 4th Armoured—a tank battalion with two companies of infantry, a battery of SP howitzers, a reconnaissance company, and an air force controller—would have "plung[ed] onward to the south towards their objective, Falaise."[8]

He went on to suggest that the advance force, commanded by a "young fanatical Communist" and assisted by ground support aircraft, would have stopped at nothing before Falaise. It would have advanced not by tactical maneuvering, but with guns blazing to either Falaise or "a glorious finish." The main body of the 4th Division would have followed at a steady pace to ensure the success of its spearhead. By attacking during the early morning hours instead of in darkness, which left the tank a "creeping pill-box" with reduced "ram-power" for lack of speed, the Red Army would have been able to strike deeply into the enemy defensive system, leaving the 12th SS absolutely no chance of reaching the Falaise road area north of Bretteville-le-Rabet. Strategic bombers, which in the Canadian case represented overkill anyway, would not have been used, since it would have "transferred the initiative from . . . leading combat elements to timetable acrobats of . . . Headquarters." Operation "Totalize" would have been accomplished in 24 hours.[9]

In consequence of the failure of "Totalize," however, Montgomery on 11 August issued a new directive that instructed the First Canadian Army to capture Falaise as "a first priority . . . [to] be done quickly." Argentan to the south was also to be secured with strong U.S. armored and mobile forces. The object of these two moves was to close the gap between the 21st and 12th Army Groups, thereby trapping German forces in the west now dangerously overextended as a result of operations against the Americans in the Mortain area.[10] This directive officially set in train the short envelopment, an idea hatched by Bradley, enthusiastically endorsed by Eisenhower, but only perfunctorily accepted by Montgomery. His preferred strategy remained to establish a bridgehead across the Seine in a longer envelopment. Indeed, he understood that classic encirclement operations called for a line of circumvallation as well as one of countervallation, which made the short envelopment an extremely perilous prospect, especially against Germans well-versed in *Keil und Kessel* operations on a grand scale. Without a blocking force at Trun-Chambois or along the Seine, any force interposed at Falaise ran the risk of being sandwiched between enemy forces breaking out and those sent to their relief.[11]

In any event, Montgomery was quick to give Bradley permission to move north of the interarmy group boundary that was established on 5 August 12 miles south of Argentan. That Bradley developed a similar caution of early encirclement was demonstrated on 12 August when he refused Patton permission to proceed north of Argentan to "drive the British into the sea." As Bradley later explained, better a "solid shoulder at Argentan to the possibility of a broken neck at Falaise." He nonetheless went to his grave blaming Montgomery for his failure to "close the trap by capping the leak at Falaise."[12] Yet, both Bradley and Montgomery appear to have believed at the time that the Canadians, only ten kilometers from Falaise, had to succeed in their second try. It was only subsequently that Bradley criticized Montgomery for not reinforcing the Canadians with the "more battle-seasoned troops of the Second Army."[13]

Within the First Canadian Army planning commenced almost immediately to launch another heavily supported attack toward Falaise, this time east of the road thrusting south from the general line of Estrées-la-Campagne–Soignolles. At 1000 hours 12 August, Simonds held a conference with all three Canadian divisional commanders on Operation "Tallulah," curiously named after Alabama actress Tallulah Brockman Bankhead. In the interests of security, he on 13 August issued only verbal orders for the operation, now more optimistically designated "Tractable." Following his orders group, which included brigadiers, he went on to personally brief all armored commanders down to unit level. Making known his extreme displeasure with their "Totalize" performance in no uncertain terms, Simonds directed that armor was henceforth neither to balk at movement by night nor expect infantry protection in harboring. He further warned that while there would probably continue to be "cases of. . . mis-employment of armour" in future operations, "this was to be no excuse for non-success." Canadian tank units and formations, in short, were to be pushed to the very limits of their endurance.[14]

"Tractable" was essentially "Totalize" in smoke. It also bore an astounding resemblance to the theoretical operation in *Current Reports From Overseas* described earlier. The principal object of "Tractable" was to dominate the northern, eastern, and southern exits from Falaise so that no enemy could escape. Physical occupation of the town was to be completed by the Second British Army following the success of "Tractable," after which the First Canadian Army was to exploit southeast to capture or dominate Trun. In this attack on Falaise, which aimed to skirt Quesnay Wood and Potigny, 2 Corps was to be assisted by the 2nd Tactical Air Force and Bomber Command.[15] Again Simonds planned to use massed armor and carrier-borne infantry to break speedily through the enemy gun screen, only this time he chose for surprise purposes to cloak their movement with smoke rather than darkness. Once more, preliminary bombardment was dispensed with in order to avoid signaling attack frontage, which enabled the enemy to bring heavy defensive fire to bear on rearward assaulting elements, thus reducing their capacity to penetrate in depth.

As explained by Simonds, the "first step" was to secure the high ground northwest of Versainville and then, during a "second," push through toward Falaise. To accomplish the former, the corps was to attack with two roughly equal divisional groups up: the 4th Division, with the 8th Brigade under command, on the left; and the remainder of the 3rd Division, with the 2nd Armoured Brigade (less the Sherbrookes) under command, on the right. The 2nd Brigade was to capture Point 184 northwest of Epaney while the 4th Division formed a pivot at Perrières, seized the Versainville high ground, and exploited to Eraines and Damblainville. One AGRA was placed in immediate support of each division until the 2nd Armoured Brigade attained its objective, after which both AGRA, less one medium regiment, were to support the 4th Division. The task of the 3rd Division was to clear

Map 12.1
Operation "Tractable"

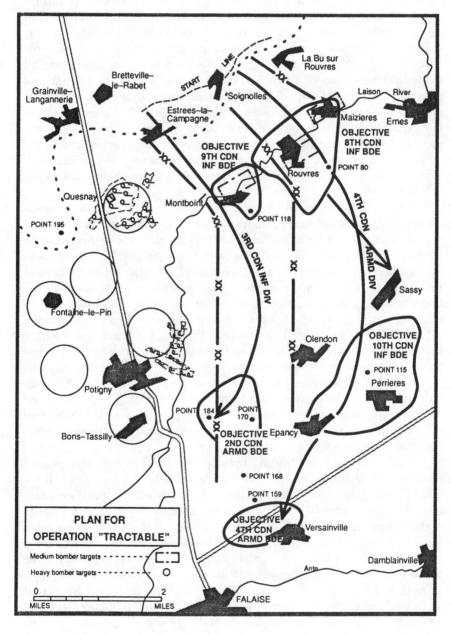

PLAN FOR
OPERATION "TRACTABLE"

Medium bomber targets
Heavy bomber targets

the intervening valley of the Laison River between Montboint and Maizieres and exploit to form a pivot at Sassy. To assist with this, the 8th Brigade was to revert to 3rd Division command upon reaching the river.[16]

As in "Totalize," 2 Corps assaulting elements were drawn up in densely packed formation with armored brigades, including special squadrons, to the forefront. Simonds appears to have listened to complaints about narrow frontages, however, for he directed the armored brigades to attack on a wide front, if possible with three units up, though he stipulated 15-yard marshaling intervals between tanks. The armored brigades were to push straight through to their objectives, advancing at a rate of 12 miles in the hour, the "proper emp[loyment] of armour . . . [being] to pos[itio]n it so that the enemy must drive it out in order to regain his freedom of man-oeuvre." A carrier-borne infantry brigade charged with dismounting and clearing the valley of the Laison followed within each divisional column; the 8th Brigade in the case of the 4th Division and the 9th Brigade in the 3rd. Last in the order of march came the marching infantry brigades, the 10th and 7th respectively, whose task it was to pass through and join the armor on objectives.

The forward movement of the columns was to be screened by artillery smoke, of impenetrable density on the flanks and of "mist" density, as controlled by FOOs with armor, on the front (the attack was to be postponed in the event of direct frontal winds). Over and above counterbombardment by all available medium artillery, concentrations on call were prearranged on known or suspected enemy 88-mm gun positions, the latter to be engaged during the advance whether they opened fire or not. From 15 minutes prior to the attack for 10 minutes, medium bombers were also to engage enemy tank, gun, and mortar positions up to the Laison valley. Two hours after commencement, heavy bombers were slated to strike Quesnay Wood, Potigny, and German defenses astride the Falaise road for one and a half hours.[17]

The enemy position to be assaulted was not considered to be posted in any great depth. It was estimated to comprise a light infantry screen backed up by a large number of 88-mm guns along the general line of the Laison and *Nebelwerfers* behind reverse slopes. While elements of the 271st Division were believed to be joining the newly arrived 85th Infantry in this area, the disposition of the 12th SS Division could not be defined. In fact, the division was but a shadow of its former self, mustering on 12 August seven Panthers and 17 Panzer IVs, four 88-mm Flak, and six understrength rifle companies of perhaps 500 men.[18] Not surprisingly, both Simonds and Crerar were apparently satisfied that they had sufficient force to deal with the situation. The 1st Polish Division and 33rd Armoured Brigade, for example, were each directed to form a firm base, the former near the start line at Estrées-la-Campagne.

When the Canadians attacked at 1200 hours 14 August, then, it was generally with the rekindled hope that they would secure Falaise the second time round. Again, save for some clear patches in the smoke, everything went well from the beginning and leading elements were on the Laison within an hour. As might be expected on a hot summer's day, however, the kilometer-wide tank phalanxes threw up huge dust clouds that combined with high-explosive concentrations and "vision limiting smoke" to plunge columns into incredible disorder. In "charge of the light brigade" fashion, tanks, carriers, and half-tracks steering only by the sun all vied for the lead as control became virtually impossible to maintain. When they arrived on the river, most units were widely dispersed and in need of reorganization. As if this self-inflicted wound were not enough, the Laison was now found not to be, as Simonds reportedly said, "fordable by tanks at almost all points."[19]

Ironically, a major observation made by Simonds after Exercise "Spartan" was that a corps plan could not await engineer ground reconnaissance, for it would then be unable "to keep up with operations." The best that could be done was to "demand [air] photographic reconnaissance of obstacles well in advance" and through a study of these and the map prepare flexibly "for the worst."[20] Given that corps planning had to look several days ahead, Simonds was essentially correct, but to have misjudged the Laison with its muddy bottom and steep banks was an error of major consequence. The 2nd Armoured Brigade in an after-action report categorized the river as a "definite tank obstacle" and recommended that, in future, tank commanders rather than engineers determine whether an obstacle was a tank obstacle or not.[21] Fortunately, AVREs carrying fascines (bundles of poles for filling ditches and streams) were eventually able to bridge the Laison's six-foot breadth for tanks that had neither bogged nor crossed by improvised fords and demolition-free bridges.

On the 4th Division front the search for crossings forced the armor northeast along the river beyond Ernes "where tanks were lined up for two hours amid scenes of great confusion."[22] Since this formation had the farthest to go to secure its final objective, delay here was critical. Although Foot Guard tanks were over the river by 1430 hours, they like other units required some reorganization before pushing onward. About this time the brigade commander, Booth, was also mortally wounded and his entire tactical headquarters effectively put out of action. Obviously, no succession of command had been detailed within the brigade, and it was not until after 1900 hours that the CO of the Foot Guards, Lieutenant-Colonel Murray Scott, received notification from Kitching to take over. Suffering from a broken ankle and considering it too late for armor to cover the remaining five kilometers to Versainville, he suspended operations for the day.[23]

First light of 15 August found the 4th Armoured Brigade beyond Olendon, which had been secured by the 10th Brigade. On the 3rd Division front, the 2nd Armoured and 7th Brigades were in possession of the greater

part of the Point 184 objective northeast of Souligny; the 8th Brigade, to
the east, held Sassy. By the time operations were resumed, however, the
First Canadian Army had been directed to capture Falaise as well as close
off its eastern exits.[24] It was thus even more imperative that the 4th Division
capture its final objective as soon as possible. The 4th Armoured brigade
under the wounded Scott, who was in some pain, accordingly renewed its
advance toward Versainville, but not until 0930 hours due to a decision to
refuel and replenish. Brigade tactical headquarters only resumed functioning
in the early afternoon. Progress was also slowed initially by fierce German
resistance from Epaney, which was eventually reduced mainly by the Algonquins of the 10th Brigade and partly by the Lake Superiors.

It was not until midafternoon that the Grenadier Guards and the reconstituted BCR of the 4th Armoured Brigade, now grown cautious for lack
of infantry and artillery support, approached the final objective above Versainville. Unfortunately, the more distant Foot Guards at 1650 hours erroneously reported that the two units had taken it, a message that was
joyfully and prematurely passed on to Simonds. Kitching shortly thereafter
relieved the injured Scott at his own request, replacing him with Halpenny.
It was only after having dined with the jubilant Simonds at corps headquarters that Kitching learned that the objective had not been captured. He
in turn informed Simonds, much to the latter's understandable disappoint-
ment and annoyance. News from the 3rd Division was likewise discon-
certing, for after having advanced to Point 168 in a costly action that
afternoon, assaulting 7th Brigade troops were thrown out of Souligny before dark.[25] As in "Totalize," the Germans had managed to deny Canadian
arms the planned goal they sought.

The ultimate failure of "Tractable" was largely obscured by a contretemps
of considerable magnitude, though it had little impact on the battle. In a
performance reminiscent of "Totalize," 77 bombers, 44 of them from No.
6 (RCAF) Bomber Group, mistakenly unloaded short on Canadian rearward
units, especially 2 Canadian AGRA, and elements of the 1st Polish Armoured Division. Troop attempts to remedy this blunder by setting out
yellow markers and letting off yellow flares and smoke, a procedure rehearsed just for such an eventuality, only brought more bombs as a similar
target indicator color was employed by the air force that day. Regrettably,
Bomber Command had never been informed of a Supreme Headquarters
Allied Expeditionary Force (SHAEF) directive that authorized the use of
this color for indicating positions of forward ground troops.[26] While in a
strict sense SHAEF should have so advised Bomber Command, the fact
that all communication with the latter funneled through Headquarters First
Canadian Army suggests, in a practical sense, a degree of accountability on
its part.

This was at least the way the COS, Brigadier Mann, initially saw it. In
a first draft memorandum to Crerar he "suggested that we (and myself in

particular) might be considered as having some responsibility" insofar as "First Canadian Army had erred in some degree by not pointing out the use of yellow smoke and flares" to indicate the positions of troops. Crerar, on the other hand, disagreed. He noted instead that "it was, if anyone's fault, that of AEAF [Allied Expeditionary Air Forces], in not drawing attention of Bomber Command to [the appropriate SHAEF directive]."[27] Clearly, however, a commander and staff at any higher headquarters have an ineluctable responsibility to ensure that all aspects of an operation, especially those related to the safety of their own troops, are thoroughly checked and coordinated. It is thus difficult to accept totally the bureaucratic shifting of blame for bombing errors in "Tractable." In any event, when all bombing was ordered stopped at 1520 hours, most of the 769 Lancasters and Halifaxes had delivered on target. With close to 400 Canadian and Polish casualties incurred, however, the raid had a devastating effect on ground force morale.[28]

Another incident that affected later assessment of "Tractable" was the capture by the Germans of an officer of the 8th Reconnaissance Regiment who had accidentally directed his scout car into their lines on the evening of 13 August. The officer was shot dead, but a copy of a 2nd Division instruction outlining the entire corps plan was found on his body. When Simonds learned what had happened, he was highly angered and quick to claim that this individual act of "carelessness" had compromised surprise and "enabled the enemy to make quick adjustments to his dispositions which undoubtedly resulted in casualties to . . . [Canadian] troops the following day." Simonds also apparently believed that it "delayed the capture of FALAISE for over twenty-four hours."[29] According to Hubert Meyer, however, no redeployment of import took place as there was insufficient time to react. The uncomfortable fact thus remains that roughly 300 tanks and four brigades of infantry supported by massive artillery and air resources failed to overcome some 41 tanks, albeit more than half Panthers and Tigers, and two reinforced infantry regiments many of whose men had not been under fire before.[30] True, the 88-mm gun line remained formidable, but Simonds's expectation that the operation should have accomplished what it set out to do still seems valid. The real seeds of failure, in short, were less extrinsic than intrinsic to "Tractable" itself.

This was most assuredly the view of the 7th Brigade commander, Brigadier Foster, who described "Tractable" as "certainly one of the strangest attack formations anyone ever dreamed up and without a hope . . . of succeeding as planned." In his judgment what "looked good to . . . [Simonds's] precise engineering mind on paper seldom worked in practice once the human element was added."[31] To be sure, just to line up formations in parade square fashion was a complex undertaking that could not possibly have been attempted without absolute air superiority. On the other hand, it solved the potentially disastrous movement problem of getting hundreds of armored vehicles to the start line in good order. Not to have expected huge amounts of dust to generate mass confusion and associated control problems, however, seems an extraordinary oversight, suggestive even of an unfamiliarity with basic armored vehicular movement. This, coupled with a misreading of the Laison, was the fatal flaw of "Tractable," from which there was simply no time left for recovery.

The operation also suffered from difficulties in getting artillery forward, for Simonds at 1810 hours had to order the CCRA to get guns into the "valley below Soignolles."[32] While bombing errors doubtless contributed to this problem, artillery insistence on having gun areas absolutely cleared of enemy may also have been a factor. An additional impediment, of course, was the tardy transference of command following Booth's incapacitation, exactly the situation that Montgomery had warned Canadians about in 1942. Since the armored regiments of the 4th Brigade had continued to progress, an extra hour or two of firm direction from that level would literally have made all the difference. Though lower echelons are often easier to blame than higher command for operational failures like "Tractable," it is impossible to fault the performance of units like the Canadian Scottish who managed, without benefit of intimate tank support, to take Point 168 while being shelled by their own artillery.[33] The performance of many other infantry and even armored units, incidentally, does not seem to suffer by comparison.

After "Tractable" the initiative that had momentarily resided with the First Canadian Army passed into other hands. It now reacted to higher direction in an increasingly fluid situation as four Allied armies converged upon the "Falaise Gap." The withdrawal of German forces through the Gap reached full flood on 18 August, the very day Falaise finally fell. Ironically, it was taken by the 2nd Division, which since 13 August had been steadily advancing from a bridgehead at Clair Tizon; but only after a most desperate last ditch stand by about 60 *Hitlerjugend*, none of whom surrendered. The 4th and 1st Armoured Divisions had meanwhile been directed toward Trun and Chambois, respectively, to link up with the Americans approaching from the south. Unlike the region of the Caen plain, the rising countryside around Trun east of the Dives was characterized by thickly wooded hills interspersed with hamlets, small fields, and numerous orchards, all ringed by valleys, streams, and winding sunken lanes. Like the area of Villers-Bocage, it was less than ideal tank country, but it was through here that the Canadian and Polish armored divisions with their insufficient infantry complements fought a series of highly disparate offensive and defensive actions.[34]

Caught in the inexorable crush of Allied forces, the Germans fought back with determination and skill. On 20 August the 1st Polish Division was sandwiched in an *Ostfront*-style operation that saw not only the Seventh German Army breaking out of the Falaise pocket past Canadian elements at St. Lambert and Polish positions at Coudehard, but the 2nd SS Panzer Corps "breaking back" on Polish defenses to the east. Between St. Lambert and Chambois up "Dead Horse Alley," the Germans ultimately managed to extricate possibly one-third of their forces. By nightfall 21 August the Gap was nonetheless closed for good and its endless controversy begun. For our purposes, however, but one thing needs to be noted: in this confused fighting, for which reinforcements were never requested by corps or army, individual Canadian soldiers and units, even when outnumbered, appear with few exceptions to have performed well.[35]

The Battle of Normandy, rightfully considered one of the world's most decisive, was over. It had cost the Canadian Army 18,444 casualties, including 5,021 dead. The 3rd Canadian Infantry Division also suffered greater losses than any other division within the 21st Army Group. The 2nd Canadian Infantry Division, though it did not arrive in France until 7 July, incurred the next highest. All told, battle casualties slightly exceeded 3,000 in June, 5,500 in July, and 7,400 for the period 1–23 August. Fighting in "Totalize" through "Tractable" up to 21 August accounted for 5,679 casualties. Significantly, the two British divisions with the highest casualty rates, the 3rd and 51st (Highland), both landed on D-Day.[36] The troublesome thing about these figures is that they cannot simply be explained away in nationalist terms of Canadians being assigned more difficult tactical tasks. As already mentioned, British engagements in the bocage to the west approached Great War proportions in their severity. Fighting in the "Epsom" offensive, for example, "reached a sustained intensity rare even in the Normandy campaign."[37] One might have expected further, from the experience of the Great War, that an all-volunteer army would have performed appreciably better than a conscripted one like the British.

To say that the Canadian government got more than it deserved from the performance of its castaway army in Normandy would nonetheless be an understatement. One cannot escape the feeling that the prime minister of Canada would personally have preferred its troops to have fought and died with as little fuss and bother as possible. That many Canadian soldiers came to look upon Britain as a surrogate homeland is not therefore surprising. After the closure of the Falaise Gap, of course, the First Canadian Army literally marched into a new world order. Whereas the battle for Normandy was directed by a British field commander, the rest of "Overlord" was not. From 1 September onward, Montgomery reverted to command an army group of roughly 15 divisions. His erstwhile subordinate, Bradley, on the other hand, rose to command close to 50 in what clearly signaled a changing of the guard. The First Canadian Army, whose British composition at one point increased to 80 percent, advanced with the rest of the British Liberation Army into an imperial retreat.

NOTES

1. Record Group (RG) 24, Vol. 15,271, WD SDG, 31 August 1944.

2. Hubert Meyer, "Report of the Battlefield Study 1987 by Canadian Forces Support Establishment Central Army Group, 20 June 1987," and his *Kriegsgeschichte der 12. SS-Panzer Division "Hitlerjugend"* (Osnabruck: Munin Verlag, 1987), Vol. II, p. 620, and MS# P–164, *12th SS Panzer Division "Hitlerjugend" June to September 1944* (HQ U.S. Army, Europe, 1954), p. 102. The 17-pounder was known to have successfully dealt with Tigers at 1,500 yards range. It was nonetheless difficult to maneuver and took 12 to 15 hours to dig in. The Tiger was also vulnerable to six-pounder fire in the flanks. Brig. A. L. Pemberton, *The Second World War, 1939–1945, Army, The Development of Artillery Tactics and Equipment* (London: War Office, 1951), pp. 162–163, 203, 223.

3. Extracts from lecture given by Simonds, 23 June 1947, DHist 693.013(D2) Ops 2 Cdn Corps, *British Army of the Rhine Battlefield Tour Operation Totalize: 2 Canadian Corps Operations Astride the Road Caen-Falaise 7–8 August 1944*, prepared under the direction of G (Training) HQ British Army of the Rhine (BAOR), p. 33.

4. Crerar papers (CP), Vol. 21, Crerar to Stacey, 10 January 1958.

5. Carlo D'Este, *Decision in Normandy: The Unwritten Story of Montgomery and the Allied Campaign* (London: Pan, 1984) p. 172; and Meyer, "Report of the Battlefield Study 1987." Dempsey told Bucknall, 30 Corps commander, to switch the 7th Armoured to the Villers-Bocage axis immediately. Crerar might have redirected the 3rd Division in the same manner. He had also given 1 British Corps the role to comply on its right with the intentions of 2 Canadian Corps, "right shoulder up" (PRO, CAB 106/1064 Crerar WD, GOC-in-C–1–0–4 Crerar to Crocker and Simonds, 6 August 1944).

6. DHist 73/1302 Interview Kurt Meyer, 3 September 1950, by Maj. James R. Millar, forwarded to Director of Chaplain Service (P) 6 September 1950; and Meyer, *12th SS*, p. 104.

7. Crerar, even as the bombing was in progress 7 August, signaled Harris: "Greatly appreciate outstanding contribution your Command. We shall hope to continue and complete this battle as well as you have commenced it. [Col. C. P. Stacey, *Official History of the Canadian Army in the Second World War*, Vol. III: *The Victory Campaign: The Operations in North-West Europe 1944–1945* (Ottawa: Queen's Printer, 1966) p. 218]. Harris later wrote to Crerar: "If, as I consider and believe you think, the heavy bombers from Caen onwards whenever they were called in to assist the army have been an outstanding success in forwarding the military design and in saving a large number of casualties amongst our own troops, then I hope you will agree that the facts should be blazoned abroad" (CP, Vol. 6, Harris to Crerar, 13 September 1944). At Walcheren, Canadians were said to be "drugged with bombs" [W. Denis and Shelagh Whitaker, *Tug of War: The Canadian Victory that Opened Antwerp* (Toronto: Stoddart, 1984), p. 372; and Jeffrey Williams, *Long Left Flank: The Hard Fought Way to Reich, 1944–1945* (Toronto: Stoddart, 1988), pp. 149–150].

8. DHist 73/1302 Interview Kurt Meyer, 3 September 1950.

9. Ibid.

10. 21 Army Group M518 General Operational Situation and Directive 11–8–44.

11. For insight into the sophistication of German operational capacity in such circumstances, see *Operations of Encircled Forces: German Experiences in Russia* (Washington: Department of the Army Pamphlet No. 20–234, 1952); and Maj. Timothy A. Wray, *Standing Fast: German Defensive Doctrine on the Russian Front During World War II, Prewar to March 1943* (Fort Leavenworth: Combat Studies Institute, 1986), pp. 25–33. On to encircle or not to encircle, see Gen. S. M. Shtemenko, *The Soviet General Staff at War, 1941–1945*, trans. Robert Daglish (Moscow: Progress, 1985), Vol. I, pp 243–244, 311–314.

12. D'Este, *Decision in Normandy*, pp. 424–430, 439–460; and Nigel Hamilton, *Monty*, Vol. II: *Master of the Battlefield 1942–1944* (Sevenoaks, U.K.: Hodder and Stoughton, 1984), pp. 770–775. D'Este covers the controversy related to the closure of the gap very thoroughly.

13. D'Este, *Decision in Normandy*, pp. 426–427, 444–445; and Eversley Belfield and H. Essame, *The Battle for Normandy* (London: Pan, 1983), p. 225.

14. RG 24, Vol. 10, 797, GOC's Activities; RG 24, Vol. 13,789, WD GS 4 CAD SEI, 13 August 1944; Stacey, *Victory Campaign*, p. 236; and Terry Copp and Robert Vogel, *Maple Leaf Route: Falaise* (Alma: Maple Leaf Route, 1983), p. 112. Had the lady's name been "bridgehead" instead of "bankhead," a diarist commented, "Tractable" would have remained "Tallulah." According to information provided by Dr. Robert L. Fraser, Simonds during his critique of armored performance on "Totalize" called some commanders yellow and directed them to command henceforth from tanks. Meyer, an infantryman, commanded from a motorcycle.

15. CP, Vol. 2, Crerar to Simonds and Crocker on Operation "Tractable," 13 August 1944. The 2nd Tactical Air Force included 2, 83, 84 Groups. "Tractable" was also called the "Mad Charge" [Alexander McKee, *Caen: Anvil of Victory* (London: Souvenir, 1964), p. 335].

16. RG 24, Vol. 13,751, WD GS 2 CID "Tallulah" Notes on Corps Comd's Outline Talk 131000 Hrs; RG 24, Vol. 14,156, WD GS 4 CAD Outline of Instrs Issued by GOC 4 Cdn Armd Div 131230 B, August 1944 Op "Tractable;" and RG 24, Vol. 10,800, 2 Canadian Corps "Immediate Report" on 2 Canadian Corps Operations "Tractable"—The Capture of Falaise, 14–16 August 1944, dated 22 August 1944.

17. Ibid.; CP, Vol. 2, Op Tallulah Notes Given Verbally by C of S 2 Cdn Corps to GSO 1 Ops First Cdn Army at HQ 2 Cdn Corps 122300B Aug; RG 24, Vol. 14,141, WD HQ 8 CIB 8 Cdn Inf Bde 00 No 17 Op "Tallulah," 14 August 1944; and Stacey, *Victory Campaign*, pp. 236–238. The 3rd Division was deployed with two armored regiments up, 1st Hussars left, and FGH right, each with two squadrons up and one in reserve; behind these came the 7th Canadian Reconnaissance Regiment (17th Duke of York's Royal Canadian Hussars), the 9th Brigade, and the 7th Brigade. The 4th Division also advanced with two armored regiments up, the Grenadiers left and Foot Guards right, both with three squadrons up; the Lake Superiors followed left rear and the British Columbia Regiment right rear. Behind these came the 8th Brigade and the 10th Brigade with the 29th Canadian Reconnaissance Regiment (The South Alberta Light Horse) [Reginald H. Roy, *1944: The Canadians in Normandy*, Canadian War Museum Historical publication No. 19 (Ottawa: Macmillan, 1984), pp. 240, 251].

18. RG 24, Vol. 13,712, 2 Cdn Corps Intelligence Summaries No. 31 of 11 August, No. 32 of 12 August, and No. 33 of 13 August 1944; RG 24, Vol. 14,141,

WD HQ 8 CIB 8 Cdn Inf Bde 00 No. 17 Op "Tallulah", 14 August 1944; Craig W. H. Luther, *Blood and Honor: The History of the 12th SS Panzer Division "Hitler Youth," 1943–1945* (San Jose, Calif.: Bender, 1987), pp. 234, 253–254; and Meyer, *12th SS*, p. 109. Stacey estimated that the 12th SS at this time had 18 Mark IVs, 9 Panthers, and 17 Tigers (Stacey, *Victory Campaign*, p. 248).

19. RG 24, Vol. 13,751, WD GS 2 CID "Tallulah" Notes on Corps Comd's Outline Talk 131000 Hrs; RG 24, Vol. 13,767, WD GS 3 CID SEI, 14 August 1944; RG 24, Vol. 14,141, WD HQ 8 CIB 8 Cdn Inf Bde 00 No. 17 Op "Tallulah"; RG 24, Vol. 15,098, WD Lake Superiors, 14 August 1944; Maj. Gen. George Kitching, *Mud and Green Fields: The Memoirs of Major General George Kitching*, (Langley, B.C.: Battleline, 1986), p. 216; and Stacey, *Victory Campaign*, pp. 240–241.

20. McNoughton Papers (MP), Vol. 161, Simonds to McNaughton, 29 April 1943.

21. RG 24, Vol. 14,117, WD HQ 2 CAB Op "Tractable," An Account of Ops by 2 Cdn Armd Bde in France, 14–16 August 1944. Canadian intelligence admitted that the "Laison River . . . turned out to be an unexpectedly difficult obstacle that . . . [photographic interpretation and intelligence] failed to estimate correctly." [Maj. S. R. Elliot, *Scarlet to Green: "A History of Intelligence in the Canadian Army 1903–1963* (Ottawa: Canadian Intelligence and Security Association, 1981), p. 271].

22. Kitching, *Mud and Green Fields*, p. 219.

23. Roy, *Canadians in Normandy*, pp. 240–249, 253–260, 262–263; and Stacey, *Victory Campaign*, p. 241. Division did not know until 1615 that Booth was wounded. He and his tactical headquarters may have been lost [Lt. M. O. Rollefson (ed.), *Green Route Up* (The Hague: Mouton and Cy, 1945), pp. 321–32].

24. RG 24, Vol. 10,797, 2 Cdn Corps COS Telephone Notes, 14 August 1944. The scribbled entry for 1720 hours ends: "Go on with Trun—though Falaise priority."

25. Stacey, *Victory Campaign*, pp. 248–249; Kitching, *Mud and Green Fields*, pp. 220–221; Roy, *Canadians in Normandy*, pp. 269–278; RG 24, Vol. 13,789, WD GS 4 CAD SEI, 15 August 1944; RG 24, Vol. 14,052, WD HQ 4 CAB SEI, 15 August 1944; and RG 24, Vol. 14,130, WD HQ 7 CIB SEI, 15 August 1944.

26. Personal Copies CLFCSC Collection, Operation "Tractable" Bombing Errors in Close Support Operation of 14 August 1944; PRO Air 14/860, XC/A/51202, First Cdn Army COS Memo on Use of Coloured Smoke and Flares to GOC-in-C, 22 August 1944 and Minute by A. T. Harris, 31 August; Report on Bombing of Our Own troops During Operation "Tractable" by Air Chief Marshal A. T. Harris, 25 August 1944; and PRO Air 14/861, XC/A/51202, RAF Proceedings of a Board of Officers 16–18 August 1944 for the purpose of investigating errors in bombing that occurred on 14 August 1944 in connection with operation "Tractable."

27. CP, Vol. 5, Memo COS to GOC-in-C Regarding the Report of the AOC in C Bomber Command, 28 August 1944.

28. RG 24, Vol. 10,797, Notes COS 2 Corps 14 Aug; Stacey, *Victory Campaign*, pp. 243–245; and Roy, *Canadians in Normandy*, pp. 238–239, 263–265. Crerar remained a believer in heavy bombers and accordingly thanked "Bomber" Harris, doubtless the price of continued friendship, not to mention support; he also took pains to point out to troops that most of the bombs that did not land on them hit their targets.

29. Personal copy from CLFCSC Collection, Simonds "To be Read by All Officers" circular, 23 August 1944.

30. Interview Meyer, 6 March 1986, and his *12th SS*, pp. 109–110; RG 24, Vol. 13,712, Extract from an order of 85 Inf Div, dated 9 August 1944, captured 16 August 1944; RG 24, Vol. 13,712, 2 Cdn Corps Intelligence Summaries No. 30 of 10 August, and No. 33 of 13 August 1944; Stacey, *Victory Campaign*, pp. 247–248; Copp and Vogel, *Falaise*, p. 116; and Kitching, *Mud and Green Fields*, p. 216. The 102nd SS Tiger battalion reinforced the line north of Falaise, coming under command of the 85th Division.

31. Tony Foster, *Meeting of Generals* (Toronto: Methuen, 1986), p. 368.

32. RG 24, Vol. 10,797, Notes COS 2 Corps, 14 Aug.

33. Roy, *Ready for the Fray*, pp. 286–294. The Canadian Scottish had 34 killed and 93 wounded in this battle, more than in any other.

34. RG 24, Vol. 10,797, GOC's Activities, 17–23 August 1944; RG 24, Vol. 13,789, WD GS 4 CAD SEI, 17–21 August 1944; RG 24, Vol. 14,052, WD HQ 4 CAB SEI, 16—20 August 1944; CP, Vol. 2, Crerar to Ralston, 1 September 1944; Stacey, *Victory Campaign*, pp. 236, 250–265; Roy, *Canadians in Normandy*, pp. 289–315; Belfield and Essame, *Battle for Normandy*, pp. 231–237; Kitching, *Mud and Green Fields*, pp. 221–225; and Lt. Gen. Sir Brian Horrocks, *Corps Commander* (London: Sidgwick and Jackson, 1977), p. 53. Kitching was relieved of command by Simonds on 21 August. Hutchinson charges that the 4th Armoured Division, which had been given the 2nd Armoured and 9th Infantry Brigades under command, reacted too slowly on 20 August (Hutchinson, "Corps Commander," pp. 229–242). It may be that Kitching was also fired for his performance on "Totalize" and "Tractable."

35. Ibid.

36. Stacey, *Victory Campaign*, p. 271; LHC, de Guingand Papers, 1-IV/3, Notes on the Operations of 21 Army Group, 6 June 1944–5 May 1945; and Copp and Vogel, *Falaise*, p. 138.

37. Belfield and Essame, *Battle for Normandy*, p. 130.

Conclusion

Final Casting

The Army is not like a limited liability company, to be reconstructed, remodeled, liquidated and refloated from week to week as the money market fluctuates. It is not an inanimate thing, like a house, to be pulled down or enlarged or structurally altered at the caprice of the tenant or the owner; it is a living thing. If it is bullied, it sulks; if it is unhappy, it pines; if it is harried it gets feverish; if it is sufficiently disturbed it will wither and dwindle and almost die; and when it comes to this serious condition, it is only to be revived by lots of time and lots of money.

Winston Churchill, 1905[1]

The operational, strategic, and political consequences of a Canadian triumph in Normandy are impossible to know. Had the First Canadian Army succeeded in its 8 August drive to Falaise, however, it is not unreasonable to presume that it might have, as in 1918, spearheaded the British Army's advance into the heartland of Europe. The tragedy was that on the morning of the 26th anniversary of the Battle of Amiens, Simonds's corps had cleanly sliced open the German defensive zone without realizing it. Coinciding as this did with Hitler's ill-advised counter attack at Mortain the previous day, an immediate push would have caught the Germans in full stride, unable to avoid the utter calamity of such an exploitation. Here indeed was the opportune juncture at which to have initiated an encirclement, for it would have allowed sufficient time to interpose ample Allied force. In fulfillment of the legacy of the Canadian Corps, the sword would have won for Canada a greater stature than all the machinations of constitutionally minded generals and diplomats. After "Totalize" the same opportunity did not exist.

Regrettably, Simonds could not be persuaded to throw caution to the wind and change the air bombardment plan. Crerar, principally concerned that movement not be delayed until long after bombardment, may not even have sensed the opportunity. In any case, residual tensions between the two commanders plus a marked disparity in their operational abilities were hardly conducive to Crerar offering Simonds any constructive military advice. The decision to await the bomber strike was an unlucky one, but in light of Simond's determination to avoid repeat performances of "Atlantic" and "Spring" it remains understandable. Less forgivable was the failure of his armored divisional commanders to employ their assigned AGRAs to blast their way forward. More aggressive injection of these heavier resources into the fighting could have redeemed a deteriorating situation.

Against any other but the German army, buttressed as it was by the formidable soldiery of the SS, the Canadian attack on *Der Schwarze Tag* should have succeeded. Given his personal doubts about his division commanders, Simonds's plan was essentially sound, and save for the rapid response of Meyer and his first staff officer it could hardly have been stayed. Since the plan involved attacking prepared rather than hasty German defensive positions, Simonds was unquestionably correct to centralize artillery and use its firepower in mass. Another factor often overlooked, which Brooke appreciated, was that enemy troop-to-space density in this area ran to two and a half times that of the Eastern Front. Though the point has been made by many analysts that the open Caen plain, unlike the bocage, favored armored offensive operations, few seem to have understood that it also offered ideal fields of fire for concealed long-range German antitank guns and tanks. But perhaps the most disturbing aspect of this action, as with most others from Carpiquet through "Tractable," is how few German soldiers actually defended against the number of Canadians who attacked.

In very large measure, responsibility for the relatively lackluster showing of Canadian arms in Normandy must be laid at the feet of division commanders. Clearly, neither Keller nor Foulkes were as tactically competent as Simonds. The available evidence plainly suggests that the "hard-fisted" Keller experienced serious personal and command failings in leading the 3rd Division. At Carpiquet he should probably have personally coordinated the efforts of his two brigades rather than assigning one an adjacent, yet removed, battalion of the other to carry out the divisional task. The confused and congested combat for Caen further revealed a growing lack of trust and confidence, among both superiors and subordinates, in Keller's leadership of the 3rd Division. His subsequent confession to Simonds that his health was not good enough to stand the strain was tantamount to admitting his inability to command. It was only for the sake of divisional morale that Simonds chose not to remove him.

Foulkes's contention that Canadian troops without air and artillery were no match for battle-experienced Germans has had the effect of camouflaging for years his own tactical shortcomings. The 12th SS, 85th, 89th, and 272nd German Divisions had not been in action as formations before Normandy. At the same time, Canadian troops when not poorly deployed gave good accounts of themselves. The action of the Canadian Scottish in taking Point 168 while being shelled by their own artillery is a case in point. It was something else, however, to have permitted the SSR and the Black Watch to advance up the open slopes of Verrières Ridge without adequate tank or artillery support. Much responsibility for this must be borne by Foulkes. It was his overly complex plan and insistence on breaking up brigades, a practice Montgomery disdained as they were trained to work together, that aggravated the situation in "Spring."

Regardless of whether "Spring" was intended as a holding attack or not, Simonds's assertion that all objectives should have been taken on 25 July cannot be lightly dismissed. The piecemeal attack by one battalion of the 3rd Division on Tilly recalled earlier British tendencies in North Africa that had confirmed the old rule of thumb, "the fewer you use, the more you risk to lose." A full-scale brigade attack against the town, on the other hand, may have saved lives in the long run. Tilly was decidedly never the two-company objective of Brigadier Jefferson's imagination. On the western flank, the redirection of the Black Watch into the built-up area of May-sur-Orne would have at least threatened the German position at Fontenay-le-Marmion. However one looks at the attack of the Black Watch, commanded at the last minute by a junior major, Brigadier Megill should have assumed more direct control. There can be little doubt that any similar action by the 12th SS would have felt the steadying grip of Meyer.

At best, Simonds's immediate subordinates were mediocre performers. Even at brigade level, with the possible exception of Foster, a lack of tactical judgement was often evident. Within the Canadian military system Simonds was, and remains, almost *sui generis*. Though by no means perfect, he was, as Montgomery so clearly perceived, the best of the lot. It is a sad commentary that had Crerar had his way in Italy, Simonds probably would have been sacked and his considerable talent lost. To a degree, the personal conflict between these two officers symbolized a deeper professional deficiency in the prewar Canadian military establishment, which had rarely displayed any interest in or appreciation of the requirements for senior field command. Simonds at 41 was one of the youngest corps commanders in any army, largely because he had ascended in a vacuum. Fifteen years, or half a generation, separated Simonds and Crerar. Yet within that bracket Simonds had no equals. In comparison, no such void existed in the U.S. Army where the youngest corps commander was seven years older than Simonds. In the German army less than two percent of corps commanders were under 45.

There was thus no natural connection between youth and superior military performance in the Canadian Army. The critical factor, as in the

German, British, and U.S. armies (Patton was 60), remained knowledge of how to conduct military operations effectively in war. The fact that Canadian commanders were young merely reflected a dearth of such knowledge amongst their seniors and, indirectly, a misplaced emphasis on other determinants of career advancement during the inter war years. If anything, youth without knowledge compromised the operations of the 4th Canadian Armoured Division during "Totalize" and "Tractable." On the other hand, in the case of Simonds, youth precluded him from being seriously considered for army command, even though he manifestly possessed more operational ability than Crerar. Lamentably, a temporary major in 1939 proved the best that the Canadian military system, despite all its expenditures during the interwar years, could put forth. The McNaughton interregnum had resulted, in short, in a lost half-generation of Canadian commanders.

The Canadian army was the direct heir of a professional tradition developed during four years of fighting in the Great War. By any standard, the Canadian Corps was one of the finest fighting formations in the forces of the British Empire. Its battlefield excellence derived not from any innate superiority born of the North American frontier, however, but primarily from British tutelage and the hard crucible of war. In its refinement of artillery methods the Canadian Corps manifested an even more pronounced affinity for firepower as a battle winner than British Army formations. Brutinel's employment of motor machine guns or armored cars was the only first-hand experience of Canadians with a mobile arm. Regrettably, the professional tradition established by the CEF was largely usurped during the post war years by an older entrenched militia tradition that perpetuated the illusion of citizen-soldier superiority and the game of political patronage.

Lack of operational focus further hastened the eclipse of Canadian military professionalism between the wars. Instead of retrenching anywhere near realistically as had the *Reichsheer* of von Seeckt, which stressed theoretical training for war, the Canadian regular force under McNaughton catered to politicians who, as blind as their electorates, could not envision another conflict. In actively seeking and assuming politically attractive nonmilitary roles ostensibly to ensure the survival of the militia as a fighting force, McNaughton virtually guaranteed the opposite: the continued erosion of whatever operational capability remained. Institutionally, there was no provision for keeping the art of war fighting alive. Least pardonable was McNaughton's assumption that military knowledge was mainly a matter of technical efficiency that any scientifically educated person could master probably better than a regular officer. These views, scarcely unique to McNaughton, were attractive and popular with civilian and academic audiences who, in turn, showered honors upon him.

The close connection between Canadian and imperial forces fortunately ensured that at least some officers were exposed to modern military thought. The 200,000-man British Army, though scattered throughout the Empire, did offer a grander horizon than a 55,000-man militia. Indeed, it spurred keener intellects such as Burns and Simonds to contemplate the higher realm of division and corps. Bearing in mind that Britain during the late 1920s led the world in mechanization, which the Germans studied, the potential benefits of such an association to the Canadian militia might have been even greater. The system of regular officer training was also satisfactory up to the level of staff college. It was, after all, at such institutions that commanders like Slim and Montgomery first learned and later refined their trade. The Canadian regular officer who successfully completed his promotion and staff college entrance examinations and subsequently passed through Camberley or Quetta during the 1930s was probably better trained and blessed with wider experience than his equivalent in the Canadian army today.

It is true, of course, that lack of equipment and collective training opportunities hampered officer development generally and the training of higher commanders in particular. What must not be lost sight of, however, is that most armies endured similar shortcomings to greater and lesser degrees. Lack of resources forced the German army, for example, to use mock tanks and dummy antitank guns in their maneuvers, which were also restricted in the early stages. Many successful higher commanders also developed their operational theories and war fighting approaches at schools and staff colleges on cloth models, by individual study, or through the medium of war games. That this was true of Montgomery and even Simonds sets them apart. Both had developed reasonably comprehensive tactical theories *before* they ever went to war. McNaughton, in contrast, seems never to have surmounted his counter battery experience of the Great War.

The problem was one of individual focus. McNaughton's emphasis on technical training and insistence on the IDC as a prerequisite for advancement ensured the general neglect of the operational level of education. After the IDC, the Canadian career officer was better prepared for diplomatic or capital staff duty at NDHQ than service in the field. This is not to imply that the IDC experience was not worthwhile. For a great oceanic empire, it was an excellent institutional means by which to encourage the three services and other branches of government to work together and to coordinate their respective actions. Yet the IDC was never intended as a training ground for field army command or troop staff appointments. In this sense it steered senior Canadian officers toward the politico-strategic arena, which created a leadership void at the operational level that left regimental officers clinging to their colors. Montgomery never went to the IDC. McNaughton and Crerar did.

McNaughton, it should also be remembered, was hand-picked by Mackenzie King to head Canada's overseas contingent. Recalled from military retirement, his was thus a political appointment, but, as events demonstrated, a far less successful one than Hughes's selection, Currie. Although reputedly a humble man, McNaughton was puffed up by the Canadian, British, and even American press to dimensions far beyond his actual military abilities. Exercise "Spartan" clearly revealed his serious limitations as a field commander. Judging from the state of Canadian Army training in 1942, after more than two years of his leadership and direction, he was the wrong man for the job. While Canadian political authorities, unlike the British or American, persisted in earmarking their senior soldier for field command, it is moot to ask whether McNaughton would have been better employed as CGS in Ottawa. Given his great energy and propensity to aggrandize and dabble, however, this too would probably have been a mistake. Perhaps he should simply have been left in retirement from where he could have just as easily in honorary uniform promoted the war effort without affecting the army he had compromised before.

The rapid expansion of the Canadian Army overseas to over 50 times its prewar regular strength, as compared to a 15-fold increase in the British Army, did not enhance its professional military depth at the lower echelons. It needed British help. While obviously demanding further investigation, the system of basic and advanced training for other ranks in Canada generally seems to have suffered from the standpoint of their morale and motivation. There also remains the question of just how good were Canadian NCOs? Did the policy of promoting officers from the ranks skim off the best and leave the weakest as the "backbone of the army"? Whatever the answer, indications are that the officer training conducted at the Brockville OTU left something to be desired. The Canadian Army had thus eventually to rely largely upon the battlefield, with all its obvious hit and miss probabilities, to throw up commanders of tactical competence like Rockingham.

As for staff training, evident shortcomings in the quality of instructors at the CWSC Kingston suggest wider imperfections in the army at large. During major exercises in Britain and operations in Normandy, even with air superiority, the intricacies of road movement seem never to have been adequately solved. Problems associated with the forward movement of the artillery and armoured divisions on phase two of "Totalize" were not exceptional. They should have been anticipated and sorted out by the staff. Indeed, one senses that had Simonds not lined up his divisions in parade square fashion initially, similar problems might have arisen during phase one. Ironically, after being fired by Simonds, Brigadier Cunningham assumed the position of staff college commandant! In a related vein, it also appears that despite Montgomery's personal advocacy of the COS system, it was never fully embraced in the spirit of the Germans. Less disposed than the latter to share command with their COSs, many Anglo-Canadian commanders usually opted to remain at headquarters from where they could neither adequately see nor develop a feel for the battle.

The sad conclusion is that the years of preparation and training in Britain prior to D-Day did not entirely expunge either those weaknesses in the Canadian military system that existed before 1939 or those attributed to rapid expansion after war was declared. Unbounded enthusiasm and amateurism doubtless contributed to the latter category. But so too did the fact that units and newly formed higher formations were left to their own devices. From virtually the beginning, serious inadequacies at the high-command level undermined Canadian training efforts in Britain. McNaughton proved incapable of training his division commanders who, in turn, failed to train their own brigades and units. Incredibly, while Montgomery observed that Canadian commanders did not know how to train for war or stage-manage battle, McNaughton worried about education courses that would benefit troops, as military training obviously would not, after hostilities were over. In all of this, Canadian regimental officers continued to carry on as best they could. When the ground swell of battle drill arose, they naturally embraced its novelty. The high command, with little evident appreciation of its less desirable implications, followed suit. Fortunately, the personal influence of Montgomery forced many Canadians back on track.

Late in the day, the dismissal of McNaughton left the First Canadian Army essentially leaderless and without a spearhead role. This was a critical point, for training time had by then boiled down to months instead of years. That left Simonds who took over 2 Corps on 30 January and Crerar who assumed army command on 20 March little room to identify and correct training shortcomings. It is significant that within 2 Corps individual rather than collective training received priority to the end of March 1944. The 3rd Division and the 2nd Armoured Brigade, which carried out combined operations training from July 1943, may have fared better. But one is at a loss to explain why Brigadier Wyman, a veteran of Italy, allowed tanks carrying infantry to lead an attack on Le Mesnil-Patry at the end of June. Here the Queen's Own Rifles were simply shot off the tanks by counter attacking German panzers. If anything, the incident may indicate the limitations of Italian armored experience on the battlefields of Normandy.

Although the Italian campaign influenced some individual Canadian commanders, the army as a whole had in the main trained according to a doctrine gradually worked out in North Africa. Indeed, the Eighth Army adhered to this doctrine as it fought its way up Italy. From Alamein onward, of course, the nature of the fighting had also begun to change. As Fuller had predicted, mobile operations begat static operations. In Russia and elsewhere *Blitzkrieg* foundered before opponents prepared to wage *Materialschlacht*, an antidotal slugging match of attrition. Attacking forces could no longer get through a prepared position in depth without hard pounding. German failure to dislodge the RHLI from Verrières amply reaffirmed the substantial holding power of infantry on suitable ground. Supported by 17-pounders, massed artillery, and air strikes, such positions withstood even the heaviest armored and infantry counter attacks. In these circumstances a defending army, like a losing hockey team, could also look good.

Fortunately, the Anglo-Canadians possessed in their artillery a powerful means for dealing with prepared enemy defenses. By bringing massive fire and smoke to bear, it countered *Panther* and *Tiger* tank superiority and the power of German mobile and entrenched antitank guns. Naturally, the emphasis accorded to the preparation of artillery fire plans often constrained maneuver, leaving little scope for infantry battle drills. With good reason, moreover, Simonds insisted that the infantry not stop to maneuver, but follow the barrage directly on to the objective. He unfortunately appeared to place little faith in infiltrating infantry elements forward on foot at night. Apart from being difficult to control, of course, infiltration on the open Caen plain was always a more risky proposition than in the bocage. Then, too, as Tuker warned, such tactics did not negate the need for detailed and thorough contingency fire planning. Still, as the Argylls demonstrated at Point 195, night infiltrations could be accomplished against an enemy that with serious manpower problems itself could not always prevent them from succeeding.

Canadian infantry, nonetheless, does not generally appear to have been as well trained as the German in fighting skills and techniques. The infiltration attack by three SS rifle companies at Putot, which drove out three defending Winnipeg companies, illustrates this point. Patrolling capability was also woefully inadequate within the 2nd Canadian Division. Here battle drill mania may have been the culprit, distracting attention from these vital areas of infantry training. One cannot escape the impression, as well, that the very nature of battle drill training, in particular its parade square facets, inculcated a rigidity of thought and action that was not typical of German troops. Be that as it may, Canadian infantry units when intelligently commanded and led were capable, despite their inferior weaponry, of more than holding their own against the enemy. If not so obviously superior an arm as the artillery, relative to the German, the infantry nevertheless performed better than Canadian armor.

Without question, the tank arm remained the weakest link in the Anglo-Canadian order of battle. It is, of course, true that the limitations of the *Sherman* left Allied armor distinctly disadvantaged in Normandy, though it should not be forgotten that the *Firefly* enabled the 21st Army Group to take on a weight of German panzer might that less well-gunned armor on such open ground could hardly have handled. Yet, as the North African experience revealed, the root of the problem concerning armored employment was as much historical and doctrinal as technological. El Hamma and "Totalize" both demonstrated that there was no reason why Canadian armor from the beginning could not have led attacks with special armor following protective barrages. That it did not, to use a boxer analogy, was almost like fighting with one arm tied behind. It seems incredible, in short, that the tank arm with a significantly lower casualty rate often remained behind while forlorn hopes of infantry, torn by enemy and friendly fire alike, plodded ever onward.

The less than successful performance of Canadian formations in Normandy can thus be partly explained in terms of doctrine. It took an able commander to exploit the peculiar strengths and weaknesses of each of the foregoing arms and use them in optimum combination to attain battlefield success. While Simonds possessed this capacity, which is not to suggest he made no serious mistakes, his division and brigade commanders, with few exceptions, did not. Frustration with their tactical shortcomings demonstrably drove Simonds to assume more rigid control, possibly with a view to showing them how all-arms operations should be conducted. Unfortunately, Simonds stood alone. Too little staff or tactical depth existed either above or below to adequately support him, or even save him from his foibles, as did Montgomery in Italy. In such circumstances, he naturally came to prefer his own counsel. The reason for such lack of depth in the Canadian system, of course, can be traced back to training in Britain and before. The ultimate cost of this wasted preparation period was that Canadian volunteer soldiers incurred notably higher casualties than their conscripted British brethern.

Study of the underpinnings and conduct of Canadian Army operations beyond the Normandy bridgehead to the closure of the Falaise Gap must take into account the legacy of the Canadian Corps and the state of the army during the interwar years. The reasons are apparent, for it was from these bases that the leadership and fighting approach of Canada's first field army sprung. There was indeed a direct, if complex, connection between those long forgotten winters in the Dominion and that now half-forgotten summer of 1944. A misplaced emphasis during the interwar years haunted the Canadian Army to the end of 1943. Those who had been paid excessively high wages to keep the military art alive, adopted instead the bankrupt policy of searching for other roles. They shamefully forgot that the main purpose of a peacetime military establishment is to prepare for the day when armed force might have to be used against a first-class enemy.

Winston Churchill most eloquently and accurately expressed what should be the proper reactions of armies during periods of peace and retrenchment. They should pine and sulk if diverted from fulfilling the principal trust with which their nation charged them. On reflection, however, the unquestionably significant corrective of money is of far less importance than time. As study of the Canadian case reveals, rapid expansion and budgetary increases do not, cannot, and will not compensate for an army's neglect of itself. "Of what use," as French historian-hero Marc Bloch asked, "is a military education which trains men for everything except war?"[2] Fortunately in 1939, certain individual officers remained serious students of their craft and appeared to understand that the workings of a large, modern army are so complex, its elements so varied, and its operations so esoteric as to demand years of undiverted attention and study. The best blood of Canada that poured forth freely on the golden sweep of Verrières Ridge in the Norman summer of 1944 remains a sad testament to this reality.

NOTES

1. Quoted in *Infantry Journal*, 6 (Winter 1976/77):1.
2. Marc Bloch, *Strange Defeat: A Statement of Evidence Written in 1940*, trans. Gerard Hopkins (New York: W.W. Norton, 1968), p. 95.

Appendix A

—————

Some General Notes on What to Look for When Visiting a Unit

1. The underlying object is obviously to find out what the C.O. is worth, and generally if it is a good or bad unit. The method adopted, and the length of time it will take, will depend entirely on the inspecting officer's own military knowledge, on his own experience in actual command, and generally on whether he can be "bluffed" by the C.O.

2. Most C.O.'s will want to lay on a tour of the unit area, looking at the training and so on. This would be quite suitable for *later* visit. But for the *first* visit, if you really want to find out all about the unit there is only one way to do it. And that is to sit with the C.O. in his orderly room and cross-examine him on certain points which are "key" points, and which will show at once whether or not he knows his job. The Brigadier should be present, but no one else. The C.O. is then put through it. And if he begins to wriggle and to give evasive answers, he is pinned down at once. The C.O. will welcome such an interview and will learn a great deal from it. On no account must he be bullied or rattled. The great point is to show him that you really want to know all about his unit, and that you are all out to find out his difficulties and worries and to help him. I have found all C.O.'s in the Canadian Corps most friendly, and very willing to tell me how they run their show. It is very important that the C.O. should realise early in the proceedings that you really do know what you are talking about, it is quite easy to show him this by cross-examining him on some point of detail about which he probably thinks you know nothing. Once he sees this, he will be perfectly frank and will welcome any ideas you may give him. Both parties will learn a great deal from the discussion—the visiting officer and the C.O. And so will the Brigadier. And all the time you are summing up the C.O. and finding out what he knows. It must all be very friendly and natural from the beginning; you then get the C.O.'s confidence; this is most important.

3. An investigation into the following points will show you at once what the unit is worth, and if the C.O. knows his job.

(a) *The system of selection, promotion, and inspection of N.C.O.'s.* This is a very important point, and its importance is not always realised by the C.O.'s. The N.C.O.'s are the backbone of the battalion; a good solid foundation must be built up on the L/Cpl. level, and the standard of this foundation must be the C.O.'s standard and NOT five different company standards. The C.O. must interest himself directly in everything connected with his N.C.O.'s and W.O.'s.

(b) *Organization of individual training, i.e., training of the rank and file.* The usual fault here is that men are not graded *before* the training begins, and put into categories in accordance with their knowledge and efficiency. This must always be done, so as to ensure that men get instruction in accordance with their needs. The principle of piece work is also very important.

(c) *Training of the N.C.O.'s.* The training of the N.C.O.'s in all duties in the field, tactical and administrative, must be carried out by the Coy. Comds. The Adjutant and the R.S.M. must take a very definite hand in keeping the N.C.O.'s up to the mark, in instruction in discipline matters, and generally in ensuring that the non-commissioned ranks are a credit to the battalion, are able to maintain a high standard in all matters, are not afraid of the men, and are trained on for promotion.

(d) *Training of the Officers.* The C.O. must handle this himself, personally. No one else can do it for him. *He must do it himself.* The best results are obtained when the C.O. has an officers day once a week. Officers have got to be taught the stage-management of the various operations of war, the technique of movement, the co-operation of all arms in battle, the technique of reconnaissance and deployment, administration in the field, and so on.

(e) *Organization and conduct of collective training.* Before beginning Coy or Bn. Training the C.O. must issue instructions as to how it is to be done. He should assemble his officers and lay down:

1. The object of the training.
2. The principles on which it is to be based.
3. The standard aimed at.
4. The phases of war to be studied.
5. His views on operations by night.
6. How he wishes the time available to be used.
etc.,

The great point in collective training is to mix the training. During platoon training the whole company should go out once a week. During company training the whole battalion should go out once every 10 days or so. During Battalion training the whole Bde. should go out once a fortnight. This is far better than having long periods devoted separately to each subject.

The next point is that when you embark on unit training every exercise must include the dusk and the dawn. These are the times when things happen in war.

A small number of exercises lasting 24 hours or more are much better than a large number of short exercises. The exercise lasting from after breakfast till tea-time is of little use. A good exercise is one that tests out the administrative arrangements, and involves the dusk and the dawn.

During collective training the following operations must be taught and practised:

(a) The set-piece attack, i.e., the Brigade battle.

(b) Breaking down the Brigade battle and carrying on the advance by means of resolute fighting in small self-contained groups of all arms.

(c) The dusk attack.

(d) The night attack.

(e) Forcing the crossing of obstacles.

(f) Re-organization and holding the ground gained.

(g) Disengagement and withdrawal.

(h) Defensive tactics.

(j) Counter-attacks.

Teaching "Training" as Distinct from Teaching "War"

4. It is the exception to find a commander who teaches his subordinates how to train troops. In the F.S.R. we have laid down the principles of war, categorically. In no book do we find laid down the principles of training; officers are supposed to know all about this subject; actually, very few know anything about it and a great deal of time is wasted in consequence.

Training is a great art; there are principles of training just as there are principles of war. Training in war time must be carried out somewhat differently to training in peacetime, as we have to be ready to meet the enemy at any time.

5. In the training of his unit the C.O. has got to consider the following points:

(a) Training of the rank and file.

(b) Training of the N.C.O.'s in their duties as leaders.

(c) Training of the officers.

(d) Organization and conduct of collective training generally.

(e) The best way to run sub-unit training, i.e., platoon and company training.

(f) Battalion training.

If he will think it out on these lines he has got a firm basis from which to start.

6. But he will do no good in his training unless he realises very clearly the importance of the following basic points, and has a good system for carrying them out:

(a) Interior economy and administration, and life generally within the unit.

(b) The training of the leaders, i.e., the officers and the N.C.O.'s.

Some C.O.'s realise the necessity for training the officers; not a great many, but only some. Very few bother about the N.C.O.'s; in fact practically none. But the N.C.O.'s are the backbone of the unit; the whole question of their selection, promotion, instruction, and welfare must be on good and sound lines. Sgts. Messes are very important.

The R.S.M.

7. The R.S.M. is one of the most important people in the unit. I always ask to see the R.S.M., treat him like an officer, and shake hands with him. When inspecting the S. Saskatchewan Regt. I called the R.S.M. out in front and shook hands with him in front of the whole Bn; It may seem a small point but in my view it means a great deal.

The R.S.M. is the senior non-commissioned rank in the unit; his authority over the N.C.O.'s is supreme, and he must be backed up and given opportunities to pull his weight. He should frequently assemble the W.O.'s and N.C.O.'s by Coys and address them, getting across to them various points in the daily life of the unit that want attention.

He and the Adjutant should work together as a team; and they should go out together round the battalion area whenever they can, keeping an eye on the general show.

It is very difficult, in fact practically impossible, to have a good cadre of N.C.O.'s without a good R.S.M.

Visiting Collective Training

8. When visiting a unit or inter-Bde exercise, or a Divisional exercise, you want to be clear as to what you want to find out. Generally I suggest that this will be as follows:

(a) What the commander is worth, and whether he is able to handle his ship when in full sail in a rough sea.

(b) Whether his machinery for exercising command is good, and runs smoothly.

(c) Broadly, how the formation or unit re-acts. Does it answer to the helm, or is it awkward and unsteady in a rough sea?

As far as the Corps Commander is concerned, or in fact any senior general officer, the above points are the ones that really matter. The points of detail such as the minor tactics, the fieldcraft, and so on, are the province of subordinate commanders. If you want to get a line on this it can be done by getting a staff officer to watch the operation in the front line and to keep an eye on such things as:

technique of movement;

deployment;

battle drill;

quick manoeuvre;

outflanking tactics;

sub-unit tactics generally;

cooperation with other arms on the sub-unit level.

9. *As regards para 8(a) and 8(b).*
The points here are:

(a) What orders did the commander receive?

(b) What did he know about the enemy when he received those orders?

(c) What orders did he then give?

Once you have got this *from the commander himself,* then you are well on the way to what you want to find out.

You then go on as follows:

(d) What are his present dispositions?

(e) What is his view as to the general situation, i.e., how does he view the problem?

(f) What are his plans for future action?

A few questions as to the layout of his H.Q., and a quick tour round his H.Q., follows. I should then leave him.

10. *As regards para 8(c).*
You now visit the next commander below, e.g. if para 9 has been done with a Brigadier you visit one of the forward battalion H.Q. There you go for the same points as outlined in para 9.

11. You have now got the answer to what you want to know. But you want to check up on it, so must find out from the Director when some important change or event in the battle is to take place. There may be a moment when a very fast ball is going to be bowled at the commander of one side.

You want to be in on this, and study the reactions. In particular it is a good thing if you can be present when the commander is giving out his orders; by listening to this you will find out a good deal.

12. In general the art lies in being at the right place at the right time, and knowing when that time is.

The next point is to get all your information from the commander himself. You want to sum *him* up; therefore you must deal with *him personally.* If he is out, you must chase him till you find him.

The last point is to remember what is the object of your visit; see para 8. You will not have time to also visit sub-units in the front line; if you want a line on how they are working, send some other officer to get that information for you.

[signed] B. L. Montgomery
Lieutenant-General.
General Officer Commanding-in-Chief.
6.Mar.42.   South Eastern Command.

Appendix B

Tank and Gun Comparisons

Canadian and German Tank Comparison (June–August 1944)

TYPE	CREW	MAX ARMOUR		ARMAMENT	MAX SPEED	RADIUS OF ACTION	WEIGHT	MECHANICAL RELIABILITY
		FRONT	SIDE					
Stuart (Honey)	4	44 mm	25 mm	37 mm	40 mph	40 miles	12 1/2 – 15 tons	Good
Sherman	5	76 mm	51 mm	75 mm 3 MG	24 mph	215 miles	30 – 32 tons	Good
Firefly (Sherman Vc)	4	76 mm	51 mm	17 pdr (76.2 mm) 2 MG	22 mph	125 miles	34 tons	Good
Mk IV (German)	5	80 mm	30 mm	75 mm Kwk 40 3 MG	25 mph	125 miles	25 tons	Good
Mk V (Panther)	5	100 mm	45 mm	75 mm Kwk 42 (Long) 3 MG	30 mph	110 miles	45 tons	Fair/Good
Mk VI E (Tiger I)	5	100 mm	80 mm	88 mm Kwk 36 3 MG	23 mph	62 miles	56 tons	Poor
Mk VI B (Tiger II)	5	180 mm	80 mm	88 mm Kwk 43 3 MG	24 mph	68 miles	68 tons	Very Poor

Allied and German Tank and Anti-tank Gun Comparison (June–August 1944)

GUN	PROJECTILE	PENETRATION AGAINST HOMOGENEOUS ARMOUR PLATE AT 30 DEGREE ANGLE				REMARKS
		100 yds	500 yds	1000 yds	2000 yds	
ALLIED						
75 mm Mk V	APCBC	74 mm	68 mm	60 mm	47 mm	Muzzle Velocity (MV) 2050 ft/sec. Sherman tank
6 pdr Mk V	APCBC	93 mm	87 mm	80 mm	67 mm	Towed anti-tank gun (MV 2675)
	APDS	143 mm	131 mm	117 mm	90 mm	Towed anti-tank gun (MV 3800)
3 in	APC	109 mm	99 mm	89 mm	73 mm	M10 tank destroyer
17 pdr Mk II	APCBC	149 mm	140 mm	130 mm	111 mm	Towed anti-tank and in some Shermans (MV 2900)
	APDS	221 mm	208 mm	192 mm	161 mm	Towed anti-tank (MV 3950) Only a few available in August 1944
GERMAN						
75 mm Kwk 40	APCBC	99 mm	92 mm	84 mm	66 mm	Mk IV tanks (MV 2,460)
75 mm Pak 40	APCBC	99 mm	92 mm	84 mm	66 mm	Anti-tank gun, towed and SP
75 mm Kwk 42	APCBC	138 mm	128 mm	118 mm	100 mm	In Mk V (Panther) (MV 3060)
88 mm Kwk 36	APCBC	120 mm	112 mm	102 mm	88 mm	In Mk VI E (Tiger)
88 mm Kwk 43	APCBC	202 mm	187 mm	168 mm	137 mm	In Mk VI B (Royal Tiger) and towed anti-tank guns (MV 3280)

Abbreviations

AA	antiaircraft
AA&QMG	Assistant Adjutant and Quartermaster-General
ADGB	Air Defence of Great Britain
AEAF	Allied Expeditionary Air Forces
AFV	armored fighting vehicle
AG	Adjutant-General
AGRA	Army Group, Royal Artillery
APC	armored personnel carrier/armor piercing capped
APCBC	armor piercing capped, ballistic cap
APDS	armor piercing discarding sabot
armd	armored
arty	artillery
ATC	Advanced Training Centre
Atk or A tk	antitank
AVRE	Assault Vehicle, Royal Engineers
BCATP	British Commonwealth Air Training Plan
bde	brigade
BEF	British Expeditionary Force

BGS	Brigadier, General Staff
BGGS	Brigadier-General, General Staff
BM	Brigade Major
bn	battalion
BRA	Brigadier, Royal Artillery
Brig.	Brigadier
BTC	Basic Training Centre
bty	battery
CAD	Canadian Armoured Division
Capt.	Captain
CASF	Canadian Active Service Force
CAGRA	Commander AGRA
CCRA	Commander Corps, Royal Artillery
Cda, Cdn	Canada, Canadian
CDQ	*Canadian Defence Quarterly*
CEF	Canadian Expeditionary Force
CGS	Chief of the General Staff
CIB	Canadian Infantry Brigade
CID	Canadian Infantry Division
CIGS	Chief of the Imperial General Staff
C-in-C	Commander-in-Chief
CJWSC	Canadian Junior War Staff Course
CMHQ	Canadian Military Headquarters
CMR	Canadian Mounted Rifles
Col.	Colonel
colm (n)	column
Comd	Commander
CO	Commanding Officer
COS	Chief of Staff
COSSAC	Chief of Staff to the Supreme Allied Commander
coy	company

CRA	Commander, Royal Artillery
CRE	Commander, Royal Engineers
CTS	Canadian Training School
CWSC	Canadian War Staff Course
DA & QMG	Deputy Adjutant and Quartermaster-General
det	detachment
DHist	Directorate of History
div	division
DND	Department of National Defence
DS	Directing Staff
ech	echelon
engr	engineer
fd	field
FDLs	forward defended localities
FGH	The Fort Garry Horse
Flak (German)	*Flugzeugabwehrkanone* (anti-aircraft gun)
FMR	Les Fusiliers Mont-Royal
FOO	forward observation officer
ft/sec	feet per second
GHQ	General Headquarters
GOC	General Officer Commanding
GOC-in-C	General Officer Commanding-in-Chief
gp	group
GS	General Staff/Service
GSO 1	General Staff Officer, First Grade (Lieutenant-Colonel)
GSO 2	General Staff Officer, Second Grade (Major)
GSO 3	General Staff Officer, Third Grade (Captain)
H-hour	time troops cross the start line in an attack
HE	high explosive
HLI	Highland Light Infantry
HQ	headquarters

Ia (German)	principal operations staff officer up to and including the division in the German army
IDC	Imperial Defence College
inf	infantry
instr	instruction/instructor
int	intelligence
Kwk	*Kampfwagenkanone*
LAA	light antiaircraft
Lieut. or Lt.	Lieutenant
Lincs	Lincoln and Welland Regiment
LMG	light machine gun
Lt.-Col.	Lieutenant-Colonel
Lt.-Gen.	Lieutenant-General
Maj.	Major
Maj.-Gen.	Major-General
max	maximum
MG	machine gun
MGO	Master-General of Ordinance
Mk	mark
mm	millimeter
msc	militia staff course qualified
MSC	advanced msc
MV	muzzle velocity
NAC	National Archives of Canada
NATO	North Atlantic Treaty Organization
NCO	noncommissioned officer
NDHQ	National Defence Headquarters, Ottawa
NPAM	non-permanent Active Militia
NRMA	National Resource Mobilization Act
OC	Officer Commanding
offr	officer

OKW (German)	*Oberkommando der Wehrmacht* (Armed Forces High Command)
OO	operation order
OP	observation post
op(s)	operation(s)
OTC	Officer Training Centre
PAD	Polish Armored Division
Pak (German)	*Panzerabwehrkanone* (German antitank gun)
pdr	pounder
PIAT	Projector, Infantry, Anti-Tank
posn	position
psc	passed staff college
Pz	Panzer
Pz.G.	Panzer Grenadier
QMG	Quartermaster-General
RAC	Royal Armoured Corps
RAF	Royal Air Force
RCAC	Royal Canadian Armoured Corps
RCA	Royal Canadian Artillery
RCAF	Royal Canadian Air Force
RCE	Royal Canadian Engineers
RCEME	Royal Canadian Electrical and Mechanical Engineers
RCHA	Royal Canadian Horse Artillery
RCN	Royal Canadian Navy
RCOC	Royal Canadian Ordnance Corps
RE	Royal Engineers
recce	reconnaissance
regt	regiment
res	reserve
RG	Record Group
RHLI	The Royal Hamilton Light Infantry

RHQ	Regimental Headquarters
RMC	Royal Military College of Canada
RN	Royal Navy
RRC	Royal Regiment of Canada
RTC	Royal Tank Corps
RTR	Royal Tank Regiment
SASO	Senior Air Staff Officer
SC	scout car
SDG	The Stormont, Dundas, and Glengarry Highlanders
SHAEF	Supreme Headquarters Allied Expeditionary Force
SL	start line
SOS	Senior Officers' School
SP	self-propelled
sp	support
sqn	squadron
SS (German)	*Schutzstaffel*
SSR	The South Saskatchewan Regiment
tac	tactical
TAF	Tactical Air Force
TEWT	tactical exercise without troops
tk	tank
TOETs	tests on elementary training
tp(s)	troop(s)
U.S.	United States
USAAF	United States Army Air Forces
WD	War Diary
yds	yards

A Note on Sources

The Canadian Army and the Normandy Cumpaign: A Study of Failure in High Command is based principally upon a reading of the records of the Department of National Defence (RG 24) and the McNaughton and Crerar papers in the National Archives of Canada. From a military standpoint, the Montgomery correspondence in the Crerar papers proved particularly revealing about the state of Canadian Army training in Britain after three years of war. For a staff college directing staff member, it was also a most humbling and enlightening exposure.

The McNaughton and Crerar papers contain an immense amount of information of the interwar and wartime army. But they are finite. RG 24, on the other hand, can be looked upon as either a gold mine or a quagmire. While the war diaries have captured the interest and attention of most researchers, there also exists a mass of material that can only be described as army "bumpfh." It includes, to name but a few subject areas, material on policy, operations, movement, intelligence, equipment, organization, and training. After-action reports on exercises and course reports on individuals, which require declassification for access, fall into this category. The historian's problem on entering this rather pure army world is that, for the Second World War period, he is attempting to cope with the paper overload produced by an army of nearly half a million soldiers. One might say it is an impossible task—unless one understands the army system, asks the right question, and knows what one is looking for. Fortunately, army correspondence formats and filing methods have changed little since the war, and those taught as assistant-adjutants to read document folders from the bottom up can cover a lot of material in a short time. Much valuable information on tactics, doctrine, enemy fighting methods, equipment problems, and so forth can be gleaned from these sources, but the supply is endless. The voluminous records of RG 24, in short, have hardly been tapped.

Other substantial sources of information are available in the NDHQ Directorate of History, which is an excellent starting point before proceeding to the NAC. The

Sawyer, Elkins, and Vokes papers in the RMC Massey Library also contain some worthwhile insights into Canadian wartime activities and operations. Although the archival section is small and rudimentary, it boasts certain other esoteric papers as well. The Sutherland Brown papers in the Queen's University Archives are much more complete and, for the interwar period, deserving of attention. The Rogers papers, while not extensive, nonetheless reveal something about initial army planning and expansion. The Liddell Hart Centre for Military Archives in King's College London, The Imperial War Museum, and the Public Records Office, Kew also contain considerable information pertinent to Canadian Army training in Britain and operations in Normandy. While not available to the public, the Canadian Land Forces Command and Staff College collection of documents on battlefield tours and military operations proved an additionally useful source.

Given the interpretative nature of this work, it has naturally been necessary to resort to synthesis. This is especially true with respect to British military posture between wars and the evolution of doctrine during hostilities. Authorities in each field were accordingly cited, but even here it was possible to supplement the discussion with some primary source material from the Sutherland Brown papers and RG 24. The *Canadian Defence Quarterly, Journal of the Royal United Service Institution, Current Reports from Overseas,* and *Canadian Army Training Memoranda* provided an additional wealth of information. For battlefield actions, war diaries and operations logs were consulted and double-checked against Stacey and Roy, both of whose research efforts were very thorough and hard to catch out. Ground, as Dominick Graham has pointed out, is evidence that is "as important as a typed letter, an operation plan, or a message torn from a signal pad" and was used as such during four battlefield tours of Normandy.

Select Bibliography

PRIMARY SOURCES, UNPUBLISHED

Government Records, Personal Papers, and Manuscript Collections

Record Group 24, National Defence 1870–1981, National Archives of Canada (NAC), Ottawa

Military Documents, Directorate of History, National Defence Headquarters, Ottawa, and Public Records Office (PRO), Kew, U.K.

"The Bartholomew Report," Bartholomew Committee Final Report (1940), Tactical Doctrine Retrieval Cell, Staff College Camberly

Alanbrooke Papers, Liddell Hart Centre for Military Archives, King's College, London (LHC)

Crerar Papers, NAC

de Guingand Papers, LHC and Imperial War Museum (IWM)

Dempsey Papers, LHC and the Public Records Office (PRO), Kew, U.K.

Elkins Papers, Royal Military College (RMC)

McNaughton Papers, NAC

Montgomery Papers, IWM

Odlum Papers, NAC

Rogers Papers, Queen's University Archives (QUA)

Sawyer Papers, RMC

Sutherland Brown Papers, QUA

Vokes Papers, RMC

Warren Papers, IWM

Collected Papers, Canadian Land Forces Command and Staff College, Kingston

Collected Papers, Tactical Doctrine Retrieval Cell, Staff College, Camberley

PRIMARY SOURCES, PUBLISHED

Official Histories and Government Publications

Bean, C. E. W., *The Official History of Australia in the War of 1914–1918, Vol. VI: The Australian Imperial Force in France During the Allied Offensive, 1918.* Sydney: Angus and Robertson, 1942.

Blumenson, Martin. *Breakout and Pursuit, United States Army in World War II, The European Theatre of Operations.* Washington: Department of the Army, 1961.

Nicholson, Col. G. W. L. *Official History of the Canadian Army in the Second World War, Vol. II: The Canadians in Italy, 1943–1945.* Ottawa: Queen's Printer, 1956.

——. *Official History of the Canadian Army in the First World War: Canadian Expeditionary Force 1914–1919.* Ottawa: Queen's Printer, 1962.

Pemberton, Brig. A. L. *The Second World War, 1939–1945, Army, The Development of Artillery Tactics and Equipment.* London: War Office, 1951.

Ralston, Honourable J. L. *The Extent of Canada's War Effort: Speech Delivered in the House of Commons February 10, 1942.* Ottawa: King's Printer, 1942.

Reports of the Department of National Defence. Ottawa: King's Printer, 1941–1944.

Stacey, Col. C. P. *Official History of the Canadian Army in the Second World War, Vol. I: Six Years of War: The Army in Canada, Britain and the Pacific.* Ottawa: Queen's Printer, 1966.

——. *Official History of the Canadian Army in the Second World War, Vol. III: The Victory Campaign: The Operations in North-West Europe, 1944–1945.* Ottawa: Queen's Printer, 1966.

——. *Arms, Men and Governments: The War Policies of Canada, 1939–1945.* Ottawa: Information Canada, 1974.

Manuals, Pamphlets, and Contemporary Periodicals

Canadian Army Training Memoranda.

Canadian Defence Quarterly.

Current Reports from Overseas.

The Instructors' Handbook on Fieldcraft and Battle Drill, December, 1942, DHist 78/463.

Journal of the Royal United Service Institution.

WO 2923 *Field Service Pocket Book. 1914,* (Reprinted with Amendments, 1916). London: HM Stationery Office, 1916.

Semi-Official Manuals and Associated Documents

"Battle Drill," Canadian Battle Drill School Lectures and Précis, originally assembled by 47th London Division and printed by Calgary Highlanders C.A.(O) in England for use in 47th Div., G.H.Q., and Calgary Highlanders Battle Drill Schools in England (October 1941). Revised and adapted to C.B.D.S., Coldstream Ranch, Vernon, B.C., for 9th Course 18 January–9 February 1943.

Bourne, Maj. R. P., and Maj. N. A. Shackleton. "Analysis of Firepower in Normandy Operations in 1944," NDHQ Operational Research and Analysis Establishment.

British Army of the Rhine Battlefield Tour Operation Totalize: 2 Canadian Corps Operations Astride the Road Caen-Falaise 7–8 August 1944. Prepared under the direction of G (Training) HQ British Army of the Rhine (BAOR), DHist 693.013(D2) Ops 2 Cdn Corps.

Calendar of the Royal Military College of Canada. Ottawa: King's Printer, 1927.

Howard, Col. John K. "Report on Canadian Battle Drill School, Vernon, British Columbia," DHist 322.009 (D590).

Meyer, Hubert. *MS # P–164, 12th SS Panzer Division "Hitlerjugend" June to September 1944.* Historical Division, Headquarters United States Army, Europe, 23 June 1954.

Owl Pie. Camberley: Staff College, 1923–1924.

Regulations and Calendar of the Royal Military College of Canada 1922. Ottawa: King's Printer, 1923.

Royal Military College of Canada Calendar 1939–40. Ottawa: King's Printer, 1939.

The Royal Military College of Canada Syllabus of the Course of Instruction. Ottawa: King's Printer, 1919.

Vernon, Lt. Col. (ed.). "Project #6 German General Staff," Vol. III: "Training and Development of German General Staff Officers," trans. G. C. Vanderstadt, Historical Division, U.S. European Command, 21 June 1951.

Memoirs, Journals, and Accounts

Allard, Gen. Jean V., in cooperation with Serge Bernier. *Memoirs.* Vancouver: University Of British Columbia Press, 1988.

As You Were! Ex-Cadets Remember. Kingston: The R.M.C. Club of Canada, 1984.

Bradley, Omar N., *A Soldier's Story.* New York: Henry Holt, 1951.

Bradley, Omar N., and Clay Blair. *A General's Life.* New York: Simon and Schuster, 1983.

Burns, Lt.-Gen. E. L. M. *General Mud: Memoirs of Two World Wars.* (Toronto: Clarke, Irwin, 1970).

Dunkelman, Ben. *Dual Allegiance.* Toronto: Macmillan, 1976.

Fuller, Maj.-Gen. J. F. C. *Memoirs of an Unconventional Soldier.* London: Ivor Nicholson and Watson, 1936.

———. *The Army in My Time.* London: Rich and Cowan, 1935.

Galloway, Strome. *The General Who Never Was.* Belleville, Ont.: Mika, 1981.

Graham, Lt.-Gen. Howard, *Citizen and Soldier.* Toronto: McClelland and Stewart, 1987.

Groom, W. H. A. *Poor Bloody Infantry: A Memoir of the First World War.* London: William Kimber, 1976.

Kippenberger, Maj.-Gen. Sir Howard. *Infantry Brigadier.* London: Oxford University Press, 1951.

Kitching, Maj.-Gen. George. *Mud and Green Fields: The Memoirs of Major General George Kitching.* Langley, B. C.: Battleline, 1986.

Malone, Col. Dick. *Missing From the Record.* Toronto: Collins, 1946.

Martel, Lt.-Gen. Sir Gifford le Q. *Our Armoured Forces*. London: Faber and Faber, 1945.

Massey, The Right Honourable Vincent. *What's Past is Prologue*. Toronto: Macmillan, 1963.

Masters, John. *The Road Past Mandalay: A Personal Narrative*. New York: Bantam, 1979.

Montgomery, Field-Marshal The Viscount. *Memoirs*. London: Collin's, 1958.

Mowat, Farley, *The Regiment*. Toronto: McClelland and Stewart, 1955.

Pearce, Donald. *Journal of a War: North-West Europe 1944–1945*. Toronto: Macmillan, 1965.

Pearson, Lester B., *Mike: The Memoirs of the Right Honourable Lester B. Pearson*, Vol. I: 1897–1948. Toronto: Signet, 1973.

Pope, Lt.-Gen. Maurice A. *Soldiers and Politicians*. Toronto: University Press, 1962.

Roberts, James Alan. *The Canadian Summer*. Toronto: University of Toronto Press, 1981.

Roberts, Maj.-Gen. G.P.B. *From the Desert to the Baltic*. London: William Kimber, 1987.

Shtemenko, Gen. S. M. *The Soviet General Staff at War, 1941–1945*, trans. Robert Daglish, 2 vols. Moscow: Progress, 1985.

Sokolov, Marshal S., and John Erickson (eds.). *Main Front*. London: Brassey's, 1987.

Stacey, C. P. *A Date With History*. Ottawa: Deneau, 1983.

Tuker, Lt.-Gen. Sir Francis, *Approach to Battle*. London: Cassell, 1963.

Vokes, Maj.-Gen. Chris, with John P. MacLean. *My Story*. Ottawa: Gallery, 1985.

von Mellenthin, Maj.-Gen. F. W. *Panzer Battles: A Study of the Employment of Armor in the Second World War*, trans. H. Betzler, ed. L. C. F. Turner. Norman, Okla.: University of Oklahoma Press, 1983.

SECONDARY SOURCES

Books and Monographs

Ahrenfeldt, Robert H. *Psychiatry in the British Army in the Second World War*. London: Routledge and Kegan Paul, 1958.

Barnett, Correlli. *The Collapse of British Power*. New York: William Morrow, 1972.

Belfield, Eversley, and H. Essame, *The Battle for Normandy*. London: Pan, 1983.

Bidwell, Shelford. *Gunners at War: A Tactical Study of the Royal Artillery in the Twentieth Century*. London: Arms and Armour, 1970.

Bidwell, Shelford, and Dominick Graham. *Fire-Power: British Army Weapons and Theories of War 1904–1945*. London: Allen and Unwin, 1982.

Bond, Brian. *The Victorian Army and the Staff College 1854–1914*. London: Eyre Methuen, 1972.

———. *British Military Policy Between the Two World Wars*. Oxford: Clarendon Press, 1980.

Carver, Field Marshal Sir Michael. *Dilemmas of the Desert War: A New Look at the Libyan Campaign 1940–1942*. London: Batsford, 1986.

Copp, Terry, and Robert Vogel. *Maple Leaf Route: Falaise.* Alma, Ont.: Maple Leaf Route, 1983.

———. *Male Leaf Route: Caen.* Alma, Ont.: Maple Leaf Route, 1983.

D'Este, Carlo. *Decision in Normandy: The Unwritten Story of Montgomery and the Allied Campaign.* London: Pan, 1984.

Eayrs, James. *In Defence of Canada: From the Great War to the Great Depression.* Toronto: University of Toronto Press, 1964.

———. *In Defence of Canada: Appeasement and Disarmament.* Toronto: University of Toronto Press, 1964.

Foster, Tony. *Meeting of Generals.* Toronto: Methuen, 1986.

Fraser, David. *And We Shall Shock Them: The British Army in the Second World War.* London: Hodder and Stoughton, 1988.

Godwin-Austin, Maj. A. R. *The Staff and the Staff College.* London: Constable, 1927.

Hamilton, Nigel. *Monty.* 3 vols. Sevenoaks, U.K.: Hodder and Stoughton, 1984.

Harris, Steven J. *Canadian Brass: The Making of a Professional Army 1860–1939.* Toronto: University of Toronto Press, 1988.

Hastings, Max. *Overlord: D-Day and the Battle for Normandy, 1944.* London: Pan, 1984.

Larson, Robert H. *The British Army and the Theory of Armored Warfare, 1918–1940.* Newark, Del.: University of Delaware Press, 1984.

Luther, Craig W. H. *Blood and Honor: The History of the 12th SS Panzer Division "Hitler Youth," 1943–1945.* San Jose, Calif.: Bender, 1987.

Macksey, Kenneth. *A History of the Royal Armoured Corps and its Predecessors 1914 to 1975.* Beaminster, U.K.: Newtown, 1983.

Meyer, Hubert. *Kriegsgeschichte der 12.SS-Panzerdivision "Hitlerjugend."* Osnabruck, Germany: Munin Verlag, 1987.

Nicholson, Col. G.W.L. *The Gunners of Canada: A History of the Royal Regiment of Canadian Artillery,* Vol. II: *1919–1967.* Toronto: McClelland and Stewart, 1972.

Roy, Reginald H. *1944: The Canadians in Normandy, Canadian War Museum Historical Publication No. 19.* Ottawa: Macmillan, 1984.

Stacey, Col. C. P. *Canada and the Age of Conflict; A History of Canadian External Policies,* Vol. I: 1867–1921. Toronto: Macmillan, 1977.

———. *Canada and the Age of Conflict; A History of Canadian External Policies,* Vol. II: *1921–1948, The Mackenzie King Era.* Toronto: University of Toronto Press, 1981.

Swettenham, John. *McNaughton.* 3 vols. Toronto: Ryerson, 1968.

Weigley, Russell F. *Eisenhower's Lieutenants: The Campaign of France and Germany, 1944–1945.* Bloomington, Ind.: Indiana University Press, 1981.

Winton, Harold R. *To Change an Army: General Sir John Burnett-Stuart and British Armoured Doctrine, 1927–1938.* Lawrence, Kans.: University Press of Kansas, 1988.

Index

About the Author

JOHN A. ENGLISH is a Research Associate with the International Institute for Strategic Studies. He recently completed a three-year tour on the Directing Staff of the Canadian Land Forces Command and Staff College, and was previously Chief of Tactics at the Canadian Combat Training Centre and a War Plans Officer in Central Army Group Headquarters, Heidelberg, Germany. An officer in Princess Patricia's Canadian Light Infantry, Lt.-Col. Dr. English has seen service with the British and Canadian armies in England, Germany, Denmark, Cyprus, Canada, and Alaska.

He is the author of the highly successful *On Infantry* (Praeger, 1981) and the principal editor of *The Mechanized Battlefield: A Tactical Analysis* (1984). His articles on military subjects have appeared in *Jane's Military Review*, *Infantry*, the *Naval War College Review*, the *Canadian Defence Quarterly*, the *Marine Corps Gazette*, and *Military Affairs*.

• Cap-Saint-Ignace
• Sainte-Marie (Beauce)
Québec, Canada
1995

«L'IMPRIMEUR»